Lakshmibai Tilak (1868–1936) was a Marathi writer, best-known for her memoir, *Smritichitre*. Apart from her memoir, she also completed her husband, Narayan Waman Tilak's, epic poem *Chirstayana* after his death.

Shanta Gokhale (1939) was born in Dahanu and educated in Mumbai, London, Bristol. A writer, translator and theatre critic, she began her career as a college lecturer, moved to a multi-national corporation as P.R. executive and was then appointed Arts Editor of the *Times of India*. Her novels in Marathi, *Rita Welinkar* (1992) and *Tya Varshi* (2005), won the Maharashtra State Award and have been translated by her into English. Her play *Avinash* (1988), also translated by her into English, was staged in Marathi, Hindi, Kannada and Malayalam. She has translated several other works from Marathi, including *Kautik on Embers* (*Dhag*) by Uddhav J. Shelke. She has authored *Playwright at the Centre: Marathi Drama from 1843 to the Present* (2000) and edited *Satyadev Dubey: A Fifty-year Journey through Theatre* (2011), *The Theatre of Veenapani Chawla: Theory, Practice, Performance* (2014) and *The Scenes We Made: An Oral History of Experimental Theatre in Mumbai* (2015).

Smritichitre

The Memoirs of a Spirited Wife

Lakshmibai Tilak

Translated from the Marathi
by Shanta Gokhale

SPEAKING
TIGER

SPEAKING TIGER BOOKS LLP
125A, Ground Floor, Shahpur Jat, near Asiad Village,
New Delhi 110049

Originally published in Marathi in two volumes in 1934 and 1936
The complete Marathi edition published by Popular Prakashan in 1973
Published in English by Speaking Tiger in paperback 2017

Photographs courtesy Mukta Tilak and Charudutt Bhagwat

ISBN: 978-93-86582-57-7
eISBN: 978-93-86582-58-4

10 9 8 7 6 5 4 3 2

Typeset in Minion Pro by SÜRYA, New Delhi

Printed at Shree Maitrey Printech Pvt. Ltd., Noida

CONTENTS

Translator's Introduction ix

PART ONE

Money Gets a Thorough Wash 3
I'll Break Your Leg 9
The Hostility of the Planets 16
Another Escape 26
Procession 31
Packed Off Home 35
Back to the Marital Home 39
The Harassment of an In-law 44
My People Support Me 50
Poetry Reading 54
The Pearl in the Nose-ring 60
The First Child 64
She Has Turned Sixteen and Yet... 68
Mr Tilak's Business and My Education 76
A Brahmin on Monsoon Monday 79
In the Butis' Garden 84
I've Gone Quite Round the Bend, Friends 90
Mahadevbhauji 94
Dattu's Birth 99
My Illness 103
Mahadev 112
The First Public Speaking Event in Hindi 118

Mr Khare's House Is Left Behind 124
From the Diary 129
Drawn to Christianity 132
Where Is My Grinding Stone? 136
Resignation 141
Conversion 145

PART TWO

Made to Sit in the Puja Room 157
A Meeting in Court 162
Teacher Tries Hard 166
Layette 173
The Bird in a Love Cage 178
Gift from a Brother-in-law 182
Meeting My First Christian Woman 187
The Gosavi's Father 192
Our Feet Refused to Move 197
A Welcome of Sorts 201
A Gift and Alms on Top 208
Poison or Nectar? 213
Transformed 217
Haushi 222
Kulkarni 228
A Memorable Incident 235
You Have Surpassed Me 240
Our Savings 244
Our Household Grows 247
We Meet Again 252

God's Design 257
All Because of Your Pampering 267
My Education 273
Rahuri 278
Ordained 282

PART THREE

Into Mr Tilak's Mind 291
Gopaji 294
Rebirth 298
Poets' Conference at Jalgaon 302
Balkavi Thombre 306
House Gone, Buffalo Gone 313
Our Days in Ahmednagar 319
Kith and Kin? 325
The Karanji and the Modak 332
Eight Years of Waiting 335
New Pots and Pans 339
A Story 345
Scaredy Me 348
Memories of Balkavi Thombre 355
The Lord's Court 362
Satara 369
Renunciation 373
An Acutely Felt Need 378
An Offering of Devotional Songs 383
Last Visit to Ahmednagar 387
Dattu's Wedding 393

Chiki 399
Not Christianity but Christ 403
Shadows Gather 410
Why Fear When the Lord Is with You? 418

PART FOUR

A New Age 427
Mumbai 434
Joy Wrapped in a Pall of Gloom 439
When Fate Takes a Hand, Good Sense Takes Leave 445
Through the Shadow of Death 455
Visitors 459
Illness Comes from Four Sides 465
Wanted, a Daughter 472
Independence 478
Karachi 483
Our Days in Karachi 488

How the Story Ended 494

Translator's Introduction

Lakshmibai Tilak's *Smritichitre* is one of those books that constantly beckons you to re-read it. If not to re-read it in its entirety, at least to dip into it occasionally to meet an old friend. When such a book beckons a translator, she does not stop at re-reading, or re-re-reading. She is keen to make it her own in the only way she knows. By translating it.

The idea of translating *Smritichitre* had been lodged in my brain from the second time I re-read it thirty-five years ago. One good reason that went beyond the personal, which I shall soon come to, was that it was one of the finest examples of literary storytelling that existed in my language, Marathi. My sense that this was enough reason to translate it was confirmed by Susan Sontag, who, in the St Jerome Lecture on Literary Translation has argued with perspicacity, panache and passion that the purpose of translation was to enlarge the readership of a book that was not just worth reading but worth re-reading. In the pyramidal structure of literary merit, she said, very few books occupied the top. The translator's 'evangelical incentive' was to translate these. Lakshmibai Tilak's *Smritichitre* sits right at the top of the pyramid. Of this there is no doubt.

With translation, there are personal and practical factors also to be considered. It is, after all, not a mechanical process of fitting word to word. One needs to get into the skin of the writer, view the world through her eyes, find words and phrases that hypothetically she would have used had she been writing in English. The question I had to ask myself was whether I had the capacity to get into Lakshmibai's skin and translate not so much her words as her world. It was all very well to be seduced by the easy flow of her crisp and colourful sentences and her vocabulary that smelt of kitchens and cowsheds rather than books and libraries. But was I equipped to find the right register to carry those lines, those phrases into English? I decided to translate the first chapter to find out. But once I had started, I could not stop.

Besides the fact that *Smritichitre* was a literary classic and therefore had to be translated, besides the fact that I was totally enamoured of Lakshmibai's storytelling persona, there was something else too that was driving me. I had to bring before the world this woman's extraordinary life. She had lived through events that would have destroyed a lesser person. They very nearly destroyed her too. She made two attempts at killing herself and failed. Looking back at them, she writes, 'Many occasions had arisen in my life when I was near to committing suicide. But I never did. I do not think I was capable of taking such a step. That is how I am. Even in the darkest hour of despair, I grope and struggle to find a way out and live. I do not stumble and fall on the way and give up on life. In short, I am like a rubber ball.'

The dark hours of despair that Lakshmibai lived through did not have the power to dent her spirit. Her father-in-law tortured her mentally; her husband, a poet and seeker, would up and leave whenever the desire came upon him, without ever leaving an address where he could be found. His conversion to Christianity separated Lakshmibai from him for five years, during which time her maternal family watched her like hawks, afraid she would run off to join him. She did join him in the end but in stages, first sharing a roof but not the kitchen with him and then, won over to Christianity herself, living with him as a wife.

This story could so easily have been written in tears. But Lakshmibai's sense of humour was too irrepressible to allow that. She describes every notable event of her life from age seven to fifty-six and every oddball character that became part of it for a while and moved on, with her unfailing comic touch. It is true that in turning everything to laughter she does not give us a rounded view of her complex relationship with her husband, or of his character or hers. However, reading between the lines, we see that living with Lakshmibai must have been quite as difficult for Reverend Narayan Waman Tilak as it was for her to live with him. She was by no means the meek, docile doormat that women were expected to be in those days. She fought tooth and nail with her husband when she disagreed with his ideas or actions, and often won her argument. But she was ready to laugh at her vanity when she lost. He, on the other hand, was a bad loser. He used physical violence to settle arguments, and when his rage subsided, became instantly contrite and remorseful.

Feminists have had a problem with Lakshmibai's endurance of her husband's ill-treatment of her. Viewed in the framework of women's rights as we see them today, she should have filed for divorce on innumerable counts. But it is not just that such an act was unheard of in those times, the thought of permanent separation from her husband did not once enter her mind. Because, quite simply, Narayan Waman Tilak and Lakshmibai Tilak loved and respected each other. Although she does not say so in the forthright way we would, her poems and his express the single-minded commitment they felt towards one another. Even more movingly, their love expresses itself in Lakshmibai's account of the few meetings they had during their separation. They were brief meetings during which she was strictly chaperoned and no more than a few words were exchanged. But those words, for the very reason that they were so few and almost formal in character, carry for us an extraordinary charge of love. The meetings and the letters he wrote to her make it clear that he pined for her as much as she did for him. John Donne speaks of such a love:

> If they be two, they are two so
> As stiff twin compasses are two;
> Thy soul, the fixed foot, makes no show
> To move, but doth, if the other do.

If Lakshmibai tells us stories about her husband that make us laugh, she tells as many about herself that are equally funny. She admits candidly to her strange idiosyncrasies and her overweening confidence in non-existent skills. She also touchingly confesses that she became a poet, a keertankar, a public speaker and a social worker entirely because her husband pushed her to study and to grow. He had an eccentric disregard for the material things in life and wished she too would extricate herself from household concerns and involve herself in public life.

Lakshmibai Tilak started writing *Smritichitre* in 1924. She wrote consistently for seven years. Beyond that, life was the present which she was living fully and creatively. She was done with reminiscing. *Smritichitre* was first published as 'Memories' in a weekly called *Sanjeevani*. There were no plans then to bring it out as a book. But later, some important literary figures suggested it should be. That is when the name was changed to *Smritichitre*. The first three parts were published in 1934. The fourth was published posthumously in 1936. Since it was incomplete, Lakshmibai's son Devdutt Narayan Tilak edited the four parts several years later, adding a chapter at the end about Lakshmibai's last years. It took thirty years for the second edition to be published. But after that, there has been a new edition every few years, including one edited and annotated by Lakshmibai's grandson Ashok Devdutt Tilak who indicates in his introduction that his father had dropped some parts from the original in his version, probably to make the book tauter and racier. He himself has edited the unabridged edition.

This is not the first translation of *Smritichitre*, nor perhaps will it or should it be the last. It was translated by E. Josephine Inkster as *I Follow After* and published by Oxford University Press in 1958. A few chapters, particularly from Part 1 were dropped in this translation and Part 4 was totally omitted. The second translation, *Sketches from Memory*, by Louis Menezes was published by Katha in 2007. His source was the third edition of *Smritichitre*, abridged and edited by Devdutt Narayan Tilak, which included the chapter on Lakshmibai's last years.

I have myself omitted three chapters out of a total of ninety-two. These three chapters are devoted entirely to Narayan Waman Tilak's poems. Chapter 24 is 'Poems on Dattu', Chapter 25 contains poems about the loving relationship between Rev. Tilak's brother Sakharam and his wife Rakhmai. Chapter 31 entitled 'To Abandon Your Religion Is Not to Abandon Your Love for Your Country' comprises one long poem that argues the proposition in the heading. While omitting the chapters, I have placed Lakshmibai's account of the poems at the end of the previous chapters.

Poems abound elsewhere too. Rev. Tilak was a poet of renown in his time. Poetry was a vital part of life for both him and Lakshmibai. But, as poems, they did not warrant in my judgement the space they occupy in the original. Written in the 'poetic' mode of the times, neither the language nor the sentiments expressed lend themselves happily to modern English, which does exceptionally well in Lakshmibai's narration. Translating the poems into a faux archaic style would do a disservice to the genuineness of the love, anguish and devotion that the poems express.

For all these reasons, I have taken recourse to paraphrasing relevant parts of those poems which take Lakshmibai's narration forward while omitting the rest.

SHANTA GOKHALE
Mumbai

PART ONE

Money Gets a Thorough Wash

Some of these memories are hearsay. Mother and my father's sister, Attyabai, once stood talking to each other in the Tryambakeshwar temple. Attyabai was childless. Mother made her a promise that day—my next will be yours, whether boy or girl. Both kept their word. It would therefore not be wrong to say that I grew up almost entirely in Attyabai's house. To tell the truth, all my siblings grew up there. We did not care much for our own home. It was a place of torture for us and for Mother and Granny, my father's mother. Father, whom we called Nana, had suffered an attack of purity. His fear of pollution was the source of our torment. This is the story, as they tell it, of how this affliction came about.

It was 1857. There was commotion and strife everywhere. My grandfather, Aai's father, had a shop in Tryambakeshwar. He was also a moneylender to the Bhil and Koli tribes. The poor worshipped him and the villagers loved him greatly. He was very prosperous. Some people found this difficult to stomach. Taking advantage of the turmoil of 1857, these people poisoned some government officials' ears against him. Grandfather and Father loved each other like father and son. Grandfather was arrested in Tryambakeshwar and hung on the spot. Nana was in Nashik at the time. When he heard the news, he rose and went directly to Tapovan forest.

My parents' home was in Jalalpur. Jalalpur is four or five miles away from Nashik. My father lived in Nashik, but Mother and Granny lived in Jalalpur with my two elder siblings. My sister was fifteen months old and my brother a month-and-a-half. Granny had heard the news of Grandfather's hanging, but had not told her daughter-in-law about it. They lived in a village. There was tumult everywhere because of the rebellion. Imagine the state that old woman must have been in at such a time. Stones would be flung at the house. Her granddaughter would say let us go out to see the fun. But the old woman guarded her grandchildren like a cat guards her kittens. After news of the hanging came, the old woman began nagging her daughter-in-law to go to her sister's place in Nashik for Diwali. 'Nana is not around,' she said. 'We are just two women. How can we manage in these terrible times? This place is a village. The children are small. There is nobody around to help us.' But Mother would have none of it. She would say, 'How can I go away and leave you alone here?'

Finally the old woman managed to persuade her daughter-in-law to go. They could find neither horse nor cart to take her. At last she was put on the back of an ox. My infant brother was tied to her back. My sister was handed over to the servant to carry. And so they left for Nashik, the old woman seeing them off. Meanwhile, Attyabai was waiting on Bhaubeej day for her brother Nana to return. His bath water was ready, but where was he? She did not even know that her sister-in-law had arrived in town. Nana had left home in the morning to return only at lamp-lighting time. He had already bathed and wore washed, wet clothes. Everybody asked him, 'Nana, where have you been? And why are you in purified clothes?' He answered, 'I went to Tapovan. A Mahar was washing his face there. A drop of water fell on me. I am polluted. I must have a bath. Throw water on me from afar.' The news of his father-in-law's hanging must have unhinged his mind. The result was this attack of purity. He suffered the attack in 1857 and it lasted for twenty-five years; that is for the rest of his life.

I was born twelve or thirteen years after the attack.

His purity rules tormented not just the family, but the whole village. If even Brahmins polluted him, why talk of other castes like the Marathas? If the women of the house visited somebody's place for haldi-kumkum, they had to bathe before re-entering the house.

There was a platform in front of the entrance to my parents' home. There was a cowshed near the entrance, beyond it a yard and beyond that an open verandah with the prayer room on its left and the kitchen at the back. The prayer room had an enormous window almost the size of a door. If you sat in that room, you could see every stone and pebble outside.

Nana would leave home at eight in the morning and return at six in the evening. There were no clocks in those days. When the first sunrays fell on the plinth of the house, it was eight o'clock in the morning; and when the cattle came home, it was six in the evening. That is how we kept approximate time. Nana came home with the cattle. This was his daily practice. Once home, he had a bath, said his evening prayers, counted his beads and said more prayers. He kept a stern eye on the kitchen. The woman in the kitchen, which was always Mother, had to do all the cooking in wet, freshly washed clothes and use only her right hand for the work. The left arm had to hang by her side, like a limb that was broken. Nana's evening prayers and other rituals lasted for a good two hours, enough time for the cooking to be done. He would eat around ten or eleven.

I had five siblings in all. Actually many more were born, but only five survived. There was a difference of about sixteen years between my eldest sister, Bhiku, and me. After her came Keshav, then Bhagirathi, then Vishnu and me at the tail end. None of us children ever sat with Nana for dinner, not even on feast days. But this did not mean that he neglected us. He kept a strict watch over everybody from the prayer-room window. If a neighbour called (all our neighbours were Brahmins of course) Mother had to follow them out, sprinkling water as they left.

Once Nana had left the house in the morning, we were free to have fun. After he went, Mother's friends would drop in. We too would gather all the neighbouring children to play. Mother hungered for company. She would bathe neighbours' children, offer a word of sympathy to daughters-in-law, give medicines to the sick and talk sweetly to all. Once she even went to a Maratha home to make puranpolis for them! All this was done on the sly, of course.

Under Nana's rule things were very different. Anything that came into the house from outside had to be washed, including salt and chili powder. One day he asked us children to wash salt. We decided to teach Nana a lesson. We put the salt in a loose-weave cloth, washed it thoroughly and hung it from a peg to dry. Instead of drying, the salt dissolved and drained away. When Nana looked inside the cloth, there was no salt. From then on salt, jaggery, sugar, oil and ghee were allowed into the kitchen unwashed.

Mother and Granny were responsible for the washing. They washed, or pretended to wash, everything Nana ordered them to. When they washed salt and sugar, it never dissolved. They used sleight of hand for the work and instructed us to lie. There were good reasons too for doing so. Nana had made a strict rule that all the grain that came in from the farm was to be washed before storing. But how could any human being wash twenty maunds and more of grain? So what Mother and Granny did was to wash some of it and spread it on top of the pile. The children would be tutored about what to say. When Nana returned, he would cross-examine all the children. If, by mischance, a child gave the wrong answer, that is, blurted out the truth, the whole house was turned upside down. The women had to wash all the polluted stuff under Nana's supervision even at that late hour of the night. The children had to be thrashed. Then, as a result of the pollution this caused, Nana had to have another bath.

Nana's purity rules were outlandish. After his morning motion, he had to have four coconut shells full of soil to scrub his hands and feet clean. Throughout the twenty-five years of his affliction, he brought this soil from a single spot a couple of miles into a remote forest where nobody went. They say there is a huge pit there now. Once the soil was collected, he would spend hours cleaning his hands and feet with it.

In the evenings we were cross-examined about everything. Did we have visitors? Who came? Was water sprinkled behind them as they left? Who washed the grain? Where did you children go? The questions went on and on. Once there were three baskets of love apples lying under the eaves. They were waiting to be sent to Nashik to be sold, but there was nobody to take them. So there they lay till the evening, by which time they were properly polluted. We children were dying to eat the fruit but none of us dared. We spent all day, till the evening, wondering how it could be done and whether it should be done at all. Finally it was decided that one of us would stand guard at the door while another ate the fruit. Everybody had their turn before me; but when my turn came, nobody was ready to stand guard. In the end I walked up to the door myself, made sure nobody was coming, picked up a fruit and bit into it. Next moment, who should present himself before me but Nana. I ran for my life and hid behind the pestle in the corner of the verandah. Nana went to the backyard, stripped a stout twig off the custard apple tree and came looking for me. 'Where's that snotnose?' He pulled me out from behind the pestle and thrashed me to his heart's content. Poor Granny was terribly upset to see this. The rest of the children were tense with worry. If I were to tell on them, not only would they all get a pasting but we would have to wash the whole house to boot.

One day I was sleeping near a heap of wheat with my doll beside me. I had fallen asleep while playing with her. I had dressed her up in a sari. One corner of the sari touched me and the other corner touched the wheat. Nana came home, took in the scene and decided the wheat had been polluted. He flew into a rage. He grabbed me and began raining blows on me. As it turned out, my middle sister and my brother had also been polluted in some other way. All three of us were sent off to the Godavari for a bath. On our way there, we decided that one of us would get drowned in the river and die. That was the only way Nana would come to his senses and not torment people.

No sooner had we thought of the plan than we prepared to act on it. We waded into the river. I had been really badly beaten so I was keener than the others to teach Nana a lesson.

I paddled around till I exhausted myself. Water began to enter my mouth and nose. My face turned east. The sun blinded my eyes. Our neighbour Krishnarao Walwekar was sitting on the bank nearby doing his puja. He noticed me, jumped into the river and pulled me out. He pumped the water out of me, brought me back to my senses and took me home. In the end, it was not Nana who learned a lesson but me. I laugh now at all these memories which are still vivid in my mind.

Once, a couple of hundred-rupee notes had arrived from a debtor. Nana had covered them with cow dung and gone away on his usual business, leaving them in the front yard. We children had been put on duty to guard the pat of cow dung all day. In the evening, Nana took the notes to the river to wash them and forgot them there. He realized this when he got back home. But what use was that? The money had disappeared. In short, even money and gold did not escape Nana's pollution and purity rules.

I'll Break Your Leg

Govindrao Khambete was Attyabai's husband. I have already said they had no children, but their house was always buzzing with them. They had a house in Nashik too. That is where I lived with them. One of Govindrao's sisters had a house close by. A family of three, a sister and two brothers, had recently come to stay there as tenants. The girl, Sakhu, was married and had come from her in-laws' home to spend some time with her people. She was about twelve or thirteen. Of her two brothers, one was in the fifth grade and the other in the sixth. Sakhu spent all her time playing. I would go over to her place to play. That would delay her cooking duties and her brothers would fret and fume and go to bed starving.

Once, the older brother decided this would not do. Their sister was gathering girls from all over the neighbourhood to play with her and starving her brothers. He decided it would be better if he played with her himself and drove her friends away when they came. So he began playing all the games the girls played with her. But when he played sagargote*, every time he dropped a stone, even in the last stage of the game, he would gather all the stones together, scrap that game and start all over again. This meant that once he had the stones, Sakhu never got to see them again.

One day when the brother was playing with Sakhu, I went over as usual. The house had two separate flights of stairs. The

---

*Sagargote are seeds of the medicinal sagargoti tree (caesalpinia bonduc). They are roundish and pale grey-brown in colour. Girls play a toss-and-gather game with five or seven of these seeds. The player scatters the seeds on the floor, picks one, tosses it in the air and sweeps up one or more seeds according to the stage of the game she is at and with both hands cupped, catches the tossed seed when it comes down. She loses her turn if she touches another seed while gathering seeds off the floor or fails to catch the tossed seed before it falls to the ground.

moment Sakhu's brother set eyes on me, he blocked one flight with a stick and said, 'Don't you dare enter our house or I'll break your leg.' But there was Sakhu, calling me from an upstairs window. So I began climbing up the other staircase. That too did not work. The same voice followed me. 'Watch out. You'll go home with a broken leg.' That day I decided I would never enter Sakhu's house and never set eyes on her brother's face again. Later the family shifted to a house right across the road from us, near the Uma-Maheshwar temple. Even then, I did not step into that house, not once. I was helped in my resolve when, later, Govindrao built a house in Jalalpur, my parents' home town, and I moved there with them. Sakhu stayed back with her brothers far away in Nashik. So there was no question of even being tempted to meet her.

Govindrao had a hunger for people. The town was small and his house was always open to everyone. Soon people grew to love him. He cultivated his land, set up as a moneylender and did extremely well for himself. In addition, he had to look after my parents' household too. He took full responsibility for tending their land, managing their financial transactions, thread ceremonies and marriages. I, as the adopted daughter, was pampered silly by Attyabai and Govindrao. By this time I was quite grown up—ten, going on eleven. In those days it was a shocking thing for an eleven-year-old girl not to be married. Attyabai and Govindrao were consumed by anxiety about my marriage. But they were not willing to make the move to find a match for me. Govindrao used to say to my people, 'That's your job. I don't want you to say later that I was tempted by money and gave your daughter away to an unsuitable man.'

Although I was only ten, I ate well, had no worries and therefore, looked big for my age. Govindrao was willing to shoulder the marriage expenses but not to look for a bridegroom. Nana was too obsessed with his purity to have the time for such trifling things as a husband for his daughter. And anyway, it was most unlikely that he would find a groom pure enough for his approval. Aai was worried sick, but as a woman, she was helpless. Finally the responsibility fell on the shoulders of my brothers-in-law Raosaheb Nanasaheb Pendse, Vamanrao Ranade and Raghunathrao Mahabal. Around this time, a young student named Narayan Waman Tilak was making a name for himself in Nashik as a poet and an orator. Nanasaheb Pendse was very keen that Manu, that is I, should marry this young man.

Nanasaheb informed Govindrao about this eligible young man. Govindrao wrote to the young man's father, Wamanrao Tilak, inviting him to see the girl. Wamanrao replied, 'I will not sell my son for a dowry. Please spend what you can and I'll spend what I can for the wedding. My only condition is that their horoscopes should match. Otherwise I will not give my consent. I also wish to say that there are no women in my house; so you will have to look after your daughter till she comes of age. I see no need for me to see her. If all our people like her, that would be enough for me.'

Everybody was very happy to read this letter. Our horoscopes had already been matched. Only Wamanrao's consent had been lacking, and that had arrived. Govindrao was more than happy to look after me till I came of age. All that remained now was to make arrangements for my prospective husband to see me. I was sent to Nashik to my sister's place. Mr Tilak came there with a group of friends. I was sitting on the swing outside with my cousin. The visitors asked, 'Is Nanasaheb at home?' I replied, 'Yes, he is.'

The visitors could not find the stairs to the house. They looked so perplexed that I burst out laughing. Then I showed them the way. When Nanasaheb saw them, he sent for me. My sister, Maisaheb, decked me up top to toe and took me upstairs. When I got there, I was ready to die. These were the people I had laughed at and, to top it, the man who had come to see me was Sakhu's brother, the one who had driven me out of his house. How firmly had I resolved never to set foot in Sakhu's house again, and how terrible it was to see my resolve about to collapse. The gentleman who had once threatened to break my leg if I stepped into his house did not ask me any questions. He simply let it transpire that his friends had approved of me and left.

Now it was time for my grandmother-in-law to test me. I passed that test too. Gangabai pinched my left earlobe hard and immediately said she approved of me. I had said neither 'eek' nor 'ouch'. Perhaps that had convinced her that she could grab me by the ear any time and turn me whichever way she liked. What still surprises me is how Mr Tilak approved of me. My colour and face were pretty plain. My features were far from chiselled. All you could say of them was that they were all there, each in its proper place.

Govindrao had planned to spend one thousand rupees on my wedding. It was obvious that nothing would be forthcoming from my father, Narayanrao Gokhale. Mother wanted so much to do her bit, but what could she do? We have already seen the torture she had to suffer at home. Her only joy in life was to help others as much as she could and work herself to the bone. The merit she had accumulated in this fashion must have earned her a relative like Govindrao to keep her children fed. Mother was illiterate, but she would entertain herself by composing songs, teaching them to the young girls of the neighbourhood and getting them to sing them. It was small pleasures like these that greased the wheels of her life of labour. What else could she do besides expressing her deepest gratitude to Govindrao with tear-filled eyes?

Govindrao, on his part, treated my marriage as his own family event. He did more for me than he would have done for his daughter had he had one. He wrote a letter to Wamanrao in which he said he had a certain standing in the town and the wedding would have to be celebrated in a style befitting that. Since this was the first big occasion in his family and the town was small, could he request Wamanrao to give the townspeople a celebratory lunch? Wamanrao agreed to the request.

Govindrao and Attyabai went into a flurry of hectic activity. Wamanrao did what he had said he would. He came with twelve cartloads of wedding guests from his family's side. The house was filled to the beams with people. An enormous shamiana had been erected in front of the house. There were four more days to the wedding. Wamanrao now saw his to-be daughter-in-law for the first time. But soon, an obstacle reared its head. The Gokhales' Kashyap gotra and the Tilaks' Shandilya gotra did not match. How then could the marriage be allowed? The problem was soon solved with a loophole in the shastras. I was to be officially adopted by Govindrao. I had been given away to the Khambetes anyway, even before I was born. It was they who had looked after me from the moment of my birth to the time of my marriage. So there was no problem in my transforming myself from a Gokhale to a Khambete for a few days.

When the appointed time for the adoption ceremony came, Nana, who had to give me away, was nowhere to be found. He had left for the forest as usual to collect soil. There was no chance of his returning till the evening. Considering that he had once sent a message to his dying mother—telling her not to die before he finished his evening prayers—he was hardly likely to make an exception for his daughter's adoption.

Govindrao was livid with rage. He was not a short-tempered man by nature, but now he was really upset. He said, 'Only a father can give a daughter away. If he is so irresponsible, why should we bother? She is his daughter. Let him do what he pleases.' Attyabai was also furious. Her tongue did not stop wagging for a single moment. Mother felt worse than dead. She began to fear that the wedding would be called off. The groom's guests looked dejected. There was confusion everywhere. Just then Govindrao's uncle Dinkarshastri Khambete came to Aai's aid. He had found a loophole in the shastras which said that, on very rare occasions, even a mother could give a daughter away for adoption. This acted like drops of cold water on milk that was about to boil over. Everything grew calm again. Aai gave me away to Govindrao in adoption, her eyes moist with tears.

Here, I will merely mention the names of my in-laws. Janakibai, wife of Waman Sakharam Tilak, had already passed away before the wedding. Their children's names were Mathura, Narayan, Sakharam, Sakhu and Mahadev. I will write more fully about them later. My husband was seventeen or eighteen when we married. I was eleven. We were married two days after the adoption. Govindrao gave me away.

It was Ekadashi, the day after the wedding, that is the eleventh lunar day. My in-laws decided, on a whim, to fast that day. A fast involved cooking special food. There were twelve cartloads of wedding guests from twelve different households, all with their own ideas of what they would like to have as fasting food. So the vast amounts of wedding sweets that had already been made, had to be set aside and Ekadashi was celebrated with fresh food made to please everybody.

All the customs were observed. The groom's side stole things from the bride's side and there was much laughter when the theft was discovered. Imagine twelve cartloads of people from twelve households laughing and you will get an idea of the commotion. According to another custom, the groom was supposed to sulk for a gift. In our wedding, the groom had been thoroughly tutored to sulk. It was not in his nature to sulk. He would lose his temper all the time, but never sulk. His friends' instructions to him were not to go when called for lunch, demand a gold ring weighing two tolas and sulk till it was produced. Having done their job, they went away to their lodging.

At one o'clock in the afternoon, my older brother Keshavrao went to call Mr Tilak for lunch. Mr Tilak said, 'I am sulking. I will come only when my people come.' The guests who were staying with us were very hungry. They quietly polished off a few snacks and waited for the son-in-law to come. The son-in-law was also hungry. He called Keshavrao aside and said, 'I'm very hungry now.' Keshavrao was overjoyed. He grabbed the chance to start serving food and sent word to the bridegroom's party, 'Lunch is served. The rice is getting cold. Our son-in-law is already here.' That did the trick. Everybody rushed over for lunch and not a word was said about the two-tola gold ring. Other customs—extracting betelnuts out of each other's tightly closed fists and feeding each other—were duly observed, although Mr Tilak could barely endure them. But, quite against the general practice, there were no fights between the two parties.

My father-in-law's lunch for the townspeople was being prepared. One of Mr Tilak's friends, Mr Khadilkar, had a brainwave. He put cannabis in the fritter batter. People were pressed extra hard to eat the fritters. They loved them. With the exception of my father-in-law who knew nothing about this, everybody else in the groom's party knew and was having a laugh. Even Mr Tilak knew. He quietly took the fritters from my plate and put them aside and did not have any himself.

By evening, with a cool breeze blowing, people began doing the oddest things. I was beside myself with laughter. One Maratha yoked up his bullocks and tied the yoke to a tree. The poor bullocks began to feel strangled. Some young people went to pick flowers and lay down amongst them, forgetting to return home. Mr Pendse went to the river bank for his evening puja. There he thought he had lost his ring and frantically searched for it with the very hand on which he was wearing it. When Bhikutai entered the kitchen, the heat from the stove and the light from the lamps intensified the effect of the cannabis. There were some coconut karanjis in the kitchen, waiting to be fried. She mixed them all together, kneaded them into a huge ball and handed it over to Attyabai!

My father-in-law was very upset when he saw this. This was not how he had intended his lunch to go. Finally we had our last wedding meal and departed for Nashik. When we arrived there, we, the couple, were sent off to Nanasaheb Pendse's house while the others went to their respective homes. The wedding procession was held the same evening. The new bride entered her new home, stepping into the very house she had sworn never to enter.

The Hostility of the Planets

When we came home, our relatives from the Konkan left. Only a few like my grandmother-in-law and my sister-in-law Sakhu stayed back. Even my father-in-law, Mamanji, left. It was his habit to come and go. The month of Chaitra dawned three months after the wedding. My grandmother-in-law got me to do a Gauri puja and invited women relatives and friends for a haldi-kumkum. Sister-in-law Sakhu had come. The people at home had decorated Gauri's shrine beautifully. It was a Friday. Mamanji was also there. The very same day he received a letter from his eldest son-in-law to say that his wife had died of fever. The letter had arrived ten days after her death so a bath was enough to free us from rituals. This sister-in-law had come for my wedding.

On Fridays, Mamanji was possessed by the goddess. Everybody in the house was expected to attend to him during these divine seizures. If he noticed somebody missing, he would get very angry. It was the first time I was seeing something like this. I was terrified. While Mamanji was possessed, people brought up all the quarrels that had happened during the previous week. They asked the goddess many questions, which she answered with great clarity. On that Friday the goddess said the new daughter-in-law who had entered the house was an inauspicious presence. There would be no joy or peace in the house because of her. Everybody would suffer misfortunes because of her. Most recently, she was the cause of the daughter of the house dying.

Mr Tilak was upset to hear what the goddess had said. The custom was for people to offer flowers and haldi-kumkum to the goddess when she began to spin. Everybody did that except Mr Tilak. He sat before Mamanji without saying a word. When the goddess departed, Mamanji asked people what she had said. He was also told that Mr Tilak had not made offerings to her.

Naturally, he lost his temper. He said to Mr Tilak, 'The goddess is angry with you because you did not worship her.' Mr Tilak said, 'The goddess has gone now. How did you come to know she was angry?' It was Mamanji who now flew into a rage, not the goddess.

The very next day Mamanji stripped me of all my wedding ornaments. He left only the kumkum on my forehead and the mangalsutra round my neck untouched. He also took back all the saris I had been given, leaving only the Paithani with me. Mr Tilak did not find anything inauspicious about what his father had done. As far as Mamanji was concerned, there were three people in the house who were like evil planets—Mr Tilak, brother-in-law Mahadev and now me. He had always had doubts about those two sons because the lines on their palms were not to his liking. His favourite children were Sakharambhau and sister-in-law Sakhu. He believed implicitly in ghosts, black magic, the evil foot, the evil eye, hostile planets and horoscopes. He liked or disliked people depending on the length and breadth of their fingers and toes. The goddess who possessed him was his very favourite deity. She always said dreadful things about the three of us. If one of us had displeased him particularly during the week, she would froth and fume about all three of us on Friday.

Mamanji had lost his job when Mr Tilak was born. That was Mr Tilak's big sin. His wife had died after Mahadevbhauji was born. That was his evil foot at work. My eldest sister-in-law had died after my marriage. That was my inauspicious arrival in the house. He found a new job when Sakharambhau was born. That made Sakharambhau's entry into the world auspicious. That is why he treated him as his own son and the other two as stepsons. At teatime he would call Sakharambhau and sister-in-law Sakhu to sit with him. He would not as much as look at the other two.

I was not fortunate enough to meet my Sasubai. But I will recount here some of the things I have heard about her and about Mr Tilak's early life. Sasubai's situation in her home was exactly like my mother's in hers. Mr Tilak and Mahadevbhauji were always disliked, and before I arrived Sasubai was the third evil person in the house. There were a couple of reasons why she was disliked. To begin with, she used to compose poems. Only two lines of one of them have survived his fiery temper and the real fires in which he burned them. They are as follows:

> A ragdoll is tiny, but great are the deeds she has done;
> She has taught girls from birth, how a home is run.

It would not be an exaggeration to say that Mr Tilak drank his first sips of poetry at this fountainhead. His father hated poetry and therefore Sasubai because she wrote it. That was perhaps the reason why Mr Tilak grew up to dearly love both his mother and poetry. Even after his siblings were born, he would snuggle up to his mother at bedtime. Every night saw furious quarrels breaking out over this. Mr Tilak played many tricks to win his mother's attention. Once when he suspected she was ignoring him, he feigned a fever. He remembered this till the end of his life. He has written about it in one of his devotional poems as recently as 1919 or thereabouts. This is what the poem says:

> I pulled up a rug to fake a fever
> Crying 'oh mother oh mother' the while.
> Mother came running, hugged me tight
> The tears in her eyes erased her smile
> 'Do not cry, it was naught but a play
> A pretense to pull you to my side.
> The fever was never real but fake,'
> Her love poured forth as she did chide
> 'You sly one, you;' and pinched my ear
> I think I feel it tingle still
> God's servant says God's love is mad
> It bends with joy to the servant's will.

'God's servant' was Mr Tilak's appellation for himself in his devotional poems.

Mamanji could not bear to see the love between the son and the mother; but his anger only intensified Mr Tilak's love. He was fascinated by the woman missionary who visited his mother and taught her how to sew and embroider. She had also given Sasubai a book of stories from the Bible, which she used to read regularly. One day Mamanji set fire to the book. Mr Tilak was so angry with his father that he vowed he would take the first opportunity to get back at him. Mamanji was addicted to tobacco. He chewed it mixed with lime. One day, when he was not looking, Mr Tilak took the little box of lime out of his tobacco pouch and flung it into the well. He was only a young boy. It was not as though one book of stories in the fire meant that fire had turned every storybook in the world to ashes; nor did one box of lime flung into a well mean that every other box of lime was queuing up to jump in. But Mamanji flew into an uncontrollable temper. He stamped and danced with rage, while Mr Tilak watched him gleefully from his bed. Mamanji lined up everybody in the house and cross-examined them. Nobody confessed to the crime. Finally he turned on Mr Tilak. He came for him with a stout cane and gave him a severe thrashing. On the third day after the beating, Mr Tilak ran away.

For the next six months, nobody knew where he was. On the day before he ran away, his behaviour had been angelic, perhaps to give his mother at least one day of complete happiness. After that, she lost all peace of mind. She prayed to every deity there was, promising to fulfil the pledges she was making to them if her son returned unharmed. She pleaded with acquaintances for help. She sent a message to her brother Govindrao Bedekar in the Konkan. He came to see her and on the same day, as it happened, an acquaintance came to the house saying, 'Kaku, I saw your Nana acting in a play in Pune yesterday.' Once she was sure he had indeed seen Nana, she asked her brother to mention it to Mamanji. Finally, somehow, they managed to bring Mr Tilak back home. Once he was back, Mamanji began to ill-treat him even more. Sasubai worried constantly that her son might run away again. Sakharambhauji was convinced that Nana had run away because of him. That is why, even as they continued going to school together, he stopped carrying tales to their father about the things that happened on the way.

Around this time, both brothers got guinea worms in their feet. Sasubai looked after them with equal care. But Mamanji would say to Mr Tilak, 'I'm glad this has happened to you. I'd be even happier if it cripples you. You need to be taught a lesson.' To Sakharambhauji, who lay next to Mr Tilak, he said, 'Don't cry, my pet. You'll soon be fine.' A barber was called in to extract the worms. Mamanji took Sakharambhauji on his lap, stroked his back and consoled him while the operation was done. Then he went into the kitchen and got a pedha for him. Needless to say, Mr Tilak got different treatment. Mamanji threatened him with a beating if he cried. These are not imaginary tales. Mr Tilak narrated them to me in Sakharambhauji's presence.

Soon the brothers recovered fully and began going to school again. When Mr Tilak had run away, one of the pledges Sasubai had made for his safe return was a garland of vadas for Maruti. She had pledged other things to other deities too and kept her word. Only this promise remained to be fulfilled. So one day she made vadas, strung them together and asked Mr Tilak and Sakharambhauji to go to the Maruti temple and garland the idol with them. 'Why can't we eat the vadas instead?' Mr Tilak asked.

'I've kept some aside for you to eat when you get back,' she said.

The two boys set off for the temple; but, instead of going there, Mr Tilak sat by the river and ate all the vadas. Sakharambhauji saw this but did not say a word at home. When they returned, Sasubai said, 'Come and have vadas.'

'I don't want any,' Mr Tilak said.

'I thought you did.'

'I've had some.'

'Which?'

'The ones you gave us.'

'You mean you ate the vadas that were meant for the God?'

'Yes.'

Sasubai was shocked to hear this.

Mr Tilak said, 'You've always told us God is never too far away from us. He is within us.'

'But that doesn't mean you eat an offering.'

Although Sasubai was upset, she also appreciated the point he was making. 'I had no idea you would take what I said this way. When I said God is in our hearts, I meant he sees all the bad things we do.' The following day, Sasubai made more vadas and went to the Maruti temple herself to garland the deity with them.

Mr Tilak used to help his mother in her chores. Mamanji would want even a glass of water to be served to him. Mr Tilak helped Sasubai fetch and store water. Every time Mamanji saw this, he would say, 'That's right. Fill water. You're going to end up as a water-carrier anyway. Look at Sakharam here. He's younger than you, but he spends his time studying.' When Sasubai imagined her son as a water-carrier she was filled with fear.

Mr Tilak would write poems during Maths class but nobody ever saw them because he would tear them up immediately. News of this filtered through to Mamanji and Sasubai. This raised his temper higher than ever and made her worry even more. She would say, 'Nana, what's to become of you? I really don't know what to do with you.' Mr Tilak's eyes would fill with tears and he would say, 'I swear I will behave exactly how you want me to.'

Both my parents-in-law abhorred the idea of borrowing money. They had never done it in their lives. Sasubai used to take in sewing to add her mite to Mamanji's earnings. They looked forward to the time when their sons would grow up and augment the family income. Sasubai also waited eagerly for the day a grandson would call her Aaji. Such was her fear of debts that she had put aside a hundred rupees for a rainy day. Mamanji knew nothing about this. As it happened, the rainy day did come, though not in the way she would have wished but as God willed. Mamanji had been transferred to a place called Mokhada. There were no schools there so he went alone leaving his wife and children in Kalyan. As soon as he left, peace, contentment and joy entered the house as new residents. Mr Tilak's pranks decreased. Or perhaps Sasubai did not notice them as much as her husband used to. Now Mr Tilak had all the time in the world to talk to his mother. When Mamanji was around she had much more work to do and he would get annoyed if he saw Mr Tilak talking to her. Things were quite different now. Now there was nobody but just them, children and mother. What more could they want!

Sasubai was an ideal mother. She took excellent care of her children. She would serve them simple but fresh food, hot off the fire. She kept an eye on their studies and their activities. Mr Tilak would never step out of the house even for a moment without his mother's permission. His behaviour in the house was always respectful. He did not trouble his younger siblings. With his Dada away, Sakharambhauji knew he had to obey his mother and elder brother now. Sasubai took her children occasionally to visit Mamanji's aunt at the Subhedar home. But one worry nagged her all the time. How was her husband managing for food? Mr Tilak would say, 'Aai, it's so nice when Dada isn't here. It'll be such fun if he stayed away forever. We'll be free of worries.'

'Who will feed you then?'

'To tell you the truth Aai, I feel terribly scared when he's here. Sometimes I even wish he were not there at all.'

'Never say such terrible things.'

'What have I done to make him so angry? Aren't I a good boy? I really don't know what I do that is so wrong.'

'You'll understand when you grow up.'

'Aai, I will never ever leave you. You have had to suffer so much for me.'

'Let's not talk about that. I only want you to continue behaving well.'

People's thoughts, plans and actions depend entirely on God's will. What happened then was like a snake spitting poison in a pitcher of gold. One day a letter came, signed by Mamanji but written by someone else, saying, 'Wamanrao is seriously ill. Come immediately if you want to see him alive. Do not delay.'

To begin with, she is a woman, impoverished, surrounded by a crowd of children. She gets this letter from her husband. The journey to his place is extremely difficult. Her mind is in turmoil. She does not know what to do, how to go. Her stomach churns with anxiety, but she musters courage and says to her children, 'Stay back here, my dears. I'll go alone.'

Mr Tilak said, 'Aai, this is what we will do. I will go with you. You'll need help. How will you manage alone? Dada is ill. You'll have to do housework, fetch water from a distance. If you take me along, I promise to behave myself. Sakharam can stay with the Subhedars.' This was like a straw to a drowning man. Sasubai agreed. The fact was, Mr Tilak did not want to stay away from his mother. Sakharambhauji was sent to the Subhedars. Mother and son prepared to leave. She took along the hundred rupees she had saved and they left. Those who remember what the road to Mokhada used to be like fifty years ago will know what lay ahead. Sasubai had Mahadevbhauji in her arms, Mr Tilak carried a small bundle of belongings and they set off.

It was high summer. The ground was hot, the sun blazed, the mind was anxious, the stomach empty, not a drop of water along the way, feet bare, pricked by thorns and stones, dense trees, fear of predatory animals, a hill to descend, another to climb, a deep valley on the other side, small villages of fisher-folk, fear of snakes slithering out of their holes, strange sounds from dry leaves—this was the terrain through which they trudged. Sasubai was crossing all the boundaries of her life. 'Let me carry the baby,' Mr Tilak offered. 'You must be tired.'

'It's all right, dear. I'm older and stronger,' she said. So they talked along the way, easing one another's burden and finally reached Mokhada. The village was on a hill. Sasubai kept saying, 'All I want is to see him happy.'

'I am sure he is perfectly fine. Don't worry. There's nothing the matter with him.'

'I hope not. That's all I ask. May God will it. I pray for nothing else. Life is a path on which we help others, and others help us to whatever extent they can. It is a difficult path and so is this.'

They climbed the rock-faced hill. The village was not very big. As soon as they entered, they heard the news. They were not too late. When they arrived at the house, Mamanji was relaxing outside chatting. Sasubai's joy knew no bounds. The great hardships she had borne no longer weighed on her. A little while later, she got down to work, sweeping and cleaning. Then she took her children down the steep incline to the well to have a bath.

'Aai, remember what I said? There's nothing wrong with him.'

'Bless your tongue. What you said was true. All I want now is that you should behave yourself as you promised.' Sasubai was carrying a pot of water on her head. Washed clothes hung over her shoulder. Mr Tilak was carrying Mahadevbhauji. Thus they trudged up the hill.

'Let me carry that water pot.'

'No, dear. It's heavy.'

'Aren't you tired, Aai?'

'Not much. Really.'

With the pot on her head and the clothes on her shoulder she entered the house thinking of the food she would now have to cook. Mamanji was sitting by the door. As she came up she said to him, 'Do you think you could give me a hand with this pot?' The moment he heard those words, he lunged at her like a tiger. 'Am I your servant?' he roared, catching her by the neck and kicking her in the back. Sasubai collapsed on the ground with Lord Rama's name on her lips. The boys saw this and began to cry in terror. Putting Mahadevbhauji down, Mr Tilak went to his mother's side and said, 'Are you badly hurt, Aai?' Sasubai signalled with her hand to say no. Mr Tilak brought her dry clothes to wear. She managed somehow to wrap herself in them and took to her bed.

The neighbours had seen what had happened. They were at a loss to understand the reason. Mamanji was sitting outside. He would come in once in a while and go back outside. Sasubai lay in bed for eight days. No word except Rama's name escaped her lips and nothing except water passed through them. On the eighth day she breathed her last, leaving Mamanji a widower and abandoning her children to the mercy of the world.

Another Escape

The heat of the sun dries up trees, cracks stones. Mamanji was after all human. Separation from his wife burned him up and broke his heart. The thought that he had brought this sorrow upon himself by his own reckless act filled him with bitter remorse. He became distracted. Life without his wife was unbearably difficult.

Mr Tilak felt completely lost. His grief was unbounded. He had always looked upon his mother as the ultimate deity. He said openly how good it would have been had Dada gone, not Aai. When her end came, she had only called upon Lord Rama. Not once had she uttered her son's name. That is why Rama took her away. Mr Tilak thought he too should do what she had done and follow her. But who would look after little Mahadev then? Such conflicting thoughts ran amok through his mind.

Mamanji stopped tormenting Mr Tilak and Mr Tilak stopped playing pranks on him. But a desperate thought lurked in his young mind, which he did not speak of to anybody. He wanted to run away from Dada and earn his own living. Mamanji decided to immerse his wife's ashes in the Godavari and conduct all the death rituals at Tryambakeshwar. That was the nearest holy place to Mokhada. He decided to leave Mahadevbhauji with the neighbours and take Mr Tilak with him. Mahadevbhauji's clothes were in the bundle his wife had brought with her. He opened it. Inside he saw another small, tightly tied bundle. Untying it, he found the hundred rupees that Sasubai had brought along for emergencies. Looking at the money, his sorrow surged up again. He sobbed uncontrollably saying, 'She saved this money for her final rituals.'

After the rituals at Tryambakeshwar, Mamanji planned to free himself by handing the children over to Sasubai's brother's care. He had asked Mr Bedekar to come down to Mokhada for this. Mr Tilak felt sure his uncle would take care of Sakharambhauji and Mahadevbhauji. That would relieve him of responsibility. If he himself stayed at his uncle's place, he would not be able to stop crying thinking of his mother. It would be better if he made other arrangements for himself. Mr Tilak must have been about twelve then. That night, when everybody had fallen asleep, he got up silently and ran away. When Mamanji woke up in the morning, there was no sign of him. It was a repetition of the earlier incident in Kalyan. Mamanji became distraught and his return to Mokhada was greatly delayed.

Mr Tilak slept in a dharamshala after he ran away. In the morning, he started walking down the road outside the dharamshala to wherever it led. It turned out to be the road to Nashik. He had nothing with him but the clothes on his back. No money. Nothing to eat. He had no idea where he was heading. All he knew was that he would keep walking straight and stand on his own feet.

Mamanji returned to Mokhada. His brother-in-law had already arrived there to take the younger children away. Mamanji was sad to see them go. He was also sad for Mr Tilak. Sasubai's face haunted Mr Tilak. Her last words 'Rama Rama' echoed in his ears. He reached Nashik around ten o'clock. But he did not know that was where he was. He had never been to Nashik before. He inquired around and when he came to know this was Nashik, he made his way to the Godavari and settled down on her bank. God neglects nobody and he did not neglect Mr Tilak. A boy of about the same age as him had come to the Godavari for a bath and had entered the river close to where Mr Tilak was sitting. The boy came up to him and said, 'Who are you?'

'I'm just a Brahmin.'

'Where have you come from?'

'From the Konkan.'

'Where are you going?'

'I don't know.'

'Don't you have a family?'

'I do, all except my mother.'

'Which of them is here?'

'None.'

'Would you like to come home with me? We have a big house. I too have no family except my mother. She'll give you something to eat.' After this, the boy spread his wet dhoti out to dry and gave it to Mr Tilak to wear after it dried. They had their baths and went home together. The boy introduced Mr Tilak to his mother, Yesubai. She turned out to be even more loving than the boy. The lady asked him to tell her everything about himself. She was saddened by what she heard. She said, 'Son, I am not rich. But I would like to do what I can for you. Don't wander around here and there. Stay with us. It's a large house with only two of us living here.' So Mr Tilak had a place to stay and somebody's support to survive. Yesubai arranged for him to eat his meals with other Brahmin families four times a week. She fed him on the remaining three days.

Yesubai was very kind, but poor. She also suffered from some stomach ailment. She had not been able to give her son much education. Despite this, she had offered to help Mr Tilak out of sheer concern and sympathy. Conscious of this, he would help her out with her daily chores, and felt guilty about eating with her three times a week knowing how poor she was. Gradually he made many friends in Nashik and found two more families willing to feed him. So now he had only one meal a week with her.

The boy who had befriended Mr Tilak was called Vishwanath Balkrishna Mylay. The love that the two boys bore one another appeared to have no limits. No morsel of food tasted sweet to either if the other was not eating. They loved each other like brothers. Concerned about the burden he was putting on the family's finances, Mr Tilak would buy vegetables and other groceries for the families he became acquainted with and give the two or three rupees he earned every month to

Yesubai. Meanwhile, he developed a great love for Sanskrit. He approached the Veda scholar Ganeshshastri for lessons. The shastri's son, the late Laxmanshastri, was still a young boy then. Sometimes Mr Tilak would go to the local seminary to learn Veda recitation. He won his teachers' love. One of his teachers was called Mr Rahalkar. Impressed by the boy's brilliance, he would also help him out financially. Mr Tilak had now forgotten his father's harassment and his mother's love. But he continued to love poetry, nature and oratory. He observed everything minutely, composed poems and always helped others to the extent he could.

Almost nine months later, Mamanji came to know that his son was living in Nashik. He felt reassured when he heard this. He wrote to his brother-in-law Govindrao Bedekar immediately, telling him that Nana was in Nashik. Educational facilities there were good and living was inexpensive. So he asked him if he would agree to set up house in Nashik with his son Shridhar and his widowed sister-in-law who stayed with them, promising to send them ten rupees a month. When the letter was read out to Nana's grandmother, Gangabai, her eyes filled with tears. She had already lost her daughter and had been terribly worried about Nana. Following Mamanji's suggestion, Mr Tilak's uncle, aunt, cousin Shridhar and brother Sakharam arrived most unexpectedly in Nashik. They tracked down Mr Tilak and the family began living together. Gradually one thing led to another, Mr Tilak's uncle returned home, leaving him at the head of this household of three brothers, and solely responsible for looking after them. It was during this time that I went to play with sister-in-law Sakhu and was driven out of the house. Mamanji and Govindrao would send Mr Tilak ten rupees each. Mr Tilak would add a little to that with his occasional earnings. Meanwhile, he continued to study Sanskrit and English.

Soon after we got married, Sakharambhauji finished his education in Nashik and went to Pune. Shridharbhauji went back to the Konkan. That left just the two of us in Nashik.

Naturally this meant that the twenty rupees that Mamanji and uncle Bedekar had been sending Mr Tilak, stopped coming. With nobody to help him, he could not immediately start fending for us by himself. So we decided to go to Jalalpur, to my parents' home.

Procession

Govindrao Mama loved Mr Tilak like his own son. He was accustomed to saying, 'Who is left now? Manu is my only child. All that I have will be hers and my nephew's after I go.' But Attyabai saw things differently. She wondered what Mr Tilak's future would be if her husband pampered him, allowing him to idle. Their difference of opinion on this matter gave rise to constant flare-ups between them. Attyabai would say, 'Mr Tilak has no sense of responsibility towards his family. He eats, washes his hands and off he goes to roam the town with his loafer friends.' To this, Mama would say, 'Let him be. That is how the young are. He will understand things better when he's older.'

Gangapur is next to Jalalpur. The Ganga is the only boundary between them. Gangapur was larger, richer and livelier than Jalalpur. Dashavatar plays used to be staged there. Mr Tilak had found many friends and admirers of his poetry there. At their insistence and by his own wish, he began to act in one of the plays. But it was all hush-hush. Everybody took great care to make sure news of this did not reach Govindrao Mama's ears. But somehow, news would break through all fortifications and reach him. Someone would say casually, 'Hey Mama, your son-in-law set the stage on fire yesterday. He played Dashrath so well, it made the audience sob loudly.' To this, Mama would say, 'That's impossible. He was at home all night.' It was Mama's habit to quietly put a lock on our door when we slept. It was on the strength of that lock that he tried to lock up people's mouths. He would feel for the keys in his pocket, find them there and conclude that people were trying to set him up against Mr Tilak with false reports.

When the night grew quiet, the sounds of the play at Gangapur would reach Jalalpur. Lying in bed, Mr Tilak would begin to mutter impatiently in the dark, 'Ganapati has entered. The first stroke has fallen on the drum. Listen to the opening song "Dance Sharada". How clearly we can hear it.' Around the same time, we would hear the murmur of voices below our window. Mr Tilak's friends would help him climb noiselessly out of the window. It was a farmer's house. There were always ropes and harnesses lying around. They would come in handy for the exercise.

Once again, on the day after Mr Tilak had run off to Gangapur and climbed back into the room with the help of the same rope, somebody told Mama about his wonderful performance the previous night. 'That is not true,' Mama said. 'I will come to see the play myself tonight. Your tongues will not stop wagging otherwise.' Mama did what he said he would. At night he slipped out quietly and went to see the play. Little did Mr Tilak know that his father-in-law was in the audience that night. It was the scene of Rama's departure from Ayodhya. King Dashrath was lamenting his fate. Mr Tilak began to sing the poems he had composed for the scene. The audience began to sob. The practice of reciting poetry publicly had not started during Mr Tilak's lifetime. He made up for that lack by singing his poems in this way. Mama's eyes began to stream with tears. The flood doused the fire of his rage. It was all very well for Mama's rage to fizzle out, but Attyabai's thunder was not to be contained. It exploded. Attyabai had spread stories in the town about Mr Tilak not doing his evening puja, but using the puja paraphernalia instead in the most sacrilegious ways. For his part, Mr Tilak would go around town saying his mother-in-law was a termagant while his father-in-law was tender-hearted. 'He's the kind who will draw the cover over me as I sleep. She's the kind who will order my wife to tear it off.' This constant bickering finally drove Mr Tilak to decide to leave Jalalpur. Back we went to Nashik. Within four days, Nashik became a bore and we felt like returning to Jalalpur. But nobody was saying come back. How could we just get up and go? In the end, we made up our minds to go anyway. The problem was, how would I walk the distance? So we hired a horse. But I refused to ride it while Mr

Tilak walked. I was also scared to sit on a horse. So Mr Tilak said, let us both ride it. But I felt shy to sit on the horse with him. Mr Tilak said, 'We will not meet anyone along the way. The bazaar must be long over. If we do meet somebody, we'll pretend to be neighbours.' That convinced me. We mounted the horse and set off at a trot. We met nobody at all till we reached Alandi. There we met the village barber. When he saw us, he burst out laughing. 'Well, well,' he said laughing all the time, 'that's a nice wedding procession you have there.'

Deeply mortified, we got off the horse. We warmed the barber's palm with a few coins. He promised not to tell anybody. We also made him an offering of the quilt we had spread on the horse's back. We could not have taken it with us to Jalalpur anyway. The barber had a nice horse-ride back to Nashik while we walked the rest of the way to Jalalpur to appear, like an apparition, at Govindrao Mama's door.

The welcome we got was lukewarm. The house was completely silent for the next four days. Then, gradually, we saw signs that Attyabai's smouldering volcano was about to erupt. Finally, it happened. Now even Mama joined Attyabai in accusing Mr Tilak of not showing any concern for home and family. Mr Tilak went into a sulk and took off by himself, abandoning me. He walked at a good clip till Gangapur. Then he slowed down. On the way he met Gopalbhat, the priest of Jalalpur. He worked hard to persuade Mr Tilak to return. So Mr Tilak forgot his anger and came back.

This time, my elder brother Keshavrao Mama received him.

'So? You ate crow again?'

'Rubbish! I didn't want to come. Gopalbhat forced me.'

'Like the old saying—Buffalo, buffalo, where are you dragging me?'

Mr Tilak laughed and so did his brother-in-law. But after this, we could not stay in Jalalpur much longer. Mr Tilak heard from people that Attyabai had been saying she had brought this curse upon herself and there was no help for it but to watch the twists and turns it was taking. There was no way we could continue staying there after this. Mr Tilak decided that we would return to Nashik. Once he made a plan, he had to execute it immediately. He set off forthwith for Nashik. He stayed in Panchavati at Wamanrao Ranade's place. Some time later, Wamanrao advised him to start a private school to teach English. Mr Tilak had studied English only up to the sixth grade, but he had read English books voraciously. So he started a school in the Krishna temple in Panchavati and began teaching there. It was near where his friend Krishnarao Bhonde lived. Some fifteen children attended the school. The fees were eight annas per head. Mr Tilak now rented his own place near Mr Ranade's in Phadniswada. This reassured me because Wamanrao's aunt was my father's sister. I would not feel out of place staying there.

Once Mr Tilak had taken the responsibility of starting a school, he saw it through to the end. He devoted himself to it heart and soul. He spent almost all his time with the children. One day he was late coming home. It was past ten o'clock. I was alone at home. I had finished cooking and was waiting for him to return. At one point, I lay down on the rug and fell asleep. When Mr Tilak returned, he knocked and knocked on the door and even threw himself at it. The neighbours tried to persuade him to have his dinner with them, saying I was obviously fast asleep and not likely to get up. But he would not have it. My aunt was also upset with me. At last my brother-in-law propped up a ladder near the window and prodded me with a long stick. I shot up startled. Mr Tilak was furious. He said 'Wait. I'll write this whole story and send it to your Waman Dada to publish in his paper.' I swore to him I would not let it happen again. I would splash cold water on my eyes if they began to close. I would not even sit down, but wait for him standing up.

Packed Off Home

Our life was running smoothly when Mamanji and Sakharambhauji turned up one day.

Mamanji's expression said he was happy to see how our life had turned out. He had wanted to do a Satyanarayan puja but had not been able to do it yet. He asked me to make all the preparations for it. I was just a girl but my Ranade aunt was a great help. She came over and did everything that was required. Mamanji was very pleased with the arrangements. He went around telling everybody, 'Our Lakshmi is not only Lakshmi in name. She is a real Lakshmi. She's still young but how clever she is. She takes such keen interest in home and family.' His words thrilled me.

Mamanji and Bhauji left after the puja. Almost immediately afterwards, we got a letter from Mamanji saying Sakharambhauji was engaged to be married and we were to go to Pune. Obeying his wish, we went to Pune. Mr Tilak was very unhappy at having to leave the school he had started. He handed over this tiny institution to Krishnarao Bhonde before we left. Readers will gradually come to recognize a characteristic of Mr Tilak's personality. He would throw himself heart and soul into whatever work he was engaged in at the time. But once it was out of sight, it went completely out of mind. What happened then to his heart and soul? His popular poem 'Little bird will you ever return' applied to him perfectly. When he went away, we were left singing, 'Oh wave upon the wind, when will your anger turn?' When he left in a fit, I would weep quietly, the family elders would fall to worrying and the young would run helter-skelter looking for him.

The wedding guests arrived. But some fly got into the ointment and the wedding was called off. The guests departed. I have mentioned earlier that the only good sari I possessed was an heirloom Paithani and the only jewellery I had was my mangalsutra. Mr Tilak knew that. He asked me for the Paithani on some pretext and went off somewhere, leaving me behind in Pune. Nobody knew where the Paithani went. One day Mamanji began to cross-examine me. I was about thirteen or fourteen then.

'Lakshmibai, where is the Paithani?'

'I don't know. I had tied it up properly and kept it in that niche.'

'I don't care where you kept it. Bring back the Paithani or face my wrath.'

When Mamanji got angry, he would address me in the respectful plural. The truth of it was that he and Bhauji had paid to retrieve the Paithani from a pawn shop. But I never set eyes on it again. Father and son must have had a tiff. The son had left. I was abandoned to Mamanji's mercy.

'Mamanji, I want bangles.'

'Oh? Why are you telling me? Bring back the Paithani, then we'll buy you bangles.'

'My saris are torn.'

'Oh? Why are you telling me? Bring back the Paithani, then we'll buy you saris.'

'I swear I haven't lost the Paithani.'

'I don't care. Grind grain for people and buy yourself bangles and saris.'

When he said these things, I would sniffle away by myself. He didn't give me shikakai to wash my hair or oil to oil it. Whatever I asked for, his answer was always the same. One day Sakharambhauji drew me aside and said, 'We have the Paithani. Nana had pawned it. It's been retrieved, but I can't give it to you. Dada will get angry.' I said, 'I don't mind if I don't get it. I have enough.'

A nephew of my aunt, Waman Balkrishna Ranade, lived in Pune. Mamanji called him over and told him to take care of me. He said, 'You are her father-in-law. We have looked after her all these days. Now it's your job to do it. If you hadn't been around, we would have been obliged to look after her and we would have done it too.' As my aunt's nephew was leaving, he took me aside and said, 'Manu, don't worry. We aren't abandoning you. We'll take care of you.' That gave me courage. I immediately said, 'I am very keen to wear Pune bangles. Mamanji says go grind grain for people and buy yourself Pune bangles.'

That afternoon when Mamanji came home, he spoke very sweetly to me.

'Lakshmibai, you want saris, don't you?'

I was thrilled.

'Yes, I do. My saris are in tatters.'

'Do you want one or two?'

'Two.'

'If you want one, I'll get you a four rupee one. If you want two, I'll get you two rupee ones.'

That was it. What could I say? I felt very bad. I went into my corner again, wiped my eyes and got back to work. Those were the first saris that Mr Tilak's family was giving me after my wedding. I remembered the love that Govindrao Mama had showered on me and wept at the memory. A little while later, I was given two saris worth two rupees each.

Mr Ranade came in the evening. Mamanji said to him, 'Ranade, I have made arrangements to send the girl away. You need not bother about it now. Goodbye.'

Next morning, I was put on the seven o'clock train to Nashik. I was accompanied by two women. I never got my Pune bangles. Bhauji had come to see me off. Just as the train was leaving, he put a rupee in my hand saying, 'Vahini, you talked so often about wanting bangles but I was too afraid of Dada to get them. Take this money now and buy bangles.'

'But I wanted Pune bangles.' The train began to move. My Pune bangles were left behind forever. We reached Nashik in the evening. My companions took me to their home in Panchavati. I had dozens of relatives in Nashik but I had to stay in the house of strangers. The women took me to an upstairs room and went down to do their work. Looking around, I saw a pair of tablas, a veena and other musical instruments. First I was curious and then scared. I had never seen such instruments before. I had grown up in a village. To top that, I was Narayanrao Gokhale's daughter. I was the kind of girl who imagined train compartments to be like laddoo containers. You packed people into them and closed the lids. I got scared of the instruments and fled from the room. Downstairs, I called out frantically to the two women, groping my way around in the dark. There was a sunken courtyard paved with stone slabs outside. I stumbled into it and fell with a thud. My hands dashed against a raised stone platform. I had not been given Pune bangles and now even my Nashik bangles broke. Luckily, although I had had a bad fall, my head was safe. The noise brought the two women out. They helped me up and took me upstairs. They took off their necklaces and wound them round my wrists as substitute bangles, and began urging me to eat something. I refused to eat food cooked by them. The poor things did not take that to heart, but stayed up with me all night and did what they could to make me comfortable. The next morning, they bought me bangles that cost an anna and I left for Nashik from where I was to go to Jalalpur. But even before I left Nashik, I ran into Govindrao Mama in Ravivar Peth. He was both surprised and pleased to see me. But he was also unhappy to hear of the journey I had made. The two of us then set off for Jalalpur together.

Back to the Marital Home

Mr Tilak's flight from Pune took him straight to Dhamak village in Varhad. There he found a teaching job in a government school on a salary of Rs 25 a month.

Fathers, mothers, brothers, sisters live in every home
But there is no place on earth untouched by my love.

These devotional lines from his pen match his own personality perfectly. There was not a soul in Dhamak that he could call kith. But he took to his heart whoever happened to be around him. That is how he peopled his world. A poor Brahmin youth was now part of his world. He had a sweet voice. Mr Tilak composed four keertans specially for him, rehearsed him and helped him perform them. The youth went on to make his living off those keertans.

Mr Tilak also met a Yogi Sadhu there and became his disciple. The Sadhu gave him a mantra which Mr Tilak would recite sitting in the river. He would also grind neem leaves, roll the paste into pellets and eat them. More people now gathered around him. But he would go off into the jungle to meditate. As a result, he had to say goodbye to the school. But his guru soon ordered him to give up this life. One day, he asked him, 'Where is your family? Do you have their permission to live this life?' Mr Tilak was forced to say 'No.' His guru instantly ordered him to return to Jalalpur, assuring him that they would meet regularly.

Meanwhile, my people had been searching for Mr Tilak high and low. One fine day, he presented himself at the door wearing a saffron robe, a long beard, matted hair and a string of rudraksha seeds as large as lemons round his neck. Govindrao Mama was shocked to see him in this state. But he resolved not to say a word of reproach to him. In his present dress, he seemed well on his way to becoming an ascetic. Mama warned Attyabai to hold her tongue. She did too. But not for long. Nature had to be given way. One day when Govindrao Mama, Attyabai and I were sitting in the inner room talking, she said to Mama, 'On which rootless stump did you find this crow?'

'Wasn't me. It was your people who found him.'

'But Attyabai, if everyone decides to sit in a palanquin, who will carry it?'

'Listen to this one taking his side. Why, you are there to carry it. He'll sit in it composing songs. You can sing them and the two of you can go beg.'

This angry exchange flew straight out the door onto the verandah where Mr Tilak was sitting. He got up like a shot and began packing his things. Mama tried hard to pacify him. He would not relent. Then Mama said, 'Your wife has now come of age. You must take her with you. I'm not prepared to look after her beyond this.'

Mamanji had been transferred to Murbad. Mr Tilak decided to take me there. My father-in-law was a man of extremely neat habits. After my mother-in-law died, he did not marry again nor did he indulge in any hanky-panky on the side. His conduct was chaste in the extreme. He looked upon every woman other than his wife as a mother. After Sasubai's death, he kept house. He did all the cooking, and in such perfect proportions, that not a grain of rice was left over at the end of a meal. He stocked the house with every small thing required to run it efficiently. A visitor would have found it difficult to believe there were no women in the house. The house was on the premises of the Ram temple. There was a homely eatery next to the temple.

When we arrived, Mamanji had had lunch and was relaxing on the verandah. Needless to say there was nothing left for us to eat. So we were sent off to the eatery next door. What a meal that was. So little rice you could hardly see it, a tiny spot of dal and roasted beans, all washed down with watery buttermilk. Mr Tilak felt nothing about it. But four generations of my people had lived on the plains. For me, this meal was worse than starvation. When we returned from lunch, Mamanji showed me around his quarters.

'Lakshumbai, I will not tolerate disorder and slovenliness in this house. Here's all the foodstuff. Here's the firewood. Out there is the well. You will now cook the evening meal.'

I was making rice bhakris for the first time in my life. Never before had I even seen them. My bhakris looked like parched earth before the first rain.

'Lakshumbai, this will not do. Your people may be animals. I am not. Your cooking must be perfect.'

When I cooked, he would sit in the front room from where he could see everything I was doing. Very often he would do his puja while simultaneously instructing me how to cook. I was a good cook but my food was what we ate on the plains. His food belonged to the Konkan. One day Mamanji said to me, 'Make a live phodni for the amti.'

'How do I make a live phodni?'

'Heat the iron ladle.'

I heated the ladle and put in mustard and cumin seeds as usual. Mamanji hit the roof.

'If you'd been a stone, you would have served perfectly as a step to the lavatory.'

'Who knows? I might have been carved into an idol.'

Of course I said this to myself.

Mamanji then instructed me to let the oil catch fire before putting in the spices.

I picked up a piece of burning wood and held it over the ladle to let the oil catch fire. The oil flared up into a fire to end all fires. Then Mamanji's rage flared up even higher. To begin with, the people from the Konkan ate food that was very different from what we ate on the plains. Two, the names they gave dishes sounded outlandish. Three, Mamanji had a satiric tongue. Taken together, it was enough to make me go berserk. One day Mamanji told me to make 'ayti'. Now what was this? 'Ayti' as far as I knew was a woman (me?) who didn't lift a finger to do any work but expected to be provided for. Another day, he told me to make 'pejbudya' rice. I had heard the word 'panbudya' meaning something that dives underwater. But 'pejbudya'? This was beyond me. Luckily I found a guru. There was a house near the well. A matron called Gangabai Joshi lived there. If Mamanji told me to make something I had never heard of, I would pick up the water pot and race down to the well. While drawing water, I would ask Gangabai softly through her window, 'Kaku, what is "pejbudya" rice?'

'Simple. Just flood the rice with water and you have pejbudya rice.'

I came home laughing, made the pejbudya rice and served it to Mamanji. After that, whenever he told me to make strange dishes, I would make them without a hitch under Gangakaku's instructions as though I'd been making them all my life. Soon Mamanji smelt a rat. He tracked down my guru. He and the Joshis were friends but the friendship curdled because of me. Mamanji said to Mr Joshi one day, 'Don't let my daughter-in-law visit you.' Mr Joshi said, 'We can't do that. Keep her tethered if you want her not to see us.' Mamanji left it at that. He did not think it wise to tether me. Instead he gave up on the Joshis.

Mr Tilak started a school here too. He had become an expert at that now. He was a past master at teaching English. His friends and brothers became his students. He did not draw a salary. He loved his students like his own children. They respected him back as a father. He earned good fees too. He designed the curriculum. His aim was to turn out cultured human beings. Perhaps the education he gave the students fell short of this aim, but his company itself was enough to make them cultured. The school was doing very well. Mr Tilak would go there as soon as lunch was over. Mamanji would then begin pacing the floor. The school was in the temple precincts. The temple and the house stood cheek-by-jowl with each other. He paced from the kitchen to the temple and back. All his attention during this time was on my movements. You would think I was born only to eat.

I tended to forget many of Mamanji's orders. When the men had eaten and I had cleared up after them, I would plaster the floor with cow dung and leave the glob of dung near the cooking vessels. Then I would wash my hands and serve myself. Mamanji would watch saying nothing till I had started eating. Once I had had a couple of mouthfuls of food, he would say, 'Lakshumbai, the cow dung glob is lying near the cooking vessels. Kindly throw it out.' So I would push my plate away and throw the cow dung out. Mamanji would tell me all the time not to leave the cow dung near the vessels and I would always forget. When the dung was thrown away, I would return to my meal. It was time now for Mamanji to say, 'Lakshumbai, have you watered the tulsi plant?' Of course I had not because it was a chore I invariably forgot. So off I went again, in the middle of my lunch.

'How is it that you never forget to eat? Will you die if you don't? And if you die, do you think the world will be desolate without you?'

This was our daytime routine. There was another routine for the night. Mamanji would say, 'Lakshumbai, make my bed before you sit down for dinner. Fill the tin-pot with water. Don't forget.' Dinner was always very late. I would get hungry. I could not spread Mamanji's bedding while the family was still sitting around. If I made the bed afterwards, I would have to change back into my polluted sari because I could not do household chores wearing the freshly washed sari I had to wear to cook and eat. If I decided I would rather change than stay hungry a moment longer, I would regret the decision. Because a few minutes into dinner and Mamanji would say, 'Lakshumbai make my bed, will you?' And Lakshumbai would get up, change into her polluted sari, make the bed, change back into her washed sari and resume eating.

The Harassment of an In-law

I was cooking one day when some students rushed in to say, 'Vahini, your father-in-law is observing yours and Nana's last rites out there.'

I got up and rushed to the temple to see what was happening. What a sight it was! Mamanji was chucking out all the puja vessels one by one from his upstairs room, landing them in Lord Rama's sabha mandap. With every object he flung, he chanted, 'My daughter-in-law is dead. This is her twelfth-day ritual. My son is dead. Here's his tenth day ritual.'

The reason for this rage was that the puja vessels were stained. They were made of copper. I washed them with well water; I scrubbed them with wood ash; and it was the rainy season. However hard I scrubbed to make them shine, clouds would appear on them within minutes. I collected all the vessels Mamanji had thrown down and went upstairs. He had set up his gods in a corner of the school. He watched me as I came up.

'Had you scrubbed the vessels?'

'Yes.'

'Swear on me.'

'I swear on you, I had scrubbed them.'

'You aren't going to weep if I die of your false oath, are you? Hold your mangalsutra in your hand and swear.'

I held my mangalsutra in my hand and swore. Why should I be scared since I was innocent?

'Wait. I'll call a meeting of the village women, put these vessels before them and ask them what they think. They'll put cow dung in your mouth for lying.'

I was sure no woman was going to put any cow dung in my mouth.

'Hold my feet and swear. Watch out. You'll turn to ashes if you touch them.'

As I moved forward to touch his feet, he moved back, 'Watch out. I'm telling you, you'll burn.'

'I don't mind. Death at your feet might not be such a bad thing.'

Finally, I flung myself flat on the ground and held his feet tight. I did not burst into flames and die. I was very disappointed. I thought it would have been a blessing to die and be done with it. But perhaps because Mamanji's divine powers fell short, or, quite simply, I had indeed scrubbed the vessels, I did not turn to ashes that day.

One day Mamanji took Mr Tilak aside and said, 'Nana, you must marry another woman. I'll get you ten girls from the Konkan.'

Mr Tilak said, 'I have problems feeding one. What do I want with a second?'

'Abandon her to her people.'

'I will never do that. I don't care how my life turns out. But I will never do something like that.'

This and the story that follows were proof of how much Mr Tilak loved me.

The water in the nearby well had dried up. There was another well in the forest. But because throngs of women went there during the day, Mamanji's instructions to me were to fetch water at night. I was afraid of the dark. But he did not care. He said, 'If someone comes to devour you, tell him my father-in-law is sitting in the temple. Eat him first, then come to get me.'

But Mr Tilak said, 'Don't worry. I'll fetch the water.'

When night fell, I'd go out of the back door with the water pot and he would go out of the front door empty-handed. He would meet me outside and fetch water. I'd loiter around outside till he came back. Then I'd carry the water pot in. Mamanji was impressed by how confidently his daughter-in-law fetched water!

One day I was washing Mamanji's spittoon. I felt squeamish and spat. This did not escape his sharp eyes. At night he said very sweetly to me, 'Lakshmi, I rather like your water tumbler. Please put that beside my bed tonight.' So I began putting my tumbler beside his bed every night. One day the woman who came to wash vessels said to me, 'Vahini, Dada uses your tumbler as a spittoon.' I could not believe her. The next day the woman showed me my tumbler. That is when light dawned on me. Later I would set the same tumbler out for his puja and he would push it away.

Although Mamanji tortured me in all these ways, there were two things about him which I must acknowledge. One was that he never used an obscenity when he cursed me; and two, he never touched me. In fact he would occasionally even have good things to say about me to people. One day he invited somebody for a meal. He cooked everything himself. I was amazed. Soon the guest arrived. I served him. He asked the guest, 'How did you like the food?' The guest said, 'It is so good, words fail me.' The guest was happy to have had such a good meal and I was still trying to get over my amazement.

However, this aspect of his nature did not reveal itself too often. If I asked him for something, he would fly into a rage. I was never given oil or shikakai to wash my hair. If I asked him for these things, he would say, 'Grind grain for people and buy oil and shikakai with your earnings.' I was reduced to cleaning my hair with mud. Halfway through my bath, he would walk off with the bucket of hot water and have a bath himself. Then I would have to complete my bath with cold water. Whenever we quarrelled over oil and shikakai, he would tell me this story: 'Once we had run out of firewood. My wife was pregnant. Even then I made her chop wood. Why should I show concern for you? My wife never answered back. When she realized she had run out of some foodstuff, she would place the remains before me without a word. I understood that she was running out of the stuff. But today's girls have become very arrogant. You'll never learn how to behave with elders.'

For 'those' three days of the month, I was left to starve. Mamanji would cook only for himself. He would cook for all of us only when Mr Tilak was around. On those days I had to sit in a dark room. I was very scared of the dark. But gradually, I lost that fear. So, in a way, the ill-treatment helped.

Mr Tilak had now made a name for himself as a poet. His reputation had reached as far as Mumbai and Pune. Although I was having a bad time, the times had turned for him. Once during that period, he was invited to Mumbai to speak. He went supposedly for eight days but did not return. Eight days went by, then ten, then fifteen. There was no sign of him and no letter from him. I began to worry. My tears would not stop. To add to that, he had told Mamanji he was going to stay at Sardar Griha in Dhobi Talao. That gave him a stick to torture me with.

'There's a letter from your husband today.'

'I want to go to Mumbai.'

'He's found a job washing dhotis in Sardar Griha.'

'Then I'll hang them out to dry.'

'He waits on people there.'

'I'll clear up after they are done. Just take me to Mumbai.'

'I have no money. Fend for yourself if that's what you want. But don't think Mumbai is Murbad. You'll be like an invisible pebble there.'

One day I was sobbing my heart out. Mamanji felt sorry for me. He sat down beside me. 'Lakshmi, I have just one daughter. The other one died. You are like my second daughter. Don't cry now. Tomorrow is the hartalika feast. Call a couple of women over in the evening. Make laddoos. I'll give you all the ingredients.' So he went to the market and got all the ingredients for besan laddoos. I got everything ready. I made the laddoos. As soon as they were made, he took all but three, put them in a box, put the box in a trunk and put a lock on the trunk. The women who came got three laddoos to celebrate the feast.

On top of that, he began complaining to the women about me. 'Lakshmi steals food,' he said. At this, Gangabai pounced on him. 'What does she steal according to you? Your foodstuff is all under lock and key. I suppose she eats firewood and drinks kerosene.' He had wanted to justify his locking up the laddoos to the women. But his preamble turned the tables on him.

There is one other incident I must relate about the torture I suffered when Mr Tilak was away. Mamanji would collect all the neighbourhood children and tell them stories. One day when he had gone out somewhere, the children came and one of them accidentally overturned his inkpot. I had gone to visit next door. The children came running there saying: 'Vahini, Dada's inkpot has fallen.' Scared out of my wits, I ran home, wiped the ink off the floor with my feet as best I could and went back next door, leaving my inky footsteps on the floor.

When Mamanji got home, he lost his temper on seeing the ink on the floor. None of the children would take the blame. He made each one of them place their feet on the footprints. None matched. Finally, he came roaring into the kitchen.

'Come along upstairs.'

I followed his order.

'Who spilt this ink?'

'I don't know.'

'Whose footprint is that? Put your foot on it. See? You spilt the ink, didn't you?'

'No, I didn't.'

'You did. It was government ink. You'll have to compensate for the loss.'

'How can I do that?'

'Go grind people's grain.'

I had gotten so used to this refrain that it no longer affected me. Nor did God ever bring me to a state where I needed to do that. Mamanji wrote two letters, one to Mr Tilak in Mumbai and the other to Govindrao Mama in Jalalpur. His letter to Mr Tilak said, 'Your wife goes out at night and returns home at dawn. Come and take her away immediately. Or abandon her. I am not responsible for her.'

The letter to Govindrao Mama said, 'Your son-in-law has gone completely astray. He has acquired all sorts of addictions.

He has deserted his wife. He smokes ganja, charas and chandol. If you want your daughter, come and get her in three days or I will abandon her in some unknown place.'

Mr Tilak had full confidence in me and knew his father's nature well. So the letter had no effect on him. But Mama and Attyabai were scared out of their wits. Attyabai said, 'I can understand ganja and charas. But how can he smoke chandol? How does he catch it? It flies in the sky doesn't it?'

To this Mama replied, 'Chandol is opium.' That scared her even more.

My father Nana was very ill at the time. There was no saying how it would turn out for him. Mama and Attyabai were in a dilemma. Should they leave him and come to their daughter's help or stay by his side and lose the daughter?

My People Support Me

Finally, Mama asked Nana hesitantly, 'Shall I fetch Manu back?'

As soon as Nana said yes, Mama left in a rush for Murbad. Meanwhile, a second letter from Mamanji had landed in Mumbai for Mr Tilak. He had got someone else to write it. It said your father is very ill. Please treat this as a telegram and come home immediately. Mr Tilak did not believe this letter even for a moment because his father's first letter, which he had received only two days earlier, had made no mention of illness. But he feared the letter was about something else. He thought I had had enough of Mamanji's ill-treatment and killed myself. That is why he left immediately for Murbad. Mamanji was overjoyed with the idea that now either Mama or Mr Tilak would come and rid him of this illiterate woman of ill-omen, born and bred on the plateau, who could not cook in the Konkani way. The two men on their part were sick with worry as they made their way to Murbad.

Murbad is close to Mumbai. Mr Tilak took a train and reached the railhead quite early. The distance from the station to Murbad town is about twelve to fifteen miles. In those days, you had to make the journey by bullock-cart. But Mr Tilak thought he would get there faster if he walked. So he set off on foot. It was the month of Bhadrapada, a time for the heaviest rains. But that did not deter him. A large river traverses the path to Murbad. It was in full spate. Mr Tilak jumped in and swam to the other bank. The road beyond the river was bad. Mr Tilak had a rough time on this journey. When he got home, he saw Mamanji sitting in the courtyard, chatting loudly with his friends. Mr Tilak's first question to him was, 'How are you feeling, Dada?'

'Why, what's wrong with me? Take your wife away. I don't want her here. She will tell you many tales about me. Don't believe her. She never talks to me.'

He had more to say but Mr Tilak did not wait to hear him out. He came straight into the kitchen. I was sitting there, crying. He consoled me and told me that he had found work and we would leave for Mumbai the next morning. The sky was not high enough to hold my joy. Mamanji was equally happy. We left for Mumbai the following day. We left in the morning and Govindrao Mama reached Murbad the same evening. When he found I was not there, his heart sank. Mamanji would not talk to him properly. All he said was, your daughter has gone to Mumbai with her husband. Mama asked him where we were staying in Mumbai. Mamanji told him he did not know.

Mama left for Mumbai immediately. But where was he to look for me? For three days he trudged around Mumbai like a madman, looking hopefully into every chawl that he passed. Meanwhile, I was in a real state. Mumbai's tall multi-storeyed buildings and trams scared me out of my wits. I was nervous from the moment I got off the train. I stared at everything around me instead of watching my feet. Mr Tilak had to tell me at least three or four times till we got home to watch where I was going. Got home? There was no home. We spent the night in an eatery. The following morning we rented a room somewhere near Prarthana Samaj in Girgaum. Mr Tilak and I set up house there. He bought stuff for the kitchen and I put it away. Still under the spell of the wonder that was Mumbai, I would pop out and look around each time I heard an unfamiliar street call. On one such occasion, as I peered out at the road, I spotted Mama. I called out loudly to him. He looked up in great surprise and shouted, 'Manu!' I cannot describe how happy we were to meet. Besides being happy, Mama was also greatly relieved. He had feared that his daughter was lost to him.

A little while later, the son-in-law and father-in-law met and had a warm chat. Mr Tilak was very happy to see Mama. Mama told Mr Tilak that Nana was on his deathbed and asked his permission to take me to Jalalpur. There was no question of Mr Tilak refusing permission. So the following day, there I was, back at Boribunder station. Mama put me in the ladies' compartment. He would come to me at every station to make sure I was all right. I kept reassuring him I was doing fine. But actually there was something else going on. This was the last month of the Simhastha period, which comes once every twelve years, when the Kumbh Mela is held in Nashik. The compartment was full of Bhatia and Gujarati women, each with arms as thick as beams. They would not make place for me to sit comfortably. I was like a little mouse caught in the middle of this crowd of Bhatia women. Even then I kept up a mousy complaint, 'I'll complain to the station master at the next station.' That was hardly going to move them. They continued elbowing me in the ribs and occasionally pinching me. At Kalyan I quietly picked up one of their children and began playing with him. It made them give me a few more inches of space. Gradually then, all the children in the compartment were thrown at me. I did not mind playing with the brats since it allowed me to travel comfortably all the way to Nashik.

When we got off at Nashik, the tongawalas demanded five rupees per seat. Mama did not have that much money. He said, 'You go by tonga,' and I said, 'You go by tonga. I'll walk.' In the end, both of us walked. Nashik was about six miles away from the station. Mama and I had walked under the midday sun for six miles to get there. Our plan was to eat a little, rest a little, send for a cart from Jalalpur and travel there in comfort. But our people are utterly insensitive. They have no notion of how to talk and what to say. As soon as we entered Nashik, we ran into Mr Upadhyay. And this is what he said: 'So, Govindrao Mama, where have you been?'

'To Mumbai to fetch Manu.'

'For how many days were you away?'

'Four.'

'Oh, so you weren't there when Nana Gokhale died?'

This came as a shock to both of us. There was no question now of refreshments and rest. We set off immediately on foot for

Jalalpur. Although Nana had never caressed me affectionately even once, his going made me profoundly sad. My mother had left me when I was twelve. I recalled her death now. She died in Jawhar. I was with her. We had halted at Mokhada on the way to Jawhar. Mother had made inquiries about the house where her mother-in-law had died. We had visited the house before leaving for Jawhar, about seven kilometres away. Exactly twelve days after her mother-in-law had died, my mother died of the same fever. Both left this world in their married state, which made their deaths auspicious. I remembered all these things and wept.

Poetry Reading

Before I came to Mumbai, Mamanji had made a trip there. He had taken forty rupees from Mr Tilak then, as though our cup of bliss was not already overflowing. Mr Tilak had found a job in Raosaheb Moropant Walwekar's printing press. Raosaheb Walwekar was very fond of Mr Tilak. Mamanji had put us in a really tight spot by taking forty rupees from Mr Tilak. Seeing our plight, Raosaheb put us up at his place, treating us like guests. Mr Tilak wrote his play *Anandrao* during this time and had it printed too.

My eldest sister Bhikutai was married to Nanasaheb Pendse. There was a difference of about fifteen years between us. Bhikutai loved me like a daughter and Nanasaheb loved Mr Tilak in the same way. Nanasaheb was posted to Karmala as the Mamlatdar. Their only daughter, Gharumai, was like a sister to me. We loved each other very much.

Gharumai's marriage was fixed during our stay in Mumbai. This was the first and last big event in Nanasaheb's home. Given the Pendses' wealth and enthusiasm, it was obviously going to be a grand affair. Nanasaheb wrote to Mr Tilak pressing him most insistently to come for the wedding. Balasaheb, Nanasaheb's nephew, also lived in Mumbai. Mr Tilak said to me, 'Get ready. Bala will come in the evening. You will go with him to Karmala for Gharumai's wedding.' And away he went.

What was I going to get ready with? It was the first celebration in my sister's family. It was my beloved niece's wedding. How could I go empty-handed? I was like Parvati in Lanka with not a single ornament to my name; and Mr Tilak was like Shankar with not a paisa to his. I remembered a similar story from Shiv-Parvati's life. It made me laugh and cry at the same time. Just then, a man turned up with samples of fabric. Mr Tilak had sent him. I chose some lengths of material but how was I going to pay for them? It was evening and Mr Tilak had still not returned. In the end, the cloth merchant got tired of waiting and left.

When Mr Tilak did return, it was with Balasaheb in tow. Balasaheb urged me to leave immediately with him. How could I talk about money to Mr Tilak in front of him? It was one thing that I had bought no material for my niece, but should I not at least have some money? At last I said to Mr Tilak in a voice that only he would hear, 'I need some…'

'Don't worry. I've given full instructions to Bala. Ask him for whatever you need.'

I had whispered my request to Mr Tilak and he boomed his answer to me.

Now Balasaheb said, 'Don't dawdle or we'll miss the train. We'll talk about what you need and don't need later. Just get ready quickly.'

Guests from the bride's side had begun to gather at Bhikutai's home since a fortnight before. Orderlies were on duty at the station where food had been laid out. As soon as the train arrived, an orderly asked, 'Has Manutai come?' Nanasaheb's sister, Godutai, who was sitting by the food said, 'Sure, sure. Manutai, Phanutai and every other tai has come.' She had taken offence because she thought nobody had inquired after her, only after Bhikutai's sister. But it turned out that the orderly had asked after Godutai's cousin Manutai who was coming from very far away. Nanasaheb had not seen this cousin for twelve years. Some ritual had to be performed. They had to go to the Maruti temple first. A curtain was to be held up between them, and they had to see each other's reflections in a vessel of oil before going home. That is why the orderly had asked after that Manutai. But I was very hurt by what Godutai had said. I was convinced that people insulted us and thought nothing of it only because we were poor.

When I reached Karmala, I found everybody busy with their own work and absorbed in their own thoughts. Or at least that is how it struck me. I had already heard Godutai's Manutai-

Phanutai remark at the station and now nobody inquired after me although I too had come from far away. I had my dinner with the other guests and lay down with the women holding Gharutai close to me. But I could not sleep till midnight. I was sobbing quietly as I thought, 'People insult me because I'm poor. Even my sister has no time for me. She is a rich man's wife. Mrs Mamlatdar, no less. Why should she bother about me? If I'd been wearing rich gold ornaments, everybody would have found time to talk to me.'

Around midnight, Bhikutai came into the room with a lamp in her hand. She went around looking at every sleeping face till she found me. She sat next to me for a while with her hand on my body. I wasn't asleep but she didn't know this and began calling to me softly. I shook off her hand and said, 'I am not your sister. Why have you come? Do you see any gold ornaments on me?'

Bhikutai choked with emotion as she said, 'Manu, you foolish girl. Aren't you dearer to me than gold? This is the first time we are meeting in three years after Nana and Aai died. How could I have talked to you without breaking down? Would it have been right for me to weep in front of guests who had to be looked after? What would they have thought of me?'

I felt mollified when Bhikutai said this. The following day, she took off all the ornaments she was wearing and put them on me. She gave me an expensive nine-yard sari to wear. The marriage ceremonies lasted four days and were conducted in grand style. Those were happy days for me. Bhikutai wanted me to go with the bride as her chaperone. 'Let us keep Manu with us for a couple of months now,' she said to Nanasaheb.

'Someone else can go as Gharu's chaperone,' Nanasaheb said. 'There's company for Manu today to go back to Mumbai, so let her go.'

'I'm meeting my sister after three years,' Bhikutai said. 'I haven't had time to say even a few words to her. How can I let her go just yet?'

In the end Nanasaheb came out with the truth. 'Mr Tilak has sent four telegrams in four days. Two of them arrived on the day of the wedding. I put them aside then. But now it's going to be impossible to keep her here.'

This shut Bhikutai's mouth and I was packed off to Mumbai the very same day. When I got home, I found that Mr Tilak had nothing more than a cold. I was furious with him. He had not allowed me to spend even a few days with my sister. Mr Tilak tried very hard to console me. He even promised to send me to Jalalpur for a few days. I said no, then yes and in the end agreed to go to Jalalpur. During my absence, he rented a room for us in Tryambakrao Vaidya Lagwankar's chawl in Mugbhat at seven rupees a month. Balasaheb Pendse had also taken a room in that chawl. After setting up our new, independent home, Mr Tilak came to Jalalpur to fetch me back.

Here I must relate an incident that happened at Nashik Road station. I will narrate many such incidents as we go along, each one to do with how Mr Tilak would lose all sense of time and place once he started talking. But this one at Nashik Road station has remained fresh in my memory. We left Jalalpur together like the divine couple Lakshmi-Narayan. I was looking forward to our new home and the beautiful life we were going to live together. I was keen to carry as much stuff as I could from Jalalpur for my new life. But Mr Tilak kept putting obstacles in my way because he hated carrying extra luggage. Even then, I managed to take as many vegetables and fruit as I could. We reached Nashik where we intended stopping over. Mr Tilak had a wealth of friends there. He lost himself so completely in their company that we missed two trains. Determined not to let this happen a third time, we left Nashik town the following day and arrived at Nashik Road station. Now we were on the platform itself. I sighed with relief. Mr Tilak called a porter and asked him to carry the luggage to the opposite platform. I went with the porter while Mr Tilak disappeared in the crowd outside the booking office. I piled our luggage neatly on the other platform and stood ready to board the train as soon as it came. The train came. The porter carried our luggage in. I boarded the train and sat down. The train blew its whistle. So I got up in a hurry, quickly threw all our luggage on the platform and jumped. The train pulled out and puffed away. I saw Mr Tilak standing on the opposite platform, deep in argument with somebody. Even after the train had come and gone, he had not bought our tickets. I stood there not knowing what to do.

Just then Mr Tilak saw his childhood friend, Bhikajipant Gorhe, who lived nearby. He insisted that Mr Tilak should go home with him. That is when Mr Tilak remembered me. Bhikajipant called a porter and got him to take our luggage to his house. We followed. I began to worry about the vegetables and fruit we were carrying. Mr Tilak, being an expert at dealing with such problems, began to give them away. It was only with the greatest cunning that I was able to save half of them for us.

The plan was to leave the following morning. I repacked our stuff. Lunch was so hurried it reminded me of the eatery where we had once eaten. There was still no guarantee that we would actually leave. Mr Tilak was talking till the very last moment. Finally, we left. This time both of us boarded the train. We passed a couple of stations. Things seemed to be going smoothly. Just then Mr Tilak noticed the vegetables and fruit I had saved. He began distributing the fruit to everybody and threw the vegetables out of the window one by one. All the while he kept muttering, 'Why do you need so much stuff?' Sticks from her parents' home are dearer to a woman's heart than bricks that make houses. But only the rice and lentils I was carrying made it to Boribunder station. On top of everything, Mr Tilak had this to say to me: 'You can buy everything except parents in Mumbai.'

We reached our new home. There we found Mr Tilak's brother Sakharambhauji waiting for us. I was very sad about all the vegetables and fruit I had lost. But I noticed there was some rice and chickpea flour in the kitchen. I resigned myself to celebrating our housewarming with a simple meal made with them. I was about to serve dinner when Mr Tilak said, 'Sakharam, better change into a fresh dhoti for dinner. I'll just pop out to the latrine.' And he disappeared. Sakharambhauji changed and waited for him. I put the rice I had served back into the pan. It was eight o'clock, then half past eight and there was still no sign of Mr Tilak. Sakharambhauji changed back into his street clothes and went to all of Mr Tilak's favourite haunts looking for him. He was nowhere there. Sakharambhauji returned crestfallen and ravenous and resumed waiting for his brother. Neither of us spoke. In the silence, we thought we heard Mr Tilak's voice reciting poetry in some room below ours, near the staircase. Sakharambhauji crept downstairs and found a poetry-reading session was on in full flow.

'You are such a fool, Sakharam,' Mr Tilak said. 'How could you think I had run off somewhere? There was no reason to be scared. What was the point of looking around for me instead of having your dinner? We were talking about such a beautiful subject and then you turn up. Now wait a while.'

The beautiful subject continued. Sakharambhauji sat there with a sad face, listening to the monologue he had interrupted. In this way, the dinner that had been served at seven o'clock got eaten at midnight.

The Pearl in the Nose-ring

Mr Tilak trusted people. A man might even be a thief, but if he said he was an honest man, Mr Tilak would believe him and would even quarrel with people who dared doubt it. He believed that human beings were not born evil. Circumstances made them so. The brakes of the Deccan Queen need to be particularly strong to halt her reckless speed. Similarly, I gradually developed strong brakes of scepticism against Mr Tilak's good nature. The moment he showed trust in somebody, as sure as anything, I would mistrust that person. This led to many quarrels between us. The goldsmith story was only one of several such incidents.

Once my nose-ring broke. Mr Tilak immediately called in a goldsmith and counted out the pearls for him to take away and restring. I said let him bring the gold wire here and do the restringing before our eyes. We quarrelled bitterly over that. Mr Tilak went against my wishes, handed over the pearls to him and sent him off. Then he gave me large doses of advice, whole tumblerfuls of it. But the medication had no effect on me. For the next two or three days, only my nose-ring and the sly goldsmith danced before my eyes. On the third day the goldsmith turned up with the nose-ring. Now it had eighteen pearls in place of sixteen. Mr Tilak said to me, 'See that? You should trust people. This man has put two extra pearls in from his pocket.' Days later, he admitted that all eighteen pearls were fake. But till then he sincerely believed that the goldsmith had added two extra pearls at his own cost.

Mr Tilak was generally mild but also hot-tempered. I have no idea how he could be both. I can only say that is how it was. He lost his temper for trivial reasons and regained it for equally trivial reasons. His friends were familiar with the rage he could get into over a game of dice. He once said to me, 'Come. Let's play dice.' Playing dice always afflicted me with a serious condition. Laughter. When Mr Tilak began losing, I would break into waves of laughter. When I began laughing, he would begin to lose his temper. That day, as the game progressed, I started winning. Mr Tilak's temperature rose and my condition grew worse. I could not stop laughing. The affliction could have proved fatal that day. I survived only by the skin of my teeth. The cloth board, pieces and dice trembled. Some found a home in the gutter below. The beds which I had made became a chaotic mess. Every object in the house mutinied. Only two things stayed where they were—the wife and the lamp. But the storm grew so violent that finally the lamp too breathed its last. A box of matches had wrapped itself in a coverlet long before this and hidden its face in the tumbled bedding. I continued to be amused. I was laughing loudly. Now Mr Tilak opened up the last front in the battle. He flung me into the stairwell which was pitch dark. I went tumbling down the stairs in a series of somersaults. Mr Tilak's rage vanished. So did my laughter. Scared out of his wits, he looked around frantically for the box of matches. He could not find it. Finally he groped his way down, picked me off the floor and led me up. I was seven months pregnant at the time.

He had started writing a farce based on his temper, but had not completed it. It is full of entire sentences that we said to each other when we quarrelled. Mr Tilak always felt terrible after he had lost his temper. Another thing—once the storm had blown over, it did not leave behind even a smidgeon of a cloud. He had begun writing the farce in one of his notebooks. Judging by the other entries there, this must have been in 1887. That was the year our first son, Vidyanand was born. I have copied the incomplete farce below.

ACT I

Mr Crabby: (*Returns home, flings his turban away and throws himself down on the floor*) Son of an ass. Dare say that again and I'll kill you. So what if I owe you money? Sure you'll take my house, my yard, my wife, my child. Go ahead. Do it. But how dare you speak to me like that? (*He boxes the floor. Mrs Virtue enters*)

MRS VIRTUE: Good heavens. What sort of behaviour is this? Such fury and for what?

CRABBY: That monkey of a man. That son of an ass. He had the guts to insult me. So what if I owe him money? I'll fling it at him tomorrow.

MRS VIRTUE: My word! That's the limit. Won't a man who has loaned you money have a few things to say to you? Why fly into a rage? That's enough now. Get up. Where's your turban? (*Notices it*) You flung it away? That's the limit. What kind of man are you? Does it suit you to throw your things around like some four-year-old?

CRABBY: That's enough. I'll throw my turban anywhere I like. It's mine. Not your father's.

MRS VIRTUE: That's right. Drag my father into it. After all he's the one who has tied me to you. What a temper. It wasn't more than two days ago that we got that turban properly bound.

CRABBY: So? I'll do what I please with my turban. I will tear it or burn it. What's it to you?

MRS VIRTUE: What's it to me? It's everything to me. Dearest, won't you listen to me? Please get up now. (*Picks up the turban*) Oh dear. It's worse than a pancake.

CRABBY: Look here. Don't go on about it.

MRS VIRTUE: All right, I won't go on.

CRABBY: Talking back, are you? I'll give you a kick you won't forget.

MRS VIRTUE: All right. I won't talk. Happy?

CRABBY: But why did you say it in the first place?

MRS VIRTUE: I was wrong. Please forgive me.

CRABBY: Still going on. Are you going to hold your tongue or not?

MRS VIRTUE: Won't you go for your bath now?

CRABBY: Get out of my sight. We will have our bath when it pleases us. Go, go, go. Out. Let me not see your face, you witch.

MRS VIRTUE: I plead with you. I beg of you. Please come. It's one o'clock.

CRABBY: Still won't hold your tongue? Take this then (*Kicks her in the back*). Demoness.

MRS VIRTUE: (*Goes to the kitchen crying*)

CRABBY: I hate, hate, hate this life (*Slaps himself across the face right and left. Just then Banya enters.*)

BANYA: (*Laughing loudly*) Mamma, hey Mamma, come out quick. Look what Baba's doing. He's so funny.

CRABBY: Son of an ass.

BANYA: I'm not an ass' son. I'm your son.

CRABBY: You pipsqueak. Are you making fun of me? Rascal (*Hits him*)

BANYA: Help. He's killing me. Run run run. Save me. Mamma help. (*His screams bring the neighbours to the door*)

RAMBHAT: What's going on, Mr Crabby? We always thought you were a wise man. Do you want to kill the boy? Come on. Let him go.

CRABBY: Get out, you bag of bones.

The First Child

One day Mamanji wrote to say he was coming to Mumbai. He did not know how to get to our new place so he wanted Mr Tilak to fetch him from Boribunder station. Mr Tilak did not show me this letter. So I had no idea he was coming. Mr Tilak put the letter in his pocket and, instead of going to meet his father, went off somewhere else.

Mamanji got off at the station. When he realized his son was not there, he was furious. He had once put Govindrao Mama in this situation. Now he found himself in it. He had a faint idea of where Balasaheb Pendse lived. He found his way there somehow. The moment he arrived, he began quarrelling with Balasaheb.

'You've spoilt my son,' he said.

'What did I do?'

'Either you or your aunt stopped my son from coming to the station.'

'Then how did you get here, Dada?'

'I knew this place. I haven't been to his place. That's why I'd asked him to meet me at the station.'

'Come then. I'll take you there.'

Balasaheb brought him home. They were climbing up the staircase, Mamanji behind Balasaheb when I heard him curse. That is when I realized for the first time that he was coming. I had cooked for just the two of us and was waiting for Mr Tilak to come home. When Mamanji arrived, I served him Mr Tilak's lunch. Then Mr Tilak came. I will leave it to the readers to imagine the storm that blew up after that and the curses that were piled on my head.

The following night, a moneylender from Gangapur, a friend of Mr Tilak's, came over to see him. Mr Tilak was sleeping inside. Mamanji was still awake. The moneylender asked for Mr Tilak. Mamanji asked him who he was. The man said, 'I'm from Gangapur.' Mamanji made no response. For him the conversation had ended. The poor visitor waited at the door for a long time and then went away. He wrote to Mr Tilak later. That is how we got to know what had happened. A few days later Mamanji left.

One of those days, I had just about three rupees left with me. Mr Tilak had no sense of money. He would spend on all kinds of impractical things. That is why I would confiscate all the money he brought home and keep it safe. But that day I had only three rupees. I put it all together and handed it over to Mr Tilak to buy rations. When he came back from the market, he was wearing a big grin on his face. He had spent the three rupees I had given him on a clock. My temper soared. Mr Tilak said nothing. He sat in front of the clock and wrote a poem titled, 'What the Clock Says'. He sold the poem the following day to somebody and gave me what he got for it. I do not remember the exact amount but it was something like twenty rupees. It was around this time that he wrote a long poem titled, 'My Deserted Village', which was published as a booklet.

When Mr Tilak realized that he was going to be a father, he took me to Jalalpur to Govindrao Mama's place. Attyabai gave me all the care and love I could have asked for. She satisfied all my cravings. But I could not stop worrying about Mr Tilak. I do not think there was a moment in my life there when I was not worried about him. I would worry and weep. Then Govindrao Mama would say to me, 'Why are you weeping, Manu? I promise I will find your husband wherever he is and bring him back. Don't worry.'

For six months there was no letter from Mr Tilak. I have no idea where he had disappeared to during those months. Soon I gave birth to a boy, a grandson for Govindrao Mama and Attyabai. Govindrao Mama's mother's name was Sakhubai. He wished his grandson to be named after her. So we called him Sakharam. But his uncle was also called Sakharam. So later his name was changed, according to Mr Tilak's wishes, to Vidyanand. Around this time, Mr Tilak wrote to say he was in the Konkan. He himself turned up on the heels of the letter. Vidyanand was not keeping well. So we took him to Nashik to Nanasaheb Pendse's place. Govindrao Mama also came with us. After a few days of treatment, the child began to bounce with good health.

In those days public speaking events were held in many places like Mumbai, Nagpur and Nashik. The best speakers were given cash prizes. Mr Tilak loved public speaking and he invariably won prizes at these events. One such event was going to take place in Nagpur. Mr Tilak mentioned it to his father-in-law and said he would like to go. Mama agreed in the hope that Mr Tilak would come back with money. I feared he would not come back at all. He did come back, very promptly too, but without the money he had won. He had given away the entire amount. All he came back with was his trophy—a metal plate.

Govindrao Mama was very upset to see him return empty-handed. 'We will not look after your wife and son now,' he said. 'You are free to settle her under a peepul tree or a banyan tree, we don't care.'

Mr Tilak said, 'Fine. I'll look after them. Don't worry.' Govindrao Mama went off in a huff and, surprise of surprises, I was going to be looked after by Mr Tilak! Whenever we shifted house, we shifted only ourselves. All our pots and pans and foodstuffs were distributed amongst the neighbours before we left. In Nashik we did not have even a cracked pitcher to our name. Nanasaheb had a large house but in the midst of all these happenings, he got his transfer orders to Sangamner. The Pendses began to pack.

Bhikutai was very worried for me. Finally, she and her mother-in-law decided to take me along to Sangamner. Nanasaheb invited Mr Tilak most enthusiastically to go with us. So we all went, bag and baggage, the Pendses and their appendages. Nanasaheb went ahead. We followed in bullock-carts.

Before we left for Sangamner, Bhikutai's mother-in-law, Maisaheb, had made many things like fenugreek laddoos which are good for a lactating mother to have. She sent two tins of them to Attyabai. Attyabai was very angry with all of us. Her regular anger was reserved for Mr Tilak, but now she was furious with Maisaheb because after Attyabai and Govindrao Mama had done so much for me, got me married, looked after me through my delivery, here was Maisaheb acting the benefactor. She is oozing with love for Manu now. Where was that love earlier? She had been more furious than usual with Mr Tilak because he had won at the public speaking event and given away all the money he had won. It was in that fit of anger that they had threatened to abandon Manu. Did that mean they would really do it? If she and Mr Tilak had pleaded a little with them, the problem would have been solved. But Bhikutai and Mr Tilak had taken what she and Mama had said at face value and that is why we were going to Sangamner now.

The tins of laddoos arrived in Jalalpur, but Attyabai did not touch them. She did more. She put Govindrao Mama under oath not to touch them. 'If you eat any stuff sent by Bhiki, it'll be like eating cow's flesh,' she said. 'You told Mr Tilak that you wouldn't look after Manu and her child. That was enough for Bhiki to take Manu off with her. I did all the work, I raised her, I spent on her, and there is Bhiki ready to pat and prick dough that's been already kneaded.' So Attyabai raged against the fenugreek laddoos as though they were us. Her rage destroyed them and the garbage heap was the richer for it.

Around that time Yeshwantrao Maharaj, the Mamlatdar of Satana, was called to God. Mr Tilak composed an elegy on him and got it published. While we were in Nashik, Mr Tilak had won prizes in public speaking events. As always, he had given away the money.

She Has Turned Sixteen and Yet…

Nanasaheb went ahead to Sangamner and we followed by bullock-cart. This is how it happened. It was Bhikutai's habit never to come before Mr Tilak or even talk to him. She was convinced he would compose a poem on her one day. After Nanasaheb had left, Mr Tilak who was having his lunch said, in a voice that Bhikutai could hear quite clearly, 'Give me a few pots and pans and two rooms in this house. I'll stay back here.'

Bhikutai fell into deep thought. The request was like the proverbial creature which bites if you hold it and runs off if you don't. Mama had abandoned me and here was Mr Tilak offering to look after me. If anything happened to me, he would easily find himself another wife. But she would not get another sister. The two women, Maisaheb and Bhikutai, sat together and thought deeply over the problem. In the end they wrote to Nanasaheb in Sangamner explaining what had happened. Nanasaheb replied by return of post that he wanted all of us to go to Sangamner, including Mr Tilak and me. So we got into a bullock-cart and left.

We were seven people in all, including a cousin of Nanasaheb's. We left at five in the morning and reached Sangamner the following day in the evening. We stopped on the way at Dubere for refreshments. On the way, whenever we passed a neem tree, Mr Tilak would grab some leaves and eat them. At such times the old lady would say to her daughter-in-law, 'Your brother-in-law is a yogi. You may criticize him as much as you like, but he is a true ascetic.'

The house where Nanasaheb was staying was known as far as Nashik for being haunted. As soon as we arrived, Bhikutai bathed Vidyanand with warm water. She gave me hot water too. We had our dinner. Then she arranged a string cot with a pot of charcoal fire underneath for me and Vidyanand who was only six weeks old. He and I slept on the cot. Bhikutai had put up a thin cotton curtain around it. Gharumai, Granny and Nanasaheb's cousin Wamankaka slept on the floor on beds made of cotton rugs and sheets. Nanasaheb, Bhikutai and Mr Tilak slept upstairs.

The house was a wada with four verandahs surrounding a central courtyard. I think the door of Nanasaheb and Bhikutai's room faced east. To the left of the courtyard, as you entered the house, stood a wall which shut off a stable. Stairs led from the courtyard to the verandahs and the upstairs rooms. The staircase leading upstairs faced the opening of my curtain.

That night I lay awake with strange thoughts running around in my mind. The saying that an idle mind is the devil's workshop is absolutely true. I had no idea that the stable was on the side in which my head was pointing. The restless stamping of horse hooves sounded ominous. Everybody else was fast asleep. I alone lay wide awake, my head unmoving but my eyes rolling around watching all four sides. Come what may, tonight I would at least see what a woman's ghost looked like. My heart was thumping in my chest. I thought I heard the sound of toe-rings on the stairs. Someone was coming down. My heart turned to water. My throat went dry. Mustering all my courage, I kept my eyes fixed on the direction of the stairs. Hoof-falls again. I could not keep my eyes open. Just as they began to close, a figure appeared on the stairs. She was dressed in a red sari. Her hair was flying, loose. Her forehead was covered with a horizontal stripe of vermillion. She held a lamp in her hand. She matched exactly the description I had heard of the ghost that haunted the wada. I was terrified. I pulled Vidyanand under me and kept my eyes on him. The woman now stood right next to my cot. She extended her hand. It fell on Vidyanand. She began drawing him slowly out from underneath me. I wanted to say to the spirit, I know who you are. But all I could do was scream 'Who-who-who.' The people sleeping on the floor now woke up and joined the chorus of 'who-who-who', all of us shouting in one voice and to one beat. The ghost, topping our voices, was shouting, 'What-what-what.' Nanasaheb came running down and he too began shouting 'Who-who-who.' Mr Tilak followed him and burst out laughing. Nothing ever scared him. The sight he saw amused him vastly.

Then the mystery was cleared. The woman was Bhikutai. I was still a young girl. She had come down fearing that I might roll over in my sleep and smother the baby. She had come to check out and found that Vidyanand was indeed under my stomach. That is why she was trying to draw him out. The horses' stamping, the sound of toe-rings, Bhikutai's wild appearance and her enormous shadow dancing on the wall in the light of the lamp—it was more than enough to petrify me.

A famous keertankar was staying in Sangamner at the time. He was very popular among the people. A new instrument had very recently entered keertan performances. The harmonium. This keertankar had a fine voice. The devotional songs he sang were melodious and his arguments well-constructed. People thronged to hear him. One evening, he had just finished his introductory remarks and was about to begin his main argument when Nanasaheb and Mr Tilak arrived and sat down. They were given places right in front, close to the keertankar. He took off the garland which they had put around his neck and garlanded Mr Tilak with it. Then he put his head on his feet before beginning his argument. Nanasaheb was very surprised to see this but could not ask about it just then. At the end of the keertan, the keertankar inquired after Mr Tilak's well-being before leaving.

Nanasaheb was most eager to find out what it was all about. Back home he asked Mr Tilak about it. Mr Tilak told him that when he was staying in Dhamak he had written a few keertans for the man and had taught him how to perform them. He had been performing them ever since. Nanasaheb was very happy to hear this. He insisted that Mr Tilak should now begin to perform keertans. Mr Tilak thought about it for a few days and in the end wrote a beautiful keertan on Subhadra's abduction.

He practised it constantly over the next two or three days. The invitation for his keertan went out to the whole town. But now Nanasaheb began to have doubts. He kept saying to Mr Tilak, 'Are you sure about this? We won't fall flat on our faces will we? I can easily put the word out that you are unwell.' But when he heard Mr Tilak rehearsing, all doubts vanished. His joy knew no bounds. Nanasaheb had always been fond of Mr Tilak. Now his love doubled. Bhikutai and Granny were also pleased.

As for me, I was fond of playing with dolls, singing, listening to and telling stories and making rangolis. Bhikutai and Granny would always scold me for spending my time on such things. When I began to tell a story, they would say, 'Women who tell stories have had to abandon their hearth and home. Heaven knows where your storytelling is going to take you.' When I sang, they would say, 'You've turned your whole married life into a silly song.' When I played with dolls, they would say, 'You've turned your whole married life into a ruinous game.' These scoldings had no effect on me. Habits die only with death.

After Nanasaheb left for work, Bhikutai and Granny would take Vidyanand and go to the darkened room upstairs to sleep. Mr Tilak too would be upstairs writing. Or he would play sagargote with Gharumai. I was the only one left with nothing to do. In those days I did not know how to read or write. Even now I can barely get by. There are letters in the alphabet which I still cannot place without counting the whole alphabet off on my fingers. So there was no question of occupying myself with reading or writing. If I was not allowed my songs, dolls and stories, how was I to pass my time? Once girls learn to read and write, dolls and kitchen sets go into the junk room. But I was the most illiterate among illiterates. So my day would begin when the two older women retired to sleep. The domestic staff looked upon me as their mistress's right hand. They waited on my every word. I would be mistress of the house from noon to four o'clock in the afternoon. That is when I would work for my dolls.

We had four domestic animals, two horses, a buffalo and a cow kept specially for Vidyanand's milk. If the servants were asked to buy grass for them, they would cut a few coins for themselves out of the money for the purchase. So I was put in charge of buying grass. I used to watch out for grass-sellers passing by, bargain hard with them, get what I could for a rupee or a rupee and a quarter and not return the change to Bhikutai but keep it for myself. Gharumai was the only one who knew exactly how much money I had collected. The servants would be sent off to buy things for my dolls with that money. They were told that the orders had come from Gharumai's mother. Soon I was able to set up a lovely home for my dolls from the money saved on grass. I once got the goldsmith to make tiny ornaments of brass for them and I also made a shrine of twigs for their gods. Gharumai would plead, 'Please aunty, don't. Aai will scold me.' I would say to her, 'What nonsense. And if she does, put the blame on me.'

One day after the two older women had slept, I told the servant that Maisaheb had asked him to get a few banana stems. He got them. I tied two to the door and four to the pillars of the verandah. I invited a band of wedding musicians to come for four days. I invited the neighbouring women for my doll's wedding. The whole celebration was organized in Maisaheb's name. I took out the silverware. Made the traditional mixture of dried coconut and sugar to distribute. I forgot totally that I was playing at dolls. The invitees began to gather. Each one wondered where Maisaheb was. Of course Maisaheb was upstairs fast asleep. She woke up when she heard some noise downstairs. When Bhikutai woke from her sleep, her eyes would usually take a while to open properly. She kept washing them with water so she could see what was going on. I distributed the coconut-sugar mix. Just then the musicians struck up. Now Granny sat up in alarm, wide awake. She stood with her hands on the door jambs, looking at the scene with her mouth wide open. Vidyanand was bawling upstairs. My sister was welcoming the guests with a smile. But inwardly she was infuriated. The musicians brought Mr Tilak down too. He was at a complete loss to understand what was happening. He drew Gharumai aside and asked her to explain. She said, 'Aunty went ahead with this plan although I was telling her not to.' He sent word with her to me saying I should take some lessons from her.

Nanasaheb came back in the evening and was not at all upset. But when the drums stopped beating outside, my heart began to drum. My sister laid out a veritable feast before me. Nothing was missing on the plate. There were cheek twists, pancake slaps, thumping laddoos, fist dumplings and ear pasties. To add to my sins, the silver bowl in which the coconut-sugar mix had been kept was nowhere to be seen. Assuming it was lost, Bhikutai burst into thunder and lightning. That's how the first day of the wedding was celebrated.

The following day when we were at lunch, the musicians began playing again. Next, as was the custom, plates of food began to arrive from our neighbours. My sister went red with anger. 'You wretch,' she said. 'You are going to be responsible for bringing shame on us. People are going to say, now that we are about to be transferred we've started exploiting them for whatever we can get.' Plates of food kept coming for four days, not just by themselves but accompanied by music. Each plate had three things—something made of milk, sweets or savoury snacks and a vegetable dish. Granny would have the milk dish, the elders would have the snacks and we were left with the vegetables. The plate that came from the posh Jinsiwales was so huge that even I felt embarrassed. There was enough food to serve twenty meals and snacks to fill half the store room. The plates would not stop coming and my sister would not stop fuming. I would say, 'If you are angry, why do you store away all the snacks without giving us any?'

She would fume and say, 'Aren't you satisfied with what you get every day?'

Besides the food plates, khanns* and coconuts rained on us. And so the fourth day dawned. I was like a mother or mother-in-law to my doll. Gharu was my assistant. I stayed behind the scenes, directing everything. Granny and Bhikutai were there to attend to Vidyanand when he cried. They looked after all his needs.

We needed a palanquin for the wedding procession the following day. I wondered who could make one for me. The doll had to have her procession. The Jinsiwales' aunt used to visit Granny now and again. I asked her secretly if they had a palanquin. She sent me one from their toy collection. My joy knew no bounds. It was as though I myself was going to be taken around in it. I slipped the palanquin under my cot. The procession would start the following morning. But custom demanded that curd-rice be shown to the doll after the procession returned and then disposed of ritually. Now how was I to get cooked rice so early in the day? There was one way. Granny used to make rice for Gharumai every morning. I told her to put aside a mouthful to show to the doll. Gharu did accordingly. Everybody else was busy with their respective chores. Mr Tilak was reading out to Nanasaheb what he had written the previous night. Just then the musicians started playing. Everybody had grown used to this now; so it did not bother them. Bhikutai was upstairs with Vidyanand. Gharu and I wore our special stoles and got ready for the procession. Afraid of the beating we would get if we went too far, we decided to do a quick turn round and come back. When we returned, I entered the kitchen from the back door. I had to quickly mix the rice and curd, nip across to the front door and show it to the doll when the procession arrived there. Mr Tilak was around somewhere. The Brahmin cook was at the stove. I was looking

---

*This is a bright, patterned handloom fabric with a broad border in a contrasting colour. It was once used for making the traditional knotted sari blouse called choli. It is part of the ritual gift offered to goddesses and married women along with coconut and rice, fertility symbols.

for the curd. I looked into the mesh container in which all dairy stuff was kept. I was peeping into it looking for the curd when Mr Tilak pounced on me. He pulled me up by the scruff of the neck like a cat caught stealing milk. Granny was in the front room telling her beads. She turned her head to look in our direction. Mr Tilak had to let go of me then, leaving my punishment incomplete. I quickly mixed the rice and curd and raced, trembling, to the front door to show it to the doll. The other girls were already waiting for me.

Vidyanand was crying. Bhikutai was sitting by the cot trying to soothe him. Seeing me, she let fly at me. 'Other people must look after your living doll while you sit there playing with your rag dolls.' Granny too came to stand before me with her hands on her hips. 'Dear Manu, when are you going to grow up? Gharu is only ten and she eats a proper rice breakfast. You are sixteen and you still play with dolls.'

My game of dolls had put poor Bhikutai to some expense. She invited all the women for a meal and presented each one with a khann and coconut. That is when Mr Tilak wrote his poem 'My Better Half'. As usual he read the poem out to Nanasaheb. Nanasaheb said, 'That's right. That's our Manu.' To which Mr Tilak replied, 'I'm the writer of the poem but I am not responsible for my subject's doings.'

Mr Tilak's Business and My Education

In Sangamner my sister and niece loved me beyond words and Nanasaheb loved Mr Tilak just as much. He used to shower him with appreciation. But Mr Tilak was not at mental peace. He felt an insistent urge to do something other than a job. He wrote to Govindrao Mama saying, 'I am looking for a business. Please take care of your daughter for some time.' Mama and Attyabai wanted nothing better than this. Everybody forgot their anger and we were all back together in Jalalpur.

While Mr Tilak was there, we heard of a couple who lived in a wadi near Jalalpur called Abhalyachi Wadi. The husband was blind. The wife spent all her time caring for him and indulging him. Some time later, he died. His wife began to live the life of a widow. In her community, widows were allowed to remarry. She was young and good-looking enough to have found a second husband. But she did not do that. Instead she had a stone image of her husband made and spent her time worshipping him and singing songs in praise of him. Mr Tilak was deeply affected by this story. His poem 'Ganga' was inspired by her. Later, Mr Tilak went to Nagpur to see if he could find himself a business.

It was the Diwali season. So he bought a shop and stocked it with firecrackers. Mr Tilak was as much a close friend of flowers and children as he was their poet. Which child would not be charmed by a friend who ran a firecracker shop? Many young friends gathered around him and they had lots of fun bursting all the firecrackers in the shop. A friend of his, Ganpatrao Khare, said to him, 'You will never be able to run a business. Come with me to Rajnandgaon. I'll find you work for which you are qualified.' So Mr Tilak went with him to Rajnandgaon and immediately found work in Balram Press. After working there for three or four months, he came to Jalalpur to take me away. Vidyanand was seriously ill at the time. He died two days after Mr Tilak arrived. Govindrao Mama was so grieved that he took to his bed. Mr Tilak was deeply saddened. He wrote a poem titled 'A Father's Tears'. It was printed, but no copies are available anywhere now. Twenty years later, he wrote his second 'A Father's Tears' when our friend in Ahmednagar, Vinayakrao Sathe, lost his son. A few days later, when Mr Tilak had come to terms with our loss, we went together to Rajnandgaon.

This is where my education began. Mr Tilak taught me the alphabet. That is where my education ended. It would be no exaggeration to say that that was the sum total of it. Mr Khare's wife Lakshmibai could read and write. That inspired Mr Tilak, who now believed even his wife should be able to do so. I was weak in reading. Even now, occasionally, I get terribly confused with some letters whether I am reading or writing. But having been in Mr Tilak's company from childhood, my understanding had matured. I was generally the first listener and critic of his poems. Mr Tilak was surprised by some of the observations I made, which he felt displayed my powers of comprehension.

Having decided that Lakshmibai Tilak should become literate like Lakshmibai Khare, Mr Tilak began to teach me. He was a very good teacher with children, but he turned out to be quite the opposite with me. To start with, I was not a child. Then I was not a stranger. And finally, I could not control my laughter. This habit worked against my education.

Once he had taken it into his head to teach me, he spent all the money he had on books prescribed for the first to the sixth grade. Our lessons began with this pile of books in the middle and we on either side. The first lesson was grammar. Mr Tilak said, 'What is a word?' I burst out laughing. What kind of a question was that? I said, 'A word is a word.' Mr Tilak said, 'But what is a word?' I answered, 'A word is a word.' He said, 'But what is a word?' Back came my answer, 'A word is a word.' Mr Tilak became very angry. The angrier he got, the funnier I found it. Finally, the flames of his rage fanned by the gale of my laughter caused him to set the books on fire. Mr Tilak tore them all to shreds and set them alight. This was our first lesson.

Mr Tilak wanted me to become as learned as him in eight days. But I was denser than dense, so how was that possible?

Gradually, he understood his mistake. So he began to teach me the alphabet, group by group, making me trace the letters over and over again. But after a few days, he got bored with this kind of teaching. Thus my lessons ended. But they had allowed me to recognize letters and that gave a fillip to my reading. Gradually I became familiar with even complex letters like diphthongs. But, as I have confessed earlier, I trip over some letters even now.

A Brahmin on Monsoon Monday

One day we received a letter from Jalalpur to say Govindrao Mama had been called away to God. We were terribly upset by the news. We left instantly for Jalalpur and I stayed back when Mr Tilak returned to Rajnandgaon. He had not been there for more than three months when he left and went to Nagpur. Mahadevbhauji was in school then. He was extremely intelligent and had quite an extraordinary nature. He loved the whole world. If he noticed a poor man who had nothing but a rag to cover him, he would give away his shirt to him and go to school bare-torsoed. He had a friend who was very close to his heart. His name was Vasudevrao Patwardhan. Mr Tilak also got to know him well. Vasudevrao was a poet and had a fine ear for poetry. It was most natural that Mr Tilak should prefer to spend time with a fellow poet. What was a job in Rajnandgaon in comparison with the company of such a man? So Mr Tilak became a Nagpurite. He managed to find many students to tutor there. This helped him settle down comfortably.

While in Nagpur, he participated very actively in the agitation for cow protection. He even wrote and published a play about it. He contributed a lot of funds to the agitation. He had drawn a picture of a cow flanked by the sun and the moon. A Sanskrit shloka was inscribed underneath. The body of the cow was covered from horns to tail with images of deities. He even had this picture printed. Mr Tilak's life in Nagpur was happy in every way. He had made many friends and earned a lot of social respect. But three or four months later, he sent a telegram to Jalalpur saying 'I am very ill. Come immediately.'

Attyabai panicked. She was already deep in grief. There was not a paisa in the house and no male. Nagpur was miles away. She had buried fifty rupees in the wall for land tax. There was no alternative but to take that money out for the journey to Nagpur. The land tax collector who was called a kulkarni after his work, had been sitting with us since the morning to collect the tax. He was also the one who had brought the telegram and read it out to us. Since that was all the money we had, Attyabai told me secretly to take the box of money out of the wall quietly and put it away while she engaged the Kulkarni in conversation. I was very scared, and the money that was supposed to be taken out quietly announced itself loudly. The lid of the box came off and all the coins rolled out on to the floor in ringing tones. The Kulkarni could see and hear this. But he continued talking to Attyabai as if nothing had happened. The water in the river was rising, but the same Kulkarni helped us and our money cross the river safely to Gangapur. From there we took a bullock-cart to the station.

When I was growing up in Jalalpur, everybody, whatever caste they belonged to and however rich or poor they were, were like one family. Untouchability was practised rigorously, but nobody thought of untouchables as not belonging to the community. Similarly, we did not think of the Kulkarni as an extortionist Pathan serving the government. We were all there for whoever was in need. Families did not have secrets. Everybody's affairs were out in the open and everybody was willing to run to another's aid.

From the moment we left Nashik, I began to worry about how we were going to find Mr Tilak's house and who was going to take us there. When the train reached Mutijapur, I remembered that a friend of Mr Tilak's, Bhikajipant Gorhe, lived there. I told a porter to send word to Bhikajipant asking him to send a telegram to Nagpur to say Mr Tilak's family was on its way. He must have got our message and sent the telegram because, when we got off at Nagpur, we found a couple of Mr Tilak's friends waiting to receive us. They escorted us to his place, but Mr Tilak had vanished. We were overjoyed to hear that he was fine and busy giving public lectures and taking part in agitations. We were greatly relieved to hear that he had never been down with a fever or anything else. We were also angry, but only momentarily.

It was Shravan Monday, a day on which the pious feed Brahmins. When Mr Tilak met his friends, they told him an elderly woman needed to feed a Brahmin so would he be willing to go. Mr Tilak readily agreed. They took him to the old woman's house around lamp-lighting time. When he saw the old woman, he was astonished. It was his mother-in-law. 'You here? And whose house is this?' he asked. We pointed to his friends who were now laughing uproariously. Mr Tilak turned to them. 'Thank you,' he said.

Mr Tilak's friends were responsible for this prank. They had rented the house, stored it with household goods and foodstuffs, brought us over and astonished Mr Tilak. Two days later, Mamanji came. Life was going to be fun and games now, he being the kind of person he was, and Attyabai being the kind of person she was.

Attyabai was a good cook and did not brook any criticism of her cooking. Mamanji was also proud of his culinary skills and took great pleasure in comparing the cooking style of the plateau people with that of the Konkan. I was in charge of serving. When I served him, he would make some snide comment on the food in a deliberately audible voice. When I went back to the kitchen, Attyabai would fume at me because my father-in-law had criticized her food. I was a two-faced drum, slapped on one side and then on the other. That is how it was until a few days later, when both went back to their respective homes.

Mr Tilak was extremely charitable. Money held no value for him. He was as happy not having it as he was having it. I used to say to him, 'When you have money, you spend your time worrying about how you can get rid of it.' I inclined the other way. I was worried about how to keep it. Spending money is much easier; so in this battle victory was always his. Moreover, people were always eager to lend him money. He would borrow and I would repay. So there was no way money could stay with me.

This story is from Nagpur. There was no food in the house. I had a lone rupee.

'Will you go to the market?' I asked.

'Of course, I will. You are the one with money. We are only servants.' Upon this, a few loving exchanges took place and finally I sent him off to buy rice. I waited for his return. Unusually for him, he did not go off somewhere else, but came back promptly. He was laughing but there was no packet of rice in his hand. I was very angry. Each time I lost my temper, he would call me Jijai, Tukaram's supposedly shrewish wife, and himself Tukaram. He took an ink-pot out of his pocket and placed it before me. 'See how beautiful this is.'

'And what am I supposed to do with this inkwell? Cook it? I tell you!'

Mr Tilak picked up the inkwell and went straight upstairs and flung it out of the window on to the street below. Then he called down to me, 'You don't understand psychology.'

I truly did not understand psychology. I still do not. I am certain Jijai did not understand it either, nor did Socrates's wife. But if they had written about their lives, the world would have known the problems they had to deal with. They might not have understood what was going on in other people's minds, but they surely understood the anxieties in their own.

Mr Tilak used to wonder why I was so concerned about running the home. Surely it was because he was so little concerned. If both of us turned ascetic, both would starve. We were always short of vegetables. In those days Brahmin women didn't go to the market. So I would prepare all sorts of preserves, papads and dry chutneys as accompaniments for rice. Once I had decided to make dry chutney of bora berries. The boras were drying on the terrace.

'What is this?' Mr Tilak asked.

'I'm drying boras for chutney.'

Mr Tilak was furious with me for being so involved with keeping house and all that went with it. He began to throw the boras down. Children gathered downstairs to wallop them as they fell. I was ready to cry but also felt like laughing. Around that time I fell seriously ill and Mr Tilak nursed me like a mother. He kept me on oranges for a whole month. One day he said, 'Let me make shira for you.'

'You don't know how to make shira. I don't want it.'

Mr Tilak said angrily, 'Why do you think I don't know how to make shira? Am I not a human being? Don't I have brains?'

I said, 'I didn't say you don't have brains. You have more brains than anybody. But you don't know how to make shira.'

He was adamant. He lit the stove and put semolina in a pan over the heat. The semolina would not cook. He added the sugar, lowered the heat but the semolina would still not cook. He did not know he had to add water. In the end he came to me and said in a low voice, 'What's to be done? The shira isn't happening.'

We both laughed and I said, 'Each one to his work.'

We were staying in Lakshmibai Buti's wada. One day a keertankar performed there. At the end, when the salver with the lamp and offerings was brought around, everybody put an anna each into it. The collection looked meagre. Mr Tilak invited the keertankar home and asked him about himself. The keertankar told him about his difficult life. This made Mr Tilak's heart bleed. He gave him all the money we had in the house—about twenty rupees—borrowed money to buy him clothes and sent him off. Then he borrowed more money for me to run the house.

This behaviour was the cause for all the quarrels between us till the very end. He used to say, 'Let me tell you. I will be like this till the day I die. But I promise you, you will not have even a paisa of debt to repay when I'm gone.' During the last year of his life we did not owe anybody any money. But, up until then, his subtractions and my additions continued uninterrupted.

In the Butis' Garden

Mr Tilak was free of desire. He had been appointed tutor to Gopalrao, the youngest son of Appasaheb Buti. Gopalrao was generally known as Bapusaheb. Appasaheb not only paid Mr Tilak well but had also given us quarters in a bungalow in his garden. One day Appasaheb said, 'Mr Tilak, I think I would like Bapusaheb to live with you.' Mr Tilak agreed instantly to this suggestion. However, he refused to take the money Appasaheb was offering for the boy's board and lodge. In his opinion, a student who lived in the home of his guru was not living in a lodging and boarding house. Gopalrao was very meek and humble and endowed with a great sense of humour. He used to get a hundred rupees spending money for himself alone and had two servants at his beck and call. The family employed several clerks just to do their accounts. Yet, when Gopalrao came to stay with us, he came like any other poor student. Not once did he betray arrogance because he came from a wealthy family. He would go about his chores quietly and with a smile. While I cooked, he set the plates, and when we finished eating he cleared up. I felt no inhibitions about addressing him in the familiar singular.

In our house outgoings were heavy, incomings light. We were the owners and we the servants. We were the employers and we the clerks. Gopal used to call Mr Tilak Guruji and me Bai. That is why our Dattu also called me Bai till we converted to Christianity. Mahadevbhauji was also living with us. He and Gopal became great friends. Every morning they would gather the dried leaves from the garden to heat their own and Mr Tilak's bath water. They would warm up last night's rice, mix it with buttermilk, eat it and go out. If Gopal was asked what he had eaten he would name a string of delicacies. There was nobody at home to care for him except his father and brother. His wife was seven years old and his brother's wife nine. He thought of our house as his home. He would say, 'There are many people who call me saheb but nobody who addresses me in the familiar singular.' We both loved him dearly.

One day when Mr Tilak had gone out, a friend of Bhauji's and Gopal's came to meet them. When all three boys had eaten and done their chores and made their beds, they said to me, 'Bai, after you've finished your work, come out to the garden. We'll sit there chatting.' When I had finished eating and clearing up and went out, all three were fast asleep. I shook them awake. Two woke up but Gopal showed no signs of moving. I became nervous. The two boys were also very frightened. Gopal's body had grown cold. By now it was midnight. I was weeping and the two boys were just looking around, scared out of their wits. Each time I said to them, 'Please go over to the big house and tell Appasaheb what has happened,' they would say, 'We are too scared.'

My imagination began to play games. The crematorium was nearby. Could this be the doing of evil spirits? Every now and then I would touch Gopal's body only to find it cold. 'I must go myself,' I said. 'One of you stay here and one come with me.' They would not agree even to that. 'There's a lock on the gate. How will you get in?'

'I will have to find a way. We can't let him die like this.'

'If you go, how can we stay here? We won't be able to breathe for fear.'

'I don't care whether you breathe or don't, I am going.' I said it firmly and left.

The garden gate was quite far from the big house. The moonlight was bright. I hitched up all the free-flowing parts of my nine-yard sari and began to climb over the gate. My mind was full of doubts. How was I to enter the big house? It was protected by a heavy guard. Would I be taken for a thief and dragged to face Appasaheb? What would I do if he did not recognize me? Such were the thoughts that ran amok in my mind. Just when I had topped the gate and was about to climb over, somebody pulled my leg from behind. When I looked back I saw something that looked like Gopal. It had to be his ghost. I broke into a cold sweat. My tongue stuck to my palate, but before my tongue got permanently stuck there, I managed to shout, 'Who are you?' Mahadevbhauji and his friend lifted me off the gate and sat me down under a tree. I was just about conscious but could not talk. Gopal held my feet tight. 'Bai, please don't tell Guruji. We were just playing a prank on you. We'll never ever do it again.'

I was very angry. Gopal said, 'Please laugh, Bai. Please laugh. I'm not going to let go of your feet until you do.' As usual I was crying and laughing at the same time. The three of them had thought up this prank together. Mahadevbhauji was against it from the start but he could do nothing before the other two who were determined to carry out the plan. Mahadevbhauji also said solemnly, 'I too think you shouldn't breathe a word about this to Nanasaheb.'

'And you will continue to harass me like this.'

'No, no. We will never harass you again.'

One day Mahadevbhauji reported to me that Mr Tilak had won a big prize and had given away the money to somebody. 'But please don't tell him I told you,' he added.

When Mr Tilak came home at night I was in bed pretending to be asleep. In my sleep I blabbered, 'So what if he gave the money away. It came one way, went out the other. It's like an April shower. It slides off the ground.' Mr Tilak shook me. 'Wake up. You're babbling. Is it a dream?' I pretended to wake up. Bhauji and Gopal were sitting nearby. They were looking down and trying not to laugh. Seeing me awake, Mr Tilak asked, 'Were you dreaming?' I said perhaps I was. 'I dreamt that you had won some money and given it away.'

'Now isn't that a wonder? I really did give away money to somebody today.'

One day Gopal said, 'Bai, I feel like eating something nice today.' I gave him four annas. He went to the market and brought back two melons. It was the season for the spring haldi-kumkum dedicated to goddess Gauri. 'I'd love to have a haldi-kumkum,' I said spontaneously.

'Don't be an idiot. A haldi-kumkum is all show. Do you have anything to show off? Anything at all?'

'So what if I don't. May only fair-skinned girls wear kajal?'

Later Gopal said, 'Bai, I have to go to the big house for lunch today.'

That ended all talk of haldi-kumkums. Gopal went to the big house and did not return the whole day. He came back only to sleep. The following day everybody set about their work as usual. Mr Tilak was busy writing something. I was busy with my chores. Just then two or three carts drew up before the bungalow and all kinds of vessels and foodstuffs began to be unloaded. I wondered if some other people had been given rooms in the bungalow. Huge pans arrived in the kitchen. Immense logs of wood and sacks of foodstuff were piled in the back verandah. This was followed by hammering noises from the living room of the bungalow. I kept running from the kitchen to the living room and back again thinking to myself, 'We shouldn't have come to stay here in the first place. We don't pay rent. Appasaheb owns the bungalow. He will do what he likes in the house. Were these preparations for a garden dinner for his guests? Why should he worry about our convenience? How am I to cook with this going on in the kitchen? What will I serve the family when they come for lunch?' While I worried about cooking, enough food for eight or ten people had already been cooked in the kitchen. The servers laid out the plates and began serving the food. Word was sent to me to come and eat. I said, 'I'm not coming. My family hasn't eaten yet. How can I eat before them?' I believed it was a sin to say no to food, but I was caught in an exceptional situation. I said, 'You've upset my cooking completely today. Has Gopal gone to the big house for lunch?'

The messenger said, 'Everybody is here, including Bapusaheb. The message is from him.' That did it. I was really angry, particularly with Mr Tilak. I sent word to say I was definitely not coming. Then Gopal himself came to me. He took my hand. I shook it free. He said, 'Bai, just listen to me. Then you can be as angry as you like.' So saying, he led me to the living room. And what did I see? Goddess Gauri installed in splendour in a beautifully decorated shrine which was as yet only half complete. I was stunned to see it. My eyes filled with tears of joy. I had no words for Gopal. All my anger against him melted away.

Mr Tilak came for lunch. He had assumed that some guests of the big house were coming for a garden party and we were invited. Obviously nobody had a clue to what was happening. After lunch Mr Tilak went to the living room and stood astonished to see Gauri in a shrine. That was it. Mr Tilak flew into a rage. 'This is your doing. You are completely thoughtless. Why should we take on the responsibility of all these valuables? If all this gold, silver, diamonds and rubies are stolen, who will be responsible?'

'Who? Those who brought them here.'

'Sorry, I don't approve of this,' he said and went off in a huff.

The Gauri shrine was so beautifully decorated, I had never seen anything like it before, nor was I likely to again. Around two o'clock in the afternoon, Gopal's sister-in-law, wife and a serving woman came over in a buggy. Mats of the fragrant khus grass were wrapped around the living room and water sprinkled on them to keep the room cool and fragrant. Tall silver oil lamps burned before Gauri and enormous silver trays filled with delicacies were placed in front of the shrine. All the paraphernalia for the haldi-kumkum was set on the side. Rose water, attar, betel leaves and betel nuts, dry coconut-sugar mix—they were all there. The girls put the haldi-kumkum on the guests' foreheads and I distributed the coconut-sugar. When the haldi-kumkum ended and I went to our room, I found plates laid out again. One by one, Mr Tilak's friends began to gather. Appasaheb came. The dinner was full of rich delicacies. Four vegetable dishes, shrikhand-puri, lots of chutneys and salads and other accompaniments. Appasaheb said, 'Mr Tilak, I am so happy to be eating with you in your house.' Mr Tilak merely smiled.

Our home was dearer to Gopal Buti than his own. If an acquaintance came to the door when we were at a meal, he would call out the names of rich delicacies which he wanted served. He had told me that on such occasions I was to insist that the visitor stay for dinner and Gopal would then say, 'Sorry, but I can't stay. I have to go over to the big house for dinner.' That is how he got rid of his acquaintances and they would go away under the impression that we were living the good life. Appasaheb realized this on the day of the haldi-kumkum. He had also heard about Mr Tilak's generosity. He appreciated Mr Tilak so much that he would have been happy to see him every day. So he thought of a strategy. He suggested that his salary should go towards running the home and he should claim two more rupees every day from Appasaheb for his own expenses. 'But I will not give the money to anybody else. You will have to come for it yourself.'

Mr Tilak turned down the offer and continued to live as before. He did a great deal of writing during our years in Nagpur. He wrote poems, two novels and a play and also edited two magazines of poetry.

I've Gone Quite Round the Bend, Friends

I was approaching the full term of my pregnancy. I was escorted to my maternal home. Attyabai was now alone. After Mama's death, her property had been lost through neglect and the house had been confiscated by the moneylender. So we went to live with my brother. Before this, Nanasaheb Pendse had been transferred to Kalwan. When they heard I was in Jalalpur, Bhikutai came to stay with me. Never before had she left her home to go anywhere, not even to our mother's home. But this time she stayed with me for three months to help during my delivery. I gave birth to a girl and we named her Narmada. We called her Nabi for short and also Mai. She was a lovely baby.

Every time I went away from Mr Tilak, he would abandon his job and home in a fit of charity and follow me. It happened again this time. We were once again left with not even a cracked pitcher to our name. Around this time, he suddenly remembered his guru from Dhamak and began living on neem leaves.

Nabi was three months old when one day Mr Tilak came back from wherever he had gone with a large bag. He set it down and sat before it. The bag appeared to be filled with what looked like brand new folded saris. The children gathered around him and began counting. One for Granny, one each for my two sisters-in-law, a couple for me perhaps? But the stack turned out to be notebooks. He picked one from the pile and read out the entire script for a keertan on Savitri. When the reading ended and he put the notebook down, we noticed that all its pages were blank. He had composed the keertan on the spot.

Soon after Bhikutai returned to Kalwan, Nanasaheb wrote an urgent letter to Mr Tilak insisting that all of us should go to stay with them at Kalwan. We accepted the invitation promptly and soon left for Kalwan. Mr Tilak's talent for composing poems even as he was busy talking to people used to make Bhikutai nervous. She feared he would one day make a poem on her. So she avoided appearing before him. Nanasaheb was busy with office work, Bhikutai was busy with housework and I with the baby. So only Gharumai was free to spend time with Mr Tilak. That's how their old bond was sealed in Kalwan.

Bhikutai had made the customary baby ornaments for Nabi. One day Gharumai pestered Mr Tilak saying other children's aunts made ornaments for them so why did he not make some for her. Mr Tilak pulled a piece of paper towards him and made a list of the ornaments she would like to have. Then he told her to come for them in a little while and sent her away. Wondering how her ornaments would be made in such a short time, Gharumai kept peeping into the room as she wandered around outside. All she saw was Mr Tilak busily writing.

At last the ornaments were ready. Mr Tilak called out to Gharumai to come in. He handed over her ornaments to her. They were exactly what she had desired and she was overjoyed. When the goldsmith lives in your house, it does not take long for you to get the ornaments you want. What Mr Tilak had done was craft a poem which bestowed a casketful of the most beautiful ornaments on Gharumai, connecting each with a moral virtue that embellished the character of a woman. Some lines from the poem went as follows:

> Anklets of modesty on her feet
> Rings bloom on her toes
> With careful grace she walks the earth
> Behold her as she goes.

Gharumai loved her ornaments. She picked up the paper casket and ran to the inner room where Bhikutai and I were sitting, admiring Nabi's ornaments. Gharumai said, 'Listen to the ornaments Mr Tilak has made for me,' and began to read out the poem. Mr Tilak had followed her to see how she liked her ornaments. Bhikutai had not noticed him. When Gharumai finished reading the poem, she said, 'What is to be done? What is the use of all this intelligence? So much learning and not a paisa to show for it. Wanders around with his wife like a naked fakir from home to home. His house is full of nothing. What is to be done? He should wear bangles.'

On hearing this Mr Tilak went to the verandah where he curled up, pulling a blanket over his head. Soon after that an astrologer came to the Pendses' house. He knew nothing about the inmates. Bhikutai asked him to read everybody's palms. The Pendses' cook was a dandy. He used to wear very stylish clothes. Reading his palm with a solemn face, the astrologer said, 'Now here is a man who will acquire much knowledge and become famous.' Then Bhikutai pointed to Mr Tilak, wrapped up in his blanket and said, 'What would you say to him?' The astrologer said roughly to Mr Tilak, 'Show your hand.' Mr Tilak held out his hand palm down. 'Is that how hands are read?' the astrologer said scornfully. Mr Tilak turned his palm up. 'Zero education. Zero money. Won't find a wife.'

Bhikutai asked in a low voice, 'What about children?'

'How will he have children if he doesn't have a wife?' the astrologer shot back and left for the other homes in town.

When Nanasaheb came back that evening, Mr Tilak said to him, 'You are always after me to perform a keertan. I'm in the mood to do that today. Please arrange for it.' Nanasaheb was thrilled. Being the Mamlatdar, he had no problem at all getting everything together for the keertan. People began to gather after dinner. The astrologer too came and sat right in front. Bhikutai sat on the other side with the women.

The introductory stanza of the keertan was all about how the stars had abandoned the keertankar, how he had no kith, no kin, no knowledge, no money. But the good Lord was with him and he was happy spending his life praising Him.

The astrologer was mortified to see the man he had taken for a menial, poking fun at him. Bhikutai thoroughly enjoyed seeing him embarrassed. But the song he sang in the next interlude which began, 'I've gone round the bend my friends / I've gone right round the bend,' went on to speak of how some people called him a fakir and not a man at all; how his learning was no use if he could not hold on to a single pie; and how he deserved to be packed off to where he came from with bangles on his wrists.

Now Bhikutai's laughter was suddenly silenced. She went red with rage and got up in a hurry to leave. She had always feared that one day Mr Tilak would compose a poem on her and it had happened. Nanasaheb had no idea why she was so upset. When she calmed down a little, she said, 'He's my sister's husband. That's why he composes keertans on me. I must tolerate it for my sister's sake. When sisters die, brothers-in-law don't even show their faces to us.' I was relieved to hear her say that, because I was between the devil and the deep blue sea.

The following day the astrologer ran away from Kalwan. Mr Tilak too decided to leave Kalwan and back we went to Jalalpur. This must have been around the year 1890, because a poem of Mr Tilak's dated 13.2.90 uses chess as an allegory for men and their moves. Nanasaheb used to play chess regularly with a friend of his, Mr Rangrao, while Mr Tilak watched.

Mahadevbhauji

We left Kalwan the day after the astrologer left and came to Jalalpur. Mr Tilak decided to leave me there and go to Saptashringi. But the problem was money. It was impossible to ask his mother-in-law for it, and to ask his brother-in-law would be embarrassing. I had Nabi's ornaments, but they were Bhikutai's gifts to her. How could I touch them? The only thing I could give was a brand new sari which I had not worn. Mr Tilak had bought it. I handed it to him and said, 'Return this to the shop and use that money to go.' At first he refused to take it. But I insisted and finally he did and so he went to Saptashringi. The following day the sari came back with a cartman accompanied by a message which said the sari had got mixed up with Mr Tilak's luggage by mistake. The fact of the matter was that the shopkeeper had loaned him the money to go to Saptashringi and asked him to keep the sari.

Anyway, he did not go to Saptashringi after all. He went to Vani. This is how it happened. Mr Tilak had made the acquaintance of a very clever vaidya, an Ayurvedic medicine man named Nana Sant in Surgane. Nana was very fond of him. Mr Tilak had picked up many skills from Nana. But he did not use them to earn money. This pair of guru and disciple decided between them that Mr Tilak should settle down in Vani where Nana had his home. Mr Tilak started a school in Vani which became the most successful of all the schools he had set up. Forty students had enrolled in it. The monthly fee was one rupee, which the students happily paid. Today, one does not see even a hundredth part of the respect that teachers used to be given by their students in those days. Mr Tilak was also a most unusual teacher. He taught English to his students and many of the young boys in Vani grew up composing poems.

Mr Tilak took up residence in his family priest Kakaji Mulye's house. His school occupied an upper floor in the same house. When I joined him a month later with Nabi, we continued living in the same place. We felt completely at home there, despite the fact that Kakaji Mulye was our respected priest. Mr Tilak loved Nabi very much. Around that time Anandibai Joshi had just returned from America. She was one of the first women from South Asia to acquire a degree in modern medicine and the first Hindu woman to set foot in America. Naturally, the papers were full of news about her. Mr Tilak would always say that Nabi would grow up to be an educated woman like Anandibai. Nabi was a sweet girl. Mr Tilak used to take her to his school. There were many people around to pamper her, not just us but all of Kakaji's family and the forty students in Mr Tilak's school. Nabi was really beautiful. If she stood beside me, nobody would guess she was my daughter.

Mr Tilak used to visit the poorhouse attached to the temple of the local goddess and feed and clothe the starving and treat the sick. This is how all the money he earned was spent. Vani was a village, so you got only the most essential things there. You did not need money for anything extra.

Mr Tilak's younger brother Mahadevbhauji was exactly like him, a whit more generous perhaps. He once went to Jalalpur. He did not have even a scrap of clothing on him besides a dhoti. No cap, no footwear. He had given them all away. He was studying at college in Nagpur at the time. He was on his way to Vani and decided to stop off at Jalalpur to see Attyabai. Attyabai asked him, 'Mahadev, why have you come with just a dhoti on you?'

Bhauji replied, 'I fell asleep on the train and everything got stolen.' Who would have believed that? Attyabai said, 'Mahadev, however fast asleep you were, how could anybody have taken the clothes off your back?'

That is how Bhauji was. When he saw someone in need, he would give away all that he had and fib when questioned. When we were in Nagpur, he got after me to get him a silk-bordered dhoti. 'I've always wanted one. Please buy it for me.' A few days after I had bought one, it disappeared. I looked for it everywhere. He helped me search. The following day a gondhal performer came to our door wearing the dhoti. It was only after I questioned Bhauji this way and that, back and forth that he finally admitted he had given it to the gondhali.

Anyway, Attyabai gave him some of Mama's clothes before sending him off to Vani. Now we were in real luck. We had two birds of the same feather in the house. The two took turns to fly away with objects and clothes from the house which they believed others needed more. Once, a copper water pot disappeared. I ran all over the house shouting, 'Where's the tambya? Who's taken the tambya? Has anyone seen the tambya?' Then I said to Mr Tilak, 'I'm sure you've given it away.' He denied the charge but would say nothing more.

Days later, when I was grinding grain, Bhauji came and began helping me to turn the stone mill. He said hesitantly, 'Vahini, don't get angry, and don't blame Nana. I gave away the tambya to a poor man.' When I heard this I laughed and said, 'Why didn't you tell me earlier?' Bhauji said, 'Because you'd have got angry. Vahini, I'm terribly scared of you.'

Once Bhauji and a friend of his decided to climb a hill fort and stay there overnight. Bhauji begged me to give him my blanket. I refused, saying he would give it away to somebody. 'No I won't. I promise,' he pleaded. 'It will be back in your hands when I return.' I gave him the blanket and he gave it away. It made me mad and that terrified him.

When we were in Nagpur, many proposals of marriage came for him. He refused to marry, saying, 'Why do you worry about me, Vahini? I'm not going to marry.' I felt a strange fear when I heard him say that. Perhaps he had a premonition of what was going to happen. One day after he returned to Nagpur, we got a letter from Vasudevrao Patwardhan saying Bhauji was very ill with fever and was constantly asking for Attyabai, Mr Tilak and me. We made instant plans to go to Nagpur. But before we left, Vasudevrao wired us to say Bhauji had breathed his last. People are right when they say that God calls away good souls like Bhauji early.

It was in Vani that Mr Tilak wrote his collection of songs,

Devicha Prasad. They were indeed what the title said they were. Poems blessed by the goddess.

Nana Sant would drop in at our place quite often when we were in Vani. 'Just as I need to eat betel leaves and betel nuts after lunch, I like to hear you two quarrel,' he would say. 'Your quarrels are so amusing.' He was right. We did quarrel all the time over all kinds of things.

At one point, there was a rash of robberies in Vani. Mr Tilak planned a trick to prevent robbers from robbing us. He decided to dig a pit in front of the door, fill it with prickly leaves, and cover it with a mat. When a robber came, he would fall into the pit and get pricked and be disabled from robbing us. I said, 'How can you be sure only a robber will fall in? How can you be sure it won't be you or me? Another thing. Won't everybody around see us digging the pit?'

'Take my word for it. That's not going to happen.' A quarrel started. Nana Sant dropped in and had a lot of fun listening to us. Both the brothers, Mahadevbhauji and Mr Tilak, were loving, charitable, short-tempered and, to some degree, eccentric souls. Once when we were in Nagpur and Mr Tilak had gone out somewhere, I found there was nothing in the house to cook for lunch. There were only two of us at home. I had two rupees which I gave Bhauji and asked him to get provisions for lunch. He came back with two rupees worth of ghee and sugar and a barber in tow to shave him. I was so mad, I said, 'You don't need the barber. Watch how I shave you good and proper. What do we do now? Eat ghee and sugar the whole day? I've had enough. I'm going to kill myself.'

I went and sat upstairs. Of course I had no plans of killing myself. I'm too tough in mind and body for that. I sat upstairs fuming and Bhauji sat downstairs sulking. After a while he noticed there was no sound from upstairs. He got scared. He went out into the garden and peered into the well. I was watching from upstairs, hugely amused. When he did not see a sign of me in the well, Bhauji set up a howl. 'Vahini, how could you have killed yourself? Where did you kill yourself? What will I say to Nana now?'

I could not stay away after this. I came down. When he saw me, he fell at my feet. Holding them tight, he said, 'I'll never do something like this again.' I had no idea of his nature then. I had allowed myself to get mad at a saint. It is only now, when he is not with us, that I recognize his value as a human being. Anyway, Bhauji wept, he promised and returned to his usual ways. When we were in Nagpur and heard the news of Mamanji's passing away, I sent Bhauji to the market to get provisions for the meal I had to serve Brahmins to mark the thirteenth-day ritual. Bhauji bought everything I had asked for. It was my practice to ask both Mr Tilak and Bhauji for an account of what they had spent, because you could never tell where money would go once it was in their hands. This time Bhauji's accounts were perfect, except for a missing four annas. I probed and probed and finally Bhauji admitted that he had given two annas to a beggar and bought and eaten jalebis with the remaining two.

'You actually ate jalebis?' I asked incredulously. 'How can you even say that?'

'Vahini, what could I do? I was hungry.'

'But Bhauji, we still haven't fed the Brahmins. Your father has died. How could you eat sweets?'

'He died far away from here, Vahini,' was Bhauji's reply. This was beyond my understanding.

After my first son died, Bhauji had been like a son to us. I used to cry over his death whenever I thought of him. So Mr Tilak bought a baby parrot for me. He tried teaching him to speak Sanskrit. But the parrot would only say 'Bho bho Mahadev' elongating Mahade-ev very musically. Mr Tilak composed a poem about how I looked after the parrot. When the baby grew into a full-grown parrot, he flew away. The three of us were plunged into grief. But he would return once in a while, sit on the tree outside our house and sing, 'Bho bho Mahade-ev' a couple of times before flying away.

Then our Mahadev left us too. For many days after Vasudevrao Patwardhan's telegram came, there was no joy in the house; and Nana Sant heard no more quarrels.

Dattu's Birth

Mr Tilak had always wanted a daughter. The daughter that came to us as God's gift was plump, beautiful, clever and sweet-tempered. She had a musical voice and her lisping prattle would send people crazy. Mr Tilak's dearest wish had been granted. Nothing else in his life was as valuable to him as his daughter.

One day, our little Nabi started a fever. We wondered if the dumpling made of new rice that she had eaten had brought it on. Since she was not seriously ill, Mr Tilak left for Nashik on some work. He had not gone very far when he met a fakir who sent him back. When he returned, Nabi asked him to sing songs from *Devicha Prasad* to her. She loved those songs. A few days later, our daughter left us. We were heartbroken. Mr Tilak was overwhelmed by grief. He had cherished such dreams and ambitions for Nabi. And now they lay shattered.

One day Mr Tilak was sitting upstairs talking to Nana Sant. He was in a state of deep depression. I was on my way upstairs when I heard him say, 'Nanasaheb, this wife of mine is a real demoness. She has devoured so many of my loved ones—my son, daughter, father, brother, sister.'

When I reached the room, I said to Nanasaheb, 'You tell me now, who does a demoness marry? This demon has devoured more of my people than I have devoured his—my son, daughter, mother, father, adopted father, aunt, father-in-law, brother-in-law and sister-in-law.'

Mr Tilak said nothing to this. But never again did he utter such inauspicious words or even think such inauspicious thoughts. Some time passed. The grief of our loss receded. I was pregnant again. I would have to go to Jalalpur for my delivery. I said I would not go. Mama is gone and Attyabai lives with other people. But he insisted I should go. 'I'll send money,' he said. He was earning well now. While we were still wrangling over this, we received a letter from my brother saying his wife had delivered a baby boy. He wanted us to go for the naming ceremony.

This gave Mr Tilak a reason to press me further. 'It would be wrong if you didn't go for your nephew's naming ceremony. If you decide to go later, you won't be able to take the long bullock-cart ride.' I still could not make up my mind. But finally I packed all the things I had made for the babies, loaded them into the cart and we set off. We arrived on a Saturday, when no auspicious work is done. To top that, it was new moon night, and the puja for the baby's fifth day was to be held that day. Attyabai said, 'Don't enter the house.'

I said, 'I will. Why should my sister-in-law's fifth day harm me? And anyway where will she go on my fifth day?' I paid no heed to Attyabai and went straight into my brother's house. Mr Tilak went back home. But he returned a month or so later. My heart sank. Had he given away everything in Vani and come, in keeping with his old habit? Fortunately not. This time Mr Tilak's pocket was well-lined. It was evening. Mangoes were ripening under straw in the house. Their heady scent filled the house. At dusk the cattle came home and herding them, my younger brother Vishnu. He put fodder out for them and came to sit with Mr Tilak. 'I have a stomach ache. You've studied medicine under a well-known vaidya. Why don't you check my pulse?'

Mr Tilak checked his pulse and said, 'You've over-eaten mango pulp and onion bhajias.'

'Oh, really? You vaidyas are very smart, I must say. The house is filled with the fragrance of mangoes and it is kandenavmi today, the day to eat onion bhajias. You tell people what's wrong with them by looking around and sniffing. If you see a mortar, you'll say the patient has swallowed the pestle. That won't do. Check Manu's pulse and tell us when she will deliver. Manu come out here. Let's test him.'

'I'll do it, but on one condition. If I am proved right, you will distribute pedhas. If I am wrong, I will.' This was agreed upon. I came out. I was not feeling too well that day but had not told anybody about it. Mr Tilak felt my pulse and said, 'She will deliver a baby boy tomorrow afternoon at two o'clock.'

I delivered a baby boy at two o'clock the following day. Mr Tilak was not with me during the first two deliveries, but this time he was. I fell seriously ill after the delivery. It was the month of Ashadh. The rain was pelting down. Mr Tilak went through that heavy rain to Nashik and brought back a doctor who charged high fees. Mr Tilak not only paid the fees but also for the doctor's tonga ride back. I had lost my first two children, so I put this third child on my sister-in-law's lap. Her baby was now six months old. When she held my baby, her milk began to flow. 'Let me feed him now,' she said to Attyabai. 'Don't say that,' Attyabai replied. 'His mother is alive and we must hope for her recovery.'

The baby was like Krishna, born to Devaki and brought up by Yashoda. My sister-in-law looked after him for three months and when we returned to Vani, two other women looked after him for another few months. Mr Tilak invited musicians to play for ten days and he distributed pedhas. My brother gave a big dinner. The baby was named on the thirteenth day. His given name was Dattatreya. Mr Tilak returned to Vani the following day.

Dattatreya was very comfortable with my sister-in-law Ramavahini, but he would cry when Attyabai or I took him. This upset Attyabai. She wondered what the reason could be. One night she had a dream. She saw Govindrao Mama in the dream. He said, 'Mr Tilak isn't interested in his family. That's why I've come to be with Manu.' Attyabai took it into her head that Mama had been born to me as Dattatreya. She was overjoyed. She invited musicians to play again. She distributed pedhas again. She held a naming ceremony again. Dattatreya was named Govind. The child was to be given three more names later.

In Vani, Kakaji's mother had asked for a boon for me and

made a promise in return. When her prayer was answered, she fulfilled her promise. She named the child Ambadas. Later when the child was about three and we had gone to Rajnandgaon, Mr Tilak became friendly with a Bengali doctor. He insisted we call Dattu Sharatchandra. Finally when Dattu was baptized, we called him Devdutt because he was a gift from God. But through all these years we continued to call him Dattu, short for Dattatreya, his first given name.

My Illness

Three months later, Mr Tilak sent a cart from Vani to fetch me back. With it he sent vests and bonnets for my sister-in-law's son and Dattu, a khann for her, a nine-yard sari for Attyabai and other gifts. The moment Attyabai set eyes on the cart she flew into a rage. She sent word back with the cartman to say, 'It is the Kojagiri full-moon night today. I'm not sending Manu back today. Tell Mr Tilak to send for her when Dattu is five months old.' Mr Tilak wrote an angry letter by return of post. 'Come away the minute you get this letter or I won't show you my face again.'

This scared me. My brother engaged a cart to take me to Vani. I went by myself with Dattu. When I arrived, I was told Mr Tilak had gone to stay with Sakharambhauji. He only returned fifteen days later. When Nabi died, Kakaji's mother had asked for a boon for me. Her pledge to the goddess on Saptashrungi hill was that if I delivered a boy safely this time, we would carry the baby's cradle up to the temple and name him Ambadas and that she would have the baby weighed and distribute jaggery equal to him in weight and also take him up to the temple when he was five to have his head shaved.

Attyabai arrived from Jalalpur for the naming ceremony at the temple. There were about twenty of us altogether, including Nana Sant. That night on the hill, I started a fever. We were to have a celebration lunch the following day. Nana Sant examined my pulse and said, 'Don't get entangled with lunch and all that. Let us go down immediately. The fever looks dangerous.'

The fever had come on because of the exhausting climb. I had climbed every step of the way up. We named the baby hurriedly and came down. I was in a palanquin with Mr Tilak running all the way beside it. The others got left behind. Dattu was with Attyabai. He was crying. Even when we came home he continued to cry loudly. Mr Tilak was sitting beside me, and the baby was howling the house down. Attyabai burned incense around him to ward off the evil eye. But nothing would stop his crying. The following morning, Kakaji's daughter took him on her lap and was gently rocking him back and forth. Every time her hand touched his bonnet he would scream even louder. She began to feel the bonnet bit by bit and at one point touched something sharp. It was a needle. I had pinned it to the bonnet when I was doing some embroidery and it had stayed there when I put it on him. He was badly pricked.

Attyabai stopped burning incense. Dattu was laughing again. But my fever would not come down. I could not nurse Dattu. But two neighbours, Mrs Bhagirathibai Mulye and Mrs Parvatibai Deshpande kept him alive partly on breast milk and partly on cow's milk. He would spend the whole day in the big house with Gopal and be handed back to Attyabai at night. Mr Tilak would say to her, 'Why don't you let him stay there?' This suggestion made her very angry. 'I send him there in the day because I have work here. But I will never part with him. If his mother doesn't survive, I'll sling him on my back and go out to work and look after him. You don't even need to send us money.'

As the days passed, I became so weak I was oblivious to my surroundings. Mr Tilak kept vigil beside me. Nana Sant would visit every day. One day he said to Mr Tilak, 'She won't survive till tomorrow. She will just about live through the night.' Vani was a small town. Word spread. A large number of people gathered. Mr Tilak's students came to be with him through the night.

Mr Tilak asked Nana, 'Are you sure this is her last night?'

When Nana said yes, Mr Tilak asked, 'Shall I give her an icchhabhedi pill* then?'

'Please don't. You'll only advance her death by two hours.'

'If she is going to die anyway, two hours earlier makes no difference.'

---

*This is an Ayurvedic pill prescribed for asitis, constipation and bloating. It induces purgation. Since it contains mercury, it is best not to self-medicate because it can bring on severe diarrhoea and may even be toxic.

'Do what you like then,' Nana said. 'I'm leaving. I don't want to be held responsible for her death.' He ran off. Mr Tilak sat with me the whole night, his fingers on my pulse. Around break of day I began to feel better. When Nana came later in the morning, he certified that I had survived the fever. He praised Mr Tilak for his courage. Gradually, I regained my strength. Attyabai had made many pledges during my illness. She fulfilled them all when I had recovered fully. A few days later, Mr Tilak shifted Dattu and me to the Deshpandes' home while he himself went away to Pune. There was neither sign nor letter from him for the next month-and-a-half. When my brother heard of this, he came to Vani and took Dattu and me to Jalalpur.

Dattu was nine months old and I was still at my brother's. One day my sister-in-law said, 'Tell me, do ghosts really exist?'

'Of course not. It's all imagination.'

'Then why have we put grandfather amongst our gods?'

A plate bearing my grandfather's name had been fixed to the wall of the prayer room in my parents' home. It was an object of worship for the family. When we went out or returned, when there was a family event like a wedding, or when difficulties arose, we took grandfather's name before doing anything. That night, we fell asleep talking about the plate. We all slept side by side in a long row. But because summer had begun we had shifted from the middle room to the verandah. Towards dawn I saw grandfather in my dream. I woke up. There was bright moonlight outside in the courtyard. By contrast the verandah seemed even darker. Four Bhil guards were asleep in the courtyard. Vishnu was sleeping in the room adjacent to the verandah, his door locked from inside. The door was made of wooden slats. The maid had gone next door to grind grain and had locked the main door of the house behind her.

The buffalo had calved recently. Her four-day-old calf was tethered to the verandah, close to my sister-in-law's feet. The calf licked her foot. Sister-in-law, still asleep, let out a scream. The next moment Attyabai was up and had grabbed her son away from her. She tried waking up sister-in-law but no word would come from her mouth. She could only scream 'Oyo oyo.' The two voices mingled and became one. I was wide awake but I too had lost my voice. So I joined their chorus of screams. Had there been a potter's cottage next door, his donkeys would have joined our chorus too. Vishnu began banging on his door shouting, 'Open the door. Let me out. I'll see what's happening.' The maid, hearing the commotion, came running from next door and started banging on the main door asking to be let in. She had forgotten that she herself had bolted the door from the outside. The Bhils sleeping in the courtyard had got up, grabbed their axes and sticks and were dancing around saying, 'The Brahmin women have died, the Brahmin women have died.' They thought we were in the locked room. While this was going on, I put my arm around sister-in-law's shoulders. It touched Attyabai who was sitting on the other side and she let out a yell, 'Why are you looking here and there? Here's the thief.' Immediately, the Bhils came for me. I sprang up, put Dattu down on the mattress and ran into the courtyard shouting, 'I'm Manu. Look at me. I'm Manu.'

When everything got sorted out we couldn't go back to sleep. We stayed up the rest of the night laughing at what had happened. We remembered the story for months afterwards and laughed.

A few days later, Mr Tilak came to Jalalpur. We had settled down very well in Vani. Mr Tilak had found work that he liked, an opportunity to do social service and time for his theological studies. But the time had come for us to leave Vani. Appasaheb Buti wrote to Mr Tilak in Jalalpur. He said he wanted to do some useful work for society and had decided to translate the Vedas from Sanskrit into Marathi, the everyday language of the people, for which he would require Mr Tilak's help. 'Please come to Nagpur as soon as you can. You will get your old living quarters,' he wrote.

We decided to go to Nagpur. Dattu was about ten months

old. Bhikajipant Gorhe had now been transferred to Nagpur. We began to live in Appasaheb's garden bungalow in Nagpur as in the old days. Mr Tilak would divide his time between teaching Gopal and writing. While there, he had begun working on a long novel. It was never completed; but as he went along, he got what he had written printed. I do not remember the name of the novel. What I do remember is that one room in our house was filled with piles of printed paper. During this time he also wrote a shorter novel called *Veerkanya*, another one called *Teen Vidhwa*, *Eka Phulacha Itihas* and his collection of poems, *Kavyakusumanjali*. He also began spending a lot of time with a sadhu who was staying with Appasaheb. There were many books in Appasaheb's house as it is. But if Mr Tilak needed more, Appasaheb would order them immediately. All in all, with the reading, writing, debate and discussion, Mr Tilak's life was made. Home and family had never meant much to him. It was not surprising that he should forget them totally now.

Mr Tilak did not go in fear of anybody. If he was afraid of anybody at all, it was God, and after Him, me. One day, when it was my time of the month, Mr Tilak had to do the cooking. Dattu was now on solids. Mr Tilak had his bath and put some dal to cook on the stove. He got into his outdoor clothes saying, 'I'm going out while the dal cooks.' I said to him, 'Why not go after lunch?' But he went anyway. Back home, the dal cooked, got burnt and finally turned to cinders. And yet there was no sign of Mr Tilak. Dattu was crying with hunger. The town was far away. I did not have a paisa on me. We had engaged the young son of an oilpresser to look after Dattu. I got him to set up three stones as a makeshift stove, put rice to cook and that is how Dattu was fed. I starved. The only outlet I had for my feelings was tears.

A Mahar woman was working in the garden. She saw my plight. She plucked some fruit from the trees and insisted I eat them. 'What can I do, lady? You Brahmins can't eat food made by us. Otherwise I would have fed the child and you.' What a caring thing to say. But she was right. We were not permitted to eat food cooked by her. Night came. The young boy made some rice again, fed Dattu and put him to sleep. Around nine o'clock at night, Bhikajipant came to make peace in advance. He brought some chivda and besan laddoos with him. A lamp was flickering in the house. I was sleeping in one corner, Dattu in the other. I lost my temper. 'What brings you here so late at night?' I asked. 'To tell you the truth, Vahini, Mr Tilak is in Hansapuri. He told me you and Dattu must be hungry. That's why he asked me to bring these things for you. He said he would have his dinner later. He is afraid of you.' Mr Tilak came back a long time later.

A few days after that, Mr Tilak and Appasaheb fell out. It might have been over a religious issue or something else. I think it was around this time that Mr Tilak had begun to feel uneasy about religion. Gopal had decided to go to Ramtek for a change of air. He wanted Mr Tilak to go with him but Mr Tilak did not feel like going. After that he disappeared somewhere for nearly a month. I had no money. I had a serving boy, his pet monkey, Dattu and myself to look after. There was not a grain of anything in the house. There were no neighbours nearby. The boy would go into town, pick up odd jobs and feed himself and the monkey.

While we were living under these conditions, I came upon two seers of jowar lying in a dark corner. I doubt if anybody has experienced the kind of joy I felt at this discovery. I would grind the grain, cook a gruel and have it with buttermilk. I'd pluck chillies from the garden and make a spicy side dish with them. We used to have a woman deliver two seers of milk every day. I'd buy and store a paisa worth of popped unhusked rice. I would soak some of it every day in milk and feed Dattu on that. That is how we lived. One thing I was sure about. Whatever happened, however much we suffered, I would not go to my brother's or let my people know about my life. So, I stayed put in Nagpur.

One day Dattu began crying for rice. Where was I to get rice from? We did not have a single grain of rice in the house. The same day the people from the big house were having dinner in the garden. Food was being cooked there for a hundred people. I felt tempted to go over and ask for a bit of rice for Dattu. An old woman was supervising things. I approached her and said, 'Granny, can you give me a small bowl of rice for Dattu? I'm feeling too lazy to light the stove.'

It was evening time. The old woman flew at me saying, 'Is this any time to ask for such a thing? We haven't had our dinner yet.' Hearing this I went back the way I had come. For me it was like the end of the world. How could this illiterate woman have spoken to me like that? I thought of my people. Our house feeds dozens of people. We grow rice. My sister cooks two or three seers of rice every day. And here I was looking for just a small bowl of rice.

Never before had I felt so aggrieved. I pacified Dattu somehow and put him to sleep. I lay down beside him but I could not sleep. Terrible thoughts gripped me. I told myself my son did not have rice now, but when he grew up, he would have enough to feed a few others. Just then there was a knock at the door. I opened the door. It was the old woman. Behind her was a Brahmin carrying a plate full of food. 'I am ashamed at the way I spoke to you. Please don't hold it against me. I've brought dinner for Dattu.'

'But he's asleep now. And he wouldn't have eaten so much anyway.'

It has been a long-cherished rule with me, not to turn my back on food. I always remember a verse from the hymns in praise of Vyankatesh. 'Oh Lord of the Universe, you make us run / In all directions in search of food.' The woman had also brought some rice.

'I don't need this. I have rice. I was just being too lazy to cook it.'

'I've brought you rice because you are lazy. Now please don't be offended. Think of me as you would of Dattu.'

'How can that be? I called you Granny.'

'Call me anything you like, but please accept this.' And the old woman left. The serving boy and I ate that food for two days and the laddoos lasted us for days after. The old woman turned out to have a human heart after all. There are others who will make people suffer and still walk around looking like innocence incarnate.

The following morning the milk woman came. She asked to be paid. For a long time I could not utter a word. Suppose this woman refused to give me milk on credit, how was I going to feed Dattu? A sob escaped me. The woman said, 'What's the matter, lady?' That was enough to bring on a flood of tears. I told her my story. 'I'm trying to track him down,' I said. 'If I can't find him, I'll go to my parents' home. Give me your address. I'll send you the money. But please don't stop giving us milk while I'm here.'

The woman said, 'Send the child with me. I'll look after him well.'

'And how will I live without him?'

'I understand. Whether I get money or not, I promise not to cut your milk for as long as you are here. One can always get money, but good people are hard to come by.' Then she pressed the two rupees she had got from another customer into my hand. 'Keep this for your expenses. Someone gave it to me today.'

I was filled with gratitude. God works in such unexpected ways. Here was a mere village woman with such a large heart. The woman's back was hardly turned when Bhikajipant came. 'Vahini, Mr Tilak hasn't been to our house for a long time. Has he gone away somewhere?'

'Yes.'

'Where?'

'I don't know.'

'How long has he been gone?'

'A month.'

'Do you have anything to eat in the house? Or shall I get you some stuff?'

'I have everything. But since you've come, can you send him a telegram?'

'To which address? And what shall I say?'

'He must be in Rajnandgaon at Ganpatrao Khare's. Tell him I'm very ill and there's nobody to look after Dattu.' Although he kept refusing, I insisted he take a rupee from the two the milk woman had given me to pay for the telegram. Bhikajipant sent the telegram. The very next day Mr Tilak came. I was busy sprinkling water in the front yard. He said, 'How stupid you are. Who'll believe you if you cry wolf like this? What was the matter with you?'

'I had sprained my ankle.'

Mr Tilak had his bath and sat down for dinner. I set some broken rice, buttermilk, salt and a side dish of chillies from the garden before him.

'What's this?' he asked.

'It's what we've been eating since you left.'

Mr Tilak was full of remorse. But it did not last. 'We are going to Rajnandgaon,' he said.

'Why? What's wrong with being here?'

'I say we have to go so we'll go. Otherwise you can go to Jalalpur.'

As it happened, the time had come for me to go to my brother's anyway.

Mahadev

Mr Tilak had expressed a wish that I should go to Jalalpur when we left Nagpur. However, the idea did not get the majority vote and so I went with him to Rajnandgaon. The following two years were the most important in Mr Tilak's life. Soon after we left Rajnandgaon, he went to Mumbai to be baptized.

Mr Tilak had always kept a diary, but the entries were irregular and desultory. However, after we arrived in Rajnandgaon around 1894, he began making minutely detailed entries in it. They were written in such a small hand that many of the pages had to be read under a magnifying glass. The diary entry for 5 February reads:

> School 3.45-5. I was talking to the headmaster Ayodhyanath when the school peon Nohar came. The headmaster told me that his wife had been in labour from the previous night but had still not delivered. The peon's income was five rupees per month. Who would not pity him? I forgot all about my other work in the courthouse and went straight to Mr Milton's house. He was not at home. A policeman stood guard outside. I told him I wished to speak to Mrs Milton. She is a midwife. I wanted to pay for her services. But she offered to come without charging fees. Mr Sharangpani loaned us his tonga. In the end, thanks to Mrs Milton's charity and by the grace of God, Nohar's wife delivered safely. I returned home at 7.30.

My first three deliveries had happened in Jalalpur. The first two were at Attyabai's place and the third at my brother's. Circumstances had now brought me to my 'mother-in-law's' place for the fourth. I had never seen my real mother-in-law. Had she been alive I would still not have suffered the torture that is reserved for daughters-in-law. But she had passed on. Then Rajnandgaon threw up a mother-in-law who gave me a royal taste of what I had missed.

We were staying at Sadashivrao Retrekar's house in Rajnandgaon. Another family lived in the same building. That tenant had an old mother. Mr Tilak used to call her Aai and respected her as a mother. The landlord's brother Govindrao and his wife Anandibai also lived in the house. Sadashivrao himself did not live in Rajnandgaon.

Govindrao and Mr Tilak's adopted mother had engaged a maid to do their work. A general pretense was made that she served both. Both paid her a salary. But as far as you could see, she spent all her time doing the old woman's bidding. When we arrived, she pestered Mr Tilak to engage the same woman to look after Dattu for four rupees a month. The maid who used to get three rupees a month from Govindrao and the old lady now began earning a monthly income of seven rupees. In return, she was bent under the burden of the great favour the old woman had done her. The old woman used to treat Govindrao's wife Anandibai like a daughter-in-law. Soon she began according me the same treatment. But I was not meek like Anandibai. I did not allow her any elbow room. So the old woman began to poison Mr Tilak's ears against me.

When we came to Rajnandgaon, we were given only two rooms, one on an upstairs floor and something like a shack in the garden. But Mr Tilak had proposed to the old woman that we would be allowed the use of her room when the time for my delivery came. However, when the time came, the old woman refused to shift into the shack. She kept saying there was still time for my delivery. It was the month of Bhadrapad and the shack was becoming damp with the rain.

One day when we were sitting together, I said to Govindrao, 'Kaka, I want another room.'

Guessing which way I was leading, Mr Tilak said, 'Go to your brother's.'

'I don't want to go to my brother's.'

'You're a very stubborn wife. If you don't want to go, stay here and die.'

'I will do just that but I will not go to my brother's. I want that room.'

Mr Tilak now turned to his adopted mother and said, 'Aai, please give her your room.'

'But the hut must be dirty. I want the floor and walls to be properly plastered with dung.'

I said, 'Employ a woman to do the job.'

'I won't live in a house that's been plastered by some serving woman.'

Anandibai said, 'I'll plaster the walls and floor.'

Kaku said, 'But why just yet? I'm older than all of you. I know what's what.'

I said, 'I don't care whether you're older or younger. I want that room now.'

Mr Tilak turned on me saying, 'You should heed what older people say.'

I said, 'I'm not going to heed anybody. Anandibai, you move into the shack and give me your room. Your husband had promised to give us the place.'

Now Govindrao decided to order the old woman to vacate her room there and then and allow the Tilaks to move in.

Anandibai plastered the hut up and down. She employed a woman to help her shift our stuff. I helped as much as I could. The old woman sat watching the fun. Mice and rats had dug holes in her room. We had to get them all sealed. Once Mr Tilak left for work, the old woman made sure that our maid did not touch our work. Anandibai and I would do all the chores ourselves. The old woman could not endure Anandibai helping me. Throughout the day she would sit muttering that I had spoilt Anandibai. When the men came home from work, she would carry tales about us to them.

On the day of my delivery, Mr Tilak had gone either to the school or elsewhere to rehearse a play he had written. Dattu was running a high temperature. I asked Anandibai to look after him that night. Women of the sweeper caste were the midwives in those parts. I did not want to be delivered by one of them. So the old woman delivered the baby boy. I had been requesting her to stock up all the things we would require for the delivery. She kept saying there was plenty of time and Mr Tilak, believing her, ignored my requests. As a result, that night, there was not even a drop of oil in the house for the oil lamp and the only person to help me was the old woman. Mr Tilak returned from his rehearsal the next morning. He was very happy to see his second son. He wired Attyabai to give her the news.

The custom in those parts was not to give the new mother anything to eat for three days and make a hundred pricks on the newborn's stomach. I revolted against the custom. I asked Anandibai to give me chapattis and quietly ate them. Somehow they were transformed into rice and buttermilk and Mr Tilak was told that evening that I had dared to eat rice and buttermilk. Mr Tilak lost his temper with me. I was the last person to tolerate this. I sat up in my cot and quarrelled bitterly with him. He promptly composed a poem on me. Naturally I did not like what it said, but as a poem it was good. I suspect he tore it up later. On the third day, Lakshmibai Khare came. Having her was a great help.

Dattu's fever had come down to normal and he was back to running around and playing. One day Mr Tilak was upstairs writing. The old woman, his adopted mother, was at the well. We all drew water from that well. There was no pulley to draw it because it was built flush with the ground. Dattu was playing in the garden and the old woman was staring at him. While playing, he happened to wander towards the well. The old woman did not say a word, nor did she pick him up or push him away. Govindrao noticed this and ran out to pick him up. From that day Mr Tilak lost trust in his adopted mother. He realized now that the old woman had made him pay four rupees to the maid for looking after Dattu, but had not allowed her do it.

Soon after that Attyabai came. She and Mr Tilak had always been at loggerheads. With her in the house, Mr Tilak was constantly away. I was like a betel nut caught in a betel nut cracker. Attyabai's constant complaint was, 'Why did you stay here? Why didn't you come to Jalalpur?' When she asked Mr Tilak to go to the market for provisions, he would go and eat out. When he returned, she would have things to say to him. He would then vanish upstairs and compose a poem on her which he would then set about reading out in a loud voice. They got on each other's nerves to such a degree that one day Mr Tilak disappeared to become an ascetic. He did not tell me about his decision but wrote to my brother and sister to say so.

Everybody in Jalalpur panicked. Boons were asked for. Sixteen Monday fasts were begun. My people wondered fearfully that if Mr Tilak returned as an ascetic as Dnyaneshwar's and Sopandev's father had done, who would look after his children? We had no clue to the chaos he had thrown my family into. We came to know what he had threatened to do only when the family started writing to us. Eight days went by. Mr Tilak returned. I threw all the letters that had come during his absence before him. 'Is this true?' I demanded.

'Yes, it is,' he said. 'But I cannot become an ascetic without your permission. That's why I have come back.'

Two days after Mr Tilak came back, the younger boy started having convulsions. The doctor said, this room is dank, the floor is damp, there is no ventilation, you should move out. We changed house to Gopalrao Joshi's place. But the very next day, the baby died. He was on my lap when he died. I put him down and then called out to Attyabai, 'Something's happened to the baby.' Attyabai tried everything in her power to revive him but to no avail. The baby was already dead. As a matter of fact, I had only called her after I had put the baby down. Otherwise she would have raised a hundred objections about pollution and other such superstitious beliefs and a bitter quarrel would have broken out again between her and Mr Tilak. It was to avoid such a thing that I sat away from the child pretending for a while that he was still alive. We had called the baby Mahadev after

Mahadevbhauji, wishing to believe that Bhauji had been reborn to me. In looks at least, he was quite like Bhauji.

After Mahadev's death, the conflicts between Attyabai and Mr Tilak grew even more bitter. She would say to him, 'It's your flightiness that's responsible for taking this golden boy from us.' To this he would reply, 'Your idiotic, illiterate beliefs were what took him.' Caught between them, I was in a terrible place.

It was after one such quarrel that Attyabai decided, in a fit of rage, to return to Jalalpur. We escorted her to the station. She had had nothing to eat since the morning. When she boarded the train, Mr Tilak gave her packets of dates and pedhas. When the train began to move she threw them out at us. She was very angry but also very sad at having to leave Dattu.

The First Public Speaking Event in Hindi

After Attyabai departed there was at least peace in the house. Mr Tilak writes in his diary, 'The old woman, the queen of cheats, is not our neighbour anymore. Mother-in-law has gone away. Peace reigns.' But there was no peace in Mr Tilak's heart. In Appasaheb he had had a soulmate with whom he could read Sanskrit literature, exchange views, debate. He was deprived of that. Here, the people around him were more involved in local politics and commerce. Meanwhile, Mr Tilak's urge to be of use to society had intensified. He writes in his diary on 3 January, 'I want to wind up everything here in six or seven years and be free to serve the country.' He had been fighting to help farm labourers who were being mercilessly exploited in Rajnandgaon. There was a real risk of his losing favour with his seniors, but he carried on regardless. People who believed in expediency and not ethics believed he was mad. Mr Tilak says in his diary dated 6 January, 'The doctor told me local people have decided I'm insane. That is natural. I am bound to be declared mad amongst men who are scoundrels, cheats and ingrates. Wherever you look, you will find that Hindus respect nobody more than boot-lickers, hypocrites and bribe-takers. The Hindu is like a dog who is tempted by the mere smell of food and will take any beating for it. Profit or no profit, there are thousands who will drool at the mere smell of money and endure kicks in return.'

This entry gives some idea of Mr Tilak's state of mind at the time. He was also reading voraciously, committing many books to memory. His diary entries often read, 'I'm memorizing *The Letter Writer*' or 'I'm memorizing *Cicero*.' The Bible formed an important part of his reading in those days as also books written by the Christian scholar Baba Pudmanjee. Moreover, since he had always done what he thought fit, he did some outrageous things during this period.

On Sasubai's death anniversary, I was after him to invite Brahmins and married women for the shraddha lunch.

'I don't want to observe her death anniversary.'

'Why not?'

'I will observe it only if you agree to serve those whom I invite.'

'Who are you going to invite?'

'The lame and the blind, of any caste and any creed.'

'The death anniversary observance means Aai will be with us. What are you saying?'

'My mother appreciated compassion. She wasn't a fanatic.'

'So what? The Brahmins will eat first. Then you can serve whomsoever you want.'

'I want the lame and the blind to come in place of Brahmins. I don't want to invite Brahmins at all.'

Finally, after more arguments, I agreed with Mr Tilak's plan and quietly went off and invited a Dravidian Brahmin and Mr Retrekar's wife as my married woman guest. Mr Tilak's lame and blind guests also came. They sat outside. My guests sat inside. Mr Tilak presented dhotis to his guests. My Brahmin began to complain. 'Why didn't you invite other Brahmins? Who are those people sitting outside?' I explained everything to them. 'If anybody questions you, you can say, "I was invited, I went. How would I know who else was coming? And once you have sat down to a meal you can't get up, can you?"'

There are entries about this in Mr Tilak's diary dated 8 January and 15 and 25 February. They are about our quarrels over various rituals.

> I got Lakshmi to read ten devotional verses. She is not interested in reading. Her Attyabai has filled her head with just one great principle which is that the only function and end of human life is to perpetuate the circumstances of life and customs that have come down to us through the ages. So if I as much as begin to talk against some custom of this kind, spirits instantly possess her. We did not celebrate

> dhanurmas with khichadi. All I said was rather than invite a mean-minded, arrogant, stupid Brahmin who's already obese with food, why not invite the poor who have never had this kind of food? That set her off.

In those days, public speaking contests used to be held in cities like Pune, Mumbai, Nashik and Nagpur. Mr Tilak would enter all of them and come away with prizes. He had a strong urge to hold one such event in Rajnandgaon. Since nobody there spoke Marathi, it was naturally decided that the speeches would be in Hindi. It is my surmise that he was encouraged in this enterprise by Mr Waman Daji Oak of Raipur. During that period Mr Tilak made many visits to Raipur. His diary is full of references to Mr Oak. I think Mr Oak was the publisher of a literary magazine. A diary entry says he had decided to place one of Mr Tilak's poems in *Vividh Dnyanavistaar*, not *Dnyanasangraha*. In another entry, Mr Tilak has listed the number of times he visited Raipur, how many days he spent there and how many in Rajnandgaon. Adding up numbers, he comes to the conclusion that in one month, he had spent twenty days in Rajnandgaon and ten in Raipur.

There is no need to tell my readers how little store Mr Tilak set by money. Invitation cards were sent out everywhere for the public speaking contest. Rajnandgaon had never seen anything like it before. There was a lot of running around and commotion in the village. Our house was like a wedding host's. Mr Tilak gave away half his salary for the kitty. Grand preparations were made for the reception of guests. I had collected all the spices and condiments I would need. Bhauji and Rakhmai were staying with us at the time.

It had been decided to organize meals for the guests elsewhere, not at home. But the cook was asking for too much money. The collection that had been made was just enough to cover prizes and some sundry expenses.

Mr Tilak said to me, 'What is your contribution going to be?' I said, 'Your contribution is my contribution.'

He said, 'How can that be? When I eat you also eat, don't you?'

'Well, yes.'

'Similarly, what I give is not what you give.'

'But I don't have any money.'

'I've thought of something. We can't find a cook. They are all asking for too much money.'

'I will cook. Then I won't have to pay a fee, will I?'

That is how I made my contribution. There were five or six women working in the kitchen. One of them said, 'Let us warm up the leftovers from lunch and serve them for dinner.'

I said, 'I will never do that. I will cook a simple rice and pithla meal but it will be fresh. These people are our guests.'

This led to a fight. I got angry and came away home. After the event was over, the guests went to the kitchen for their evening meal and found I wasn't there. Mr Tilak lost his temper. He came home with the guests.

'Are the guests going to have cold snacks for dinner?' Mr Tilak demanded.

'Certainly not,' I said. 'Sit outside talking while I get dinner ready.'

'But why did you come away like that?'

'I had a fight.'

There was a week's store of provisions in the house. I used it all up for the dinner. I cooked and Bhauji's wife Rakhmai served. The guests had their fill. Mr Tilak was very happy. The event was over. Mr Tilak has made the following diary entry about the event, dated 20 May 1894:

> Plans for the event are afoot. I had invited Dewansaheb today but he did not turn up. Milton did not come because he was working. Shankarprasad, Anandiprasad, Appaji Modak are not in town so they did not come. I hear H.M. Ayodhyanath did not come because he would have had to pay a month's salary today as promised. Be that as it may, the meeting started with Mr V. Sharangpani being elected president. The

idea of the event was explained and then discussions about how to organize it began. A managing committee of thirteen people was elected to work under Sharangpani. Bhagwandutt and I were appointed secretaries, Laxmanrao Modak, the treasurer. When expenses were calculated, it looked like we would require 200 rupees in all. At this point people began to leave the meeting till only twelve of the original twenty-five remained. It was clear that the collection we had made would not stretch to that amount. I knew I was not rich enough to make up the shortfall. So I offered to host the people who were coming from other parts. Initially people objected, knowing how poor I was. But later, when I insisted, they submitted to my offer. Even then a group of men pounced on me. I have heard them brag although they have not done a shred of work for the country. All they wanted was to pull me down because they were jealous and petty-minded. This enraged me and a quarrel broke out. I am told it was my fault. Quite right. They expect peace from me. We made a collection of 135 rupees today.

21 May:

Bhagwandutt comments at length about yesterday's argument. My decision: If my temper obstructs my work for the people, I must instantly control it.

12 July:

The first Hindi public speaking event began here today. There are twelve guests from Nagpur—Haripant Pandit, Shankar Laxman Gokhale (M.A.), Mr Atre (B.A.) Ghanashyam Deuskar, Krishnashastri Dhule, etc. There are about eight from Raipur, three from Kamthi and altogether ten from four other places. The event began at two o'clock in the afternoon and ended at six in the evening. The Raja and the Dewan are in a panic because of what one that I shall call X has told them. You can see how this idiot's fearful nature is allowing that scoundrel to exploit him. Today Sakharam comes with his family.

13 July:

> Vishwanath Sharma and other teachers from Balod were deeply impressed by the speeches. Nine contestants spoke on the first topic, nine on the second and nine again on the third. I doubt if we are going to get the hundred rupees the Raja has promised.

14 July:

> The whole of today was spent trying to get a hundred rupees of the hundred and eighty-five promised. We managed to squeeze them out of him with great difficulty. I don't know what can be done with this evil man.

The entry dated 15 July lists who won what prizes. It ends with, 'We as secretaries won curses from two Maithili Brahmins.'

Mr Khare's House Is Left Behind

Mr Tilak read voraciously in Rajnandgaon and also devoted time to studying. He had engaged a munshi to teach him Urdu. He read many books in English. I cannot say what they were, but his diaries tell us that he was studying the Bible and the Christian religion with intense attention. He corresponded regularly with the well-known Christian writer Baba Pudmanjee and Rev. Dr Abbot. It is perhaps at their suggestion that he read the autobiographies of Rev. Pudmanjee, Rev. Karmarkar, Rev. Modak and Rev. Hari Ramchandra Christi and many comparative studies of Hinduism and Christianity. He was a prolific writer and many visitors came to discuss and debate with him. I could understand this. But the Christian business was completely beyond my understanding at the time.

I too read and wrote. Although my writing did not win Mr Tilak's approval, I have continued to be an avid reader and writer from then till now. I write with any implement that is at hand—a lead pencil, a penholder, a quill or even a matchstick. An entry in Mr Tilak's diary reads, 'I am teaching Lakshmi a shloka. She is taking it down with a matchstick. Even if I repeat a stanza one hundred times, there's nothing on paper. And what there is, is filled with mistakes. She works like a workhorse, but shoots her mouth off and loses people's love.'

In another entry he says, 'Vishnupant Gore came over. He returned Rev. Baba's autobiography which he had finished reading. He used filthy words about the Bible. We talked about this. Lakshmi lost her temper, and she said something quite idiotic. We had a small fight.' Mr Tilak was strongly influenced by the Bible and particularly the Sermon on the Mount. He regretted the small fight we had and he refers to it in his diary. He writes, 'There is no forgiveness or peace in me. Shiva, Shiva. What use is all the reading and thinking I do?'

In an entry dated 19 February 1894 he says:

> I feel drawn towards Christianity. It strikes me as a religion that brings peace, devotion, morality, tenderness and salvation to the human being. I might feel happier living in the ever joyous and fertile garden of this religion than amongst the trees and thorns, deep ravines and terrifying mountains, arid deserts and sweet mango groves that crowd the Hindu religion. But at this point, I dare not even utter the thoughts that are in my mind. Lakshmi does not even want to read. It is nothing but my fear of her and the fullness of her love for me that hold me back. Dear God, show us both the right way.

Mr Tilak had been going somewhere every night. There was no way to know where. How could I find out? I could not tell the landlady's son to tail him. He was too young. And if he was discovered, Mr Tilak might even beat him in a rage. So one day I decided I would investigate this myself. We had had a quarrel so our dinner thalipeeth had made it to the stove at nine o'clock. I had fed Dattu and he was asleep. Mr Tilak said, 'I'll go over to see Mr Khare and come back.' I closed the door but kept my eye on the crack. Mr Tilak turned towards Mr Khare's house, allowing his shoes to creak loudly. After a few steps, he turned round and walked in the opposite direction, making sure that his shoes did not creak. It was bright moonlight outside. Leaving the pan with the thalipeeth on the stove, I threw the door wide open and walked swiftly after him, while keeping a safe distance between us. Some way down the road it struck me that it would not be right to have a showdown in somebody else's house. It would be better if I returned home before Dattu woke up. But I said, loudly enough for him to hear me, 'That's not the way to Mr Khare's house.' The moment he heard me, Mr Tilak spun around. I too turned. I could barely see the road ahead. I wished the earth would split and swallow me. I rushed home, bolted the door from inside and sat in the kitchen. The thalipeeth had turned to cinders.

Mr Tilak had followed me home and was now banging on the door. I dared not open it. Finally when the door seemed on the verge of collapse, I was forced to open it. Mr Tilak then gave me a proper pasting. When his rage was spent, we ate a cold dinner. The following morning, Mr Tilak was genuinely grieved to see my swollen back.

That day he had been on his way to visit an Englishman named Mr Milton. The following entry from his diary makes it clear that he used to visit him, read the Bible with him, discuss religious subjects and even eat with him:

> At Milton's. Introduced to Mrs Milton. My impressions about Christianity and discussion with Milton about them. Read out several poems form the diary, etc. Am beginning to believe that of all religions, Christianity assures greatest joy on earth, is easiest to understand and the most blissful. I do not believe that Jesus is the son of God. I see him as a great soul with a generous heart. This I frankly confess. Home at 10. (13-2-1894)

Mr Tilak writes about what happened when he was eating with Milton:

> One of the constables here, Yeshwantrao, came in under some pretext four times to see this uncommon sight. Just then Milton's daughter came in with rice and rotis. This convinced the man. For people like him, even to eat with somebody from another caste is one of the ultimate sins. But I too felt a moment of hesitation when I saw Yeshwantrao. See how lame one's ideas are unsupported by courage. (19-02-1894)

> Met two American missionaries who wish to work in Chhattisgarh. One was elderly but the other was only eighteen. They, Mr Milton and I talked, read the Bible, had dinner, prayed. (26-02-1894)

Mr Tilak's correspondence had increased a great deal these days. I had no idea whom he wrote letters to and who wrote letters to him. Many people told me that I should keep an eye on the letters that came for him and pass them on secretly to the local people. I did not consent to doing such a thing. I was once advised to burn the Bible that was kept on Mr Tilak's table. My response to the advisor was, 'I have no idea what a Bible is. But suppose I did burn it, will it be impossible for him to get another? Will my burning one burn all the Bibles in the world? No. So I won't burn this one.'

The diary discloses that Mr Tilak was corresponding with religious leaders in Mumbai and particularly with Rev. Baba Pudmanjee. The following reference to Mr Tilak's letters may be found on pages 269–70 of Rev. Baba's collection of experiences published in 1895:

> A few days ago I received a letter from an unknown scholar. He wrote to say that he had read my book *Arunodaya* (The Rising of the Sun), amongst others. He says, 'This book is not embellished by any literary graces nor is it marked by a scientific perspective. Yet I have felt compelled to read it over and over again. It is filled with true feeling, devotion, simplicity and freedom from desire. I am in the process of reading your autobiography for the sixth time now.' This scholar met a Christian gentleman with whom he had a discussion of which he provides a succinct account in the letter. 'The Christian gentleman asked me if I had read the Bible. I answered that I had studied the Vedas and the Puranas. They are written by men who are even baser in nature than me. Now my Bible is this sky, this earth, these forests. In short, I am reading God's life in Nature.' When he heard this, the gentleman said in English, 'I do not have the powers to debate this point with you. But take this Bible and read it at least three times. I agreed and began reading it reluctantly only to keep my word. But as I read on, it began to seem to me that, as I have said above, this was not a fearful jungle but a lovely little garden.' I sent the gentleman many books on his request.

To judge by his diary entry for 13 September, Mr Tilak appears to have gone on to make a detailed study of the Bible. Instead of his customary beginning, 'Got up in the morning', he has filled the page with notes like a student studying for an examination.

When we were in Rajnandgaon, Mr Tilak composed several poems on Dattu. Very few of them have survived the assault of time. Those which have were composed during the time he took Dattu to Raipur. One contains a description of the games the child, 'barely thirty months old', played. Another gives an account of Dattu's laughter and merry chatter when his father gave him a mouth organ. A third describes his feelings on kissing Dattu. 'Even a thousand kisses do not suffice / But he must have one more.' There is one poem about the games Dattu played with a visitor's son and another about his illness. 'A child who is never still / Now lies unmoving / A child who never stops talking / Will not answer his mother's calls.'

Dattu was indeed the apple of his father's eye.

From the Diary

During our time in Rajnandgaon, Mr Tilak became good friends with Mr Waman Daji Oak. He used to visit him very often in Raipur. He had gone there once with the Raja of Rajnandgaon to attend the Commissioner's durbar. Mr Oak's children had come to stay with us on a couple of occasions.

Mr Tilak has said the following about the children in his diary:

> Monday 29-01-1894. Raipur. Mr Waman Daji Oak's elder son is called Ganapati. He is about sixteen years old. The younger son Gopal is twelve or thirteen, daughters Bayo, twenty, Kashi, six or seven. His nephew Shivram is twenty-two or twenty-three and another nephew Damu is sixteen. Ganapati is open-hearted, loving and of a noble nature. Gopal seems mild and meek. Shivram is self-contained but appears to be far-sighted. Damu is going to be the spitting image of Wamanrao. Ganu and Damu are both very intelligent. Bayo is timid, of good character, affectionate and modest. Kashi will grow up to be like her but a bit short-tempered.

We knew nothing about the progress or lack of it that these children had made in the world thereafter. But thirty-five or forty years later, we all met in Nagpur during the Annual Literary Confernece. Damu, now Damodarpant, is the principal of the Normal School in Nagpur. Kashitai did not show any temper at all and Gopalrao's meek temperament in childhood continues to be so even now.

The English speech that was read on behalf of the Raja in the Commissioner's durbar was written by Mr Tilak. He had also composed some poems for the high school children. It would appear that Mr Tilak was particularly close to Ganu and Damu in Raipur. He writes in his diary that he once misplaced his spectacles and Damu spent a long time helping him look for them. Elsewhere he notes that both boys saw him off at the station and were very saddened at having to say goodbye. Returning home from that visit, he wrote a small poem about Dattu:

> Nana, Nana cried the child, seeing me
> Pick me up he said and clung to me
> With tear-filled eyes I held and kissed him
> And tiredness fled as though it had never been.

Once a pearl-seller was passing by the house. Mr Tilak said, 'Don't you think a bhikbali* would look good on my ear?' Mr Tilak had never been interested in fancy clothes and ornaments. I felt saddened when I heard him express a wish to own a bhikbali. We were not direly poor, but Mr Tilak's ways often put us in great financial difficulties. It wasn't possible at the time to buy pearls and get them strung in a bhikbali. Moreover, had I bought pearls, he would have been very angry with me. I once bought a bijwara, a hair ornament of red stones. What a to-do he created over it. He refers to it in his diary entry of 16-01-1894:

> My wife insists I go to the market. Only this will prove I am involved with the family. Today Lakshmi bought a bijwara made of fake stones and base gold for three rupees. That left a balance of eight rupees in the house. That is supposed to last us the rest of the month. To top that, she loaned three rupees to Janaki, that so-and-so Patwari's wife. Had I done something like that, she would have made it difficult for me to live.

(It was true. I did indeed believe he threw money away. But I will let that pass.)

I decided to break my nose-ring and make Mr Tilak a bhikbali from the pearls. It was the same nose-ring in which that

---

*This is an ear ornament worn by men in the old days. It has become fashionable today with young men. The bhikbali, which hangs from the top rim of the right ear, consists of a gold ring strung with two pearls between which dangles a small tear-shaped stone.

Mumbai goldsmith had cheated us, using false pearls instead of the real ones we had given him. I had a ring made from the one-and-a-half tola gold bracelet that Keshav Mama had given Dattu and put it on Mr Tilak's finger. Mr Tilak makes this incident the subject of a poem in his diary entry dated 14-02-1894, introducing the poem with, 'Today a heart-wrenching thing happened. This is how it was.' After describing the incident, the poem ends with lines that say I had broken an old nose-ring which was very dear to me and had strung it into a bhikbali for him with my own hands. This, for him, was a sign of the deepest love and it was this love that had filled his life with bliss.

Drawn to Christianity

Around this time Mr Tilak had begun to suffer from health problems. He made things worse for himself by imagining he might be suffering from tuberculosis or asthma or some third thing. As a result, along with value payable post (VPP) parcels of books, VPP parcels of medicines began to arrive home. He had his chest checked in Raipur. The doctor told him that he was suffering from dyspepsia, which had caused two lungs near his liver to become non-functional. Who knows whether the doctor was joking or whether he had thought up this incredible problem to fleece Mr Tilak. Whatever the case, if Mr Tilak had been in the condition he described, we would have had to register his death twenty-five years before it happened.

It was becoming clearer by the day that Mr Tilak was being drawn towards Christianity. Some of his writings in *Dnyanodaya* bore witness to that. In a diary entry dated 18-2-94, he says, 'Finished reading Hari Ramchandra Christi's biography. I feel greater joy when I read these Christian books than I have felt during my intense study of the Vedas and other scriptures, or heard the passionate speeches of Muslim thinkers. I have torn up and thrown away books that Christian missionaries had lovingly given me. But that was in my younger years.'

One day, Mr Tilak went out as usual. I had put the child to sleep and was sitting by myself with a heavy heart and anxious mind. You need someone to share your joys and sorrows with. Whom did I have? I had only the child who knew nothing beyond eating and sleeping. There were some people in the town, but they were hostile to Mr Tilak. I used to be afraid to talk to anybody. The local language too was different. There was talk everywhere that Mr Tilak was going to convert to Christianity. When he came back I asked him, 'Are you really going to become a Christian?'

'Who told you?'

'People.'

'Are you married to me or people?'

'You.'

'So am I telling the truth or are they?'

'You.'

'So I'm telling you, I'm not going to become a Christian.'

Having said this, he went out again. I bolted the door from inside and howled my heart out. I felt a little lighter after that. A breeze only ruffles the surface of water causing ripples. But my heart was heaving with a tempest that had blown in from the past and was threatening the present and the future. I wrote my first poem that day.

> My lord says he is going away
> Whose arms can I run to now?
> You the omniscient, tell me, pray,
> Whose feet can I fall at now?

Even as I wrote the last line of the poem, there was a loud knock at the door. I screwed up the paper on which I had written it and threw it into the waste paper basket. Meanwhile, the knocking on the door had continued. Mr Tilak was furious because I had taken so long to open the door.

'You never bolt the door. Why did you do that today?' He suspected me of something. 'What were you doing?'

'I was resting.'

'Couldn't you open the door?'

'It takes time to get up. Am I a machine?'

'Alright. Serve lunch.'

I went in to get lunch. Mr Tilak looked around the room. He thought I had been writing a letter to someone. Finally, he upturned the waste paper basket. Looking through the stuff, he came upon my verse. He was overjoyed to read it. He locked it away in his cupboard. These days Mr Tilak had taken to locking all his papers in this cupboard. When he was away, several people would ask to see his writings. I would say, 'I will not show you any of his papers even if it is in my interests.'

'At least burn the copy of the Bible that is on his desk then.'

I would say, 'Suppose I do, will all the copies of the Bible on earth disappear? If you say they will, I'll burn this one.' The people would go away then. I had a reason for not showing them the papers. We were living in a princely State. I had the impression that Brahmins from the Deccan were under watch here. Many of them had been thrown into prison for one reason or another. Suppose there was something against the king in Mr Tilak's papers? He was doing a lot of work to better the lives of forced unpaid labourers. In a diary entry dated 4 February, he writes, 'A hundred labourers from the fort are going to Mr Khare's to lift a tiger's iron cage from his place, guarded by five or six sepoys. Yesterday the labourers could not lift the cage which measures a full twenty arm-lengths. They had had nothing to eat from the morning till three in the afternoon. With the cage on their heads, they could hardly breathe. At one point, one of the labourers hurt his foot. Naturally, he was driven mad by the pain and could not lend his full strength to the work. So a sepoy whipped him as you would a draft animal. What brutality. What heartlessness. And what fear, what endurance from these Chhatisgarhi idiots. Would a couple of sepoys have the power to oppress hundred men like that in any western country? If only our king would see the terrible condition of these labourers with his own eyes. First an application had to be made to him in this regard. I wrote that out in Hindi on behalf of some four or five labourers. I have handed it over to Mr Sharangpani and Sadashivrao to submit to the king. It has been decided that I should speak to the king about this application when the two of them are present. Many people think I'm mad for doing this. The head clerk thinks I am overdoing things. Dear Lord, pity these poor souls; give me courage and the king compassion. As for me, come what may, I will put my trust in You and do my best.' Elsewhere he has written, 'I am planning to write a book to open the king's eyes.'

This must have been the reason why people were so keen

to see his papers. Or perhaps this business gave them an excuse to ask for them while the real reason was their suspicion that he was preparing to convert to Christianity. That is why I was extra wary. Here we were living in a princely State and Mr Tilak was openly writing all kinds of things. What would we do if somebody deliberately twisted what he had written to get him into trouble? I began to guard every scrap of paper on which he had written.

During this time we suddenly began getting streams of visitors. There were new faces every day and Mr Tilak would have animated discussions with them. One day I asked him who these people were and why they came to our place. He said, 'They come to influence my mind.' One gentleman told him, 'Mr Tilak, I don't have any kin. I have a large estate. I shall will it all to you.' He was willing to adopt him. Mr Tilak said, 'I have no plans to convert. And if I did, it wouldn't be for money.'

Appasaheb Buti sent Bapusaheb to Rajnandgaon to tell Mr Tilak that Appasaheb was willing to pay him one hundred rupees a month for his lifetime, give him a house and look after Dattu's education if he would give up the idea of converting. Mr Tilak set Bapusaheb's mind at rest and sent him away. The news that Mr Tilak was going to convert to Christianity reached the Pendses in Nashik. Mr Pendse wrote to Mr Tilak saying, 'Come and stay with me. I will look after you forever and pay for Dattu's education. You may eat meat and fish in my house if you wish and drink whatever you want. But please don't become a Christian.'

Appasaheb had offices in many places. They were all under instruction to keep an eye on Mr Tilak's movements. Bapusaheb told me of this before he went back and also gave me some money. 'If you sense something untoward is happening, let us know immediately. We will take care of him. We'll stop him. If need be we'll have him arrested and jailed for not repaying a debt. Whatever happens, we will not let him convert to Christianity. Please don't worry.'

Where Is My Grinding Stone?

I have already mentioned that I went to Pandharpur with Bhauji for Rakhmai's delivery. On the very date that she had been given for her delivery, a telegram came from Rajnandgaon from Mr Tilak. 'I am ill. Please send my wife back as soon as possible.' Mr Tilak preferred sending telegrams to writing letters. They were speedier. You needed to have money in your pocket to send them. Whenever Mr Tilak had money he would send telegrams at the oddest times.

Bhauji's tender heart trembled with fear when he read the telegram. He instantly set about making preparations for sending me back. It was a difficult time in Bhauji's home, but he gave no thought to his problems. He said to me, 'Vahini, you've been here for a long time. Nana has been without home-cooked food all this time. You must leave today.'

He gave me my train fare. I had to go by bullock-cart to Kurduwadi and take a train from there. One had to change trains a few times after that. Little Dattu was with me. I told Bhauji, 'Please arrange for someone to go with me. How can I go alone?' But Bhauji gave me detailed instructions in writing for getting there. So finally, I agreed to go, with no company except little Dattu.

An overseer called Tatyasaheb Kane lived in Pandharpur. His wife was Bhikutai's friend. I went to bid goodbye to them. 'I'm leaving today,' I said.

'Who is going with you?'

'Nobody. I'm going alone.'

'What will Bhikutai say to that? Nothing doing. I'll find a woman to go with you. Take this money.' So saying she put twenty rupees in my hand.

I set off with my companion. She was a widow. The telegram had scared me. I had taken nothing with me to eat and drink on the way. The two of us starved. We bought things for Dattu to have. We reached Bhusaval. Rakhmai's father lived there. Bhauji must have wired him to say we were going to pass through. He came to the station with lots of food. He tried to persuade us to stay the night. I told him I could not. I had to get back as soon as I could because of the telegram. The old man was very blunt. He was very affectionate but often said terrible things. Now he said to me, 'Look here. Tilak isn't going to die if you stay here one night.'

'Kaka, what a dreadful thing to say.' I was on the point of tears. The train began to move. At eight o'clock that night it reached Nagpur. I got off with my companion. I asked around for Bhikajipant's house and finally found it. The door was closed. The two of us were faint with hunger. Dattu was whining. I was nervous about Mr Tilak's health. I pushed at the door hard. It was a long time before it was opened. And the first words that fell on my ears were, 'Vahini, where is my grinding stone?'

'It's in hell. I'm dying of hunger. Give me some food first.'

'Come. Bhikajipant's dinner is already served. He's gone out. But you can eat before him.'

I had dinner. My companion also had something to eat.

Five or six years ago, when we first came to Nagpur and were staying in Mr Buti's rooms, I had borrowed the grinding stone that Bhikajipant's wife was talking about. After that we had lost three or four homes. It was in the course of those upheavals that Mr Tilak had given away the grinding stone to someone.

When Bhikajipant returned, he tried hard to persuade us to stay. But I had received this telegram. There was no way I was going to stay. We caught the seven o'clock train the next morning and were in Rajnandgaon at eleven. There was no coolie at the station. So I picked up our baggage, my companion carried Dattu and we trudged home. When we reached, we found the door locked. My heart missed a beat. I went over to the Khares'. There we discovered that Mr Tilak was as fit as a fiddle. We had lunch with them and went back. We sat in the courtyard waiting for Mr Tilak to come. He returned at four o'clock. 'What's this? Why did you send the telegram?' I asked.

'So you wouldn't exhaust yourself working there.'

'I was there for so many days. Would ten more days have exhausted me? They needed me.'

'They'll fend for themselves.'

As usual there were some angry exchanges, some banging around till tempers cooled and we were back to normal life.

One day Mr Tilak said, 'I met two missionaries today. They said a prayer in English. Never before in my life have I heard anything so beautiful.' I was not really listening to him. I was thinking about what this was leading to. A few days later, Mr Tilak was preparing to go to Mumbai. I asked him, 'Why are you going to Mumbai?'

He said, 'I have to buy horses for the Raja.'

He alone knew whether this was true or false. Neighbours used to tell me not to let him go. He was going to become a Christian. I was at wit's end. If I challenged him he would ask, are you married to me or to the neighbours? Then he would go and have a tiff with them. I decided it was best not to say anything. But I could not stop thinking. Then I struck on a ruse. I said to Mr Tilak, 'Why don't you take Dattu with you?'

'Why would I do that?'

'Just like that.' My idea was that he would not become a Christian if Dattu was with him. After much yessing and noing, he agreed to take him and I stopped worrying. Mr Tilak got off on the way at Nashik, left Dattu with the Pendses and went on to Mumbai alone. Dattu was only two years old. He had never stayed away from his parents. He cried the whole day. So they sent him to my brothers' in Jalalpur. When problems come through the door, illnesses also jump in through the windows. In Jalalpur, Dattu went down with measles. My people became anxious. But neither Dattu's mother nor father knew of his illness. As usual I was sitting by myself in Rajnandgaon like an abandoned Parvati. Of the five rupees Bapusaheb Buti had given me to send a telegram if required, two remained. Three had been spent on running the house.

After Mr Tilak left, the neighbours gathered around me and scolded me. 'What's this you've done? Why did you send Dattu with Mr Tilak? He's only a child. He will not understand anything. Did you not think Mr Tilak would have the child converted too?'

How true. Why had I not thought of that? Now there were two daggers in my heart. But outwardly I stayed calm and pacified the neighbours saying, 'Mr Tilak might have a change of heart because of Dattu.' But I was very depressed. I spent nights crying, separated as I was from husband and child and 500 miles away from the nearest relatives.

It was three weeks since Mr Tilak had left. I had no news of him or Dattu. I blamed myself bitterly for sending Dattu with him. At such times, even an enemy will not think the things that your fearful mind does. The railway station was close by. I would make two trips there every day, suffer disappointment and return home crestfallen.

There was a jailor in Rajnandgaon called Sakharampant. He was a friend of Mr Tilak's. They visited each other frequently. Thinking he might know something of Mr Tilak's whereabouts, I decided to go over to his place and ask. But then I had second thoughts. What would people say if I went to see him? Still, I decided to go. I was told he had gone out. I left word asking him to come over and returned home in a nervous state.

Now everybody in the town began saying that Mr Tilak was sure to lose his job. One well-wisher said, 'Lady, better fall at the dewan's feet. That's the only way your husband will retain his job. Otherwise he is bound to lose it.'

My true counsellor was God. I could not bring myself to fall at the dewan's feet. Even then I went to his house because people pressed me to. I was at his door. A thought came to me then that if I fell at his feet and Mr Tilak retained his job because of that, people would say his wife was responsible for his having a job. It did not matter if he lost his job, but she was not going to give people a chance to say that. Even if he were to lose his job, we would not be reduced to begging. And if we were, I would follow him holding my sari pallu out for alms. With this thought in mind I turned back even as I stood on the dewan's threshold.

The jailor came at four o'clock. I asked him, 'Where has Mr Tilak gone?'

'I have no idea.'

'Is that the absolute truth?'

'Absolute truth.'

'I thought you might know.'

'Truly, I don't.'

'Can you send a telegram for me?'

'To whom?'

'To Narayan Krishna Pendse at Nashik.'

'What shall I write?'

'Has Mr Tilak come there?'

I gave him a rupee and he sent the telegram.

Resignation

On the day that my telegram reached Nashik, Mr Tilak too arrived there from Mumbai. The moment she set eyes on him, Bhikutai put fifty rupees in his hand and said, 'Go immediately to Rajnandgaon and bring Manu here. I haven't met her for two years and there's a chance we'll soon be transferred to some other place far away from here.' When he heard this, Mr Tilak instantly set off for Rajnandgaon. In accordance with my routine, I was present at the station when he came. I was overjoyed to see him, but I did not see Dattu with him. I became nervous.

'Where's Dattu?'

'At his uncle's.'

'Why?'

'We'll go there now.'

'I'm not coming.'

'Your brother-in-law is going to be transferred far away. Bhikutai has sent for you because after that you won't meet each other for a long time. She has even given me train fare.'

'Even if she has, I'm not coming.'

'How stubborn you are. You don't even feel like meeting your sister. You're heartless.'

'Say what you like but I'm not coming.'

'Then what will you do?'

'What will I do? Stay here.'

'But I am coming with you.'

'And your job?'

'I'm resigning.'

'So what do we do with all our stuff?'

'Come back for it.'

I was in a trap. As the proverb goes, hold it and it bites; let go and it runs away. Whenever we moved, I would pack all our stuff into boxes, seal them and put my name on them. Else

Mr Tilak was likely to simply give them away. Of course, it was not as if sealed stuff escaped him. Most times when we moved, I would never again set eyes on the place or on the stuff we had left behind. But I always had innumerable keys to various houses in my keep. A collection of such keys weighing a seer or two, were lying around the house when Mr Tilak died. He now said, 'We're coming back soon. So don't carry too much luggage.'

Even then I managed to stuff two new saris, one tattered one and a cracked tambya in his bag just before we left. We bid farewell to Rajnandgaon and set off on the next part of our journey. Mr Tilak was with me till we reached Nagpur. But as soon as the train drew into the station, he suddenly remembered he had some urgent work there. He said, 'You go on ahead. I'll follow. I need to do something urgently here.'

Mr Tilak always had urgent work which I did not necessarily know about. Nor could I argue with him about it. That would be like trying to confine a wild wind in a box. So I left Nagpur station by myself. I did not have a paisa on me, nor any jewellery except for the gold wire ring in my nose. Mr Tilak had given away the ring I had made for him from Dattu's two-tola gold bracelet to somebody and told me it was lost.

The train arrived at Nashik at three o'clock. Here I was, Lakshmi, with only the gold wire ring in my nose to show for the name, a ragged sari wrapped around me and a bag in my hand bearing Mr Tilak's name in large letters and not a paisa on me even for a tonga. Such was the apparition that descended from the train at Nashik. There two men came rushing at me and tried to relieve me of my bag. I was scared out of my wits. I looked at them open-jawed wondering why these strangers were behaving like this. They said, 'Aunty, haven't you recognized us? We are the Pendses' men. We've come in a tonga to take you home.'

Bhikutai was waiting at the door, eager to see me. She hurried to help me out of the tonga as soon as it stopped. She was very sad to see the condition I was in. She held me close and said in a tearful voice, 'Manu, what a terrible state you are in.' For a while we chatted about this and that, then I had a bath and sat down to dinner. I had just finished when my brother arrived with a bullock-cart. 'Manu, Dattu has a dreadful cough. Please come to Jalalpur with me.'

Bhikutai said, 'Yes, please take her. Sita is in exile with demons on her tail. Mother and son have been separated for nearly a month and a quarter.'

When I saw Dattu in Jalalpur, I broke into sobs. On the third day, Bhikutai sent a tonga to fetch us back. We were soon there. Now our only worry was about Mr Tilak. He came seven or eight days later and we relaxed. Everybody had some advice to give him. Gharumai said, 'You must become an itinerant keertan performer.'

Mr Pendse said, 'Don't go anywhere at all now. You can all stay with us. You will eat with us and I'll give you twenty-five rupees a month for your personal expenses.'

Mr Tilak said, 'I don't want to be beholden to anybody. I'll perform keertans. I will have to go to Mumbai to pick up the things I'll need.'

Mr Pendse said, 'Why go all the way there for just that? I'll write to Balasaheb. He'll immediately send you everything you need.'

Mr Tilak did not care for the idea. He said, 'That won't do. It has to be a personal choice.'

What could Nanasaheb say to that? Nanasaheb had a house guest at the time, the jahagirdar of Chandori. Mr Pendse took him aside and told him about Mr Tilak. He requested him to persuade Mr Tilak to go with him to Chandori where he could keep a close eye on him. The jahagirdar agreed. A while later Mr Tilak said to Mr Pendse, 'The jahagirdar is asking me to go with him to Chandori for a few days.'

Mr Pendse said, 'That's good. Why don't you go then?'

When he left, he said goodbye to everybody in the house. He sat Dattu on his lap and as he kissed him again and again, his eyes flowed with tears. Everybody thought he was regretting his behaviour. Now, at last, he would take an interest in home and family. Ten days later, Mr Tilak went to Mumbai directly from Chandori. He had made his last visit to the Pendse home. After Mr Tilak left Chandori, the jahagirdar wrote to Mr Pendse. Mr Pendse took Bhikutai aside and showed her the letter. She took to her bed and never rose from it again. Within a couple of days several newspapers published the news. Mr Tilak had converted to Christianity.

Conversion

I shall give a full account in Part Two of what happened after Mr Tilak became a Christian. I shall conclude Part One with what he himself set down about his conversion.

> All of you know that the miracles performed by Jesus Christ as described in the New Testament stand like mountains in the path of truth-seekers who depend on their own inadequate mental powers to assess the sacred scriptures. These people become familiar with the son of man but they do not have the ability to know the son of God. They recognize the man who was crucified, but find it difficult to recognize the One who rose from the dead. The best way to bring such people to God is to pray with them, lead them again and again through the golden gate of prayer to stand them before God and to arouse true love in their hearts for that merciful Father of the Universe. That is how they will know the Father and in the process have all their doubts regarding miracles settled. I am convinced that God Himself clarifies such problems to the true seeker.
>
> When a man converts to Christianity—I am such a man having converted barely eleven months ago—he finds himself surrounded by men who, rather than being seekers of truth, are inveterate image worshippers, nay-saying heretics and men of little understanding, who lack the will to comprehend and who have no ability to do anything other than mock and ridicule. Many of these people are laughing at me even now and wondering how I could have lost my wits to the extent of believing in these miracles. Those amongst them who know me well consider this an even deeper mystery. I have only one answer for them all. It is this: Look, I am myself a walking and talking miracle. Look at me. Those of you who know me will surely see that I am a miracle. Am I not a Christian? Am I not a total believer in Christ? Around two years ago was I not a sworn enemy of this very Christ? Did I not scribble page upon page of criticism against Christ with

these very hands which are now so eager to serve Him? Was this not the tongue, so ready to bear witness to His every act of grace today, the same that I once used to heap insults upon his sacred name? Did anyone dream then that this man would one day become a Christian? Could anybody then have imagined that this man, who had such immense pride in the Hindu religion, would one day abandon it and submit himself to God's will as the Bible says? It would not surprise me if people were astonished that I should be standing before God holding Christ's finger, because I am myself surprised. What bigger miracle can there be than this? This miracle calls for no evidence.

Truly brothers and sisters, this miracle can be attributed only to the mercy of the Lord. I have no other words to explain it further. I am not the one who has become a Christian. It is the Good Shepherd himself, who neglected ninety-nine of his lambs to look for and pull out this one lost amongst the most terrible mountains. How proud and unbending I was. I had planned to found a new religion. And yet, here I am, a disciple of Christ. Praise be to the Lord. Truly, it is to Him that I owe the profoundest gratitude.

I had been striving to create a new religion for India. It was to be a religion which would bind all the countries of the world together in a spirit of brotherhood. I had been lost in this dream for years. It had been fixed in my soul by the merciful hand of God like the bedrock on which I could later build a great temple to Christian thought.

Nothing comes to pass all at once. I became a Christian, but I have no time to describe in detail the direct and indirect processes which led to this result. I will say only this: My mother was a pious woman and very loving. I have no idea what made her like that. I don't remember her ever uttering the name of Jesus Christ; but she always told us to fear God in our every action and to work for the welfare of others. As regards the fulfilment of the ideals of motherhood, I doubt I have ever met any other woman like her. There is no need to wonder how this could be since she was a worshipper of idols. The fact is, as we all know, God often grants virtues to idol worshippers in order to make them the means of some special aspects of his work. Besides her, I was fortunate to have a teacher at a very young age, who did not understand how to serve the country but whose heart overflowed with patriotism. He filled the little heads studying under him with a passionate love for the country.

It was these and other such circumstances that gave my mind an unexpected turn. I remember well that as a child I would be lost in my own thoughts during a Geography lesson. Only my body would be present in the class. My mind would be wandering to far-off lands, wondering what was to become of India in the future. Even at that young age, I would be filled with disgust at the caste discrimination in our society.

When I was about fourteen or fifteen, I had spoken in an assembly of boys on the subject, 'Why do Brahmins have a monopoly over religious matters?' I now remember my father's remark, made half in jest and half angrily, 'This boy will convert to Christianity one of these days.' I do not think I was ever taught by a single teacher who stuck to old customs. All my teachers were reformists. They inculcated in me the habit of keeping an open mind on every issue. These teachers gave me the confidence to think, speak and behave as I thought right. My mother died while I was still a boy, but I was fortunate that nobody used coercion to thwart my freedom of thought. I was convinced that if India was to make progress it would have to be through religion. That is why I threw myself headlong into the study of religion and philosophy. I finally found a true patron in Nagpur.

Till today I look upon this honourable man as my father. I began working with this individual about five years ago. Our work was to discuss and debate religion. He spent thousands of rupees on books pertaining to the Hindu religion, especially the Vedas and other spiritual literature. For three whole years I was afloat on the sea of religious knowledge and ideas. I had a great thirst for knowledge and this individual quenched it. Ultimately I came to setting down the following fundamental principles of my new religion:

1) The Creator of the universe is one for whom every human being is an equal child.

2) All religions have been created by Man and the only book that acquaints us with God is the world itself.

3) There is no such thing as reincarnation. Human joy and sorrow are the result of an individual's genetic make-up and the manner in which he carries out his duties towards himself and society.

4) To revere God and brotherhood towards all is the essence of religion.

5) There is no sin equal to idol worship.

If I were to establish these principles, I would have to turn into a sage. I began to study the lives of men who had founded new religions. I did not see eye-to-eye with many of them. The man I made friends with was Gautam Buddha. I decided to follow his example while leaving out his mistakes. Surprisingly, Christ and the Bible did not figure even in my dreams. The first reason for this was the simple language in which the Bible was written. The Brahmin seems to find only such literature interesting as is written in a language that makes you struggle and turn somersaults in your head in order to comprehend it. This seems to be a hereditary trait of the Brahmin. I am certain that if the Hindu scriptures were translated from Sanskrit into a vernacular language, Brahmins would treat them as junk and fling them as far away as they could. They are happiest when somebody chants a mantra of which nobody understands a word. But if somebody chants a translation, you can be sure that he will be mocked and ridiculed.

So this was the first reason not to turn to Christianity. But the second reason was much bigger. I did not come across a missionary, nor did I find books in Marathi about the religion, which would draw me in and hold my attention. Further, I had read and heard much criticism of the Bible of which I had myself not read even one full page. Lastly, the spiritual state of Indian converts to Christianity was so poor that there was no chance of their drawing me into the religion. It seemed to me that the only factors that separated these people from idol worshippers was a difference in food habits and customs. All these factors taken together worked towards keeping me away from Christianity.

In 1893, in accordance with the wishes of my patron, I took upon myself the responsibility of editing a monthly magazine devoted to religion and philosophy. However, because of the change in my opinions, I had to give up this work after I had brought out two issues. Around this time I was offered work by the Raja of Rajnandgaon which is located some 85 kilometres from Nagpur. I bought myself a ticket for the intermediate class which falls between the second and third class on the Bengal–Nagpur railway. When I approached the compartment, I noticed a white man sitting there. Our normal experience told me that he would throw me out of the compartment. He did not do that. Instead, he smiled and made room for me to sit.

At this point and with your permission, I would like to point out that the behaviour of white men working with and travelling on the railways stands like a mountain in the path of the spread of Christianity. There is a laughable ignorance amongst Hindus about Christianity. However, they are able to build an idea of how Christians are supposed to behave from what they see. The belief is that every white man is a Christian. Add to that the fact that for some reason the railways are full of these ill-behaved whites which is causing great harm to ideas about Christianity. I always wonder with great sadness why these men behave like that. I hope the Good Lord in his wisdom will send some missionaries their way to teach them what love means.

My travelling companion was extremely gracious and humble, so much so that whoever saw him was bound to be instantly filled with goodwill. I was carrying only one book with me on this journey. Bhavabhuti's *Uttarramcharit*. Of all Sanskrit poets, I find his poetry the most sublime. The two of us got talking at length about poets and poetry. I found his conversation most enjoyable. Soon I discovered that this gentleman had a smattering of Sanskrit and was very knowledgeable about Sanskrit literature. Gradually, he changed the subject and began to ask me about my opinion of Christianity and things like that. I told him about the new religion I had been thinking about. He heard me out and then said, with utmost gravity, 'I think within two years from today you will become a Christian.'

I was very surprised to hear him say that. What he had said was quite insane. But we continued to talk for a long time after. Then he said, 'Young man, God is calling you. Study the Bible, read about Christ's life. You will truly become a Christian.' I thought he was thoroughly misguided. Secretly, I dismissed what he was saying with contempt. Finally, he prayed and gave me a copy of the New Testament. Although I did not care for the book on first sight, I promised to read it. I did not make the promise because I believed the book held something of worth for me. I made it only because I felt I owed it to that very kind man. When we reached my destination, we bid each other a fond farewell and I got off the train. The surprising thing is that neither of us had exchanged any information about who we were and where we came from.

In Rajnandgaon I had served as a teacher, as a clerk to the Raja and as a head clerk. The last included doing sheriff's work too. There was nothing in the place, however, to engage the mind of a man who loved reading. Moreover, my favourite Sanskrit books were all left behind in Nagpur. This obliged me to keep my word to the gentleman in the train. That is how I came to read and reflect upon the New Testament.

In keeping with my usual habit, I had planned to read the book from beginning to end, marking places where I had doubts. But when I came to the Sermon on the Mount, I could not proceed further, so captivated was I by the love, compassion and truth that filled those beautiful words to bursting. I found answers to the most difficult questions in Hindu philosophy in these three chapters of Matthew. I was surprised to discover here an exhaustive discussion of the problematic question of life after life. It was with a deep urge to acquaint myself further with Christ's life that I read the Bible till the end.

There was a Christian police superintendent in Rajnandgaon. He gave me a bunch of booklets and pamphlets. I found Bushnell's *Character of Jesus* in the bunch. Reading that book sharpened even more my hunger for more knowledge of Jesus Christ. Christ has said, 'Ask and it shall be given.' Being full of doubt regarding this statement, I decided one day, like some wilful youth, to put it to the test. I prayed, 'I would like to have here and now a book that will tell me the history of Palestine and describe the conditions that prevailed during Christ's days.' I even added, 'If my prayer goes in vain I will decide that it is complete falsehood to say God listens to prayers and answers them.' This was pure folly. But God had pity on this unhappy child. The very next day I was transferred from one office to another. There I discovered three books under a heap of old papers. Two of them were Bibles as large as Webster's dictionary. The third was a book entitled, 'A beautiful story and gems of religious thought'. The three together contained all the information I was looking for. Thereafter God answered my prayers one after the other. I was astonished. This drew me, heart and soul, to Christ. On March 10 1894, I wrote my first letter to a Christian man. I knew the gentleman as a writer. (See Rev. Baba Pudmanjee's collection of experiences, page 269.) A few months later it began to seem to me that I was a Christian in my innermost being. Base creature that I am, I had hidden this fact from myself for the sake of popularity and honours. I had read 'The History of Christians' and 'Chronicle of those who laid down their lives for Christ'. Once somebody had needlessly criticized missionaries. I felt hurt. In response I wrote a poem titled 'Missionaries and Their Work' and sent it to *Dnyanodaya* (See issue dated 30-09-94 or *A Garland of Flowers*, page 15). After that, many of my writings were published in that journal. Although they were written under a pen name, my Hindu friends saw through it to who the writer was. They knew then that I had become a Christian in heart and soul. It is difficult for others to understand what a high caste man goes through when he converts to Christianity. And yet, like a mother who might not always be around her child but never leaves his side when he is ill, God stayed by my side during those difficult days. He saved me from all kinds of dangers. How many people did I play hide-and-seek with for fear of the opprobrium. But God did not forsake this sinner.

I lost my job. I became desperately poor. I had to abandon my only child. My wife and I had lived together like object and shadow. But now she preferred to be with her maternal relatives. God alone did not forsake me. In November 1894, somebody appeared to me in a dream on three consecutive nights saying, 'Follow Him. Do not be afraid.' I could wait no longer. Although there were many obstacles in the way of my baptism, I wanted to announce to the world immediately that I was a Christian. Accordingly, I requested Rev. J. E Abbot of the American Board Mission to make it known that I had become a Christian. He published the news in *Dnyanodaya* and I felt a great sense of relief.

Had I not had the deepest regard for my compatriots, I would have set down here all the events that followed. But I will not. It is best to forget such things. God be praised that soon, on 10 February 1895, I was baptized in the American Mission Church in Mumbai. What the gentleman in the train had predicted two years ago had come true. God took me to His bosom and till today he has cared for and looked after this feeble child with the boundless love of a mother.

A friend once asked Mr Tilak, 'After you become a Christian, will you continue to be the fierce patriot you are? Will you continue to love us as much?' Mr Tilak answered with a long poem in which he said he was not surprised by the question. The most sublime love, a mother's love, is always fearful in separation. Let her child go but a short distance away to play, her heart begins at once to beat with fear. I therefore assure you my friend that for as long as I breathe, I will remain your brother.

About the second question, the poem says, a lotus blooms under the rays of the sun but it does not forsake the water. Even as a Christian I will not turn my back on the soil that bore me.

After many couplets describing Christianity as a fount of love and brotherhood, he ends the poem by saying he will weep, work, yearn, even lay down his life for his country. If he failed to do so, he would be failing in his service to Christ and be but a hypocritical Christian. But enough of this self-praise, he says. People will laugh at me, not having towards me the goodwill that you, my friends bear me.

PART TWO

Made to Sit in the Puja Room

Mr Tilak left the residence of the jahagirdar of Chandori to climb the stairs of Rev. Dr Justin Abbot's home in Mumbai. Getting off at Byculla, he inquired his way to the American Mission High School which was located there. Rev. Anandrao Hivale who was to go to America later under his own steam, was then a student of the school. Mr Tilak met him at the door. Anandrao introduced him to Rev. Abbot and Rev. E.M. Hume. Rev. Abbot and Mr Tilak had already been in correspondence. They kept him with them for four months during which time he made a study of Christianity. After that he was baptized in the American Mission Church in Bhendi Bazaar.

It could be said that after his baptism, Mr Tilak introduced a different way of being a Christian. Despite the fact that Rev. Abbot was his religious teacher, Mr Tilak announced his desire to be baptized by an Indian Christian. And so he was baptized by Rev. Tukaramji Nathoji who was the editor of *Dnyanodaya* then. After his baptism, Mr Tilak went to Vasai to stay at Rev. Sumantrao Karmarkar's place.

The news of Mr Tilak's conversion spread like wildfire. Within no time, it reached Nashik. Friends and well-wishers of the Pendses made frequent visits to their house. But Nanasaheb had made sure that nobody in the house would talk about what had happened. So even the visitors said nothing. Once in a while they would glance at me and Dattu, make sad faces and wipe their eyes. I was thoroughly confused. I had no idea what had happened. I wondered if Mr Tilak had lost his life in an accident. The mind thinks thoughts that an enemy would not.

Throughout, Nanasaheb sat facing the window and holding his head tight in both hands. People looked at one another wordlessly, blankly, at most wiping their eyes occasionally. Even Dattu was baffled. People would keep picking him up and giving him things to eat. But they would not talk. Watching these goings-on, all the strength drained away from my limbs.

One day, Nanasaheb hired two or three bullock-carts and packed everybody in the house off to see the Pandava Caves. Only Bhikutai stayed back. Then Nanasaheb sent a tonga to Jalalpur to fetch Keshavrao Mama. The idea was that while I was away, Bhikutai and our brothers should freely discuss what had happened and what should be done about it. As soon as the tonga reached Jalalpur, Keshavrao Mama hastened to Nashik. Nanasaheb said, 'What's happened has happened. What do we do now?'

Mama said, 'We are two brothers. We will treat her as a third invalid brother.'

Mr Pendse said, 'I wasn't referring to her. We'll deal with that later. First we need to find out the truth about Tilak. Why don't you go to Mumbai to Bal's place and try to track down Tilak with him? If he has really converted, nothing can be done. But if he hasn't, take this ring and drop it in his pocket or somewhere on his person and report the theft to the police. The trial will have to be held before me. We'll see what can be done then. Take these twenty-five rupees and go.'

Keshavrao left immediately. Balasaheb was the eldest son of Nanasaheb's elder brother. The two made inquiries about Mr Tilak in all the missions in Mumbai. Finally, they heard that he was in Vasai. They met Mr Tilak there. He asked them, 'Why have you come?'

Keshavrao Mama said, 'We came to inquire about you.'

Mr Tilak said, 'I am a Christian now. Please look after your sister. The Ganga flows through Nashik and Jalalpur. She might throw herself in it. So please keep a watch on her.'

Keshavrao Mama said, 'Whether she lives or dies, you will certainly have nothing to do with her now.'

The two left Vasai with a heavy heart. As they turned to go, Keshavrao Mama caught sight of Mr Tilak's tuft and a sob choked him. Even earlier, although he had assumed an air of being angry, his eyes had been filling with tears. Now the dam burst.

My niece Gharumai used to call my brother Mama, uncle. So everybody called him that. And I was maushi, aunt. As soon as Keshavrao entered the Pendses' house, he went straight to where Bhikutai was laid up in bed. He told her what had transpired. Tears choked her. She said, 'You tell Manu about this. I can't bring myself to tell her.'

I was called upstairs. I was filled with such intense fear that I could hardly walk. I crawled up on all fours like a little child and sat before my brother and sister. My brother began to deliver a homily. 'There were many chaste women in olden times like Sita, Savitri, Tara, Draupadi, whose fame spread in the entire world.'

'I have read all the scriptures. Did you call me upstairs to lecture me? You went to Mumbai to find out what had happened to Mr Tilak. Just tell me first that he is alive.'

'Oh yes, he is. He is alive and happy. He has a teaching job there. But…but…'

'But what?'

'He has become a Christian.'

'So let him. As long as he is safe and well wherever he is. He may have gone away but he hasn't torn the skin off my forehead and taken it with him, has he? My marriage mark is still intact.' Having said this, I sprang up and went downstairs in great anger. But once I was there, all the strength drained from me. The other women of the household were standing around expectantly. They held me and helped me sit down. They had heard the news before me. They began to console me. 'If he's gone, he's gone. But God has given him a lovely son. One son is worth the world. He will make amends for everything. Your joy will far surpass the sorrows you have suffered.' But all those predictions were like water off a duck's back. I had become stone. Not a single tear flowed from my eyes. I could not talk.

At night, most of our relatives would come to sleep at Mr Pendse's house. Nobody ate dinner. Nor did anyone speak. They would just come in, pick up whatever bed linen came to hand, spread it on the floor and sleep. Nobody had invited them, asked them to sit or eat or sleep. But the bungalow was full of sleeping people. I had Keshavrao Mama on one side and Bhikutai on the other. Both their arms rested on my body.

Around two in the morning, sleep began to weave her web. Everybody except me got caught in it. I moved my brother's and sister's arms gently from my body, rose, tucked up my sari and looked around for Dattu. I could not see him anywhere so I decided to go alone. I walked to the front door, and just as I was sliding the bolt, I heard the beat policeman outside announcing that all was well in the town. That started off a stream of thoughts in my mind: If the police arrest me and take me to the chowki and start an inquiry tomorrow, people will say this is so-and-so's sister-in-law and poor Nanasaheb will have to hang his head in shame. I had planned to throw myself into the deep part of the river at Sundarnarayan. But the thoughts in my head made me change my mind. I turned instead to the well in the yard. It was a narrow well. Once again I began to ask myself, 'If I kill myself in this well, how will people take me out? And when the panchanama is done tomorrow, Nanasaheb will have to hang his head on my account anyway.' This thought made my head spin. I could not see any way out. I returned to my place and lay down. After a while, I squeezed Keshavrao Mama's hand so hard that his eyes flew open. He woke up Bhikutai. 'Look at Manu. See what she's doing.'

Everybody in the room got up asking what had happened. Mama somehow loosened my grip on his hand. Then my limbs became motionless. I could not move them. I was fully conscious. I knew what was going on around me. Everybody had some advice or the other to offer. Some said it was lock-jaw. Some said it was the effect of extreme rage. Some said she's swallowed poison. Bhikutai said, 'She does not have a paisa on her. Where would she get poison from?' To that somebody said she must have eaten ground glass. A new kind of yellow bangle had recently come into the market. Bhikutai had had the bangle-man put nine bangles on each of Gharumai's and my wrists. She quickly counted the bangles on my wrists.

A vaidya was called in. He found no sign of my pulse. He too gave his opinion. I had poisoned myself. Then there was a great attempt to prise open my locked jaw and feed me amla preserve, milk, herbal medications. I knew what was going on but I was like a log of wood. My tongue had receded way back and had grown prickles that did not go away for the next month.

Bhikutai's illness vanished. She rolled up her bedding and stood beside me twenty-four hours of the day for days. She had to do everything for me. I lay flat on my back, unable to help myself. She even had to clean my teeth. She would feed me milk and buttermilk at frequent intervals. Finally, after many days, some strength returned to my body. I began to sit up in bed. Now the tears began to pour from my eyes. It was an incessant flow, broken only when I slept. I did not say a word to anybody. One day, I walked to a nearby house and sat there crying. Dattu spent all his time with his aunt. But this time he saw me crying in the neighbour's house. He came to me, took my hand, raised me up and led me into the puja room.

After he made me sit down there, he said, 'Mother, please cry in your sister's house, not in other people's homes. Tell me what you want. Do you want tons of jewellery like Gharumai? Or do you want necklaces and armbands like aunty's? Or do you want saris with broad gold thread borders? Tell me what you want but don't cry like this.' Bhikutai was nearby. She pulled Dattu to her and said to me, 'Learn a little wisdom from him.'

But I only felt a fresh surge of tears to hear Dattu speak with such concern.

A Meeting in Court

As soon as Bapusaheb Buti heard of Mr Tilak's conversion, he rushed to Vasai to meet him and came directly from there to Nashik to see me. When I saw him, a sob rose to my throat. He was also choking with emotion. Through his tears, he said, 'Bai, please regard me as your elder son and Dattu your younger.' Saying so, he left and sent me ten rupees from Panchavati. It was his wish to send me a like sum every month. However, my brothers and sister did not think that would be proper, so they requested him not to, but in such a way as not to hurt his feelings. He wrote back to say he would at least bring his wife and children to see me, but that too did not happen.

That same summer Mr Tilak went to Mahabaleshwar. Bapusaheb hired a bungalow there. The plan was to take Dattu and me to meet Mr Tilak. But for some unavoidable reason, which I cannot now recall, that plan too came to nothing. In Mahabaleshwar, Mr Tilak wrote his first poems about children and flowers. He was staying with Rev. Dr Hume of Ahmednagar whose house was full of his own and his brother-in-law's children. Mahabaleshwar was blooming with wild flowers. Mr Tilak's sensibility was just right for composing such poems. He wrote his well-known poem 'Her Misty Hair Trails Freely down Her Back' on the lovely little Miss Fairbank. There was happiness all round. In such an environment, his imagined tuberculosis flew right out of the window. He left Mahabaleshwar to go to Ahmednagar to Dr Hume's school of theology where he studied and also taught a few subjects.

Nanasaheb Pendse was transferred to Pandharpur. Sakharambhauji also lived there. I went to Pandharpur with the Pendses, but my condition remained unchanged. My tears did not stop flowing and no words came from my mouth. Bhikutai and her sister-in-law had to take total care of me. This sister-in-law was Balasaheb's step-mother. She was a child widow. Dattu was very fond of her. Because of the red colour of her widow's sari, Dattu used to call her Red Aunt. That is how he had named all his aunts. There was a Shorty Aunt and a Skinny Aunt. And because Bhikutai was fat she was Fatty Aunt. They all loved the names he had given them.

As soon as we reached Pandharpur, Bhikutai engaged a tutor for Dattu. She hoped that the boy would study well and become a responsible man. After that she would not have to worry about me. She nagged him constantly to sit with his books. Nanasaheb would say, 'Why don't you leave him alone? Let him play. He is just a child. He'll study as he grows older.' But she did not give up. Nanasaheb pampered Dattu a lot. He would not eat anything without sharing it with him. Bhikutai did not like Dattu being present during Nanasaheb's teatime. So she would call out loudly to say it was teatime. Dattu would take the hint and tell her he was playing outside. She was saddened to have to do this and to hear his response. But she worried that Dattu would trouble Nanasaheb if he was around. On his part, Nanasaheb would insist on Dattu's sharing his snacks with him. He used to call him 'Tilak'. When he returned from work he would look for Dattu asking, 'Where's Tilak? Call him for tea. Tilak, hey Tilak, come and get your laddoo.' This was a daily routine. Red Aunty would first consult Dattu about what she should make for tea, and follow his suggestions.

Meanwhile, I would be lying in bed. I had to be forced to eat. Later, I began to tear up saris. Bhikutai was afraid I was going insane. She thought I would be better off dead. Who would care for me after she was gone? Mr Tilak heard about my condition. He sent a telegram and followed it with a letter in which he enclosed some self-addressed envelopes. He had not written a single letter to me till this moment. I wrote back to him secretly, because I was not allowed to correspond with him. My letters were always poems. I remember only three lines of the first: 'My imagination tortures me / It is like enduring the other woman / Then hope rises and the mind feels free.'

Another poem was about him as a husband. It began with the lines, 'He was so dear to me in virtue and in face / Then he went insane / What kind of a husband is this, would you say?' The final couplet was, 'I had devoted myself to you Narayana / But you have forgotten your Lakshmi.'

This new activity made me feel a little better. Mr Tilak could not believe that the poems were written by me.

Sakharambhauji who lived in Pandharpur would visit me every day. A rumour was going around that he was sending Mr Tilak one hundred rupees every month for his expenses. Although Mr Tilak had become a Christian and Bhikutai was very angry with him for that, she was also proud of him. She was furious with Bhauji when she heard the news. One day, he came over when Nanasaheb was having dinner. She placed a paat for him next to Nanasaheb and stood before him saying, 'Since when has your brother taken to carrying around a bag for alms?' Bhauji understood neither her words nor their drift. He said, 'I'm afraid I don't know what you mean.'

'Of course you don't know. You're busy sending a hundred rupees every month to your brother but you have no eyes for your sister-in-law's torn saris.' Bhauji heard Bhikutai out with lowered head. The next day, he sent a sari for me and two shirts for Dattu. Another day, he came and sat by me. He talked about this and that and quietly introduced Mr Tilak into the conversation. He said, 'Vahini, you are ill. So many people are looking after you. Does Nana have anybody to look after him? Tell me. Why don't you divorce him and set him free? There are enough people to look after you.'

When I heard this I sat up and said, 'And did he not have people to look after him here? And in which way is he bound now? What do I say in my divorce application? Did I run away? Did I abandon him? He has nobody, you say. But neither do I. I have no money, no education. I have a small child. What am I to do with myself? Clean your pots and pans, right? Stop mediating on your brother's behalf. Write to him. Tell him to see his wife married properly, only then can he himself marry. Do you have any idea who you are speaking to?' I was standing now and he was seated before me with lowered head.

Now Mr Tilak wrote to me every day. Sometimes he would write three letters in one day. I would write back once in a while, always a poem. I had nothing to ask of him nor did he have anything to tell me. One day, Nanasaheb received a telegram from him saying he would like to come and meet me. Nanasaheb wired back, 'Not in my house.' I was in the dark about this exchange. But that day was exactly like the one in Nashik. Nobody ate, nobody slept, nobody talked.

Mr Tilak arrived in Pandharpur at eight o'clock in the morning. He let Nanasaheb know of his arrival. He sent message after message but by two o'clock he had still not heard back from Nanasaheb. Mr Tilak grew very angry. Finally, he wrote a message which said, 'I came to meet my wife because I heard she was not well. I have sent several conciliatory letters to you since my arrival. You have not responded. That has saddened me. I will not leave this place without meeting her. Since I do not want to act against your wishes, I will meet her in court tomorrow.'

Teacher Tries Hard

The letter put Nanasaheb in a quandary. He talked to Bhikutai to see if she could think of a way out of this problem. 'Do what is best and what will befit us. I don't understand laws. But I think instead of waiting to see our reputation hung out to dry tomorrow in the court, why not send Manu to meet him today? Tilak will go away then.'

'We'll do that. We'll send her to meet him. Don't worry. I'll take every care that she does not go with him. Vahini will accompany her. I'll send two sepoys along as well.'

Nanasaheb sent a note to Mr Tilak that he would send Manu to meet him at nine o'clock at night. If this arrangement suited him, well and good. If not, Nanasaheb could do nothing further in the matter.

I only knew that Mr Tilak had come to Pandharpur. I had no idea about what had transpired between him and Nanasaheb. He and Bhikutai were sitting in the living room and I, as had become my custom, was lying in bed. Just then Yesu came to call me. She was Nanasaheb's granddaughter and wife of Dr Bhat of Yevle. She was around nine years old at the time. She told me Nanasaheb wished to speak to me. I hurried out to present myself to him. He said, 'Maushi, do you want to meet Tilak?' I said I did. Then he said, 'In that case put your hands on my feet and swear that you will not go with him.' I placed my hands on his feet and said, 'I swear I will not go with Mr Tilak.' With that I went straight back to my room. Bhikutai followed me, muttering, 'Really. All I did was ask to see my sister and we get caught up in courts and laws.' I was affected in the strangest way to hear her say that. Suddenly, I was walking all over the house. I went upstairs, then came down to the middle room, then went up to the terrace, then returned to my bed, then repeated the whole cycle. It upset Bhikutai greatly. She said, 'What are you doing? That's right. Go mad and turn this lovely child's life into hell. Your husband has shown the world his tricks; now you show yours.'

I heard her. I understood what she was saying. Yet I continued to walk upstairs and downstairs as before. Evening fell. Dinner was eaten. Every now and then, a doubt would rise in my mind about whether I was going to be sent to meet Mr Tilak or not. I kept a watch on the tonga, the horses and the servants. I was not free to talk to anybody because I was being watched by everybody—the sepoys, the servants, the maids, the water drawers, the cooks, Bhikutai, Bai, Yesu, Nanasaheb. I could do nothing without being asked what I was doing, what I was eating, where I was going, what I was writing. Questions followed me wherever I went. Even when I went to answer nature's call, somebody would go with me.

As the clock struck nine, my heartbeat quickened. I began to fear that I was not going to meet Mr Tilak after all. My eyes were fixed on the yard to see if there was any movement there. Soon I noticed that the tonga was being harnessed. I heard Bai calling 'Maushi.' I stepped out immediately. I noticed she had draped a shawl around her shoulders. Nanasaheb saw me and said, 'Manu, I hope you remember what I told you. You had better, otherwise I'll send the police after you. You know who I am, don't you?' I nodded. Then Bhikutai stepped forward to attack me from another front: 'Manu, pity this child at least.' Again I nodded. I was fearful of what I was going to see or hear. My heart was thumping, my limbs were trembling, my mouth was dry. The only part of my stiff body that was moist were my eyes. Only the end of my sari with which I wiped them knew that secret. I managed somehow to descend the stairs. I was helped into the tonga. Besides Bai, me and the tonga driver, there were two sepoys with us. So we set off with a prayer on our lips to the god of five faces.

Mr Tilak was standing at the door of the dharamshala where he was staying. He turned to go in as soon as he saw the tonga approach. Two people helped me out and stood me before him. The moment I set eyes on him I put my head down on his feet. 'What crime had I committed against you that you should have taken this extreme step? I won't leave your feet until you answer me.'

'You have never committed a crime against me,' he said as he freed his feet from my grasp.

That is all we said to each other. Mr Tilak was leaning against a pillar. Neither of us could say another word. Bai said, 'Manu, let's go. Dattu must be waiting for you. It's getting late.' I turned to go. Once again I was lifted into the tonga by the servants. Mr Tilak stood outside the dharamshala looking at the tonga till it disappeared.

Back home Bhikutai and Nanasaheb had been waiting anxiously. As soon as the tonga returned, Nanasaheb rushed out wishing to know what had happened. Both were extremely relieved when Bai told them what had transpired. Dattu was asleep. Bhikutai sat down beside him and stroking him said, 'Little one, let us hope that God will grant your mother some sense now.'

That night everybody slept soundly. Mr Tilak, having seen the condition I was in, spent the night tossing and turning. He was supposed to leave the next day. But when Bhauji went to meet him he said, 'I'm not going just yet. I'll go after her health improves.' Bhauji conveyed the news to Nanasaheb, saying, 'I will send him his meals but you will have to detail somebody to take them to him.'

Nanasaheb said, 'That would not be right. We will send him food.' When Bhikutai was packing Mr Tilak's lunch for him, her eyes began to stream with tears. She was saddened at the thought that other hands would carry his lunch to him in a dharamshala of all places when her own hands had served him with so much love in her own home. If she had known this was to be her sister's life, she would rather not have had a sister.

The family sat down to lunch after Mr Tilak's meal was sent. They would all sit together while the cook served. Nanasaheb found it difficult to eat. 'I feel very bad,' he said, his eyes filling with tears. 'We don't mind a Muslim sepoy coming into our house. He eats in our house. Muslims eat all sorts of things. Why then should Tilak eat by himself in a dharamshala?'

'But what will people say?'

'What if they do? I am not looking to marry off my daughter, nor am I looking to bring a daughter-in-law into this house. My only daughter is safely married. I am going to invite Tilak to stay here. I don't care what the world says.'

After lunch, Nanasaheb told a sepoy to harness the tonga and go to the place where he had gone the previous night and bring back the guest staying there. After the tonga left, Nanasaheb's gaze remained fixed on the road, so impatient was he to meet Mr Tilak. The tonga returned. The whole family had gathered at the door. Mr Tilak came. He picked Dattu up. Dattu couldn't recognize him. His appearance had changed a lot. Dattu first clung to Nanasaheb and then took shelter with his Red Aunty.

Nanasaheb said to Dattu, 'Tilak, ask them to get us some tea, will you?'

Two cups of tea arrived. The two men began to sip their tea. Bhikutai came and sat before Mr Tilak. 'I'm not afraid of you now, Mr Tilak. You can write and publish as many poems about me as you like.'

Nanasaheb said, 'What's this? He was going to take us to court today. Are we going to quarrel with him instead?'

Bhikutai said, 'I have nothing to do with courts and laws. That's men's business. I want to know what wrong I had done in calling my sister to meet me that you should have gone off and done this?'

Mr Tilak said, 'Scold me as much as you like, Bhikutai. I have no intention of writing or publishing poems about you.'

'Manu, aren't you coming out to meet Tilak?'

I had been standing behind the door listening to everything. My health had improved considerably after Mr Tilak's arrival in town. But that did not stop my tears from flowing incessantly.

Since Nanasaheb was a Mamlatdar, many people used to visit him and their conversations would go on till late at night. One of his regular visitors was a school principal. Nanasaheb introduced Mr Tilak to all of them. Mr Tilak took the opportunity to make rigorous inquiries about which of them was writing my poems for me. Finally, he was convinced that they were all my work. He was overjoyed. He made corrections to many of them and sent them off to be published.

Mr Tilak used to have his meals in the front room. The rest of the family ate inside. Sakharambhauji used to visit him every day. One day Bhikutai asked him, 'Tell me, Sakharampant. Is there no way to bring your brother back into the caste?'

Nanasaheb said, 'Why not? Everything is possible if you have money and are willing to make an effort.'

'In that case I'll donate all my ornaments. I will say to myself, would I not have spent the amount on my sisters' marriages if I had had four instead of one? How much will you contribute, Sakharampant?'

'A thousand rupees.'

Nanasaheb said, 'I'll give the rest.'

Just then we heard someone talking very loudly to Mr Tilak in the front room. 'Can you go out and see who it is?' Nanasaheb said to Bhauji. Bhauji returned with the news that it was the school principal arguing animatedly with Mr Tilak.

'Mr Principal. Good you've come. What's out there? Why don't you come in or are you planning to go with him?' When the principal came in, he was consulted about the plan that had just been mooted. He said, 'Don't mention any of this to Tilak just yet. We'll call a meeting of Brahmins tomorrow. Once we've discussed the plan, we'll see what we can do next.'

The principal could not sleep a wink that night. His mind was full of questions about whom to invite, how to present the subject and what people would say. Bhikutai could not sleep because she was excited and happy. She dreamt all night with wide open eyes about how Manu was going to be settled back into a proper life. Why worry about the ornaments, she thought. She was hardly going to sit in their shade forever. Dattu and Mr Tilak slept soundly. Dattu had started sleeping with his Nana now. Mr Tilak would tell him story after story and both would fall asleep in the middle of one.

The following day the principal came with Bhauji to meet Nanasaheb. A meeting had been called that evening in which the principal was going to discuss religious conversion. Nanasaheb said, 'I'm with you in this, but please don't let anybody know that I have played a part in it.'

The meeting took place as planned. The principal's speech was very effective. His persuasive tongue and intense involvement in the subject brought most people round to his way of thinking. He took their signatures and asked them to return the following day with their friends. And so the meeting ended. The process of addressing meetings and collecting signatures went on for three more days. After that the townspeople and the town leaders took the responsibility of Mr Tilak's reconversion upon themselves. Meetings were organized for another eight days. The principal would be present at every meeting and return to us with a full report of what had happened. We began to feel optimistic. But nobody had been able to find support in the scriptures for what they planned to do. Meanwhile, Nanasaheb and Bhikutai were feeling their way cautiously around how Mr Tilak would respond to their plans.

Mr Tilak said, 'Why go through all this expense? Suppose you spend all this money and I go away?'

'Well, we'll ask for our money back.'

Mr Tilak said nothing. My health was improving and perhaps he did not want to do or say anything that would upset me again. So he kept quiet. When no support was to be found in the scriptures, Nanasaheb appealed to Mr Tilak himself to find it for them. And he did. Things should have moved forward now. But they did not. The assembly of Brahmins said Mr Tilak would first have to confess that he had erred, ask for forgiveness and fall at their feet. Mr Tilak refused to submit to this demand. The principal pleaded with him but Mr Tilak would not budge from his stand. In the end, the principal asked for forgiveness on Mr Tilak's behalf and prostrated himself at the Brahmins' feet. The papers would now be sent to two holy places and then to Jagadguru Shankaracharya before Mr Tilak could be purified.

Around this time, cholera, which came regularly to claim its tax, arrived and picked up people of all ages—the old, the middle-aged and the young. A young visitor to the town who was staying close to Nanasaheb's house, was here one moment and gone the next. Mr Tilak said to Nanasaheb, 'What will you do if I go the same way as this young man? The townspeople will torment you. It would be better if you let me go now. It will be some time before you get a response from the Shankaracharya. By then the cholera menace will have abated. We will decide then how to go about it.'

Nanasaheb gave him permission to go, along with money for his fare to Mumbai, and sent him off.

Layette

This time I was not too upset when Mr Tilak went away. Everybody believed he would come back. My health continued to improve. After Mr Tilak left, Dattu fell seriously ill. When we were in Vani, Mr Tilak's priest's wife had made a promise that she would take Dattu to the temple on Saptashrungi hill when he turned five and have his hair ritually shaved. Bhikutai decided to redeem that pledge now. She wrote to my brothers in Jalalpur asking them to get rations for twenty-five meals. She would carry money so that together they could redeem the pledge. I did not accompany her to Vani.

When she had gone, I received a notice from a lawyer on behalf of Mr Tilak, saying that he had an unquestionable claim on his son. If you do not hand over the boy to me within the time stipulated here, I will have to file for custody in the court. Mr Tilak had raised a lethal weapon against me. He wrote to me every day demanding that I either send Dattu to him or go there myself with him. People advised me not to reply to his letters. They went further and said do not accept or read his letters. When I was in Nashik, some remote relatives of mine had warned me that if I went to Mr Tilak, he would marry me off to somebody else and make me do a sweeper's work. He would also force me to cook meat. My own experience of Mr Tilak deepened my fear. Suppose I went to him and he decided to convert to Islam? At the moment, my relatives were concerned about me. But if that happened they would give up on me completely. Women who lose their husbands say if the husbands were alive, they would at least have the satisfaction of seeing them occasionally wherever they were. And was I not to even reply to his letters?

My heart began to grow heavy again. I would sit in the Vithoba temple for hours on end weeping. I had got to know all the women who came there. Some of them would advise me: 'Why do you weep like this? Eat and drink your fill. Grind people's grain for a livelihood, or start an eatery. How much longer will you go on depending on your sister? Be independent.' I would listen to them in silence.

Once I said to a couple of them, 'Why should I grind grain for others? I would rather do it for my near and dear ones. Why should I serve and clean up after strangers have eaten? I would rather serve and clean up after my loving brothers and sister. Why bow before strangers? I would rather bow before my loved ones. If this is not acceptable to them, I will go to my master.' This stopped the women from giving me advice.

When Bhikutai returned from Vani and heard about Mr Tilak's notice, she was grieved. 'He is like a serpent,' she muttered, 'ready to strike when least expected.' Mr Tilak continued to write to me every day. His letters used to be loving or angry or troubled. Once in a while a letter would come accusing me of not caring for him. 'Give me a divorce so I can marry again.' He wanted me very much to abandon my relatives and go to live with him. In the end, Dr Abbot had a long talk with him when both of them were teaching in the mission school in Mumbai. Dr Abott said to him, 'Look, Tilak, judging by everything that has happened, it is very obvious to me that Lakshmibai loves you deeply. Instead of sending her angry letters, try and win her over gently. Come, I'll go with you.' Mr Tilak agreed. He had great faith in prayer. He decided to pray to God for help and soon after that, he sent a telegram saying he was coming to Pandharpur. It was not possible for Mr Tilak to stay at Nanasaheb's place this time. Bhauji was living in the Ram Mandir area. He would not be allowed there either. So he stayed with Dr Kashibai Jhankar and came to see Nanasaheb the following morning. He had not climbed more than a couple of steps when Bhikutai came and stood before him, her arms spread out. 'Don't you dare climb another step. The courts are open for you. Go there.'

Mr Tilak turned back. Dattu was down with measles again,

and I had to deal with this other headache. I was torn in two. That night, Dr Kashibai's mother came in a great hurry to see me. She said, 'Please come quickly. Kashi has been bitten by a scorpion. You know how to neutralize the poison.' I had learned the skill from Mr Tilak who knew how to deal with scorpion bites. We did not know that Mr Tilak was staying with them. So Bhikutai sent me with her. When I arrived, what do I see but Mr Tilak waiting for me.

'How are you feeling now?'

'As before.'

'How is Dattu?'

'He has a fever.'

'All right. You can go now.'

That is all we said to each other. Mr Tilak looked happy to see me well. When I returned home, I went straight to my bed and lay down. Dattu was with Bhikutai. When Nanasaheb returned, she told him about my visit to Dr Kashibai's house. He sent a servant across asking her to come and see him. She told him everything that had transpired.

Nanasaheb said, 'What does maushi seem inclined towards doing, in your opinion?'

'She wants to go.'

'Why do you say that?'

'She once asked me for poison. She said she had nothing to pay me with except the rings on her toes. But she wanted a poison that would kill her slowly because she didn't want an inquiry about her death afterwards which would get other people into trouble.'

'What did you say to her?'

'I calmed her down and sent her back.'

'Thank you. But please don't do things like this again.' With that he got a servant to escort her home. I had no idea about all this. Those days I found myself constantly overcome by sleep. When I got back, I had lain down in bed and fallen asleep to get up only the next morning. When I woke up, I noticed a whole lot of things arranged on a wooden seat beside my bed. There were two saris, two cholis, a layette for a baby and a long-tailed bonnet. Nanasaheb's niece had come to stay. She was there. I asked her, 'Sai, who is this layette for?'

'For you,' she said. I could not think of what to say. Then Bhikutai and Bai came. Bhikutai said, 'Manu, you're free to go wherever you like. I have kept some clothes for you and your baby there.'

I was totally confused. But if I was being told to go, I should go. I could live in the Vani hills as an ascetic. So I picked up one sari and a small box of kumkum and left.

Sai said, 'Maushi, where are you going?'

'Wherever God takes me,' I answered.

'You have so little strength and no money.'

'I don't need money or anything else. I didn't have anything when I came from God. Why do I need it when I'm going to him?'

Bhikutai said, 'Sai, they must have planned to meet at night. Why else would she get up so quickly to go?'

I was now in the front room. Nanasaheb saw me and said, 'Where are you going?'

'Wherever God takes me. He won't abandon me just because human beings wish to.'

'Tell me, why do you behave so stupidly? Go in this minute and lie down.'

During the sodmunja ritual of a young Brahmin, his maternal uncle persuades him not to go on pilgrimage to Kashi, and the young Brahmin consents. So did I and did as I was told. Many occasions had arisen in my life when I was near to committing suicide. But I never did. I do not think I was capable of taking such a step. That is how I am. Even in the darkest hour of despair, I grope and struggle to find my way out and live. I do not stumble and fall on the way and give up on life. In short, I am like a rubber ball.

Mr Tilak left Dr Kashibai's home to go to where

Rev. Dr Abbot was staying in Gopalpura. Dr Abbot asked him, 'Did you meet her? What do you think?'

'I was under the wrong impression. She loves me no less than she did.'

'So what is your plan now? Don't let people mislead you.' After that he read from the Bible to show Mr Tilak the Christian ideal of the husband–wife relationship. Then the two prayed together and Mr Tilak vowed, 'I will wait for my wife till she decides to come to me.'

Mr Tilak left Pandharpur and wrote a very nice letter to me: 'Take care of your health and of Dattu. I will not give you a moment's trouble. Come to me with our son when God gives you the will to do so. I shall wait for you. I will do nothing from now on that will distress you and your people. I will never marry again. You have no cause to worry about that.' There was much more in the same vein.

The Bird in a Love Cage

Bhikutai and Nanasaheb were good to me now. They had never been bad to me, but earlier they had always felt I might go off with Mr Tilak. Bhikutai made me thick bangles of different patterns and other gold ornaments. However, every time Mr Tilak wrote to me, she would worry and get angry with me. But Dattu and I were very well cared for there.

One day, an order arrived for Nanasaheb's transfer to Ahmednagar. That plunged everybody into deep thought. Although Mr Tilak was not living in Ahmednagar, the town was full of Christians. How could they take Manu there? Even as they were pondering this question, a letter arrived from Mr Tilak enclosing self-addressed envelopes. He had found a job in Ahmednagar and would soon be shifting there. It was clearly impossible for me to go with Bhikutai now. With her permission, Nanasaheb wrote to our brothers to say that he had been transferred to Ahmednagar and they could not take Manu with them, so they were sending her to Jalalpur. He assured them that the responsibility for the cost of our food and clothes would rest with Nanasaheb. He requested them to do just one thing—take care of my body and mind.

My brothers talked to their wives. They said, 'Our sister has been supported by our brother-in-law for three years. We must bring her to her rightful home now. We don't want to create the kind of scenes we see in other people's homes. We will bring her here only if you give us your word that you will treat her as a guest or as an invalid brother of ours. If she causes us losses of any kind, we will be responsible for that. You must not do anything to hurt her.'

Both my sisters-in-law said, 'Please bring her. We will not say a word to hurt her.' Nanasaheb had to report on duty immediately. So he left for Ahmednagar. Bhikutai, Bai, Yesu, Dattu and I left for Jalalpur. When we reached there, Bhikutai opened my trunk and showed my brothers and their wives every article that it contained. The trunk was chockfull of saris, cholis, ornaments, money. 'Fortune hasn't treated Manu well as it is. I don't want your wives ever to say that she has taken this or that of ours. Or question why the trunk is locked. That's why I am showing you all that she possesses. Yes, better to have the bitter first and the sweet later than the other way around.'

Bhikutai stayed for a day and then left with a heavy heart. Her eyes welled up with tears. Even as she turned to go, she said to our brothers, 'Don't cut Dattu's milk.'

The next few days were very difficult for me. On the third or fourth day, I received a letter from Mr Tilak. I have no idea how he discovered I was in Jalalpur. My sisters-in-law were very good to me. They would not let me lift a finger to help them in the house. They divided even my personal work between them. The older one looked after Dattu's needs and the younger one after mine to the extent that she would not even let me wash my sari. She would draw hot water for my bath, pleat up my sari, set my puja things out.

'You do so much for me, Vahini,' I would say, and she would respond with, 'God will only bless me for what I do, as he would not if I helped Bhikutai. If I do things for her, God and people will say I was doing it in self-interest. Whereas in your case there can be no self-interest.' It was this sister-in-law who had looked after Dattu when he was a baby.

In Jalalpur, I stopped lying around in bed. I became very religious. I had no household responsibilities. I would get up in the morning, and after finishing my morning ablutions and bath, I would read holy books, do puja and sit counting my beads. I had only one meal a day. Besides that, I kept many fasts. I would fast for four Fridays in one month, four Saturdays in another and four Tuesdays in the third, breaking my fast at night with special food. On Fridays, it was rice and milk, on Saturdays, just vadas. On Tuesdays, I would make nine kanolas, give six to the cow and eat three myself. There were other regular fasting days as well. I was doing all this to get Mr Tilak to do penance and return to his proper religion. On days when I was not fasting, my elder sister-in-law would come to where I was lying and coax me and persuade me and finally force me to eat pohe with milk. While doing so, she would counsel me. 'You know, the riches of good health are more precious than material riches. If you lose your health, who will look after you? If your arms are strong, women will inquire after you.'

I was not satisfied with only fasts to bring Mr Tilak back. I tried a whole lot of other things. But my two sisters-in-law never said a word to me about this. They said to each other, 'She isn't harming anybody, so why hurt her feelings?'

There is a huge idol of Maruti in Jalalpur. I would put a cane in his hand. The idea was that he should go after Mr Tilak with it and bring him back. The villagers wondered who was doing this. Occasionally, I would put a stone on the idol's head. We say, don't we: Has someone put a stone on your head to force you to do this? Well, my stone on Maruti's head was to force him to bring Mr Tilak back. Then I began to write Lord Rama's name on scraps of paper and sticking them on the idol's body from top to toe. I would have to do this at the crack of dawn before people were up and about. The idea was that Maruti would answer my prayer before he sinned by allowing Rama's name to touch his feet. A cane in Maruti's hand, a stone on his head and scraps of paper with Rama's name all over his body caused much concern in the village. People suspected that some form of black magic was going on. The village elders decided to catch the witch and give her a good thrashing. Accordingly, one morning, some villagers hid near the temple. I arrived wrapped in my wet, purified sari and began sticking paper scraps on the idol. The villagers ran out of their hiding place ready to beat me up. Dawn was just breaking, making things visible. They recognized me as soon as they were close enough. Dada Kulkarni said, 'We didn't imagine it could be you. Thank heavens the boy didn't lose his mother because of our mistake.

Please carry on with your attempts to try and get Tilak back. I hope you succeed.'

Another thing I used to do was to draw footprints all the way from the Ganga to our home. Similarly, I had vowed to offer a red flower to the goddess every day. If I did not find a red flower, I would fast. My sisters-in-law would get me a red flower from somewhere, somehow, to prevent me from fasting. If God occupied most of my time, the rest was taken up teaching children. I was Dattu's first teacher. I was also his children's first teacher when they came. Whenever I found the time, I would teach Dattu and my brothers' sons to write. One day, when I was teaching the boys, my brothers came home from work and started talking about the crop. The boys put their slates and pencils away and also began to talk. The boys said to Dattu, 'See our fields, our ploughs and our bullocks.' My brothers said to them, 'They are not yours alone, boys. They also belong to Dattu. He's your brother, remember?' The boys refused to accept that. 'How can he be our brother? He is Tilak. We are Gokhale.'

Dattu held out his slate and said, 'See my field.' Holding out his pencil, he said, 'That's my plough. My fingers are my bullocks.'

'But this field of yours doesn't produce grain,' the boys said. Upon which Dattu said, 'These letters are my grain.'

Tears sprang to my brothers' eyes to hear Dattu say that. My elder brother hugged him. Readers may imagine how I must have felt then.

The reason why Bhikutai had left me in Jalalpur was because she suspected I would run off to Mr Tilak if I was anywhere near him. She would often sing a song that referred to my plight. It said, 'Little bird you are in a cage of love.' Yes, I was caged but the cage was not a prison, Bhikutai said. 'We lock you up out of love. Otherwise you might fly away.'

Gift from a Brother-in-law

Mr Tilak continued to write a letter a day even when I was in Jalalpur. Sometimes his letters were full of anger. Sometimes the rage was so intense that he would send me blank sheets. Blank letters made me weep. If people asked why I was weeping, I would show them the blank sheets. But people would say that they were not blank sheets. It was a trick. Nobody sends blank letters. Surely Manu maushi knows how to read them. That would make me weep even harder.

Mr Tilak came to meet me in Jalalpur three times. He was looking very well. The first time he came, my younger brother planned to beat him up. He was pacing around with an axe. I said to him, 'Say what you want to him. Fight with him, but please don't beat or kill him.'

Dattu said, 'Let me see who beats my Nana. I'll beat them.'

Mr Tilak came. He was followed by a crowd of the old and young from the neighbourhood. When a stranger comes to a village, he automatically collects a crowd around him. In this case Mr Tilak was not a stranger, and yet he looked strange. That first time my younger brother did not come out at all. My older brother was not at home. Mr Tilak stood outside the house in the middle of the crowd and said a couple of words to me and left.

The second time he came, Keshavrao Mama was at home. He invited him in and offered him a seat. He was not beaten up. He came the third time, six months later. Neither of my brothers was in. My hair was hanging loose because I had just washed it. Besides, in retaliation against the things the old women of the village said, I used to practically cover my forehead with kumkum. Standing before Mr Tilak, with that hair and kumkum and hands on hips, I must have looked like the fierce form of the mother goddess. He was accompanied this time by a European lady. They stood outside the house in the yard. The lady said to me, 'See what a good husband you have. He hasn't married again.'

I flew into a rage. Pointing to Mr Tilak, I said, 'So he's brought you along as his lawyer, has he? So he is good because he has not married again, is he? And what makes me bad? I've not married again either. We have both married only once and that is each other. Let him speak for himself. You don't need to mediate.'

The woman fell silent after that. This is how the scene went. My brothers' children and wives stood behind me. A medley group of villagers stood behind Mr Tilak and the woman.

Mr Tilak said, 'I hope you are doing well.'

I said, 'I am doing well in accordance with the life you have arranged for me. There is no need to worry on any score.'

After this exchange, Mr Tilak, the white madam and the accompanying villagers left.

The reason I wore a large band of kumkum across my forehead was because the village women did not consider me a married woman. My sister-in-law realized this one day. I was once invited as a married woman to the village astrologer's house. My sister-in-law had accepted the invitation without my knowledge. When she went to the river, she heard mention of my name in a group of women gathered on the steps leading to the river. My sister-in-law stopped in her tracks.

'What is this, Aunty? Manu's husband has converted and you've invited her as a married woman for a religious ritual?'

'Oh dear! That didn't strike me. What shall I do now?'

'Nothing. Let her have lunch but invite another woman for the ritual.'

My sister-in-law came back and reported this to my older sister-in-law and me. Then she said, 'Why don't you also take a vow not to eat food cooked by other people?'

I never went against my sisters-in-law's wishes. I took the vow. In all the time I stayed in Jalalpur, even my sisters-in-law did not eat at other people's places. It was by God's grace that

I had sisters-in-law who would not tolerate a single word said against me. The madam who had come with Mr Tilak to Jalalpur told him, 'Your wife will come to you. Sooner than later. I am certain of that.'

A few days later, this madam wrote to me. 'Come to live with your husband. I will pay you ten rupees a month.' I wrote back, 'I don't want to go back to my husband for money.' This madam was Miss Harvey, the famous 'mother' of the Zenana Mission in Nashik. Thirty years later when we were living in Nashik, we experienced her love in full measure. Even in the last throes of death, she took my name at least three or four times. But the first reception I accorded her was as I have described it.

Both my brothers' sons were now entering their seventh year. Dattu had completed five. There were discussions in the house about celebrating their thread ceremonies. Many people were of the opinion that Dattu's thread ceremony should not be held just yet. Suppose his father were to take him away they said, then all that expense will go waste.

Keshavrao Mama said, 'That is not a problem. It doesn't cost money to take the sacred thread off. In fact, I will perform his thread ceremony first and then my sons.' Mama had been to Nashik to get an astrologer's opinion on whether the time was good for the three boys to have their thread ceremonies. He was assured that the time was good for all three. When he returned from Nashik, he brought news that Nashik was going to become another Mumbai and Jalalpur another Nashik. Everybody was overjoyed that their village would soon be transformed into a town. Mama had to visit Nashik several times to make arrangements for the thread ceremonies. On one of these trips, he brought news of a new disease. The victim would get a couple of lumps in his armpits and before you knew what was happening he was dead. The villagers panicked when they heard this story.

Preparations for the big day were in full swing. My sisters-in-law had warned their husbands not to cut corners in Dattu's case. If money had to be saved, let it be done from their sons' rituals. 'Please don't do anything that will hurt Vansa. This is the only big occasion in her life.' To this Keshavrao Mama replied, 'Don't worry. I will spend the maximum amount on Dattu's thread ceremony.' The more serious problem was that a child cannot have his thread ceremony sitting on his maternal uncle's lap. Mama wrote to Sakharambhauji asking him to come to Jalalpur to host Dattu's thread ceremony. Bhauji wrote back saying, 'I invite all of you to come here instead. I will bear the cost of all three boys' thread ceremonies.'

Mama was saddened by his reply. When he asked him to host his nephew's thread ceremony, he had not meant to ask him to pay for it. The surprising thing was that Bhauji, who had offered to pay for all three ceremonies, did not finally contribute a single paisa for his nephew's.

Then Mama wrote to Nanasaheb asking him to be Dattu's host. Nanasaheb wrote back saying, 'I have not taken a pledge before God that Tilak should abscond and his son should sit on my lap for his thread ceremony. I am prepared to spend any amount. But I shall find it very difficult to be present. If I come, it will only be out of goodwill.'

My brothers had decided to conduct Dattu's ceremony first and then their sons'. They had prepared invitations accordingly. But they merely informed invitees of the impending event without mentioning the date. This was done to prevent Mr Tilak from creating problems. As it happened, everybody, the guests and the family, wept all through the three days of the ceremony for Dattu who had had to sit on the priest's lap for the entire ritual. The priest also wept. He did not have a son. He said, 'Pity this boy because he has a father. Pity me because I don't have a son.' And so everybody together shed a great deal of salt water throughout those three days. But somehow, despite the pervading wetness, the ceremony was completed without a hitch.

During the last day's ritual, four fat letters arrived from

Mr Tilak. Two were for each of my brothers, one for Nanasaheb and one for me. The letters were like scenes from a film that was unfolding in his mind. There was everything there, including a string of curses and the threat of law courts.

Mama said, 'This is my brother-in-law's gift on this auspicious occasion.'

Meeting My First Christian Woman

Mr Tilak contented himself with pouring out his feelings in letters. He gave me no further trouble. The guests who had come for the thread ceremonies were still with us when, one day, after lunch, the maid who had gone to the river to wash our cooking utensils, left them wet on the bank and ran back through the village shouting, 'The saheb is coming.' That did it. Everybody ran helter-skelter. There were no men-folk in the village. They were all working in their fields. Even Attyabai, my sisters-in-law and the older children were all on the farm. There was just Dattu, a nephew and I at home. I hoisted Dattu over the back wall and said, 'Run. Go anywhere. Just go.' My nephew was down with high fever. I could not leave him and go with Dattu. I stood firm with my hands against the frame of the front door waiting for the saheb to come. Women were running amok through the street. One woman held only the end of her sari in her hand with the rest flapping behind her. Another had run out with a broom. Many women were running with their babies at their breasts. Others were running with ladles, spatulas and tin lamps.

My heart was beating fast, but I stood firm, waiting for the calamity that was coming my way to strike. Soon it presented itself before me in the form of the saheb. He was accompanied by a train of village worthies, the village head, the revenue collector, the overseer and the village gate-keeper. The saheb asked, 'Who else is in the house?'

'Nobody. All the women ran away when they heard you were coming.'

'Is anybody ill in the house?'

'Nobody. Come in and see.'

He peered here and there and left. Everybody returned to their homes after a while. My brothers heard the news on the farm and rushed back. Our cooking utensils, left wet on the river bank, came home the following day.

I had received a lot of money as gifts for Dattu's thread ceremony. It began to wriggle impatiently in my hands. I said to my brothers, 'I have sixty or seventy rupees. Let me take a groundnut field on contract. Money makes money. This is a profitable business. Then I won't need to worry about Dattu's education.'

My brothers said, 'You have no idea how tough it is to do business. You won't be able to manage it. Why don't you lend money on interest instead?' I saw their point. Then little by little, I lent them money whenever they needed it. In all these years, neither the principal nor the interest that must have accumulated on it have shown themselves to me.

Dattu was not keeping as well here as he had kept in Pandharpur. He had ague which gave him two or three shivering fits a day. His uncles tried many medications on him but none worked. I wondered why Dattu, who kept such good health in Nagpur and Pandharpur, should not keep well here. Why, I thought, should I stay in a place where the one person for whom I was enduring this life, was constantly ill? Yet where else could I go? My people would not let me go anywhere out of their sight for fear of Mr Tilak. Finally, I decided to go to my brother-in-law's place in Pandharpur. How to go was a problem. My money was on loan to my brothers. I could ask Mr Tilak for money. But Nanasaheb was in Ahmednagar and Mama had gone there recently. If Mr Tilak told them of my request, that would be the end. Ultimately, I did write to Mr Tilak. 'I am going to tell you something in the strictest confidence. I want you to promise me that you won't tell anyone.' Mr Tilak wrote back, 'Man is a fallible creature. The greatest sages have erred. Don't feel bad about what has happened. Even if your people and the rest of the world abandon you, I will never do so. If you want me to, I could come and fetch you here. Take care of your health.'

This reply left me stunned. It was sad but also funny. One gain from the letter was to know the extent to which Mr Tilak loved me. I wrote to him by return of post. 'I have not erred. My people haven't abandoned me. The world hasn't abandoned me. Dattu has been having fever for three months. I feel I should go to Pandharpur with him. But I have no money. If my people discover that I've been asking for money, they will not let me go. That is why I want you to send me railway fare for three people without letting anybody know. I will go to Bhauji's place in Pandharpur.'

Mr Tilak sent the money promptly and also promised to send ten rupees a month to Bhauji. As soon as the money arrived, I got ready to go to Pandharpur. I was sure Attyabai would worry about Dattu so I took her along. My brother was against my going. 'I don't care for the idea that you are going uninvited to the place of a person who did not contribute a paisa to your son's thread ceremony. If you still insist on going, please don't show me your face again.'

'I'm not doing this to please myself. I'm going for Dattu's sake.'

My sisters-in-law said, 'If you must go for Dattu's sake, please go. But remember you are not a burden on us.' My younger sister-in-law felt particularly sad. She had breast fed and looked after Dattu from the time he was eleven days old.

I went to Nashik by bullock-cart. I spent one night there at a cousin's place. He too was against my going to Pandharpur. Many people in Nashik tried to put hurdles in my way. All I said to them was, 'I have to go for Dattu's sake.'

Dattu still had fever. Passengers were being checked for plague at the station. I knew nothing about it. Our train left in the evening. I was in a panic. My heart was beating as fast as the speed of the train. I hoped desperately that I had made the right decision and Dattu would get well soon. I did not want to go back abjectly to my brother, as he had predicted I would do. The train reached Ahmednagar around nine the next morning. That is where Mr Tilak lived. So I naturally began to look expectantly around the station for him. But a totally unknown woman came towards our compartment. I asked her to come in and sit by me. I suspected from her dress that she was a Christian. She wore a six-yard sari, not a nine-yard sari tucked between the legs as we did. She wore a long-sleeved blouse and two bangles on each wrist. Her forehead was bare of the kumkum mark and she spoke chaste Marathi. I was relieved that Attyabai and Kashibai, our companion, were sitting on the other side of the compartment with Dattu. Particularly Attyabai who tended to be scatter-brained. You could never tell what she would say to whom. I was very keen to find out about Mr Tilak in case this woman knew him. So I started a hesitant conversation.

'Where are you going, Bai?'

'To Kedgaon.'

'You have relatives in Ahmednagar?'

'I live in Ahmednagar. My sister lives in Kedgaon. I am going to visit her. But why are you weeping?'

'Because none of the children I had after this one, survived. And now this one is so unwell.'

'Where have you come from?'

'From Rajnandgaon.'

'And where are you going?'

'To my brother-in-law's place in Pandharpur.'

'What's your name?'

'Manu.'

'No I meant your full name.'

'Manu Joshi.'

'A Mr Tilak used to live in Rajnandgaon. Did you know him?'

'Yes. But he's become a Christian now. He used to live next door to us.'

'We are also Christians.'

After that the woman spoke at length about Mr Tilak. Dattu's temperature was rising. I said to the woman, 'I'm worried about the child's fever. They are checking for plague at the station. I don't know what to do.'

She said, 'Just before we reach the station bathe his hands

and feet in cold water and leave them uncovered. That will save you from the checking.'

'Where are you changing trains?'

'At Daund.'

'We are also getting off there. Do you think you can help me transfer to the other train?'

'Don't worry about it. It's quite simple. The train that comes after this one will take you to Pandharpur. Just tell the coolie to put you on it.'

'What is your name?'

'Rajas Kukade.'

We continued talking in this fashion till we reached Daund. I did as she suggested. Dattu's temperature came down. As the woman was preparing to get off, I held her hand tight.

'Please help me. Do you know who I am?'

'How will I know?'

'I am the wife of the same Mr Tilak about whom we've been speaking all along.'

The Gosavi's Father

When she heard I was Mr Tilak's wife, Rajasbai felt a little awkward. Had she said something to me that she should not have? But now that she knew who I was, she made all necessary arrangements for my forward journey and only then left for Kedgaon.

As we got off the train, we were cordoned off. All the compartments were instantly locked. Before each compartment stood doctors, sepoys and police who created a cordon to hem people in like cattle in a pen. The doctor would examine every passenger and only those who passed were allowed to go ahead. The people in our pen were examined. I was very scared for Dattu. But his hands and feet were cold and he got through. Then we went to sit in another part of the platform to wait for the train to Kurduwadi. The train came on time and we were in Kurduwadi around ten at night.

As soon as we got off, a crowd of Brahmins who served at the temple laid siege to us. I told them we were guests of the Tilaks, not pilgrims. That sent them away. We hired a bullock-cart. The cartman said he would go only after moonrise. He suggested we catch some sleep in the dharamshala till then and he would call us when it was time to go.

We went to the dharamshala to sleep. I was carrying gold ornaments and a little cash. Together they amounted to a thousand odd rupees. My nose-ring alone was worth three hundred rupees. I put the bundle containing all these things under my head when I slept. Attyabai lay next to me. We were all tired and fell asleep instantly. Sometime later I felt somebody pinching my foot. I had heard stories about thieves pinching feet and lifting valuables from under people's heads. I woke up but stayed put. I called to Attyabai and asked her to light a candle. Then I got up holding my bundle to my chest. A man was standing at my feet. I shouted at him, 'Who are you? You want me to call the police?'

The man said, 'I'm like you. A traveller. Please go back to sleep. There is still time for the moon to rise.' But who would be so foolish as to believe a thief's words? We spent the rest of the time sitting up. Attyabai chose this time to start talking about our wealth. I made signs to her to stop, but she went on talking merrily about the Pendses' riches and the ornaments we were carrying.

The moon rose. Our bullock-cart set off. There was no other cart on the road. But I noticed a man running behind the cart. I said to him, 'Why are you running behind us?'

He said, 'There's fear of thieves up ahead that's why I'm coming along.'

A thief to catch a thief! 'Dear man, why tire yourself out like this? What will a thief do to us? What do we have for him? We are going to Pandharpur to make chapatis for pilgrims who come for free meals.' After this our guard left us and we had one thing less to worry about.

Bhauji had received letters from Mr Tilak and me. He and his wife were waiting for us. They bent to touch my feet and said, 'Treat this house as yours. Think of me as your son.'

Once we had done our oblations to the household gods, Attyabai and Kashibai, who had accompanied us, left. I was treated with the respect that was due to a family elder. Not once did we sisters-in-law quarrel. If somebody came to ask for something, my sister-in-law would point to me and say, 'Please ask her. I am not the mistress of the house.' Rakhmai handed over all decision making in the house to me and began working under my instructions. Here too I continued with my religious observances with the same rigour as earlier.

All my attention was now concentrated on Dattu. I had enrolled him in a school but over and above that, I also taught him myself. He used to go to school regularly. One day when he was on his way to school, a horse came galloping towards him. Fearful of being run down, he threw himself flat on the ground and the horse passed over him, leaving him unhurt.

When I heard about this, I began taking him to school and fetching him back every day myself.

Mr Tilak kept his word. A money order for ten rupees came from him. We continued our frequent exchange of letters. Once in while he would write very mean letters. I would go to the temple and sit weeping for hours. I had the time to do that because I ate only one meal a day. I would also weep when people taunted me. Some barbs were so sharp that they tore through my heart. Occasionally, even Bhauji would add to my torment. I was going berserk but there was no way out of the situation.

One day, I said to Bhauji, 'Tell me, do you ever feel pity for me? This is beyond endurance. Will you do something for me?'

'Tell me what and I will.'

'Write to everybody saying I've run away with Dattu. I don't care now about keeping reputations intact or losing them. I've had enough of this. Make an inventory of every bit and piece of the things that my sister has given me and keep it. I don't want her to say the bathwater's gone and the baby with it.'

'Where will you go?'

'Wherever the road takes me. I haven't decided yet. When I reach wherever it is, I'll write. I live now for Dattu. I'll find ways to put him through school and fill our stomachs. I'll be free from people's ill-treatment at least for some time.'

Bhauji liked the idea. The previous evening I had met a woman in the Vithoba temple. When she saw me weeping, she sat beside me and listened with the greatest sympathy to my tragic story. Her story was also tragic. She was very old and her husband even older. Their only son had died recently. They had nobody to call their own in their old age. They had been visiting all the holy places and were now in Pandharpur. They were planning to go to Gangapur the next day. They intended to spend the rest of their days there.

I said to the lady, 'I am young. I need somebody to shelter me for a few more years. Please take me with you. Think of yourself as my mother. I have no choice except to hide for some time.'

The woman agreed. The day after that, I had the conversation with Bhauji which I have reported above. There was universal agreement to my plan and I began to pack. The following day, we received a telegram saying, 'Gosavi's father coming.' There was no name or signature attached. We were completely baffled. Who was Gosavi and why was his father coming?

The next day, Mr Tilak stood at the door. His telegram should have read, 'Go says Father. Coming.' But who bothers about the Almighty and His messages in the telegraph office? The clerk must have used his head to interpret the message as best he could and sent it off.

Mr Tilak had come to Pandharpur from Wai. This is how it happened. A very good-natured, pious and loving Christian woman called Ashammabai Sheikh Umar lived in Wai. Mr Tilak used to call her Mother. Many nosey people had been after him to marry again. Little hope remained of my going to him. It was five years since he had converted. There is a jotting in his diary dated six months after the event, which says, 'When I hear a buggy approaching my door, I throw the window open to see if my family has come. Then I cannot sleep. I stay awake till the early hours. Dear God, please have pity on this poor servant and also on that poor woman and innocent child. Bring us together for Your glory. I will receive an answer to my prayer this week.' (26 August 1895)

The entry dated the day before this reads, 'Dear Lord, I know it is Your will that my family should come to me. But I am impatient. Please forgive me.'

The diary reveals Mr Tilak's state of mind in those early days. This was the state in which he had lived through the next five years. There were times when the idea of a second marriage tempted him, but only momentarily. One day, somebody had persuaded him to at least consider the possibility and had introduced him to a young and beautiful woman. He had responded to that well-wisher's urgings with a poem which said:

I have no desire for a garland of stars.
I have no use for sublime flowers.
I want my jasmine, my champak.
These are like pearls to me.
For these flowers I am willing to give up my life.
My dusky flower is simple but wonderful fun to be with.
If I sing its praises, even the nectar-collecting bee will stop
flitting around.
Why do you try to persuade me?
Give me what is mine.
My dear flower, I shall sing songs to you forever.
Your delicate heart I will worship with my tears.
It is enough for me if I die pining for you.
This will be the very zenith of my happiness.

The poem was published in the May 1899 issue of *Suvicharsamagam*. A footnote to the poem reads, 'This is the response of a faithful husband, suffering separation from his wife, to an individual's suggestion that he should abandon his wife and marry again.'

It was within a fortnight of his writing the poem that Mr Tilak came to meet me. He used to make a point of spending a few days with his mother in Wai on his way to and from Mahabaleshwar. Ashammabai's entire family had passed on. But like her name, she was hope incarnate. As always, Mr Tilak had stopped over with Ashammabai on his way from Mahabaleshwar. Every day, morning and evening, the two would pray together for me. On one occasion, their prayers were particularly intense. 'Dear Lord, it isn't for me that I ask for that mother and child to come to me, but for Your glory.' After they prayed Ashammabai gave Mr Tilak ten rupees and said, 'Send a telegram and go immediately to Pandharpur. Lakshmibai will definitely come with you.' Both were convinced that God had given Mr Tilak a message not to go to Ahmednagar but directly to Pandharpur. Mr Tilak left for Pandharpur and arrived twelve hours before I was to leave for Gangapur.

Our Feet Refused to Move

I was overjoyed to see Mr Tilak. My plan of going to Gangapur fizzled out on the spot. The next three days were full of happiness for me. Mr Phadnis, an old colleague of Nanasaheb's, lived in Pandharpur. He sent for me. When I went to his place, he said, 'If you want to leave this place, go to Jalalpur. I will give you money. But if you go with Tilak, I will take appropriate steps. Remember that.'

I said, 'I will not go to Jalalpur. Dattu does not keep well there. I will stay here.'

As I left, Mr Phadnis warned me again, 'Be careful.'

When I came home, Mr Tilak asked me why Mr Phadnis had called me.

I said, 'Just like that.'

'Really? How is it nobody ever calls me just like that?'

He was so insistent that I finally told him what had happened. Two days later, this Mr Phadnis was transferred out of Pandharpur. How that happened has been a mystery. Then Sakharambhauji stopped communicating with people. Not only did he stop talking to his wife, brother, sister-in-law and Dattu, but also to his eleven-month-old daughter. His wife and I had no idea what had caused this sudden silence. Since he was not talking to anybody, gradually the others also stopped talking to one another. However, we soon grew tired of not talking. Finally, Mr Tilak broke the silence. He said, 'I must make arrangements for Dattu's education. These are his school years. If he stays back now, he will be ruined for life. Come with me to Ahmednagar. I will set up a separate house for you.'

'Why Ahmednagar? Give me a separate house here. I'll stay by myself.'

'You love throwing challenges at me. I don't remember a single occasion in our entire life when I have asked you to do something and you have agreed. I've put up with that till now.

But I can't sacrifice Dattu's future because of your stubbornness. I will give you time up to five-thirty this evening. Make up your mind either way till then. I have given you five-and-a-half years to think. I cannot afford to give you more. I shall take Dattu with me. If you stand in my way, I will have to use other means to do it.' His voice had been rising gradually and at the end, it hit the very top note in the highest octave.

We sisters-in-law felt very scared. We could only look at one another speechlessly. Mr Tilak repeated his warning. 'I will give you time up to five-thirty. Otherwise you will see within the week what I can do.'

That said, he went for a walk. I went to the kitchen. It was like being in a jungle with a wild fire raging all around. My sister-in-law followed me in. She hugged me. Then the two of us sobbed bitterly.

'Bai, tell me what I can do for you. I'm ready to do anything you ask.'

'What can you do? God will do whatever is in His mind. I am under siege from all sides. You heard what he said. What he meant was he will take Dattu away and I can stay on in somebody else's house, toiling.'

'Bai, don't do that. Why don't you go with him instead? He is not asking you to convert or anything like that. If such a danger does arise, write to me and I will send you money to come back.'

'Where will you find the money?'

'That's my lookout. Nobody seems to give you advice that's in your best interests. Your brother-in-law will think this is the worst thing you could do. You will continue to be squashed in the middle. People say Christians make you marry again. They make you cook meat. Can we stop people from saying such things? You are free to come back, whatever the circumstances, whatever the time. I will share with you every morsel I eat. You have as much right over this house as I have. If Mr Tilak can come here, why cannot his wife, my sister-in-law?'

The brothers returned home together. Nobody said

anything. We had our dinner. It was difficult to swallow the food. The following day, Rakhmai began packing my things. She packed so many spices, condiments, chutneys and pickles that I could not lift the bag with one hand. While she packed, she wept. We asked Sakharambhauji if I should go. He put his hands to his ears. That was his answer. Rakhmabai helped me get bathed and dressed. She was still weeping and saying, 'Now whose feet will I touch for blessings when Mali marries? From today my Bai will be as good as dead to me.'

The bullock-cart came. Mr Tilak, Dattu and I climbed in. Bhauji went away the moment he saw the cart coming. Rakhmai was in her washed, unpolluted sari. She ran after the cart in that sari, barefoot, holding Mali in her arms. We had to leave without saying farewell to Bhauji. Mr Tilak was trying to console his sister-in-law. 'Go back,' he kept repeating. She kept saying, 'Take care of my Bai. Take care of Dattu.' He answered, 'She is your sister-in-law. But she is also my wife. If you are feeling so bad for her, imagine how I am feeling.' My eyes were fixed on the Vithoba temple. It had been my solace in recent times. I said to myself, 'Dear God, I am jumping into this water holding a torch in each hand. If it pleases you to keep me afloat, do so. Else let me die. But don't let me have to bow my head before anybody again.' Both Rakhmai and I were weeping continuously. Although Mr Tilak was trying to assume a stony expression, his naturally tender heart was wrenched to see the state we were in.

Dattu was thrilled to be riding in a cart. Later he was going to travel by train. Rakhmai continued to follow the cart for as long as she could keep up with it. When the cart picked up speed, she fell behind and then stood fixed to the spot, watching it disappear. I had not stopped sobbing.

Mr Tilak said, 'Please don't go on like that. I will never force you to convert. The religion appealed to me, so I accepted it. If it appeals to you and you wish to convert, I will be only too happy. But I will never force you. Whatever you have heard about it is false. You are not going to be married off to anybody.

You will not have to cook meat. Who has put these ideas into your head? Dr Hume has written to me to say he has rented a place for you and Dattu for twenty-five rupees a month. It is owned by a Brahmin. He has furnished it with everything you require. It is close to the Pendses' house. Why cry?'

My experience matched what Mr Tilak was saying. Meat has never been cooked in our house in the last thirty-five years. Mr Tilak bought us some fruit in Kurduwadi. He himself ate in a restaurant, unmindful of what caste or creed the owner belonged to. We boarded the train to Ahmednagar. It arrived around three in the afternoon. As it approached the station, my heart and Dattu's began to beat faster. We were under the impression that the Pendses did not know we were coming. But the very thing we feared stood before us. Even as the train came to a halt at the station, there they were right outside our compartment: Nanasaheb, Kakasaheb Mirikar and a whole group of others. They said they were there to receive or see off somebody. Dattu's and my feet would not move when we saw them. Mr Tilak walked on fearlessly.

When Nanasaheb saw me, he said, 'Manu, what brings you here?'

'I am here for Dattu's education. He has not been keeping well. I am going to find a place to live here.'

'So where are you going now?'

'I will go wherever you say I should.'

Nanasaheb sent Dattu, me and our luggage off to his house. Mr Tilak went to his home.

A Welcome of Sorts

That day I was welcomed to the Pendses' house in the strangest manner. When I entered, there was not a soul around. Only little Yesu came forward and said, 'Maushi, why have you come?'

I said, 'Just like that,' to satisfy her curiosity. I handed over to Yesu every article Bhikutai had given me for her to give back to her—brand-new saris, cholis, ornaments and other valuables. A Brahmin servant heated my bath water for me. I had a bath, washed the sari I was wearing, got Yesu to help me locate the house Mr Tilak had rented for us and hung up the sari there to dry. This house was close to the Pendses' home. When I stepped in, a throng of women followed me. There was much signalling going on between them, eye signals, hand signals, neck signals. They thought I had not noticed them. But of course I had.

I looked around at the set-up in my new home. Dr Hume had organized everything just as it should be. But there were things there which I had never seen before. There were no brass plates and bowls. Instead, there was crockery—cups and saucers and dinner plates. Instead of brass spoons and ladles, there were knives and forks. After I had hung my sari out to dry, a message came from Mr Tilak, 'I want tea.' Mr Tilak had his own home but his wife could not yet claim her house as her own. I made tea and took it over to him. 'You must be tired. Better have dinner at the Pendses. I am not home for dinner. I'll eat with you tomorrow.'

Before I arrived in Ahmednagar, the landlord had told Mr Tilak not to visit his house. If he wanted to visit me, he would have to find me another house. I had no knowledge of this. I went over to the Pendses' and Mr Tilak went home. I was secretly pleased that Bhikutai and I would now be living next door to each other. When I arrived at the Pendses', they had already eaten dinner. Nobody spoke to me. An enormous pot of mango jam with jaggery was boiling away on the fire. The cook placed a plate before me with a quarter of a millet bhakri and salt. There was nobody around in the kitchen. My eyes were streaming with tears. Dattu had eaten and fallen asleep. Mr Tilak must have had his dinner in his home and must be quietly writing.

Mr Tilak was not the worrying kind by nature. When my landlord had told him to look for another place if he intended visiting me, he must have said to himself, this too is God's will. Why worry? The landlord had been paid advance rent. Mr Tilak was coming the following day. I had to cook something. So as soon as I got up in the morning, I went across to my home. I had eaten nothing in three days besides the quarter of a bhakri and salt of the previous night. I had not been able to swallow any food before leaving Pandharpur. There was nothing to eat along the way. And at the Pendses', bhakri and salt were what I was served.

When I went to my home, I first put it in proper order, cooked and sat waiting for Mr Tilak to come. My mind was in turmoil. I was pacing the floor from door to window and back again. Dattu was with the Pendses, I was here and Mr Tilak was in some third place. We were in the same town but we had not met each other all day.

Mr Tilak did not come through the day or night. I had not eaten anything all day. I waited all night. I did not go to my sister's till eleven o'clock at night the following day. So that was two days of starvation. At eleven a sepoy came from the Pendses and escorted me to their place. Everything was quiet in the house when I arrived. Nanasaheb was sitting in his office. The sepoy said, 'She is here.' Those were the only words I had heard throughout the day. Nanasaheb replied, 'Show her in.' I went in.

'So is all well with you, Maushi? And what are your plans now?'

'Dattu's education.'

'Do you think only you are concerned about that, not we?'

'That's not what I meant. We are all concerned about it.'

'Good. So now go to Jalalpur. I'll give you the train fare.'

'I don't want money. Jalalpur doesn't suit Dattu. That's why I'm here.'

'That's just an excuse. What's wrong with the Jalalpur air? Don't other people live there?'

'It suits them. It doesn't suit Dattu.'

'Look. Think again.'

'I have thought. If the one for whose sake I live does not feel well, what's the point of my life?'

'Don't be too smart. Listen to me. I will make over some farmland to you. I will send you ten rupees a month and give you twenty gold coins.'

'I have not come here hoping to get something from you. I am only thinking of Dattu's health and education. I wouldn't want your entire wealth if you offered it to me. You have already done a lot for me. But I will not go back now, come what may.'

'Fine. In that case, return to me everything that I have given you.'

'I had put it aside when I left Jalalpur. I handed it over to Yesu the moment I stepped in. I have no desire for anything. I am fully aware that what man gives is never enough and what God gives never ends.'

'You are becoming too clever by half. All right. It is one o'clock now. Go to sleep. Give her a bed, somebody.'

'No bed for her. Give her a horse saddle,' came a voice from within the house. The servant immediately fetched a saddle for me to sleep on. They say if you're hungry even bran tastes good and if you're sleepy, even a stone makes a good pillow. I had not even had bran for two days. So a saddle for a pillow was welcome. I slept soundly on it.

I got up in the morning and came to my home. The first thing I did was to offer yesterday's untasted tea and uneaten food to Mother Earth. Then I set about cooking fresh food. For two days Dattu, Mr Tilak and I had not met. Dattu was being well looked after by his aunt. I had no need to worry about him. But what about Mr Tilak? Where was I to look for him? I was living in a town but it felt like a jungle to me. I was being constantly buoyed up by hope and dashed down by disappointment. Just then Mr Tilak arrived with two servants and a cart.

'I waited for you the whole of yesterday. You didn't turn up. Dattu was not with me. All the food was wasted.'

'I've found another place for you.'

'Why? I'm not coming.'

'If you don't come, remember, this landlord doesn't want you in his house.'

'Why not?'

'He's the owner. The other house also belongs to a Brahmin. There's a Maratha woman to clean the vessels and a Gujarati Brahmin to fetch water. I was running around all day trying to organize these things. That's why I didn't come yesterday.'

I fetched Dattu. All my stuff was loaded on to the cart while the three of us rode in a tonga. I had still not met my sister. I set up my second home. Now all the things that Rakhmabai had packed could be used. I made rice and pithla and the three of us fell on it. Mr Tilak went back to his home which was about one hundred steps away. Now all our troubles are over, I thought. Dattu and I slept a peaceful sleep. But the landlady sent a message first thing in the morning. 'You can't use our lavatory.' Even lavatories had to follow bigoted caste rules.

'Where do we go then, madam?'

'To the public lavatory.'

Even Lakshmi must fall at a landlady's feet when she is in trouble. Nature does not observe pollution and non-pollution. The woman who had been hired to clean our vessels, did her job one day but then came to say she could not continue. 'I will be ostracized from my caste.' The poor Gujarati Brahmin's water was cut. He pleaded with his people, 'The lady observes pollution and non-pollution. She does puja every day. Why do you cut my water?' He was told her husband is a Christian. You must do penance. He had to do penance and on top of that pay a fine of five rupees all because of me. We were faced by three insurmountable problems. There was no alternative now but to move to a third house.

'We will now move to the Fergusson Gate compound,' Mr Tilak said.

'Where is that?'

'Close by. It's a Christian colony.'

'I won't live next door to them.'

'Where do we go then? You've seen the Brahminism of Brahmins for yourself now. This is what Brahma is all about for them. I am not creating problems for you. It's your people who are abandoning you. I am helpless.'

Dr Hume got to know about my ordeal with houses. He also heard that I was unwilling to live next door to Christians. It was the rainy season. Where could the residents of Fergusson Gate be shifted? Each family had half-a-dozen children. Despite this, the poor people vacated the compound for me. It was now all mine. There were three houses of four rooms each. All three were handed over to us. Now there was no need for Mr Tilak to live apart. The Christians did not visit the compound since it was unacceptable to me. We hired bullock-carts to take us to the new house, our third in the same town. Dattu and I lived in two houses and Mr Tilak in the third.

It was in this house that Dr Julia and Miss Emily Bissel came to meet me. Never before had I met two white women who spoke such beautiful Marathi. Come to think of it, the only other white woman I had met before was Miss Harvey. Mr Tilak had warned people about me so no Christians came to visit me. But gradually, people began visiting Mr Tilak's house where morning and evening prayers, hymn singing and scripture readings were held. I had all my gods, including Ganapati, around me in my house. I would pray to them and to the holy tulsi plant every day with great fervour. He had servants. I had nobody. Marathas refused to work for me and I could not accept anybody of a lower caste. I did all my work myself. Mr Tilak ate with me.

There was no water in the compound. I had to fetch it from the Committee garden. The tap there was truly public. Or it might be nearer to the truth to say it was used entirely by non-Brahmins. One day, when I went to the tap to fetch water, I saw two women from some other caste. One of the two women's bodies was covered with feathers.

I said, 'Move a little will you? I want to take water.'

She came back with, 'You move. What's it to us if you're a Brahmin and all? And if you are, what are you doing at this tap?'

I filled my water vessel after the women left and came home. I had made some chutney. Two feathers had come floating in and fallen in it. I was ready to go mad when I saw this. So rivers of tears again. When Mr Tilak came, he wanted to know what had happened. I told him the whole story from the tap to the chutney.

He said, 'What can I do about it? The breeze must have blown them in.' That shut me up and made me cry more. Mr Tilak used to go to the church every Sunday and Dattu would go with him. One day after church, he went with his father to Malanbai Kukade's house. A Brahmin man was also there, busy guzzling tea and biscuits. He offered some to Dattu but Dattu would not eat anything there.

A few days later when Dattu was at the Pendses', the same gentleman turned up there. Tea was served. The gentleman rose from his seat, went far away and gulped a cupful down. Wiping his mouth, he said to Dattu, 'So your Pop has converted, hasn't he?'

'Better that he has converted. He's not like you. He drinks tea and eats biscuits openly. You do it on the sly.'

'When did I eat anything, you rascal?'

'On Sunday at that lady's house, didn't you drink tea and eat something? I didn't.'

Then Nanasaheb made him shut up.

Bhikutai had taken to her bed after I arrived. Once, her nephew came to visit her and later came over to see me. I was cooking in my unpolluted sari. An oil lamp was burning near the gods. They were anointed with sandalwood paste and flowers had been offered. He noted all this and laughed. 'Why do you laugh?' I asked.

He said, 'Back there your sister has fallen ill because she thinks you have become a Christian. And here I see something else altogether.'

Even now some things troubled me. But on the whole it had been a happy month. Now we were not worried that some Brahmin would turn up to torment us. Although no Brahmins came to eject us from our home, Lord Ganapati, the remover of obstacles was very much with us. He ordered his vehicle, the Rat, to arrange for our eviction. We were at lunch one day when a large rat came out of nowhere and began nibbling at the food Dattu had put outside his plate as the ritual offering to the gods. Ahmednagar rats are not scared of anyone, we said to ourselves and got up. Just then another rat arrived and also started eating the ritual food offering. Then both spun around and fell dead. I had heard a lot about rats dying in this fashion, but this was the first time I had seen it. When Mr Tilak saw the dead rats he confirmed immediately that they were plague-carrying rats.

They were sent off to be tested. The result confirmed they were plague rats. When Dr Hume heard the news, he came by and invited us to shift to his bungalow. But how was I going to follow my pollution rituals there? So only Mr Tilak went to stay with him and Dattu and I went to Malanbai Kukade's house. Only women lived in the compound where she stayed. I was given a side room and I settled down there. Rajasbai also stayed there. When we met, we recalled the time we had spent on the train and were most amused.

A Gift and Alms on Top

We came together for a brief while and then the plague separated us. Mr Tilak moved to Dr Hume's house and I, with Dattu, to Malanbai Kukade's compound. Women ruled in this place and men were barred from entering except from four to five in the evening. If by chance Mr Tilak got too absorbed in writing or talking and missed the time, we would have to wait for another twenty-four hours to meet.

There was an uneducated Christian woman here. She and her two daughters were very pious. She was very sensitive to other people's feelings. These two were company for me. The woman had a very sweet way of talking and I preferred her company to that of the educated women in the place. When she saw me weep for my relatives whom I missed, she would console me.

The compound was thick with trees of many kinds. Several varieties of birds would perch on them. Dattu would try to catch them. Rajasbai told Dattu, put salt on their tails. They will not move an inch then. Dattu did not realize that the birds would not wait for him to put salt on their tails. He spent days raiding the kitchen for salt, but not a single bird came to the poor soul's hand.

The plague intensified in Ahmednagar. The missionary in Rahuri, Rev. Ballantyne was an MD and very well known for his medical skill. He was appointed on plague duty in Ahmednagar and Mr Tilak was posted to his place. In Rahuri, the Christians live to the west of the town. Rev. Ballantyne's bungalow was located about half a furlong away from there. We all moved into this bungalow. Now I was surrounded entirely by Christians. There was an outhouse in the compound where I cooked my food and did my puja and observed my rituals of pollution and non-pollution.

The ayah who looked after Rev. Ballantyne's children lived

in the room next to me. Everybody called her Ayahbai. Ayahbai was uneducated but had been taught so well to be considerate towards others that I remember her to this day. Here I was, the daughter of Narayanrao Gokhale, which information alone was enough to indicate how strictly I followed the rules of pollution, and there was Ayahbai right next door, who was irredeemably polluted. So there was sufficient scope for quarrels to break out. But they did not. Although Ayahbai did not give up her food habits, she conducted herself with great tact. Sometimes, she invited Mr Tilak to eat with her but I never came to know what she cooked for him. On these occasions, she would send me rations to cook for myself. She always hung clothes on a string in her room which blocked the view in. When I asked her why she did that, she would say. 'There's plague around. Clothes should be aired.' She would close her door when she was having her meals. That used to surprise me. I would ask her why. Her answer was, 'That's our custom.'

At times when she was having lunch or dinner, I could hear a loud beating sound. I would ask her what she banged when she ate her meals. Her answer was, 'I fill up rat holes. Rats have become such pests.' Once from behind her closed door I heard the strangest conversation. One voice said I want the feet. Another said I want the head. I was very curious to know what was going on. I said to her, 'I heard a very strange conversation from your room. What was it about?'

She quickly answered, 'A storyteller was telling us a story about a demon.'

I had no servant to do my work. Ayahbai gradually began to do all my top work, beginning with the question, 'What harm does a bit of sweeping do, right?' Because she was so sweet-natured I let her do the work. She did not touch my cooking space or my water.

This is where I met my first Christian brother. His clothes and manners were exactly like a pure Brahmin's. His name was Bapu Namaji Adhav. I asked Mr Tilak which sub-caste of

Brahmins he belonged to. Mr Tilak said, 'He's a Gudshastha Brahmin.' I had heard of Konkanastha, Deshastha and Karhade Brahmins but never this sub-caste. But I went along with what Mr Tilak said. Years later, when I realized that gudsa meant meat, I understood who a Gudshastha Brahmin was.

Bapurao stayed with us for two or three days. I would often weep at the thought of my relatives. I had wept for Mr Tilak all these years. Now it was for my relatives. Bapurao would console me, saying, 'Please don't cry. Think of me as your brother.' And indeed he was a true brother to me till the end.

I must narrate something that happened before we left Ahmednagar and came to Rahuri. A man turned up to see Mr Tilak. He wanted to become a Christian. He began calling Mr Tilak papa, and me aai or mother. Mr Tilak grew very fond of him and treated him like a son. Was there any person on earth that Mr Tilak would not grow fond of in time? He would trust whosoever came to meet him, on first sight. His belief in himself as a good judge of people was implicit. I believed the opposite. I believed I had a better judgment of people. In my opinion, this fellow was a scoundrel; in Mr Tilak's opinion, a messenger from God.

'You don't understand human psychology,' he would say to me.

'Maybe not,' I would reply. 'But I have practical knowledge, and on that basis I say, this man is a scoundrel.'

He would say, 'You are terribly prejudiced. This man is going to be a great servant of God. You'll see.'

'He'll be nothing of the kind,' I would say. 'One day he will rob you blind and vanish.'

He came with us to Rahuri. He was baptized there. A few days later Mr Tilak found him some kind of job in Visapur. I packed him off with a tumbler, some edibles and bedding. He wrote to us regularly from Visapur. Mr Tilak, thinking the poor man had nobody else in the world but us, would send him parcels of sweet limes once in a while.

One day, Mr Tilak went to Ahmednagar on work. I got a letter from him the following day. Our house had been burgled. The surprising thing was that the house had not been broken into. The doors were all closed and the locks intact. But every single article from the tin pot in the lavatory to bed linen, silver buttons, shirts, coats, honey jar had vanished. I immediately suspected Mr Tilak's adopted son. I was convinced that this was that scoundrel's work. Mr Tilak returned soon after. He spun a lot of tall stories as preface to the main event which was, 'The thief has been finally caught.'

I asked hopefully, 'And all the stuff recovered?'

'Have patience. I'll tell you everything.'

'So tell me.'

'You know that our son is in Visapur, right? We recovered all the stuff because of him. If it hadn't been for him, we would not have got back even a cracked coin.'

'Why? Has he joined the police force or something?'

'Of course not. See, the thief was foolish enough to try and sell a pot that had our name engraved on it. Our son recognized the pot. He grabbed the thief and handed him over to the police. Such a clever man.'

'Say what you like, but what will a thief do with a rolling board and pin and a tin pot? This scoundrel must be an insider. An ordinary thief would have no use for these things.'

'You have no idea. Thieves make money even from things like that.'

'So then? What happened?'

'What can happen? He's written to me saying send me ten rupees. I have collected all the stuff. As soon as I get the money I will bring it to you.'

'So now we will send him money?'

'Of course! These jobs can't be done without money. Get me the money. Or I will have to go myself to fetch our stuff back.'

I went indoors to fetch the money. As usual, a few people were sitting with him outside. Mr Tilak continued to talk about the theft. He made no distinction between private and public talk. From the inner room I clearly heard what he was saying. 'He's the thief. He got the keys from Dr Hume. Came to the house with four carts and loaded all the stuff on them. The ironsmith's wife next door asked him where he was taking the stuff. He told her that I had sent him from here to bring it to Rahuri.'

I heard everything but since I had a large store of practical knowledge, I decided it did not matter since we were getting back all our belongings for a mere ten rupees. I came out and put the money in Mr Tilak's hand. He went to Visapur and gave the money to the man and said to him, 'I'll go ahead. You bring the stuff.'

Mr Tilak returned. I said, 'Where are all our things?'

He said, 'They're coming.'

I said, 'You'd already gifted him all our possessions. Only the alms remained. Now you've given him those as well.'

Mr Tilak continued to believe for a long time that the man would come with the loot. He never did.

Poison or Nectar?

Four or five months later, the plague abated and Dr Ballantyne returned to Rahuri. After Mr Tilak became a Christian, he went regularly to Mahabaleshwar in the summer to teach European and American missionaries Marathi. He earned a lot of money from this. He would be away for three months. He spent the remaining nine months in Ahmednagar. When Dr Ballantyne returned to Rahuri, Mr Tilak was busy getting ready to go to Mahabaleshwar. This time Dattu and I were going with him. He had written to his 'mother', Ashammabai in Wai informing her that we too were going to Mahabaleshwar with him, and inviting her to go with us. She accepted the invitation instantly. Some people in Wai said to her, 'Don't go. You won't get on with Mr Tilak's wife. What will you do if that happens?'

Ashammabai said, 'If that happens I'll come back. I have not made a contract with Mr Tilak to stay there even if I don't want to.'

Mr Tilak had written to Rev. Ganpatrao Malhar in Pune too. His wife Mathurabai was familiar with all the Brahmin rituals regarding purity and impurity. I was stunned to see how clean and tidy her house was. She had set up a separate corner for me to cook and pray in. We spent two very happy days with the Malhars in Pune.

Arrangements were made for me in Wai too to cook in a segregated place, and mangoes and pedhas aplenty had been laid up for Dattu. I cooked and we all ate together. After lunch, Ashammabai packed and we left for Mahabaleshwar by bullock-cart. All of us had been inoculated against the plague but even then, people arriving by bullock-cart were suspect. So we had to spend ten days in quarantine in a hut in Dandeghar. Even there I had my gods and wore my purified sari when I cooked. People in the huts around us wondered what kind of family we were. The man looks like a Muslim, the old woman looks like a Christian, the younger one is clearly Brahmin and the boy wanders around with a Brahmin's sacred thread across his chest.

Water was a problem for me here. It was brought by water carriers. But the water came in leather bags and the carriers were Muslims. So I myself went to fetch drinking and cooking water for us. The water from leather bags was good enough for other uses. One day there was some leftover food. I offered it to a Mang woman. She said, 'Lady, we don't eat food made by a Christian.' I was very upset to hear that. I sobbed my heart out. Mr Tilak and Ashammabai tried to console me, but there was just one thought in my head. If even lower-caste people don't want to touch food cooked by me, my relatives will not allow even my shadow to fall on them.

Ashammabai said, 'Please don't cry, Lakshmibai. Everything will sort itself out. Your relatives will visit you. You will visit them. You need to endure this for just a few days.' All she got in return for this gentle advice was my raving and ranting. The poor woman put up with it only because she was so sweet-tempered.

When our ten-day quarantine ended, we were given permission to leave. It was bullock-carts once again with our luggage and our guests. And so we arrived in Mahabaleshwar. Mr Tilak never changed his staff and house. From the time he had started going to Mahabaleshwar, he had rented the same house, Saidu Mistry's. He had written to him on this occasion too, and Mistry had organized everything for our arrival. He had laid out the bedding, bought milk, butter, ghee, vegetables and stocked up firewood. This was not all. This bearded Muslim had even stored water. What he had stopped short of doing was cooking.

We reached Mahabaleshwar at around ten o'clock. As soon as the house was opened and our luggage brought in, everybody got down to their respective work. Dattu went out to play, Mr Tilak started writing, Ashammabai began to decorate the drawing room and I went into the kitchen to cook. The well was a short distance away from the house. I felt greedy at the thought of abundant water so near at hand. I drew some instantly. The water was cold, the air cool, the food sweet and the heart at peace. I served Mr Tilak and Ashammabai first. Then Dattu and I sat down to lunch. In the middle of this togetherness, I began talking about how happy I was to have a well close by. But the minute I mentioned the well, it was like nectar turning to poison.

Mr Tilak said, 'You are not to draw water. It doesn't become my status. I will engage a Brahmin to draw your water.'

Fear entered my heart. I recalled the incident in Ahmednagar which was still fresh in my mind. That poor Brahmin had had to pay a fine because of me and was almost ostracized from the caste. We argued a little but only for a while. We finished the rest of the meal in silence.

We were Brahmins surrounded by Muslims. Where was a Brahmin to be found to draw water the next day? And did Mr Tilak have the time to go looking for one? He was working from six in the morning till six in the evening. But I still hoped he would. We had a large vessel and a half of water left. My sleep wandered away at night searching for water and returned at four in the morning. When I woke up, all I could see was the vessel and a half of water we had. I eked it out in miserly fashion through the day. Despite that, at the end of the day, there was just enough left for Dattu and me. I was now in despair. Much water began flowing from my eyes. But of what use was that?

Mr Tilak said, 'Make do with this other water for today. I'll arrange for something else from tomorrow.'

'If I drink this water once, that's the end anyway.'

We sat down to dinner. I felt choked. I managed somehow to push half the food down, but the last morsel stuck in my throat.

Mr Tilak said, 'That which guards the body is religion. Moreover, the Hindu religion tells you that if you let water flow, it loses its pollution. So drink this water.'

I raised the water drawn by a Muslim to my lips. I hesitated, shut my eyes tight and took a sip. It did not stay in for long. It surged up immediately, bringing with it whatever food there was in my stomach. This put an end to everybody's dinner.

I collapsed on the spot. I started a fever. Mr Tilak now regretted having been so adamant. Ashammabai said to him it would have done nobody harm if he had allowed me to draw water. Mr Tilak agreed.

Transformed

Lying in bed I was watering my pillow. Nobody came anywhere near me till three in the morning. Mr Tilak was feeling very guilty now. In my mind I was howling before God. 'Dear Lord, what have I done today? What must my ancestors in heaven be saying about me? What penance will I have to do to absolve myself of this sin?' A thousand such thoughts coursed through my mind.

My eyes were closed. Then suddenly a light shone on them. This is not a metaphor. I really experienced the sensation of being engulfed by a bright light like the light of the sun. The turmoil in my mind vanished and other thoughts such as I had never experienced before began to whirl around in my mind. Dattu could not understand why there was this dense silence in the house. He escaped it by going out to play and forgetting us. Mr Tilak had supreme faith in God. His prayer was answered. The chains of caste consciousness that had bound my heart snapped and fell to the ground. This happened in a trice. The thoughts in my mind at the time were so clear that I am putting them down here exactly as they came to me.

Did God create castes or was it Man? Had God created them, would He not have made them look different from one another? Instead, life and death, bones and flesh, the heart and the mind, the ability to tell right from wrong, joys and sorrows, were they not common to all men? And if God had created castes among humans, why not among animals? Why are there no Brahmin bulls and Shudra bulls, Vaishya crows and untouchable crows? No Nandi horn adorns the Shudra crow's head nor Shiva's linga the Brahmin crow's head. If any difference exists among humans and animals, it is between male and female.

That was it. My mind was free of caste. I was not going to think of any human being as low. Everybody was going to be equal to me. I would eat and drink from everybody's hands without discrimination. While this train of thought was running in my mind, Ashammabai came to console me. 'Please get up now, draw your water and start cooking,' she said. I said, 'I am not going to draw water. I am not going to cook. I'd like you to cook. I will eat what you cook.' She did not immediately understand what I was trying to say. She told Mr Tilak about it. He too came and told me to fetch water and cook. I told him categorically that I was not going to cook. He said, 'You torment yourself for no reason. I will not say a single word to you about water and cooking. Just do what makes you happy.'

I said, 'I am speaking from my heart, not out of anger.' When he was finally convinced of my sincerity, he exclaimed, 'Thank God,' and instantly knelt down to pray. Ashammabai cooked and we ate together in great happiness. It was the first time I had eaten food cooked by a non-Brahmin. But it did not upset me as drinking that sip of water the previous night had.

Ashammabai left after a few days to return to her work in Wai. I felt very sad to see her go. I had never had to work under a mother-in-law's instructions. My mother-in-law had died before my marriage. I have already written about how my adopted mother-in-law in Rajnandgaon had tortured me. But although Ashammabai was also an adopted mother-in-law, she was more like a mother.

Mr Tilak now settled down to his new married life. Eating and drinking were no longer problems. Although I had not converted to Christianity nor did I plan to, I had lost all trace of caste consciousness. Because of that, the two kitchens that we had run till then became one. Mr Tilak put no obstacles in the way of my idol worship and when it was his prayer time I made a point of sitting with him quietly.

Living together meant Mr Tilak had to earn more money. He began taking as much work as he could find. He used to earn twenty-five or thirty rupees per hour and he could work eight or nine hours a day. His fondness for spending money continued without abate. When there was money in the pocket, it got frisky and gambolled around. When we got married, he had put a garland of responsibility around my neck and I had put a garland of irresponsibility around his. Money made in Mumbai stays in Mumbai. The gold bricks from Lanka do not travel to Hindustan. Similarly, Mr Tilak began to show old signs of wanting to finish off all the money he made in Mahabaleshwar in Mahabaleshwar itself.

Occasionally, he felt an urge to visit the market. He believed nobody else had as much practical knowledge as he; whereas, I was of the opinion that he had so little practical knowledge that anybody could cheat him. Now that his wife and son had joined him and he was making good money, he went on spending sprees. Initially, objects of household use came home. Cups and saucers, knives and forks, milk pots and sugar pots, butter dishes, kettles, soup plates, dinner plates, wash basins. All modern stuff. He also bought a lot of cane furniture. He had not given a thought to what I would find useful. All the things that we were supposed to eat off and drink from were alien to me. I was not happy to have them around. I would say, 'Why do you fill the house with these breakables?' That would upset him. He would say I did not have the capacity to appreciate.

Once he had stocked the kitchen, he turned to clothes. He had four suits made for himself and two gowns for me. I said, 'What's wrong with you? Why didn't you get me two saris?' He said, 'You have no idea of human psychology. When somebody does something to please you, you shouldn't throw cold water on it. That's the real reason why we don't get along. Nothing I have done has ever pleased you.'

He had three pairs of shoes made for each one of us. Mine alone cost twenty-four rupees. Not in my whole life had I worn even an ordinary slipper on my feet. Although I had already heard two lectures on psychology and appreciation, I had to blurt out, 'What a waste of money. If you had bought some gold instead, it would have helped on a rainy day.' A third lecture was delivered to me, the gist of which was, 'You are the limit of idiocy. Is it better to wear gold and go out into the jungle barefoot or use things like footwear and umbrellas and reduce the chance of illness?'

All the money that he had earned in Mahabaleshwar was spent in this way. When we left, the household stuff that he had bought was given away to Saidu Mistry. This allowed him to rent out his house in the future at 'fully furnished' rates. When we returned, we paid him at that rate for using our own stuff.

It has to be said though that our days in Mahabaleshwar were very happy and full of fun. I learned how to bake bread. I had managed to acquire some hop leaves from somebody as leavener. I have always had a problem with stomach pains. One day my stomach began to hurt very badly. Mr Tilak used to leave the house for work early in the morning. Nobody would be around to help me after he left. He asked me what he could do for me. I told him to take some sonamukhi* leaves from the cupboard and brew them for me. He made tea for himself, made me my brew and left for work.

Soon my stomach began to bloat. It came to a point where I began to feel distinctly uneasy. I was sure I was going to die, and there was nobody at home except Dattu and me. Finally, Dattu said, 'I'll go fetch Dr Julia Bissel.' He used to go to her house with Mr Tilak so he knew where she lived. Dr Bissel asked what I had eaten and drunk. She wondered why sonamukhi should increase my stomach ache and make me bloat. She thought hard. Then she went to the kitchen where everything was in disorder. She picked up the pan in which the sonamukhi had been brewed and discovered it was hop leaves. 'You've drunk leavening,' she told me. 'No wonder your stomach has bloated.' The medicine she gave me brought instant relief.

When we left Mahabaleshwar, our luggage had been reduced to a neat and manageable amount. We had two trunks, two suitcases and some bedding. When we had gone to Mahabaleshwar, we had required an entire cart for just our

---

*These are leaves from the senna tree. Dried and powdered, they are used to strengthen immunity and cure disease.

luggage. Now we fitted into one cart along with our luggage. While we had put on weight in the balmy air of Mahabaleshwar, our luggage had lost weight.

Ashammabai was waiting for us in Wai. Known for her hospitality, she had made every arrangement necessary for our stay. Everything was in its proper place in her house. She was surprised to see the reduced quantity of our luggage. I made complaining noises. Mr Tilak said, 'The amount we'd have had to pay to transport all that stuff would have equalled buying it in Ahmednagar.' He was right of course, and it is difficult to say if there was a counter argument to that.

Mr Tilak gave a lecture on Christianity in front of the Ganapati temple. A huge crowd gathered to hear him. The lecture was followed by questions and answers. I would like to give an example of how Mr Tilak's talent for thinking on his feet helped him in such situations. One of those present at the lecture said, 'I believe you people have thirty fathers and one mother, is that right?' The man was punning on the word baptism which was 'baptisma' in Marathi; so 'bap' (father) was 'tis' (thirty) and 'ma' (mother) was alone.

When people asked such questions, other missionaries would get confused. But Mr Tilak had an answer to every question he was asked whether genuine or mocking. To this question he said, 'Why only Christians? All human beings have thirty fathers and they have one mother, which makes her our grandmother. So count. The five mahabhutas: earth, air, fire, water, light. The five breaths that give us life; our five senses; our five limbs; four inner qualities, heart, intellect, ego, mind. One soul. Add to this the five ancestors that you worship according to your shastras. There you are. That makes thirty. And who is the mother of these thirty fathers? It is God's will—mother to the thirty fathers and therefore grandmother to us.'

The doubter was left speechless. This is not what Mr Tilak believed baptism to be. But with this answer he stopped once and for all the taunts that the people of Wai flung at missionaries. We left Wai a couple of days later.

Haushi

We talked and planned as we journeyed. We were now three or four miles from Vathar. There is a bridge there with water flowing beneath. So it is a good place to unharness cart horses and bullocks. There is a village called Pipurde nearby. We got down and opened our containers of snacks. After we had eaten our fill, Mr Tilak and Dattu went wandering. My mind wandered back to Ahmednagar and our plans. We had decided to stop over at Pune for a couple of days on the way.

Seeing two or three baskets of food before me, beggars began gathering around. With my head always on my shoulders, I put our cash away and began distributing the food. There were some girls amongst the beggars. I am garrulous by nature. So I started a conversation with them. I inquired about where they lived. Then I asked one of them, 'Tell me, why do you beg?' She said, 'Bai, I have no family.'

'Will you go with me then?' She accepted the invitation with alacrity. She gave away all the money and food she had collected to her friend, whispered something in her ear and came and sat beside me.

'I hope you won't cry.'

'I won't.'

'Then go wash yourself. Leave your dhoti behind. Wear this sari and this blouse.'

When she did that, there was a huge change in her appearance. She was dark-skinned but had sharp features. If anybody saw her now, they would not think that five minutes ago she was begging. She must have been twelve or thirteen.

'What should I call you?' she asked.

'My name is Lakshmi. My son calls me Bai. You can call me whatever you like.'

She too began to call me Bai.

I was not a Christian, but since Mr Tilak's Bible was lying

beside me, I picked it up and prayed silently, 'Dear God, tell me if what I am doing is right or wrong.' Then I opened the Bible at random and the line that I read said: 'When a tree is planted beside a stream, it produces an early fruit and its leaves do not wilt.' Whatever doubts remained in my mind faded away when I read the line. I was convinced that God was guiding my actions. I did not ask the girl her caste because caste, purity, pollution were ideas that I had shed in the cool climes of Mahabaleshwar.

'What is your name, my child?'

'My name is Nakoshi.'

'Your name says you're unwanted, but for me you're "haveshi". I want you. So let me name you Haushi.' By the time I had named her, Mr Tilak and Dattu had returned. My new daughter and I were chatting. The father and son assumed she was a wayfarer. But when Mr Tilak realized the girl was wearing my sari, he said, 'Who is this?'

'A girl,' I said.

'I can see that. But whose daughter is she?'

'Ours.'

'Ours? What's this all about?'

'She has no family. The famine has driven her to begging. At night, she finds shelter under the eaves of some hut. She has agreed to come with us. So I'm taking her along.'

'Oh? All right then.'

Of course, I had known all along that he would never object to such a thing. We might not agree on most things, but when it came to helping others, we were both of one mind.

When we left Pipurde, we loaded our luggage into the cart and climbed into the tonga. The girl refused to get in. She ran behind it, making us feel very bad. We asked the driver to slow down. I threw her a pair of slippers. She would not wear them. So she ran barefoot behind the tonga all the way to the station three miles away. The moment we entered the station we heard the clang of the bell announcing the arrival of our train. Mr Tilak hurried to buy our tickets and found that the girl was talking to an old man at the station. He said to us, 'If you're taking my daughter, you will have to pay me.'

Mr Tilak said, 'I don't deal in human beings. You're welcome to take your daughter back.'

He said, 'I can't take her back. She has eaten your food. She has worn your clothes. How can I accept her back?'

Mr Tilak said, 'If you can't, just too bad. We are going.'

Just then the train pulled in. We boarded it. Haushi left her father and boarded it with us. When the train started, I said to her, 'Why did you lie to me?'

'I told my friend to ask my father to come and meet me. I didn't tell him to ask for money. He shouldn't have done that. I have a stepmother. She has young children of her own. Prices have risen in our village. I have a hard life. That's why I lied.'

'It's all right. But remember, you have starved because of the famine. So don't eat too much all of a sudden. Go slow.' The girl was very good. She remembered what I had said and did accordingly.

My thoughts ran in keeping with the train. I had impulsively taken this girl on but how would she behave around the house? Would she spill food, spit in the house? How was I to know what her habits were? At one point, I thought we should send her to a boarding school. I even wondered whether we should leave her behind at Pune station. But would that not be a betrayal of her trust? She had come with me as mine, putting her faith in me. She called me Bai as my son did. How could I let her down? At last I made up my mind. I would not part with her on any account.

We were to stop over in Pune as planned for two days. We were staying with a Christian couple. The day went smoothly, but at night they said to me, 'We can't let the girl sleep indoors.' Mr Tilak was not around then and I did not tell him. If he had heard of this discrimination, who knows what he would have said to our hosts in anger. So, keeping the whole thing to myself, I gave her two saris to lie on and sent her out to sleep.

I lay down on my bed but could not sleep. I was thinking that if Dattu had been treated this way, would I have stayed in this house even for a sip of water? How could I have sent this girl, whom I had brought along as my own, to sleep outside? Why did I bring another's child with me if I could not look after her? But the house was not mine. I had no say here. So why think such thoughts? And yet these people were Christians. Why should they discriminate against the girl?

Haushi was sleeping just outside the room where I was sleeping. I would keep getting up to look at her from the window. She seemed totally untroubled. She was sleeping soundly. But for me the night seemed interminable. It would not pass and day would not break. I decided to take both children and go to Ahmednagar the very next day. Mr Tilak would not object. Of course, I was not going to tell him about the night.

In the morning while we were having tea, I said to Mr Tilak, 'I think I'll go ahead to Ahmednagar today with the children. You can come later.' Mr Tilak agreed. We had enough money for the train fare, plus one rupee. The money that Mr Tilak had earned in Mahabaleshwar had been left behind with the cobbler and the cloth merchant. I gave Mr Tilak's fare to him and took our fare and the rupee with me and got into the Ahmednagar-bound train. Haushi had no bangles to wear. She got after me to buy her some. So I sent her off to the bazaar with a maid and the rupee I had brought with me. Haushi returned with a wrist covered in bangles and happily showed them to me.

'Haushi, why did you buy such cheap bangles?' I asked.

'Don't we need some money for our expenses?'

I was full of appreciation for this girl. But she had folded the remaining money into the sari and it had dropped somewhere along the way. She turned the folds of the sari this way and that and when she realized she had lost the money she sobbed her heart out. I had no regrets about the loss. I did regret though that she had not spent the money on better quality bangles. As for the lost money, I knew that Mr Tilak would take an advance from the bank as soon as he returned. This bank was in Dr Hume's bungalow. That is where Mr Tilak used to get his advances from. So when he returned, he came home with fifteen rupees from this bank.

Mr Tilak always went to the same barber, dhobi and tailor. He never changed shops either. He was convinced that nobody cheated him. When we returned, the cloth-shop owner reminded him of the yards of cloth he had taken on credit. The shopkeeper broached the subject with him gently and told him the amount he was owed. Mr Tilak assured him that he would send the amount immediately. Back home, he asked me if I had bought anything for Haushi on credit from the cloth shop. I had not bought anything on credit. We suspected the servant who had not shown his face to us since we returned. He was pretending to be ill. Mr Tilak went to his house. He was full of remorse. He fell at Mr Tilak's feet and begged his forgiveness. That was good enough for Mr Tilak. He returned home and consoled me. 'I have threatened him that if he does such a thing again, I will send him to prison. Let me not hear of any such thing again. Remember, you'll have to face me.'

'Was I not telling you not to trust these people so completely? Why didn't you hand him over to the police?'

'Poverty drove him to fall for this temptation. But I've put fear into him now. What would we have gained by handing him over to the police? It would have been a waste of money and time. Anyway, our money would have got spent in other ways. Why put him into trouble? Besides, he has already sold the stuff and eaten it. I have warned him.'

That he had warned him continued to be Mr Tilak's refrain. But of course, this was pretence. What had actually happened was that the man had wept and Mr Tilak had melted.

Then there was our Balutai, our dhobin. She had taken the first lot of our clothes after we came back from Mahabaleshwar. All the new clothes we had got there were in this lot. A few days later, she came crying and beating her breast. She was carrying one shirt. 'Saheb, I've lost everything. My pots and pans, my money, my gold and all your clothes with them.' We felt very sad. Balutai said to Mr Tilak, 'Please make a complaint for me.'

He said, 'You'll never find the stuff. It's gone forever.'

She said, 'I will compensate your loss.'

She earned a rupee per month. How was she going to pay back out of that?

Mr Tilak said, 'Balutai even if you worked for free for the rest of your life, you wouldn't be able to make up for our loss. Don't worry. You've also lost your things with mine. From next month, I'll pay you two rupees instead of one. Go now. Don't cry.' Thus Balutai earned two rupees a month till her next pay hike.

Kulkarni

So far, I have not said as much as I should have about Jalalpur. They say that people in cities have a broader outlook on life. I have a different opinion. When I wrote about my experience of that couple in Pune with regard to Haushi, I remembered an incident that had happened in connection with Mr Kulkarni of Jalalpur. I should have written about the incident in the previous part, but I think it will sit well beside the picture I have drawn of the incident in Pune. That is why I will write about it here.

Life in a village is great fun. The entire community is like one family. Every individual in a village feels concern for and curiosity about every other individual. Since there is much empathy amongst people, caste consciousness is not so glaringly visible. The lower castes do not feel insulted because of upper-caste observances of purity and pollution. Similarly, the upper castes are not contemptuous of the lower castes. Caste does not become the cause for friction in the village family. On the contrary, people become one another's friends and counsellors on all occasions, whether it is financial difficulties, illness or life's joys and sorrows. That, at least, has been my experience. Perhaps the situation has changed now. I am writing about how it was thirty-odd years ago. Today trains and cars have turned villages into the backyards and front porches of cities.

The month of Jyeshtha dawned. A woman came with the news that the Kulkarnis' house had been burgled and Uma Kaku was sobbing uncontrollably. The woman did not tell us when this had happened and what had been stolen. When I heard about it, I asked my sisters-in-law if I could go over. I found Kaku crying her eyes out.

'What's the matter, Kaku?' I asked.

'What can I say? Your cousin's gone to Nashik. He's making plans for Baba's wedding. And here we've lost valuables worth six or seven lakhs. There isn't enough gold left even for the thinnest mangalsutra.'

The Kulkarnis were a large family of ten. Two sons were married. One was still young.

'When did this happen? Who's getting married? I don't understand what you're saying, Kaku.'

Kaku grabbed my hand and led me upstairs to show me from where the stuff had been stolen. I had been up there hundreds of times, but had never suspected that this was where they kept their treasure. There was a cupboard set into one wall. It was very small to look at, but inside there was space enough for a man to stand doubled up. Who would have thought the contents of this cupboard were special? As children we used to play in this room. We could stand in the cupboard. Above our heads was a roof of planks. There were crescent-moon-shaped holes in the planks. You could push your fingers through one and shift the planks to climb up and slide around on your stomach. Kaku sent me into the cupboard. 'Now move that plank to one side,' she said. 'Now hoist yourself up, lie on your stomach and creep forward. See if you find anything.'

I did what she said and became breathless with the effort. There was a bit of light inside. There was an urn there with a couple of silver vessels in it.

I said, 'There's nothing here. Just a couple of silver vessels.'

Those were days of famine. Many burglaries were taking place. It was impossible that an outsider had burgled this house. Fearing theft, every single ornament worn by the women, down to the gold-wire rings in babies' ears, had been stuffed into that urn. Even the women's nose-rings had been trusted to it. I was convinced that my eldest cousin, Dada, had stolen the ornaments to prevent his younger brothers from getting their share, and run off to Nashik to avoid being discovered. His excuse for going to Nashik was to fix his middle brother's marriage. But Baba was already married.

The following day, Dada and Geeta Vahini came to our house to invite us formally to the wedding. They pressed me repeatedly to go for the wedding. 'You sit here crying all day.

If you come to Tryambak, it will take your mind off your problems.'

I hesitated but finally Dattu and I set off for the wedding. It was a seven-kilometre long journey. The wedding guests were travelling by bullock-carts. Some of the carts were covered with cane mats while others were uncovered. It rained on the way. The cart carrying rations got soaked. The flour turned into dough and the sugar melted into syrup. Yet Dada stood firm. Although thieves had cleaned out everything indoors and the rain poured down outdoors, his spirit neither melted nor wilted.

We were about twenty-five guests in all. Although I had agreed to attend the wedding, I did not feel comfortable being there. I was against the wedding. I saw no flaw in Baba's first wife, whether it was her looks, her nature or her work. She was so modest that she always moved around with lowered head. I was maushi to her and tai to her husband. So I had a double relationship with the couple. Although we were Konkanastha Brahmins and the Kulkarnis were Deshasthas, we still felt very close to them. I did not approve of a co-wife for such a good-hearted girl.

Dada girded up his loins and saw the wedding through in two days. He borrowed ornaments from his family guests and adorned the new bride with them. There was consternation amongst the bride's people. Forget armbands and bracelets, could they not have given her at least a nose-ring from the family collection? Dada got to hear of this but he remained as calm as ever. This strengthened my suspicion. I said, 'Dada, I don't think the house has been burgled.'

He said, 'Lord Rama knows and Ganga knows what has happened.'

I said, 'Why call on Rama? I think Dada and Geeta know what happened.'

To this he only said, 'And suppose we do?'

On Monday, the wedding guests began to arrive for lunch. Vishwanath Bhat and his daughter Sundari came and then wished to go to Tryambakeshwar to see the Lord's palanquin procession. Sundari said to me, 'Tai, even if you can't come, can I take Dattu along?'

I said, 'Yes, but do take care of him.' They left and the guests sat down to lunch. They had hardly finished eating the first course of rice when everybody got up, washed their hands and left. Suddenly, there were only four women left in the house. Uma Kaku was in the kitchen. Bhima Kaku was in the store room. Geeta and I were upstairs. The house was in a mess but not a soul seemed concerned about it. I felt very uneasy. I said, 'Vahini, how could they have finished lunch so fast?'

She said, 'The guests must have got fed up of eating sweets every day.'

A little while later, somebody shouted out my name 'Lakshmibai Tilak' from down below. Nobody calls me by my full name. My heart began to pound. My hair stood on end. I was sure Mr Tilak had sent a warrant for my arrest. The same call came again. Now my heart jumped into my mouth. I saw a constable downstairs. He asked me to come down. Geeta Vahini followed me. The constable said, 'Where is your son?'

I said, 'What's it to you? Isn't it enough that I'm here?'

'That's not what I meant. Has he lost his way somewhere?'

When she heard that, Geeta Vahini stepped forward and said, 'He has. Where is he?'

'Was he wearing any gold?'

'No, he wasn't. Where is he?'

The constable had asked Dattu to stand outside. He brought him in now and my heart returned to its place. Dattu had got lost in Kushavarta. His hand had slipped out of Sundari's. After that he kept trying to hold the hand of any woman he saw in a red sari. But those women would not hold his. Walking through the crowd, he soon found himself at Nashik police chowki. He said to the constable, 'Take me to my uncle's house. They have made a lot of laddoos there. They will give you a whole basketful.' When he was asked whose son he was, he said

Nana's and Lakshmibai Tilak's. There were only two weddings happening in the town that day. One was of Jalalpur people and the other of local Nashik people. It did not take the constable long to track me down.

It dawned on me now that Dattu had been the cause of everybody leaving their lunch halfway through and running out. Long ago, the only son of a rich man had disappeared in the same way. The following day, they thought he had jumped off the fort because he lay dead down below. When Dattu returned, all the guests poured back into the wedding home. Sundari's heart had contracted to nothing. Uncle and Dada had rushed out in their puja dhotis. They had returned in despair. When they heard Dattu had been found, Dada hurried indoors and filled a basket with three paylies* of laddoos and offered it to the constable along with five rupees. He said, 'Baba, you have erased the shame from my face today and returned my cousin's wealth to her.' Our Dada, who had not lost heart when the house was burgled or when the rations got soaked, was scared out of his wits when Dattu could not be found. Today I recall poet Govindagraj's line, 'Blest are those who have the generosity of a Deshastha's heart.' My experience confirms that Deshasthas are more affectionate and generous than Konkanasthas. The constable did not touch a grain of the laddoos nor a paisa of the money he was offered. He was very happy to hear that Dattu was Govindrao Mama's grand-nephew. The constable and his family were invited to lunch the following day.

We left Nashik to return to Jalalpur. Baba's first wife was at the river. She called out to me and asked, 'So Maushi, you're taking your new niece home?' It hurt me very much to hear her say that. I did not say anything, but came home wondering about her destiny. As soon as the ceremony of crossing the threshold of the Jalalpur house was over, the new bride went to her parents' house and the old one was brought back home.

*A payli, according to the old Indian system of weights, was equal to four seers and 1/16th of a maund. But this varied from region to region.

Now a thorough inquiry began into the burglary. She was asked, 'Why had you come back here while we were away at the Nagnarayan sacrifice?'

'Manu maushi asked me to come.'

I had indeed asked her to come. I had composed a sad song about the turn of events in her life. I had wanted to teach it to her. When he heard of this, her husband came to call me. His lips were trembling and his eyes were shot with rage. He said, 'Tai, Dada has asked you to come over.'

'Why is that?'

'You'll know when you come.'

I knew that they were making inquiries about the burglary. It was Friday, my fast day. My brothers were not at home. My sisters-in-law did not think I should go. They said, 'Be careful, Bai. You might get blamed.'

I said, 'For what? God stands by the truthful.'

When I arrived, Dada and Uma Kaku were on the front verandah. 'Why did you send for me, Kaku?' I asked. She said, 'Listen to what your niece is saying.'

I went indoors and hugged her to my chest. Weeping, I said, 'Look at the state you are in. You are the same to me as Gharu. You don't have a mother. How will you survive?' Our sorrows became one, our tears flowed as a single stream. She was feeling bad for me. She threw her arms round my neck and said, 'I wish I hadn't named you.'

'Is it true that you have all the stuff? Did you take it? Give it back then.'

'It's not here. It's in Gangapur.'

I said to Uma Kaku, 'It's all there. Let me go home now.'

'Not yet,' she said. 'First get it all back, please.'

We left Jalalpur for Gangapur. The water in the river was up to our knees. I felt the current pulling us. It struck me that I would be very happy to be drawn right down into the river's womb. But then I thought of Dattu. What would he do without me? We reached her father's place in Gangapur. She brought out the two tins of valuables. A voice came from a dark inner room, 'Why did you confess, you idiot?'

'Because Maushi was being harassed on my account.'

Just as the two of us were leaving, Dada came. I said, 'It's all there.'

'Did you open the tins to see?'

'No.'

'You're such a fool. What if they are full of stones?'

We opened the tins. All the ornaments were there, but some were crushed and some broken. We reached home with the tins around eight in the evening. Kaku was overjoyed. She said to me, 'Manu, you are truly Lakshmi. You have brought back my lost Lakshmi. Geeta, honour her with an oti* before we let her go.'

*A ritual in which a married woman extends the loose end of her sari to receive fertility symbols like rice and coconut.

A Memorable Incident

After our return from Mahabaleshwar, we went to Rahuri for a few days at Dr Ballantyne's invitation. We were put up in a small house. Our food would come from Dr Ballantyne's kitchen. Back home, meetings were held every day morning and evening, for Bible-reading and hymn-singing. Mr Tilak would sing his own compositions, filled with love. Everybody from the neighbourhood would attend. They would all read verses of their choice from the Bible. This routine did not change in Rahuri. Although Dattu and I were Hindus, we would always be present at the prayer meetings. I began to like this form of prayer. It was a new and joyous experience for me that we could talk to the God who was in our hearts. Over time, I had also become well acquainted with the Bible.

It was a Saturday. People had gathered for the usual prayer meeting. They were taking turns to say something to or about God. When it was Dattu's turn, he said, 'God is love.'

When it was my turn, I said, 'Dear Lord, have pity on me.'

Mr Tilak said, 'God will never have pity on you.'

'Why not?'

'If you are bound to me and yet keep your distance from me, how do you think I would feel about it? It is the same with Christ. If you have faith in Him but still hold aloof, what would God think of your betrayal? How can he have pity on you?'

I got up at the end of prayers and went out. I did not tell anybody where I was going. I went straight to Dr Ballantyne's house and knocked. He opened the door and was astonished to see me.

'Why have you come alone, Lakshmibai?'

'Sir, I want to be baptized tomorrow.'

'Dear lady, you have no knowledge of the scriptures. You will have to study Christianity for at least five or six months.'

'I am fully acquainted with the religion. I want to be baptized tomorrow.'

'But why the hurry?'

'If you don't want to baptize me, say so.'

'But you'll have to answer questions before the baptism.'

'I don't know about all that. Just tell me if you are willing to baptize me or not. Else I'll leave.'

'Please go now. I cannot give you an answer today.'

'Sir, it is Sunday tomorrow. I want you to baptize Dattu, Haushi and me tomorrow. Even if I don't pass the test, isn't it enough that I have faith in Christ? I am not lying about it.' Then Dr Ballantyne and I prayed and it was decided that we would be baptized the next day. That day he told me a story. I do not remember every detail of it, but the essence of it was this: There was once a man. A guest came to his house one night. The man had no food in the house to serve the guest. So he borrowed food from his neighbour and served it to him. I had not understood then what the story meant. Later I forgot it. But now, as I write this, I realize what the story was saying.

I came back home happy that I was going to be baptized the very next day. Dr Ballantyne sent a man with a lantern to light my way home. When Mr Tilak asked me where I had been, he was overjoyed to hear the story from my lips. I had to pass the test before I was baptized. A pastor from another place, Rev. Annaji Kshirsagar had come to Rahuri. He was a kindly man and old enough to be my father. He sat beside me, softly prompting me with the answers to the examiner's questions, and I answered accordingly.

I refused to be baptized by a foreign missionary. I insisted on being baptized by the pastor of the Congregation, Rev. Vaniramji Bapuji Ohol. My wish was granted and thus Dattu, Haushi and I were baptized in the church at Rahuri. I was admitted to the Congregation that very day and could receive Holy Communion. We returned to Ahmednagar on Monday. People there were very happy to hear that we had been baptized. There was only some disappointment that it had happened in Rahuri and not in Ahmednagar.

Another memorable event that happened in the same year was my public speech. Every year during Diwali, a huge meeting known as the Unity Gathering used to be held in Ahmednagar. Christians from Satara, Solapur and other districts would come, which made the gathering look like a pilgrim fair. Nearly one-and-a-half thousand men and women from Ahmednagar alone would turn up. Add to that about five hundred or so from other places and you had a gathering of two thousand people. The old church in Ahmednagar would be packed to bursting.

That year, people crowded every open space, including doors and windows. They were curious to hear Mr Tilak's wife speak. Mr Tilak had a great desire to see his wife become a well-known personality, to see her establish herself as a writer, poet and public speaker. He would always pray for this. Initially, he was greatly disappointed in me, but began to feel hopeful later. However, this was the first time I had been called upon to speak. Someone who had never lit a lamp was off to light a furnace! Before this I had not only never spoken publicly but had not even heard a public speech. I had once attended an elocution competition in Rajnandgaon. But that was as a cook and 'waiter'.

Mr Tilak wrote my speech for me and got me to memorize it. He rehearsed it with me several times. We went to a wood where I orated it in a public speaking voice. Our preparation was long and arduous. Each speaker had been allotted ten minutes. There were three or four speakers before me. As soon as my name was called, I took my place at the lectern in great style. A sea of people swam before my eyes. Dr Hume and Mr Tilak were in the front row. I was dressed in my usual clothes—a nine-yard sari that was pulled up tight between the legs, a large kumkum, nose-ring and ear ornaments. Christian women dress in a distinctly different way. I presented a most uncommon sight for them. The general curiosity was sharpened because I had become a Christian only recently.

So there I was, standing in style at the lectern. However, of the ten minutes assigned to me, my mouth remained resolutely shut for nine. I stood like a log of wood and the audience sat before me like a painting. Many prayed that I should manage to utter at least a few words. Somebody brought me a glass of water. Someone else brought me a clove. But my throat was not dry. What use was either of them to me? Some people thought, 'the lady has papers in her hand; if only God would give her the wisdom to read from them.' I had a handkerchief in one hand but that too refused to move to my face. I was not used to carrying a handkerchief. And the idea of reading from my papers did not strike me. There were other speakers lined up after me, so Dr Hume got up to thank me. At that moment, my obstructed faculty of speech returned. I spoke then with such clarity and fluency that the audience sat stunned. I was sure I had forgotten something from the prepared speech. So I showed great presence of mind and spoke extempore as ideas occurred to me. I ended my speech saying, 'Mr Tilak will now speak of the things I've left out.' Standing at the lectern, Mr Tilak confessed, 'She has left nothing for me to say.'

Back home I scolded him roundly for what he had put me through. He said, 'You can't swim unless you take the plunge.'

I said, 'If you ever want me to speak anywhere again, I will not make a memorized speech. I will say what I want to say. Other people's words create confusion in my mind.' Since then I have made many speeches in many meetings but I have never written and memorized them. If I am to credit anybody with giving me confidence, it is the Christian community. That day I could speak after nine minutes of silence entirely because they had sat quietly through my silence. This community observes a disciplined and sympathetic silence during such meetings.

When I became a Christian, or rather when I began to incline towards becoming a Christian, I had brought a Mahar girl home as my own daughter. Later in Ahmednagar, Mr Tilak adopted a Mahar boy called Bhikya. He had gone once to a village and found the eighteen-month-old boy lying under a tree, weak with hunger. Mr Tilak tried very hard for two days to track down his relatives but nobody came forward. He asked the police chief to arrange for the child's care. He too turned a deaf ear. He stayed with the child for two more days to make inquiries about his kith and kin in neighbouring villages. But when he found nobody, he brought him home. At home the child was greatly pampered. Mr Tilak would teach him Sanskrit every day, saying he would make the child a shastri, scholar. That is why we began to call Bhikya, Shastribuwa.

You Have Surpassed Me

Then God gave me another gift. For ten years after Dattu, no child had prattled in the house. My brothers' children were a great solace while I was staying there. But that was not like having a child of my own. But now we had a girl. We called her Tara. We both adored Tara, but we had a difficult time pulling her through. She was only five or six days old when some problem started up in her stomach and it looked as though she would soon leave us. But she pulled through. By then it was time for us to go to Mahabaleshwar. But Mr Tilak decided to give that year's visit a miss. Tara was three weeks old. She would not have survived the cold in Mahabaleshwar nor the heat of the Ahmednagar summer. So we decided to go to Wai.

The trains from Pune to Vathar were overcrowded during this season. We were travelling second class. Dr Hume, who was going to Mahabaleshwar, was on the same train. He would get off at every station to come to our compartment to inquire after us. He had reserved the entire compartment for us because we were six—Dattu, Haushi, Mr Tilak, Baby Tara, the eighteen-month-old Bhikya and I. And a whole lot of luggage.

While the rest of us sat in one place, Mr Tilak kept moving from seat to seat and from one sleeping berth to the other. I said to him, 'For heaven's sake, why don't you settle down?' He thought I was being very old-fashioned. In my opinion, once you were on a train, you kept to your seat, and before that, you got to the station four hours in advance to avoid missing the train, and that telegrams were not to be sent unless somebody was on his deathbed. In keeping with these principles, I felt Mr Tilak should sit in one place and not move. But he would not listen to me.

And so it came about that, as he leapt from one top berth to the other, his gleaming pate encountered the gleaming glass cover of the light and both came to calamitous grief. A stream of blood began to flow from Mr Tilak's head and tiny pieces of glass from the broken light scattered over the faces of the children sleeping below. While I worried that the children might suddenly open their eyes and glass pieces would go in, Mr Tilak stood stock still as though nothing out of the ordinary had happened while the blood from his head bathed him. Later he went to the washroom and held his head under a stream of cold water. That staunched the flow, but the gash was quite deep. I got busy picking the tiny glass pieces off the children's faces as gently as I could. Then, using a sari, I wiped the floor clean of blood.

'How are you feeling?' I asked.

'There's nothing the matter with me.'

'And what's that on your head?'

'These things happen and they should. That's the fun of life.'

'Now we'll be fined for breaking the light.'

'If we are, we'll pay up. Nothing can stop us from being fined and no amount of worry will close this wound.'

When Dr Hume looked in at the next station he got very worried. Mr Tilak assured him, 'I'm not hurt. I'm as fit as a fiddle. Minor things like this happen all the time.' Mr Tilak's body was as strong as his mind.

When we arrived at Wai, we found that Ashammabai and the local pastor Hariba Gaekwad had organized everything necessary for our stay. Here, too, Mr Tilak was constantly preoccupied with lectures, meetings, debates and his writing. One day, a woman came to our door, wearing a lovely sari and decked out in a jangle of traditional jewellery. I had spent a year now in the Christian community and had got accustomed to their ways and manners. When I saw the woman at the door, I offered her a chair and extended my hand to shake hers. But the woman would not take my hand or come into the house. She stood outside and only asked, 'Where is saheb?'

'He's gone out,' I said.

'He has asked me to do your housework.'

'But there's no work to be done.' Looking at her, I could not see her doing household chores. What would she do? We had brought along two people from Ahmednagar as house helps. The woman went away. I told myself Mr Tilak must have wanted her help in his writing work.

When Mr Tilak returned in the evening, he said, 'Did the sweeper woman come? I'd asked her to come from tomorrow to wash the children's soiled clothes.' The riddle was solved.

'Was that a sweeper woman?'

'Yes. Why do you ask?'

'Well, she wouldn't take the chair I offered her or my hand. Since she was wearing a nice, clean six-yard sari, I took her to be a Christian. But the ring on her finger was of typically Hindu design. She had me completely confused.'

'Why do you believe that only your people dress cleanly and neatly?'

The woman began work the following day. She swept the yard, washed the children's soiled clothes and did other odd jobs. One day, I said to her, 'Tell me, you look so clean and neat. Do you keep your house in the same condition?'

'Come with me now, just as you are, and see it for yourself. Otherwise you'll say I tidied it up for your visit.' I went with her. I did not bother to ask which community lived in that colony. But I noticed that its streets and homes looked clean. Her house had a wide doorway. I saw that her brass cooking pots, tumblers and plates were scrubbed till they shone. The floor was swept and swabbed, the yard had been sprinkled with water. I was astonished. My belief that cleanliness and tidiness had little to do with caste was now reinforced. We were like the Koyna and Krishna rivers which meet at Wai. I threw my arms around her neck and said, 'Why don't you people eat food cooked by us?'

She said, 'Our community disapproves.'

I said, 'Now that you have seen me and my house, you should have no objections to eating my food.'

She said, 'Would you be prepared to eat mine?'

'Of course. Why not?'

And so the sweeper woman brought out snacks and sweets she had made. Mr Tilak was away in Mahabaleshwar to meet Dr Hume, but the children were with me. I accepted the snacks. The servants were unhappy. I said, 'I won't force you to eat the food if you don't wish to. My children and I will eat it.' The sweeper woman was overjoyed to see me eat what she had cooked. When Mr Tilak returned the next day and heard about this, he said, 'You have surpassed me.'

Our Savings

It was raining one day. Dattu and Haushi were at school. Mr Tilak had gone to teach at the religious-knowledge class. I was alone at home. I was sitting in the open doorway, picking grain. A girl came to the door begging. She was just a skeleton topped by a large head, and no strength in the body. Her eyes were dead. There was only a scrap of cloth on her body, just big enough to cover her shame. She stood at the door with a tin-pot in her hand, under the pouring rain. There were fresh signs of branding on her face.

I asked her to come into the house and began asking her about herself.

'Do you like to beg or live in a house?'

'Beg.'

'Will you stay here with me?'

'Yes.'

'Where's your family?'

'I have nobody. They have all left me. My village is very far away.'

I made up my mind to keep her with me. First, I bathed her and gave her one of Haushi's saris to wear. This alone was enough to alter her appearance. When the children and Mr Tilak came home in the evening, they were full of curiosity about the girl.

'What's this?'

'This is a picture of famine. I've adopted her.'

'Why? We have Haushi and Tara, God's gift to us.'

'And now we have Daya. I felt sorry for her. It was God's mercy that brought her to us.'

'Oh well, all right. Let her stay.' We called her Daya.

Soon after, a number of Christian women from the neighbourhood came to our house. 'Saheb, do you know whose daughter this girl is?'

'No. Whose?'

'She's the daughter of a Mang.'

'And so?'

'Doesn't it bother you?'

'No it doesn't. Mangs, Mahars, Brahmins are all the same to us.'

'But they are not to us. We will not accept this.'

The women left, and for many days after, they boycotted our house. Then Mr Tilak deliberately hired Mahars and Mangs to work in the house. The day after Daya came, an elderly Mang woman descended on us to quarrel with Mr Tilak. From her blabbering, we gathered the following information: Daya had gone begging down her street and reached the old woman's house. The woman had given her shelter in exchange for the money Daya would bring. It was enough to buy both of them food.

'How many days was she with you?'

'Eight days.'

'And you are trying to claim proprietorship over her on the strength of that, are you? And who branded her on her cheeks?'

'I don't know.'

'Don't lie, you hag. These are fresh marks. Admit it. You don't want to be sent to prison, do you?'

Finally, the old woman said, 'The girl wasn't bringing enough money so I put just a bit of firewood to her cheeks.' That sent Mr Tilak into a real rage. Terrified, the old woman ran away. She never showed us her face again. After that we heard other things about her. She would lure strong young girls and sell them. Truly, God showed Daya much mercy in sending her to us.

Both girls were at school now. They were in the same class, the third grade. They were no trouble at all. They did not lie or steal. They treated our home as their real home. They went to school and returned without loitering anywhere or stopping off to chat with people. I had feared that they might litter the place or not clean the leftovers properly. But I need not have feared. They modelled their behaviour on ours. They learned the rules of cleanliness by imitation. They learned how to make salads, pickles, chutneys and papads. Gradually, they even learned to cook.

The famine grew worse as time progressed. The Mission suffered some losses around this time, or at least some calamity befell it which caused them to throw out twenty boarders from the residential school that the Mission supported. There was consternation in the town. The boys had no other support. The raging famine meant they would starve. Mr Tilak was very upset when Mr Sugandhrao Karmarkar gave him the news. He had not known about this before.

He said to me, 'Twenty-two boys have been thrown out of our school. They will starve. What do you think we can do for them?'

That day we had a rupee and a quarter left in the house and a seer and a quarter of millets in the storeroom. But we also had a store of something bigger. Our faith in God. The two of us bowed our heads to the floor and prayed fervently to God. Then we took a pledge, 'We will make no difference between what we feed these children and what we eat. If they eat bhakri made of millets, we will do the same.' We called Dattu and said, 'See, many of your brothers will be forced to forage for food in the forest if we don't take them in. You will have to eat what they eat. Would you be willing to do that?'

Dattu said, 'I will eat what they eat and won't quarrel with them.' Mr Tilak told Mr Karmarkar to bring the boys. From the time they came to the day they left, Dattu kept his word. But meanwhile the problem was where to keep Haushi and Daya. Mr Tilak wrote to Sundarabai Powar in Pune to ask if she would admit them to her school. She wrote back by return of post that she would willingly admit them. We sent both girls off to Pune and the boys came to stay. This was the time that Mr Tilak brought our Shastribuwa home from Khare Karjune village. I have written about that in an earlier chapter.

Our Household Grows

The famine was beginning to look grimmer. There was little food to be had; but worse, it became difficult to find water to drink. A water carrier had been serving Mr Tilak since 1895. He said he was now selling water at one rupee a bag but would continue to sell it to us at the old rate. However, he wanted some leeway in the time when he could bring it. He began bringing it at two in the morning. We had locked the back door from outside and given him the key. Every night without fail, he would bring us two bags brimming with water and store it for us. Most of our water storage pots were of potter's clay. He would not only fill those but every other vessel that he saw, down to our tumblers. We had this comfort entirely on account of the credit system, the convenience of having a water carrier and Mr Tilak's immense generosity to people which ensured that the famine raging outside the door did not enter our house.

We made shirts, coats, pants and caps for the boys with cloth bought on credit. We also ordered a heap of coir from which we made twenty-two mattresses for them. Naturally, these were accompanied by as many dhurries, sheets, blankets and pillows. Each boy had his own dinner plate and tumbler. Bhikya was given a full set of clothes made to measure. Bhikya was a great favourite with everybody. But Mr Tilak used to give him a good beating because he was such a dunce. Mr Tilak wanted him to become a Shastribuwa and here he was unable to say even 'Ramah Ramau'. So every day he would receive his goodies even before he washed up. The first act of this drama was the Sanskrit lesson. The next was Bhikya's sad song. The third was Mr Tilak's rage. And the last act brought all of us together to console both. This became our daily entertainment.

Mr Tilak put some of the twenty-two boys in school. Some others he apprenticed to a printing press and the remaining were sent to other places to pick up various trades. With their altered circumstances, the boys began to look better and happier. They were well-behaved and honest. Dattu was like one of them. We had engaged two women to help me with the housework. But, despite my working alongside them, we could not cope with all of it. Grinding grain was the most onerous job. If we gave the grain out to be ground, it would cost us. So I called a meeting with the boys and placed the problem before them. 'If I engage another woman to grind, we'll have to send one of you away. We can't cope with the grinding by ourselves. We require three measures of flour every day. So if we decide not to engage a third woman, the younger boys will have to grind one measure and the older boys two measures.'

The boys agreed to help. That's how we saved money. If a boy fell ill, I would wash his clothes. If we engaged a sweeper woman for the job, once again it would cost us. Instead, my doing the work meant money to buy vegetables.

While the household was running smoothly and happily in this fashion, an unexpected problem raised its head. Dr Hume was unhappy with the way we, particularly I, were spending money. He thought I was throwing it away. Just as, in the old days, I used to constantly worry about Mr Tilak's extravagance, Dr Hume now worried about our extravagance. He disapproved thoroughly of our taking in the boys.

He was right. On the first of the month, we would have already used up even the following month's salary. He felt this kind of charity was excessive. It was like inviting trouble upon ourselves. This concern was a natural result of his genuine love for Mr Tilak. That is why, when he interfered in our private life, we did not harbour any ill-feelings towards him.

Now he started saying things like, 'Send the boys away. Your salary doesn't even cover your own expenses.'

To this our answer was, 'We can't let them go. We will look after them until some other arrangements are made for them.'

'If you're so keen on being called Aai-Papa, I'll tell the children in all the schools in Ahmednagar to call you that.'

This upset us badly. But we were firm. 'God has given us children who call us Aai-Papa. We aren't taking all this trouble for such a ridiculous reason. We are doing it because of the state the boys are in. Unless arrangements are made for their care, we will not abandon them.'

Dr Hume always prefixed everything he said to Mr Tilak with bhau, brother.

'But bhau, this is completely beyond your means.'

'The money we earn isn't meant only to pamper ourselves. God has planned that many should have a share in it.'

'But bhau, it will get you into difficulties.'

I said, 'How can you say that, saheb? The boys' condition will then be like the proverb—mother won't feed you and father won't let you beg.'

'Dear bahini, I do not understand what you mean.'

'It means you aren't willing to arrange for their care nor will you let us care for them. That's not fair.'

'Bhau, I'll go now. But think about it seriously. I will do the same.' Dr Hume left.

We thought things over very seriously. Mr Tilak said, 'These missionaries have made our people weak. It's as if they alone have the monopoly over helping them. Somebody needs help? Point him to a missionary's bungalow. That's the extent of the charity our Christian people show. It's become a habit with them. Come what may, we will not abandon the boys.'

As things turned out, we looked after the boys for eleven months. I had become obsessed with looking after children. In the midst of caring for the boys, I brought in two other children, a two-month-old boy and a fifteen-day-old girl. Tara, whom we called Baby, was herself still an infant. My hands would be occupied permanently with either the babies' cradle strings or their feeding bottles.

Then one day, Dr Hume came and stood before me holding out his cap. 'Please give me alms. Give me the boys.'

'I won't.'

This became a daily farce. When I heard the scrambled words of one of Mr Tilak's hymns sung at the gate, I would know Dr Hume had arrived. He always came singing, 'He need have no fear who has God beside him.'

One day, he looked really fed up. He said, 'See bhau, you've adopted these boys, your finances are under strain, you two will fight over that and you'll bring the fights to my door.'

I said, 'Saheb, we did not get married in your bungalow. So if we do fight, we won't trouble you with making peace between us.'

'Bahini, what can I do for you then?'

'Pray for us.'

One day, we received a letter from Dr Hume. He wrote to say, 'I have made arrangements for all your boys in my hostel. They will not return to their dormitory to be thrown out on the streets again. And I will never throw them out either.'

We felt very sad to read the letter but also happy. Sad because the boys were going to leave us, and happy because they were going to be cared for well. That night I made sweet saffron rice for them. We sat talking till after midnight. As we talked, tears streamed from our eyes. At last Mr Tilak prayed and we retired to bed. Our large family was going to be broken up the following day. We had all grown very fond of each other.

We had run up a debt during the time the boys were with us. Mr Tilak calculated the extent of it the day the boys were leaving. He said to them, 'Boys, I had thought we owed a large sum of money to our creditors. But by God's grace I find it is not so. The debt is only five hundred rupees. We did what we did without any ulterior motive. So I'm certain God will help us pay off this debt.'

And so indeed He did. The very next day some American gentleman sent Mr Tilak a cheque for five hundred rupees. Even before the boys stepped out of the house, the grocer and cloth merchant had been paid off. The boys left. We were free of debt.

We now had three babies and Bhikya with us. Of the two adopted children, the father of one turned up to take him away.

The third baby was very weak. However hard we tried, she did not put on weight. One night, she went to sleep never to wake up. I was grief-stricken. I made up my mind never to adopt a baby that had not been weaned.

Three years later, Shastribuwa's father tracked him down to our place. Bhikya did not recognize him, which saddened him immensely. He stayed with us for four days trying to win the child over. Nothing worked. Finally he said, 'Can I take him away for a few days?' Mr Tilak gave him permission to do that. The father brought the child back in four days as promised. But meanwhile, he had pampered the boy silly. Bhikya started asking for jalebis every day. Mr Tilak had warned the father not to indulge him beyond limits. Within eight days of his return, we had had enough of this new Bhikya. We did the only thing we could. We engaged a man, handed over all Bhikya's belongings to him, gave him two rupees and packed him off to his father's.

We Meet Again

When we were going to Rahuri for my baptism, a servant had come running after our cart all the way to the station. After Mr Tilak had bought the tickets and helped us into the train, we saw him talking to somebody on the platform. Meanwhile, this man came to our compartment and said, 'My employer says you must pay up her two hundred rupees before you move.'

I died with shame. If I had had the money, I would have given it instantly. But we were back to our usual state. Owners of nothing. I looked at Mr Tilak. He only smiled. The train moved. The servant naturally jumped off. The train was hardly going to put on the brakes just for him.

After my baptism, we were returning from Rahuri to Ahmednagar. Mr Tilak was working then in the seminary for religious knowledge. His students were like us, family people. Twenty or twenty-five students would come with their families and enrol every four or five years. When they had completed the course and were ready to go back to their homes, we would usually invite them and their families for tea and snacks.

This happened after we returned from Rahuri. We invited the students to tea. I fried a whole pile of shev for them. I was suddenly ravenous. There was a heap of work to do. I got up from the stove and stuffed some food into my stomach and gulped down water. Soon after that, my body turned red. My head felt numb. I could not think straight. My women helpers were just as smart as me. They said, Bai, you have a cold. But I could not lift a finger to work. My sister Shahbai Misal and her daughter Tarabai took over. I was running a high fever. The doctor came and said this was measles. I was given a separate room where I was quarantined.

After my mother died, it was my sister Bhikutai who had taken her place in my heart. She was very loving, but also proud.

Although we lived in the same town, we had not met. The last time I had seen her was during Dattu's thread ceremony. The last words I had heard from her when we came to Ahmednagar were, 'Give her a saddle to sleep on.' She took ill after we arrived and when she heard of our baptism she took to her bed.

It was difficult for her to reconcile her pride with her love. The intense conflict that these two emotions were engaged in within her heart had brought on her illness. Nanasaheb also loved me like a daughter. But he too had abjured us because of his wife. However, when news reached them that I had come down with measles, Nanasaheb could not stay away. He came to see me without letting anybody know. When we saw each other, we shed tears of happiness mixed with sorrow. He spent a long time with me. I said to him, 'Please arrange for me to meet my sister.'

'That's simply not possible, Maushi. She's not only upset over you. She's also worried about Gharumai.' Never before, as far as I could remember, had my sister had serious problems in life. But now two daggers had been plunged into her back. One was me. The other was Gharumai. Gharumai's husband had brought home a second wife. All his money was going to liquor distillers. He lost his job. Gharumai was in dire straits. It came to a point where Nanasaheb had to send her a fixed sum every month for their survival. But that did not ensure her happiness.

Caught in the terrible vortex of this situation, my sister became completely disoriented. Nanasaheb had shifted to a bungalow near the station because he thought a change would do her some good. When we were going to Rahuri, our tonga had passed the house. When she saw it, she had instantly sent her servant running after us to demand two hundred rupees.

Nanasaheb went home. One day after I had recovered from measles, he sent a tonga to fetch me. Gharumai was waiting for me. Our meeting brought forth floods of tears and smiles. That was the kind of love we shared. Although she was my niece and I her aunt, the stronger bond between us was of close friends.

Now, in her present state of grief she desperately needed a close friend. She had nobody else but me in whom she could confide all that she had suffered. But on that day we could do nothing else but smile and weep. After we spent a long time in this fashion, she went to my sister's room and told her I had come. Instantly Bhikutai turned her face to the wall. No amount of Gharumai's pleading would make her open up to me.

Gharumai took me to a room next to where Bhikutai was lying. I peeped in at her. What I saw was what Nanasaheb had described. He had warned me that I would hasten her death if I went to meet her. His words rang in my ears as I tiptoed to her room and bent over her to look at her face. Gharumai said once again, 'Maushi is here.' Bhikutai did not turn her face from the wall. All she said as I left was, 'Put something into that low-caste woman's hands.'

It was Diwali time and even before her mother gave her the order, Gharumai had already put aside a basketful of fireworks and lots of sweets and savouries for me to take home. There is no shame when love reigns in two hearts. The woman who had sent her servant after me for money had now ordered something to be given to this low-caste woman.

Now every festival saw sweets and savouries coming to us from there. I went over to Bhikutai's practically every day. Dattu would often go with me and so, occasionally, would Haushi. One day Dattu was alone in Bhikutai's room. That was when her true feelings surfaced, pushing aside all her attempts to show us that her love for us was dead.

Seeing Dattu alone she said, 'Come to me, my pet.'

He went to her. 'Nearer,' she said. Then, lifting the cover off her body, she said, 'Come close. Lie down next to me.'

'But Maushi, my touch will pollute you.'

'If it does, so be it. No matter.' So saying she drew him close to her. I was watching her unseen from another room. She was sobbing her heart out and so was I.

'Dattu, you and Haushi must come to see me every day. It's all right if your mother doesn't come.' He assured her they would and after that the two went to see her every day. Later she reconciled herself to seeing me too. Then came a time when, if she did not see me some day, she would become restless. She would keep looking out of the window from where she lay, wondering when Manu would come. I often stayed overnight at her place. Mr Tilak would also drop in to see her every day. The woman who had once told her servants to lay out a saddle for me to sleep on, would now scold them if they gave me a plain rug. 'What's that?' she would ask. 'Is she some roadside thief? Give her a good mattress to sleep on.'

If somebody said something critical about me, she would feel sad and tell them off roundly. A woman once said to her, 'What was the use of doing so much for your sister? Finally she left, didn't she?'

Bhikutai instantly shut her up. 'What do you mean she left? She did not elope with somebody, did she?'

I would often take Tara with me to her place. She made much of her too. One day she picked her up. Then said, 'How heavy your little girl is! I can barely carry her.'

But the truth was that she herself had grown very weak. Carrying the baby was beyond her strength. Now she had lost all her misgivings about me. She would say, 'Manu, the best thing you did was to leave. It took a real load off my mind.'

Mr Tilak was not unpredictable now as he had earlier been. It gave her great joy to see the new life we had made together. And yet something was missing—the good health she had once enjoyed. She continued to grow weaker. Finally, Nanasaheb thought she might improve if she was back in her place of birth. It was decided that she should go to Nashik. I saw her off at the station. Once again she said, 'Manu, you did very well to go to your husband.'

Summer had come. It was time for Mr Tilak to go to Mahabaleshwar. But this year he decided not to go. There was a mountain of work to be done. It was not the mission's work but people's work. People's businesses had sunk on account of the famine. Mr Tilak had thrown himself headlong into helping them. He arranged loans for some, bought looms for others, gave small sums of money to vegetable vendors and small-time shopkeepers to restart their business. He had personally gone from door to door to collect funds for this work. Hearing about his work, the government too had contributed some money. He had also taken on the responsibility of distributing saris. When we realized that some women would arrive in a different dress every day and take away three or four saris, the job of taking away their old saris and keeping them fell to me. As always, I had doubts about Mr Tilak's ability to look after finances. So I became the treasurer. That kept me bound to the house.

It took us three or four months to escape from this terrible ordeal. In this period I had not had any time to visit Bhikutai. As soon as we were through with this work, anxiety about her took its place. We wrote letter after letter to her in Nashik but there was no reply. I was like a mad woman, asking whomsoever I met for news of her. One day, a gentleman came to visit us and, as was my practice, I asked him if he had any news of my sister.

'Don't you know?'

'Know what? I'm very worried about her.'

'Dear lady, she passed away ten or twelve days ago.'

My limbs turned to water. It was as though a bolt had hit me. She had been so tormented because of me that she had fallen ill and had now passed away. How this news affected me is better imagined than described. Mr Tilak sent a telegram. We received a letter back. Nanasaheb wrote to say his leave was over and that he would return to Ahmednagar in a couple of days. People in Nashik were known to be extra conservative. That is why he had not informed me earlier. If he had told me and I had gone to Nashik, there would have been hell to pay over my polluting touch. I went to meet him when he returned. What we felt when we met cannot be described in words.

Nanasaheb was to have dinner with some other people. But he would not let me go without dinner. 'Maushi, think that it's your brother-in-law who's gone and your sister is here. I will always be with you.' And he sat with me till I had finished dinner.

God's Design

Around this time I thought I should study something. I did not wish to become a scholar as Mr Tilak hoped I would be. I wanted to study something that would help me in difficult times and also be useful to others. Dr Julia Bissel was a very affectionate woman. Her Marathi too was like ours. You would think it was a Brahmin woman speaking. We had become good friends and, with her encouragement, I decided to train as a nurse. I began training with her, but she had to return to America soon after. Two young and enthusiastic doctors, Dr Beals and Dr Harding, came from America to take her place.

As soon as they arrived, Dr Harding began taking nursing classes. In those days I could barely read and write Marathi. How was I going to deal with English? But my audacity was great. I went to Dr Harding asking to be admitted to his classes. He instantly enrolled me, no doubt because he assumed being Mr Tilak's wife I was bound to be clever.

The classes were in full swing. I would attend them with my notebook and pencil. But merely having those objects was hardly going to ensure progress. By the time I managed to remember and write down a couple of letters, the others would have written two sentences. And when I had finished writing two sentences, they would have completed two paragraphs. Finally, I began to ask fellow students to help me complete my work after class. All in all, what with Dr Harding teaching us in English and I lacking knowledge of the language, my training was all happiness! But God's design is inscrutable. I took the three-month examination and passed. Or did the good doctor arrange for me to pass?

I had always been interested in home remedies. I already had a stock of native medications, and whenever I met someone who shared my interest, we would exchange notes. That is how my stock of native medicines kept increasing. Now I was adding knowledge of modern medicine to it. And it was not confined to books either. It stepped out of the covers of books and wandered around quite freely. That is how, one day, I came to conduct an experiment on Tara's eyes. A woman named Sagunabai, who lived up to her name by being a truly good person, had come to stay with us because of the famine. We were looking after her and her eight-year-old daughter and, besides food and clothes, we were paying her eight annas a month for the work she did around the house.

The inside of Tara's eyelids had erupted in grainy pimples. She was moaning continuously with the irritation. Here I was, a nurse who had passed her three-month examination. So I asked Sagunabai to hold Tara's eyes open and vigorously rubbed the eyelids with a crystal of copper sulphate. Tara yelled in protest. When Mr Tilak came home he was all praise for my smartness. 'Did you think you were a doctor? Now if the child loses her eyesight, are you going to lead her through life by the hand?'

'Oh Lord, blind me but save the child's eyes,' I kept praying. I had conducted my experiment at eight in the morning. At five in the evening, the girl had still not opened her eyes. Now I really lost heart. Mr Tilak had gone out. When he returned, he tried to open her eyes. Drops of blood oozed out. He had been right. Her eyes had ruptured. What was I to do? I washed one eyelid with boric acid lotion. Something resembling a tamarind seed fell out. That's her pupil I thought, terrified. Perhaps I should treat the other eyelid with boric acid to see if at least one eye could be saved. Again something similar fell out. Suspecting the worst, I clanged two metal vessels together. Tara opened her eyes and looked in that direction. My joy knew no bounds. Her eyes were fine. The pimples had been shed. Mr Tilak was overjoyed. But Tara was still not well. She had been running a fever for some time.

The plague had returned to Ahmednagar. Rats had declared their manifesto. Inoculations had begun. A young man named Patros Vitthal Hivale had been staying with us. He left for his village. Other people too were leaving. Mr Tilak took Dattu to Rahuri to stay with an acquaintance. Tara's fever continued unabated. We asked Dr Harding to examine her. He said the fever was ordinary; nothing to worry about.

'But,' I said, 'what are these nodules?'

'Children often have them,' he said.

'Can we be sure it isn't plague?'

'Yes. But all of you should get inoculated.'

Mr Tilak had gone to see Dattu in Rahuri. He was against inoculations. He said so every time I asked him. That is why I had agreed to send Dattu to Rahuri. When Mr Tilak left to see him, he told me, 'I sent Dattu away because I didn't want him to be inoculated. I don't want Tara to be inoculated either. You are free to do it. I will not stop you.'

Daya had come to Ahmednagar for a few days. A Brahmin named Santkaka had recently converted. He had sent us a message saying, 'I have plague. Please send me twenty-five rupees as soon as you get this letter.' Mr Tilak was away and as usual I did not have a single paisa on me. So I let the letter lie. Daya, Sagunabai, her daughter and I went to Dr Harding for our inoculations. He left immediately after for a surgery in Wadala. When Mr Tilak returned from Rahuri, he spotted Santkaka's letter. He instantly sold Tara's bracelet and wired the money to him. Meanwhile, news that Dr Harding had been struck by blood poisoning spread rapidly in Ahmednagar.

At our place, all of us who had been inoculated were running fevers and our injected arms had swollen up. The practice of inoculation was new in those days. We were not used to it. Tara, who had not been inoculated, ate and slept with us. One day a rat scampered around on her bed and fell dead. Everybody in the house was down with fever. There was one servant, but he was new. In the midst of this, somebody came with a message to say that Dr Harding had asked all his nursing students to go and meet him immediately. I did not have the heart to leave Tara alone and go. At the same time I wanted to see Dr Harding, who was suffering from blood poisoning. Finally, I left Tara to Daya's and Sagunabai's care and went. This was to be our last meeting with Dr Harding. He was very pleased to see all of us there. He said, 'I am going to another place now. My work here is over. Please do not give up your training. Nursing is a fine profession. You have all been good students. So please continue to study.'

He had a raging fever. At last he said goodbye. We did not feel like bidding him goodbye. We asked him instead what we could do for him. 'Pray,' he said. Then he turned away from us. His wife was beside him. There was nobody else. She was pregnant. She was not too old either. We said to her, 'Do call us if you need our help.' From there we went to church and prayed before dispersing to our homes.

When I got home, Sagunabai said Tara had been running around the house saying take me to the church and dress me up in good clothes. Tara had a very high fever and was not responding to questions. Mr Tilak said to Sagunabai, 'You take her all over the place. That's why she's got fever now. If anything happens to her, will you give me back my daughter?' Poor Sagunabai, who was familiar with his temper, heard him out without saying a word. We called Nanaji Bhosle from next door. He gave us some native medicine which we gave Tara. She slept on our laps all night, but she was barely conscious.

Next morning we sent a cart for Dr Sorabji. He said, 'Don't worry. I'll send some medicine.' The servant whom we sent with him for the medicine ran away directly from there. Just then we got news of Dr Harding's death. The throngs that gathered for his funeral proved how much love he had won from people of all religions and castes during his six months with us. There was no tonga to be had in the town throughout the day. Mr Tilak had gone there. I was looking for a way to go. But Tara was screaming so much that I found it impossible to leave.

The doctor had failed us. Our arms were swollen. There was not a paisa in the house. I sent for Nanaji Bhosle and asked him to sell a gold signet ring. He returned with the news that all the shops were closed. When he asked somebody why, the man said, 'Are we going to look after our precious lives or buy precious metals?' I was at wit's end. I did not know what to do. The boys from the hostel ground our grain. We cooked with our good hands. We still did not know what the girl was ailing from.

Dr Umrao came. He took one look at Tara and said it was plague. Mr Tilak returned at noon. When we gave him the news, he said, 'Let's leave town before anybody tells us to.' We prayed. Mr Tilak said, 'This too must be part of God's design.'

The big worry was money. It was not the right time to ask Dr Hume. Mr Tilak had gone again to Dr Harding's bungalow. The rest of us were ill. Tara's screams reached fever pitch. There was no money for carts and no manservant to fetch them. Just then I saw a man walking quickly past the house. The news of Tara's plague had got around. Nobody dared enter our house. I had loaned three rupees to this man sometime in the past. I ran out to the compound wall and stopped him. I did not invite him in nor did he look inclined to come. I asked him for my money. He quickly took out a five rupee note, handed it over to me and hurried away. That was all I wanted.

I began packing as though we were leaving for a long stay away. I filled a cart with everything from a grinding stone and pestle to spices and condiments and sent it off to the quarantine centre. It was four o'clock now. I sent Sagunabai for a tonga, but all the tongas were at Dr Harding's funeral. Just then the cart with our luggage returned. We could not keep so much stuff at the quarantine centre, I was told. I unloaded some and sent the rest back. This meant I had to unpack and rearrange what I had kept back. It was dark now. Mr Tilak was writing something by the light of a lantern. We were still waiting for a cart to take us. I said to Sagunabai, 'The servant has run away. If you are feeling afraid of staying, you can go too.'

She said, 'Bai, death is waiting for us all. You gave us shelter when we had nowhere to go during the famine. How can I forget that? How can I be so ungrateful?' What a large heart that illiterate woman had.

When the boys we had looked after heard about our problems, they remembered how we had shared the little food we had with them during the famine and wanted to help us. They asked their warden if they could come over. The warden said, 'What you want to do is right. There can be no two opinions about that. But I can't let you go under these circumstances. You can ask saheb for permission tomorrow.'

The boys said, 'They need help today. What's the use of asking saheb for permission tomorrow?'

The warden said, 'Do as you please. But remember you don't have my permission.'

The boys said, 'Even if you don't take us back in the hostel, we don't mind. But we must go.'

When I saw them, I asked them why they had come.

'To help you,' they said.

'What if you're thrown out of the hostel tomorrow?'

'God is with us.'

'Can you find a cart or tonga for us?'

One boy found a bullock-cart ready to take us on condition that no plague victim travelled in it. When the cool air outside touched Tara, she began to talk. The cartman assumed the plague victim had gone ahead. Tara was talking to all the boys by name. I wondered if we should be taking her to the camp at all. The journey was made pleasant with her questions and the boys' answers. The night was pitch-dark. We did not have a lantern. The cart rattled, the girl prattled while my heart thudded. Thus we proceeded, through pits and potholes, by the light of the lantern that swung up ahead. Finally we reached the camp. Mr Tilak came out of one of the tents in the midst of his writing to welcome us.

'We've been given three cottages. One is for cooking, one is for Tara and one for me to write,' he said. The doctor examined Tara. Her temperature was one hundred and five degrees. He said, 'Bai, don't sit with the girl. You'll catch plague. Let this woman sit with her.'

I said, 'Why? Who had the girl sat with to get plague? And can you say I won't get it if I stay away? And if I am to stay away from my daughter, why should this poor lady sit with her?'

That shut the doctor up. The boys and Daya left. Sagunabai and I sat with Tara in our cottage. Mr Tilak gave the boys and Daya something to eat and brought something over for us. But that something was hardly edible or drinkable. It was the month of Paush and the winter cold was freezing. The jowar bhakri had been made in the morning and was dry. The water in the clay pot was icy. My heart was full of worry. We gave two rupees to the cartman. Now we had nothing left.

The cottages were ventilated by openings about a span-long, running along the top and bottom of the walls. The walls were made of tin. They got so cold at night that we felt we would freeze over. We were surrounded by the sick. They screamed and beat on the tin walls. At times, a patient would climb on to a wall and jump with a loud thud into the neighbouring room. The floors of the cottages had not been levelled. When you walked, pebbles bit into the soles of your feet. There was no food in our stomachs and no sleep in our eyes. Tara's screams were heart-rending. I thought if Yama had a kingdom anywhere, it had to be here. The place was terrifying, the night was terrifying, the surroundings were terrifying and the state of my heart was terrifying.

Patients' relatives who were looking after them would get into fights. 'Your patient screams too loudly. Shut him up, will you? Our patient was just about to fall asleep.' Some screamed because they were sick; others because they were scared. When the doctor came the following day, I said to him, 'Doctor Saheb, you go back home at night and sleep peacefully. Do you have any idea what happens here?'

I described the whole thing to him and suggested that he give the patients something to make them sleep. The doctor took my suggestion and made some changes in the patients' medication. After that, the nights became peaceful.

The clinic was in the camp. The patients were given Belladonna. The same glass was used for all the patients to drink from. The thermometer too was the same. I had kept a separate set for Tara and I would go to fetch the medicine myself. I had installed a stove in our room and I used to foment her with a warm cloth. Sagunabai and I took turns to hold her on our laps.

Patients and their families would get food from the camp kitchen. We were given rations. Daya used to cook. We were ten people in all. She would cook for all of us single-handed. Nobody was allowed to visit us. But the boys would come through the barbed wire when they saw that nobody was around.

Mr Tilak continued with his reading, writing and prayers. His prayer was, 'Dear Lord, I still don't know why You have visited this affliction upon us. But I know that You have a purpose in doing so. Give me the wisdom to understand what it is. If You did not have a purpose, why did the plague spare us and catch this little girl?' Mr Tilak had refused to be inoculated. But the doctor had forced him to have it done. He had a bad time of it. In the early days, the organization at the camp was inefficient. Only ten per cent of patients survived. At the end of fourteen days, the civil surgeon came. He and another doctor examined Tara and told us we should give up hope.

Mr Tilak was near to tears. God had given us one daughter. He had hoped to make a scholar of her like Anandibai Joshi. But God was taking her away. Sagunabai sat by herself and wept. She had grown very fond of Tara. She had shared with me the difficult job of looking after her. In accordance with my habit of always doing more than required, like going to hunt a fox as though I was hunting a tiger, I had carried with me many useful things like a seer of flax seed flour, castor oil and coals. I had lost hope. Tara's back had not touched her mattress in ten or twelve days. We had cradled her on our laps throughout. But that day I put her down. She lay on her mattress quietly. I cooked all the flax seed flour on the stove. I plastered Tara's entire body from chest to stomach with this poultice. I heated up the castor oil with milk and sugar and somehow got her to swallow it. I placed the stove by her feet. I wrapped her up in a blanket. Then I said to her, 'Now you are free to die. I didn't want to feel I had left anything undone.'

I shut the door, left her alone in the room and walked far away into the jungle. When I saw I was completely alone, I shouted out to God, 'My Lord, please let this child live. She is not my child. She is Yours. You gave her to me. I only nurtured her. If it is Your will, You will take her. But if she recovers, I will stay here to care for other patients.' Then I let myself go. I howled.

I returned to the camp. I did not dare open the door to our cottage. Never before had I knelt to pray the way I had done that day. My heart was filled with fear. I forced myself to open the door. When I opened it, I heard Tara say, 'Where did you go, Mamma? And where is Papa?' She used to call us mamma and papa when she was a child. I was so happy, I wanted to pick her up and hold her close. But I feared her heart might be too weak to endure that. So I closed the door and ran to Mr Tilak's cottage. He was praying with some people. Seeing me, he feared the worst. But I was laughing as I said, 'Tara is calling you.' He could not believe his ears. I continued to laugh and tell him Tara was calling him. He thought I had gone crazy. Finally we went together to Tara's cottage. The minute she set eyes on him, she said, 'Why did you leave me and go away? Please get me some mangoes.'

Mr Tilak gave the boys a rupee and sent them to the market for oranges. There were hardly any people there. The boys managed somehow to get half a dozen small, dried up oranges. When the doctor came the following day, he too was astonished. We left the camp after eighteen days. Mr Tilak discovered God's design in afflicting the girl with plague. One day there was a complaint about the milk that was being served in the camp. Hearing the commotion, Mr Tilak went there and asked to see the notebook in which the accounts were kept. He was told, 'You won't understand it, saheb.' He grabbed the notebook and saw that the figure entered in it was much higher than the milk that had been distributed.

Mr Tilak said to me, 'I have found the answer to my question. I now understand why Tara was given the plague. We have a shortage of honest people. Men need to be supervised; however small or big the amount of money involved. That is how it is here too. If the patients are looked after well, if they are given proper food, they will not die. I just saw that the quantity of milk distributed is a third of the milk that comes in. For barbers and priests, holy days are happy days. It's the same here. Plague is a blessing. My mind is made up. I will stay here and do what I can to help the patients. Are you willing to stay?'

I said, 'Yes, I am.'

God gave the two of us great courage and a generosity of spirit during that time. He gave us the work of sweepers who do not fear disease and are not bothered about filth. A sweeper serves ungrateful Man in ways that even mothers would not. Both of us threw ourselves into the work, heart and soul.

All Because of Your Pampering

A small hut had been built for us near the camp. We were not given rations now. The skin-bag of water continued to be delivered. The saheb accepted the boys back in school. Sagunabai went to see her daughter in her village. Mr Tilak gave her a new sari and choli, four rupees spending money, increased her salary from eight annas to two rupees and gave her paid leave for four months. There were now only four of us in the house. But even here, after I had weighed the pros and cons carefully, I adopted two girls whose mothers had died of plague in the camp.

We busied ourselves serving the patients in every way we could. We were made responsible for looking after their food, medicines, teeth brushing, sponging and cleaning them up if they soiled themselves. People from every religion and caste came. When the news that we were working there spread, they lost their fear of the camp and more and more patients came. They would mention our name and come at any time of the night. A local man named Shidiksheth made and sent warm clothes for us. We had not asked for them, but he sent them just the same.

There was a man from the oil-pressing caste in the camp who was kept under lock and key. Nobody had the courage to take him even a drink or water. When we were entrusted with the management of the camp, we asked a new nurse to join. She was a Christian and a willing worker. On Jaibai's first day at work, we set off together for the oilman's hut. We were stopped at the locked door by a sentry. He said, 'Don't go in. He's a terror.'

We said, 'Terror or not, it is our duty to give him milk and medicines. So please unlock the door.' He did so but warned us, 'Be careful. He'll charge at you.'

Sure enough, when we entered, he came charging at us. I gave him a sound slap across the face. I have no idea why it had the effect it did on him, but he fell at my feet. When I told him to drink milk, he did. When I asked him to take his medicine, he did. There was another man from the goldsmith caste called Nana Sonar. He said to me, 'Mother, if I recover, I will cover you from top to toe with gold. As goldsmiths, our one arm is made of gold and the other of silver.'

I said, 'Sure, cover me with gold. But right now let me clean the walls which you've covered with gold.'

In difficult times, servants can hold you to ransom. One day the sweepers asked for a raise and went on strike. They sat around doing nothing while we did their work for two days. We had been well trained in their work by the goldsmith anyway. On the third day, we had to lift corpses. Mr Tilak got ready for the work. I too hitched up my sari. We lifted two corpses into the cart. This gave the sweepers a real scare. They came running to Mr Tilak and said, 'You can beat us on our backs but don't tread on our stomachs please.'

Mr Tilak said, 'I am not saying that you shouldn't get a raise. But it says nothing for your humanity if you hold up work for the patients in times like these. We will most certainly try to get you a raise. Your brothers are dying and you are putting obstacles in our way. This is really bad. This time I will make every effort to get your salaries raised. But do this again and I can promise you I'll do nothing to help you.'

When Mr Tilak began working for plague victims, some people said, 'His daughter's illness has been beneficial for him. Look how he's making money hand over fist.' Others said, 'Poor man. See how he is working himself to the bone for the sick.' Mr Tilak said:

> Good words and ill are but a side-show
> Let it pass you by
> Whether you are honoured or insulted
> Neither laugh nor cry.

The patients' health improved. The number of deaths slid down to ten for every hundred infected. A group photo was taken.

Colonel Corkery presented Mr Tilak with a certificate. Mr Tilak said, 'What do I need a certificate for?' But he praised Mr Tilak's work in fulsome words and pressed the certificate in his hands. Mr Tilak put it on the letter spike. Later it got thrown out with all our old letters.

This year we decided to go to Mahabaleshwar for Tara's sake. Dattu was in Rahuri. We asked him to join us at Ahmednagar station. We were going to meet Haushi and Daya in Pune. We left for Ahmednagar. We took two of our boys, Anand and Patros, with us. Of the two girls I had adopted in the camp, we handed one over to her father and God took away the second.

Mr Tilak's motive in adopting children was only to save them from hardship and set them up on the path to a bright future. He did not make them an excuse for fleecing people nor did he grab other people's children by force. 'If we adopt children,' he would say, 'we must make sure we can help them all the way. We mustn't ruin their lives.'

The thing to note about Mr Tilak's nature was that he loved work for itself. He had no desire for honours or fame. When he asked that his life be written about as he had lived it, what he meant was that his faults should not be covered up. It was also true that his intense idealism made an immediate impact on people. Otherwise it would have been impossible for Narayanrao Gokhale's daughter to do a sweeper's work willingly and enthusiastically. The merest suspicion that a drop off a Mahar's body had touched him had driven Narayanrao to wash and clean his home and family for the rest of his life. And here I was, the daughter of that father, eating in a sweeper's house in Wai and running off to a clinic in Ahmednagar to do work that was considered low. If anybody is to be given credit for this, it has to be Mr Tilak. He was my guru. He only had to point the way and I would run down that path with closed eyes and without a second thought. If I am to take credit for anything at all, it would be for this: I unhesitatingly followed the path he charted for us.

I was a dedicated housewife and had a strange penchant for accumulating things. These twin virtues remain with me even today. Mr Tilak was a stickler for cleanliness. During his spring-cleaning sprees, he even cleaned out his cloth purse and the cash-box. I, on the other hand, would hold on to every bit of junk. I guarded this treasure like a serpent. Mr Tilak would wait impatiently for me to leave the house so he could clean it out. It was festival time for him the moment I stepped out. It was mourning time for me the moment I stepped in.

There was no telling what odds and ends my storehouse held. It could throw up bundles of rags, bottles, torn slippers, a broken winnowing pan, rusted tin containers, bits of string, old mesh baskets, a broken seat, lengths of cotton tape, the wheels of toy carts, knives, nails and even a broken clay pot and its shards.

I collected this stuff not to make money by selling it, but because one could never tell what would be needed and when. After the boys left, we ripped open their mattresses. I gave the covers to the washerwoman and stood, arms akimbo, contemplating the mountain of coir that had tumbled out, wondering how to accommodate it in my storehouse. Curious neighbours gathered to see what would happen. Just then Mr Tilak announced an auction. People were invited to take away as much coir as they could accommodate in two armsful. In no time at all, the mountains of coir had dwindled into molehills. Mr Tilak's job was accomplished. He dusted his hands and went off to write. I was like a beggar who gathers what's left in the field after the corn has been transported to the threshing floor. I collected the remnants and tied them into bundles which I secreted away in my storehouse.

Tara had recovered from the plague. We were going away to Mahabaleshwar for three months. So I went to make my farewell calls on friends in the town. I rarely left the house. But when I did, I would walk through it, ringing every familiar doorbell. When I returned, I noticed that the remaining coir had disappeared from my storehouse along with some other stuff.

In Mahabaleshwar, we were back in our old landlord's house. Everything was the same. Only this time, Dattu and I ate the food the landlord had cooked and drank the water he had stored. Our life had been fully organized for us. We did not even have to look out for a house help. We instantly settled down to our respective routines. We hired a pram for Tara in which Dattu and Ananda would take her out for a stroll.

One day Daya said, 'You know, fresh coconut kernel is available here. I wish you'd buy us a slice each.' I sent Patros off to buy tender coconut kernel. When he returned, he held the slices out to Daya and said, 'Milady, you first.' That did it. Daya flew into such rage, we could do nothing about it. She changed into a torn sari and choli; she would not let anybody touch any part of the housework because she was going to do it all. She ate chapatti and chili off the floor not off her plate. Meanwhile, Ananda was also sulking over something else. We tried pacifying them, but nothing worked. That day I had clarified five or six rupees worth of butter and pushed the hot pan of ghee under the bed. The two sulking children did not eat lunch. I got tired of telling them to eat. I did not want to report them to Mr Tilak. Although he was affectionate, he was very short-tempered too. Ananda went out to sit by the roadside. Daya finished her work and went to stand in the backyard. I said to Patros, 'I am at wit's end. Go and tell him.'

Mr Tilak was not taking Marathi tuitions this year. He was giving ticketed lectures in English. He spent his time reading up for them or thinking about them. It was about three in the afternoon. I was sitting on the bed with Tara. When Mr Tilak heard the news, he came.

'Where are they?'

'One's in the backyard. The other's by the roadside.'

'Daya, come in this minute. What's all this about? Get into a proper sari at once. And you there, idiot! Get me that cane. Stand straight. Put your hand out and count.'

After two or three strokes of the cane, Ananda started

howling and clung to me. The cane came down on Ananda's back then. I was holding Tara so I freed myself from him. Now the cane whistled down on his hand again. He ran to hide under the bed.

'Come on out. Wash your face and all of you go out for a walk.' They had not gone too far when Ananda's hand happened to touch his backside. It came away covered in fat.

'Patros, I think I sat in the ghee pan under the bed. What will Aai say now? Dattubhau, I think I sat in the ghee pan. What will happen now?'

'Nothing. Just come home quietly and change your dhoti.'

When they returned, Mr Tilak was busy giving me a lecture. 'You go and collect all these children around you. And who's to discipline them? You have spoilt them with your pampering.'

My Education

That year in Mahabaleshwar, a man living behind our house died of fever. Mahabaleshwar was organized in such a way that no disease could enter it. So when this suspicious case came to light, Mr Tilak said, 'Patros, you'd better take the girls and Ananda back. Who knows what this man died of. The rules here are very strict. We don't want to get into any trouble later. Leave the girls in Pune and go with Ananda to Ahmednagar.' The four of them left while the four of us stayed back.

Not for long though. Mr Tilak's nature was such that not a day went by in his entire life when there were no guests in the house. Santkaka had been through the plague and recovered. He had come to Mahabaleshwar for a change of air. Whenever he came to stay with us he would take over our shopping. He did that this time too. Meanwhile, we received a letter from Patros telling us of his and Ananda's safe arrival in Ahmednagar. He also told us that he had proposed marriage to Haushi and asked if we could help him find work. Mr Tilak found him a job in Sangli.

The monsoons set in early. On a previous visit to Mahabaleshwar, I had put by a whole stack of firewood. I had had to give much of it away when we left. So this time I had decided not to make the same mistake, but buy firewood as and when we needed it. This was working well till the rains began all of a sudden and firewood disappeared from the market. My neighbours had piles of firewood stored, but they said, 'We will not give you a single stick even if you give us ten rupees for it. This is our store for the rains.' Mr Tilak reminded me once again of what he had often said before. I was pennywise and pound foolish.

We had to pack up immediately. There was still time for Mr Tilak to resume duty so, instead of going directly to Ahmednagar, we went to Sangli. We stayed there for two days to check on how Patros was doing and then went to Miraj. There was a couple known to Mr Tilak here. Dr Bhaskarrao Govande and his wife Ramabai were both studying there. We stayed with them. The local hospital, its management, and the couple's warmth and kind encouragement gave a new fillip to my urge to study. But the pull of home, husband and storehouse made me hesitate. Tara was still a baby and had just recovered from her illness. Dattu did not look too strong either. But Mr Tilak had no qualms. He said, 'Don't worry. I'll manage everything. I'll send you ten rupees every month.'

Mr Tilak met Dr Wanless who agreed to accommodate me. He gave me a room. Mr Tilak had no money for his return fare. We sold a ring and he returned to Ahmednagar with Tara and Dattu. My education in nursing resumed. There were no regular classes there. You were expected to learn on the job. Patros would come once a week and do my shopping. Jaibai's son was studying medicine here. He started giving me lessons in English. I needed to know the language to be able to at least read the labels on medicine bottles. Many students from Ahmednagar were studying there. They too helped me out.

It was four months since I had been in Miraj. I missed the children desperately. One day I simply got up and left for Ahmednagar. The Govandes had finished their course and had left Miraj for Kedgaon to work with Pandita Ramabai. It was four o'clock in the afternoon when I reached home. Tara was playing. Dattu was at school. Mr Tilak had gone out. When Tara saw me she ran to hug me, singing, 'Aai has come, Aai has come, my Aai has come / The game is done the story's told, my Aai has come.'

She clung to me singing away. I was overjoyed to see her. When Mr Tilak and Dattu got home, they too were very pleased to see me. I was there for just a day. Dr Hume came over to invite us to dinner. After dinner, in the course of conversation, Dr Hume said, 'My dear lady, your real education is looking after your husband and children. I don't think you should go back to Miraj.'

'You are right, saheb. Do you think I'm happy living away from the family in Miraj? But you can never tell what will befall us in the future. One should make preparations to face any eventuality.'

'What do you think, bhau?'

'I agree with her completely.'

'Saheb, I am not educated. Should I not have some skill that will help me earn my bread and serve people?'

'Well, think about it seriously. You are always short of money. The children also don't look too well.' We continued to talk in this fashion and then we came home. My train was to leave at seven in the morning. Dr Hume was at the station before us. Just as the train began to move, he thrust a ten-rupee note in my hand.

'Study well. When you have finished your studies, look after your husband and children well. This is just a very small gift from me.'

'But I have money, saheb. I don't need this. I'll ask for money when I need it.'

'Think of it as a brother's gift.' Yes, the children did look weak but Mr Tilak and I believed firmly that I should complete my studies. I was tearful as I bid goodbye to Mr Tilak. He said, 'Don't worry. Yes, you are the children's mother. But I love them equally as their father. I'll take good care of them.'

For two days after I returned to Miraj, everything was as it had been. On the third day, Dr Wanless came to me and said, 'Bai, we need your room. Please vacate it and go back to Ahmednagar. You don't have the strength to lift adult patients.'

'But doctor, I must study.'

'But you are not capable of doing this work.'

'Why not? I'm a human being too.'

'I don't have the time to talk to you. Please vacate the room today.'

I was in a terrible state. I did not know what to do. I took all my stuff out of the room into the compound and sat on it.

Prasadrao Waghchauray from Ahmednagar lived nearby. He was on his way home when he saw me.

'What is this, Aunty? Why is your stuff out here? Are there bedbugs in the room?'

'No, dear man. Saheb has thrown me out.'

'Why? You are paying to study. Why would he do that?'

'I don't know the reason. I broke his thermometer once. But I replaced it immediately. He says he has come to the conclusion that I'm not capable of doing this work. You can't lift adult patients, he says.'

As I spoke I wept. I wondered how I could be blamed for not being able to lift adult patients. Prasadrao tried to persuade me to have dinner with his family. I said, 'I don't want to eat. I will sit here till I know why I have been thrown out.'

Prasadrao went to meet the doctor. The doctor kept repeating the same thing that I was not capable of handling the work. Prasadrao said, 'The lady says she will not budge till she knows what her fault is.' Then Dr Wanless showed him Dr Hume's letter. 'See this. Dr Hume says send the lady back immediately. Her husband and children are badly off. There's nothing wrong with her work. Then Dr Hume adds, don't tell her I've written to you. What can I do?'

Prasadrao reported the whole conversation to me. Now the ten rupees Dr Hume had given me made sense. It was meant to pay for my train fare back. I felt very aggrieved. How could I show my face in Ahmednagar now? What would people say? Perhaps I should befriend a deep well in some remote place. The wives of our students consoled me. They helped me a lot and saw me off on the train.

At every station through the entire journey I felt like jumping out and vanishing. Dr Hume might have the power to interfere in the Miraj hospital's working, but I had my own identity, did I not? However, none of these thoughts got translated into action. Mr Tilak had just stepped out into the yard after tea when my tonga drew up.

'What's wrong? Why are you back?'

'Because I am not capable of doing hospital work.' Then I told him the whole story.

'I know now why students commit suicide when they fail. I know now what education and exams are all about.'

Dr Hume heard that I was back, but he did not come to see me.

Rahuri

Back home I made a beautiful garden in front of our house. I bought fifty pots and filled them with plants. Our garden blossomed. But nothing blossomed for too long with us. Came a day when Mr Tilak got rid of all the plants. The missionary at Rahuri, Dr Ballantyne, was preparing to go on leave. Mr Tilak was appointed in his place. Before we left for Rahuri, he gave away all my plants.

We loved Rahuri. Mr Tilak said, 'If I could build myself a house in such a place, far away in the fields where all is quiet, I could write so many books.' When a missionary named Dr Fairbank came to see us, Mr Tilak muttered something about his dream house. Mr Fairbank said, 'Some money was supposed to be coming to me. I've given up hope of it now. But if it ever comes, I will build you your house, out in the open. Then you can write as many books as you wish.' After this, the two men prayed together and all talk about the house ended.

Two days later, saheb came and said, 'Tilak, you will have your house. My money has come today. Come on. Show me where you want to build.' They walked a couple of miles from Rahuri. Dr Ballantyne had a farm there. That was the place Mr Tilak chose. They applied to Dr Ballantyne for permission to build and bought the land for some 250 rupees. When I heard about it, we had a big showdown. If he had to build a house, I argued, should it not be in town instead of way out in the jungle? There was no company there, no neighbours. There was nobody within earshot to hear us if we called for help. Mr Tilak said, 'You do not understand a thing, but I can always trust you to put a spoke in the wheel when I plan something. Water can be fetched. We can keep dogs for company. And why do we need people? You can call me for help and I can call you.'

The construction of the house started immediately. Dr Fairbank himself stood shoulder to shoulder with the labourers to build the house. He came to the site in style with a cask of water, a loaf of bread and an umbrella to protect him from the sun. He did not waste a single minute. There was neither a drop of water nor the shade of a single tree in the place. The sun beat down relentlessly and the wind turned umbrellas inside out.

I would say, 'What a lot of trouble this is for you, saheb.'

He would say, 'No trouble at all. I need to do this myself. Tilak doesn't understand anything about it.'

The cost grew from five hundred to a thousand rupees. Had we not built it with our own labour, it would have cost us two thousand. Each one to his trade is a wise saying. Saheb handed it to us, ready for use, in a month; but we had nothing to warm it with. We borrowed money to perform the house-warming ritual before moving in.

We got to know Mr Rajaramji Chandekar during this time. He was a school teacher. He was the first important teacher in Dattu's life. He taught and encouraged him from the first to the seventh grade. He would constantly complain to Mr Tilak that Dattu was not studying hard enough. He was just about scraping through his exams. I would be after Mr Tilak to scold, beat, do anything to get Dattu to study. Mr Tilak would merely say 'hunh' and keep quiet. Dattu passed the first standard. Mr Tilak sent him to Mr Bhaskar Nanji Kotak in Pune to study. He was the first Christian student in the Nutan Marathi Vidyalaya.

The idea behind living out in the jungle was that Mr Tilak would spend all his spare time—after doing Dr Ballantyne's work—writing. But Mr Tilak forgot all about that. He took to farming instead. I was a farmer's daughter and knew a thing or two about farming. But I was sidelined, put on the job of shooing away imaginary birds while Mr Tilak farmed. The field was ploughed. Somebody said, 'Sir, cotton will grow well here.' So cotton seeds were sown. Soon there were span-high shoots. But there was no rain for four days. Somebody said, 'What have you gone and done, Sir? There's no rain and no water. How will the cotton grow? Sow gram.'

Right. The next day farmhands were hired to pull out the cotton plants and re-plough the land and sow two measures of gram seeds there instead. The gram grew well. The plants bore gram pods. Many people came to meet Mr Tilak. They would say, 'What a fine field of gram you have. Can we take some?' Mr Tilak happily gave them permission and armfuls of gram disappeared. It worked well for the farmhands. There was not much gram left to harvest. It had all been done for them. Now, of the two paylies of gram sown, two seers came back into the house.

From the time we entered the new house, Mr Tilak had begun to think of giving up his salaried job with the Mission. He was of the opinion that God's work should not be done for money. Instead he began gathering volunteers around him to form a society. He resigned from the Mission and soon the volunteers began arriving. One volunteer came complete with family and set up camp in our house. There were six members in his family. A large posse of people comprising four farmhands and one watchman with his family of three wives also occupied the field.

Dattu was studying in Pune. He had to be sent ten rupees. Dr Hume did not put a stop to this new activity of Mr Tilak's. But he knew the truth of the saying that when the cock struts the hen suffers. Without Mr Tilak's knowledge, he managed to get work worth a hundred rupees a month for him from the Tract Society. So, despite his voluntary service, he earned money for us to live on. We were back on a smooth path. But of course, one hundred rupees found one hundred ways to leave us. Once, Mr Tilak called an urgent meeting of his volunteers for which train fares had to be paid. Once, four volunteers from Ahmednagar missed their train. God alone knows why, but they hired bicycles and cycled all the way to Rahuri. When they went back, they took all the fifteen or twenty rupees left from the month's salary to pay hiring charges for the bicycles.

The volunteer who had camped in our house with family used to shave Mr Tilak for which he got paid four annas. Later he asked Mr Tilak for money for shaving his own sons' heads, and Mr Tilak gave it to him. One day I told him straight out, 'I will not pay him this money. What kind of volunteer is this who fleeces you for shaving his own sons' heads?'

That led to a bitter quarrel. Mr Tilak said, 'You are brainless. It is your miserliness that creates hurdles in my work. You don't even realize that the whole world criticizes you.'

I said, 'Let them criticize me. But I refuse to be cheated by these hypocrites. That man's burden is his laziness. He can't feed his four children but gets married a second time as soon as the first wife dies. Such a man tells you things and you accept them?' That was a terrible night for us. Mr Tilak was writing. I was crying. We had our morning tea in silence. Then Mr Tilak rode off on his bicycle. In town, he went from door to door inviting the women of the house to tea on my behalf. After that, he went on to do his work.

Around four o'clock, when I was having my siesta, women began to gather one by one in front of the house. I was still snoring inside. When I came out a while later, there was a crowd of women at the door. They stared at me. I stared at them. Both sides were thoroughly bewildered. What a scene it was! Amongst the women was Savitribai, the wife of my adopted brother Bapu Namaji Adhav and their two daughters Saru and Waru. Savitribai whispered in my ear, 'What's going on, Vansa? Saheb asked us to come for tea but nothing seems to be moving here.'

Light dawned on me then. I said to her, 'Vahini, take Saru and Waru to help you and make the tea.' Savitribai put a pan of water to boil. The girls got the tea things ready. I made wheat flour sweets with jaggery. I had one rupee with me. I sent a servant off to buy melons. That is how we had our merry tea party.

When Mr Tilak returned, I said, 'Why did you invite all those women to tea?'

'You weren't talking to me. How else was I going to get you to talk again?'

That was the end of my sulk.

Ordained

Mr Tilak was ordained a minister. From being a simple mister he became a reverend. This is how it happened. When he started his Voluntary Service Group, many religious scholars started coming to meet him. Mr Tilak maintained that anybody who was called by God was free to baptize those desirous of receiving baptism. The man need not be an ordained clergyman to do so. Accordingly, he had himself conducted several baptisms.

This shocked people. But once he was convinced about the rightness of something, not even Lord Brahma could move him from his purpose. It put people in a quandary. Mr Tilak had never been concerned with what others thought. If somebody came to him asking to be baptized, he would do it himself instead of sending him to a priest. Nor did he do it quietly. He argued loudly about it. After he had baptized a few people in Rahuri, we heard rumours that he was going to be ordained. The rumours were true. It was decided that Mr Tilak would be ordained at a large gathering that was scheduled to take place in Rahuri.

It was the first of the month. The ordination was scheduled for fifteen days later. Now there was no regular salary coming from Dr Hume. Earlier, we could go to him for an advance whenever we needed money. Although he was very upset over our extravagance, he would give us even as much as two months' salary in advance. But now Mr Tilak's salary did not reach us even on the fifth or sixth of the month. He had invited all those who were coming for the meeting from out of town to lunch, tea and dinner. I was merely informed of this. I became anxious about how this was to be managed. I did not have a single paisa. No cash, no food. The moment Mr Tilak told me of his plan, I started off like the miser I was supposed to be.

'Where's the money?'

'Why are you bothered about that? It will be alright.'

'Alright for you. I will have to manage.'

'You're so impatient. There are still eight or ten days to go. We'll see.'

'That's you. We'll see when the train comes. We'll see when the train goes. What's the use of seeing then?'

'I am held in such high respect in the town. But that means nothing to you.'

'How is that? If it meant nothing to me, why would I be sick with worry over what your guests will eat and drink? People will always say what a good man and what a terrible wife. There isn't even sufficient water to drink. I had told you not to build a house in the jungle.'

'Why are you worried about water? We'll order ten skin-bags in place of one.'

'And where will I store ten skins of water?'

'I have no time to stand here arguing with you. Everything will work out in good time.'

And so Mr Tilak went off for his work. In the evening, he went to Solapur for six or seven days. While he was gone, thieves drove us mad. Fortunately, nothing was stolen. I went to Rajaramji Chandekar and Bhaskarrao Bhambal. I said, 'This is how it is. Now I will have to depend on you to see me through. I'll return what you spend when our salary comes.'

They said, 'Bai, please don't worry. We'll look after everything.' And they did too.

Mr Tilak always collected a lot of sadhus and mendicants and fake sanyasis around him. They would tell Mr Tilak of their troubles and he would believe them. But most of them were cunning hypocrites. They would stay with us for a few days, eat, drink, get clothes out of us and quietly go their way. Some did all of this and harassed me and the children besides. Mr Tilak noticed none of this. On the contrary, he would quarrel with me on their behalf. He gave shelter to one such fraud and even baptized him later and found him work. His highness turned up at the time of Mr Tilak's ordination, accompanied by four sadhus. He was carrying a bottle with him. He gave it to me saying in Hindi, 'Mother, this is my medicine. Keep it safe.' I locked up the bottle.

Mr Tilak was in the church. The girls were busy with minor household chores. Women were cooking in the kitchen. I was mopping up whatever work remained to be done. My bunch of keys was at my waist. Around one o'clock was the sadhu's time to have his medicine. 'Mother, can I have the key?' I gave him the key. The sadhu had his medicine and went to the stove. He squatted there and started throwing balls of dough into it. The women began to scream. The girls were terrified. The sadhu got up and ran to attack them. Just as I realized what was going on, Neelkanthrao Mama came over. I said, 'Just look at this riot. Please drive this man out.'

When Mama went to pull him way, he went for Mama with a knife.

Mama said, 'You're a scoundrel. I will see to it that you are not baptized.' There was a scuffle between them. If the man had stabbed Mama, it would have been his end. I took the knife from the sadhu almost without his noticing. Then I signalled to Mama to go to the other room. He went and locked himself in. I said to the sadhu, 'You know what? That man is a terrible fellow. Even I don't trust him. Come. Would you like to have your medicine?'

The man's eyes lit up. I took him to the room where his medicine was kept and gave him a couple of such hard slaps that he saw stars. He sobered up instantly and fell at my feet. 'Mother, I beg of you. Don't tell Father.' Emboldened by his timidity, I ordered him to sit in a corner. He obeyed meekly. Then I hurried out of the room and locked him in. I went to the other room and set Mama free.

Mr Tilak came home after the ordination. When he sat down to his meal, he remembered the sadhu. I told him the whole story. Mr Tilak was wearing brand new slippers. He used them to beat the life out of the sadhu. Then he packed him into a tonga along with his disciples and sent him off to the station. We received a letter from him two years later saying his conduct was greatly reformed since his time with us. We heard nothing more from him after that.

The guests who had come for Mr Tilak's ordination were looked after without his having to lift a finger. Santkaka had come. He had brought thirty rupees with him. Instead of buying things in advance, his routine was to buy stuff as and when we needed it. He said, 'Tai, don't worry. I don't get cheated. Just tell me when something is over and I'll get it for you.'

Consequently, he had to make many trips to the market. Rajaramji and Bhaskarrao also helped me. Bapu Namaji Adhav's whole family worked in the house. But in all this, something Bapu Namaji said upset some people. They sat on the river bank sulking. I was very angry. I was hurrying down to the river to pacify them when I ran into Dr Fairbank. He said, 'Bai, where are you off to in such a rush?'

I said, 'My sons-in-law and fathers-in-law are sulking. I'm going to pacify them.'

He said, 'All right. But you don't go. I'll go and pacify them.'

Dinner had been served by Rajaramji Chandekar. Kamble and others had eaten by eight o'clock that night. Then I stood before the guests and said, 'You are the leaders of our community. This is not the way to lead. When you speak from the pulpit you say, Christ came down to serve, not to be served. And here you get upset with me for no reason. Actually, you should have been helping me. You speak of everybody being God's children and brothers and sisters to each other. If I came to your house, I would go into the kitchen and ask my sister how I could help her. And what did you do? You sulked and made me run after you to plead with you.'

My audience said, 'Bai, we weren't angry with you.'

'Then you were angry with Bapurao Adhav, right? So what did he say to make you so angry? All he said was, "Don't hurry through your baths. Take your time." And yet, when you were asked not to hurry through your dinner but eat at your leisure, you didn't get angry. What was so upsetting about what Bapurao said? Have you cooled down now? Raise your hands those who are no longer angry.'

They all raised their hands. While I was lecturing them, food was being stolen from the kitchen. When we went to serve ourselves after the guests had departed, we found all the rice stolen. We had to make do with what was left.

The following day, I quarrelled with Mr Tilak again over building the house in the jungle.

'See how much trouble it is when things can't be organized in advance.'

'What trouble? I didn't see any trouble.'

'Naturally. You weren't troubled. But look at the trouble we had to go through.'

'You bring trouble upon yourself. Who can help that? Do things not happen if you don't worry? When the time comes, everything gets done.'

'What gets done? There was no water. There simply wasn't enough. I had told you from the beginning, don't build a house in this place. No water, no manpower and lots of thieves.'

'What do you mean no water? Chimbaba, get your pickaxe and shovel. We'll dig a well.'

Chimbaba was not only old, he was bent in three places. He stood with his hands on his hips gaping at Mr Tilak.

'Sir, there's no water here.'

'What do you mean no water? Come on. Start digging where I tell you to.'

Being a servant, Chimbaba had no choice but to obey. He got his pickaxe and shovel and Mr Tilak went off to dig a well. The place where they started digging was three or four hundred armlengths away from the house. Mr Tilak and Chimbaba dug. Tara, Dattu and I carried the dug-up soil away. Our guests stood around watching the fun. Bit by bit the well was knee deep. News of our well got around in no time at all.

One day, some stone diggers turned up. Mr Tilak fixed a digging rate with them of ten annas per foot dug. When Chandekar heard this, he rushed over. He said to Mr Tilak, 'You are being cheated. Don't agree to these rates.' Mr Tilak refused to believe him. Bhaskarrao Bhambal was ill. He came even while he was running a fever and ordered the workers out. By then they had dug the well waist deep. When the wages for that much digging were calculated, Mr Tilak realized his mistake. He had thought that when the whole well was dug a foot deep, he would have to pay ten annas. But the rate was by cubit feet. According to that rate, the amount came to something outrageous. Our salary had just arrived. The stone diggers were somehow appeased. Even then they took away forty-five rupees for four hours of work.

Then Bhaskarrao found other labourers for us. Their rate was ten rupees for digging the first man height, fifteen rupees for the next and so on. It meant a lot of money but it was still within our means. We struck water at a depth of five man heights. The supply was abundant and the water sweet.

PART THREE

Lakshmibai Tilak

Lakshmibai and Mr Tilak, 1918

Mr Tilak, Dattu, Lakshmibai and Tara

Lakshmibai, Tara, Dattu and Mr Tilak, 1909

Bhikutai Pendse

Balkavi Thombre

Tara and Dattu

Ashok, Ruth, Devdutt, Lakshmibai, Nana, Tara and Meera, 1924

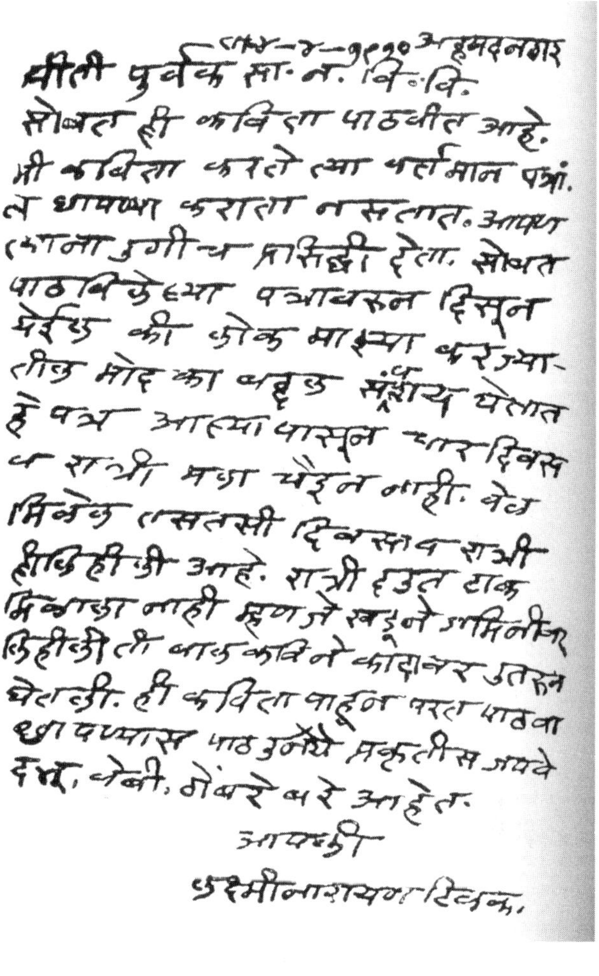

४-४-१९१० अहमदनगर
प्रीती पूर्वक सा. न. वि. वि.
सोबत ही कविता पाठवीत आहे.
मी कविता करते त्या वर्तमान पत्रां-
त छापण्या कराता नसतात. आपण
त्यांना उगीच प्रसिद्धी देता. सोबत
पाठविलेल्या पत्रावरून दिसून
येईल की लोक माझ्या करंज्या-
तील मोदकाबद्दल संशय घेतात
हे पत्र आल्यापासून चार दिवस
व रात्री मला चैन नाही. वेळ
मिळेल तसतसी दिवसाव रात्री
लिहिली आहे. रात्री दउत टाक
मिळाला नाही म्हणजे खडूने जमिनीवर
लिहीली ती बाळकविने कागदावर उतरून
घेतली. ही कविता वाचून परत पाठवा
छापण्यास पाठवू नये प्रकृतीस जपावे
दत्तू, बेबी, ठोंबरे बरे आहेत.
आपली
लक्ष्मीनारायण टिळक.

A letter by Lakshmibai Tilak

Translation

4-4-1910 Ahmednagar

Humble greeting with love.

I am enclosing this poem. The poems I write are not for publishing in newspapers. You give them needless publicity. You will see from the enclosed letter that people are expressing doubts about my poem about the modak made with karanjis. I have been upset for four days and nights since this letter came. I have written this poem as and when I got time. When I did not find inkpot and penholder in the night, I wrote on the floor with chalk and Balkavi copied it on paper in the morning. Send this poem back after you have read it. Please do not send it for publishing. Take care of your health. Dattu, Baby, Thombre are well.

Yours

Lakshmi Narayan Tilak

Lakshmibai Tilak, 1935

Into Mr Tilak's Mind

The well was dug. We were all happy. Now the stonework had to be done. There was a Vadari there, a man from the stonebreaker tribe. He promised to build the well for five hundred rupees. He was to be paid fifty rupees a month. Mr Tilak was paid a hundred rupees by the Tract Society. Of that fifty would go to the Vadari. Twenty-two to the farmhands and servants. Dattu was living away from home. He had to be sent ten rupees. That left us with eighteen rupees in which to run the house.

We had four servants and one watchman, a Bhil tribesman. Having him was vital, even though he was not always around. Once he was paid, thieves would not come to check us out. That was the unspoken arrangement. While we were settling into this life, we received two letters, one from Haushi and the other from Sugandhrao Karmarkar. Haushi wanted to come for her confinement. It was her first baby. Sugandhrao Karmarkar wanted to come for a change of air.

It was not in Mr Tilak's nature to say no. But neither was it in his nature to insist that people come and stay. So if someone wanted to come, he would say come. If someone wanted to go, he would say go. He wrote to both to say come. Haushi came with her husband and mother-in-law. Sugandhrao came with his wife and four children. There were already four of us in the house, including Mr Matekar. Twelve people's needs had to be catered for in eighteen rupees.

We grew potatoes, onions, tomatoes, green chilies, mint and coriander. There was enough farm produce to see us through. Also there was enough milk, butter and ghee in the house, thanks to our cow. There was sweet well water to chase it all down. All this and our guests' kind dispositions ensured that none of us found the time difficult to get through. We ate our jowar and bajra bhakris happily together. In all those ten months, we did not need to buy anything from the market except oil, salt, tea, sugar, kerosene, matchboxes and other such sundries.

There was no shortage of amusing incidents to keep us entertained either. One night when we had sat down to dinner, we smelt something burning. The bicycle lantern had been placed, still alight, on top of the cupboard containing books. It flared up and there was a huge conflagration. We all rushed out, including Dattu who had come home.

I kept saying, 'Throw ash on it.'

Mr Tilak kept saying, 'No. Throw water.'

The fire was spreading. Mr Tilak was shouting, 'This is how she always slights me.'

Just then Dattu knocked the lantern down with a stick and threw ash on it. A lot of time had been lost in our argument. Mr Tilak said, 'Dattu, you always insult me. You don't value me.'

'I do value you, but this isn't the time for valuing. The wind is blowing. Water will make the fire blaze.'

'Let it. What's it to you? My house will burn down. I am the owner.'

Meanwhile, the ash had extinguished the blazing lantern. Mr Tilak's rage had also simmered down. He went into his office and came out a short while later with a poem. He had grown aware of his flaws and was struggling hard to overcome them. This poem expressed the anguish in his heart.

> As long as you rage, you are a sinner, no less.
> Held in the claws of rage, how can you respect yourself?
> A garland one moment, a vicious serpent the next.
> You float on knowledge, but spin on temptation.
> Surrender to Jesus; then submit to your flaws.
> You may preach to people only if you are saved.
> Nail your ego to a post, if it is still not dead.

Mr Tilak wrote many devotional songs and hymns when we were in Rahuri. One day, when he was out walking with some Christian friends, a procession of a bhakti sect passed by. Mr

Tilak was convinced that the domination of the western form of Christian worship and of English hymns must end. The very same day he composed several of his best-known hymns. Many of his compositions, immersed in devotion to God, were written here. These poems belong to the period from 1905 to 1906. Of the six hundred and eighty-two hymns sung today, two hundred and fifty-four are his. His book of prayers and collection of devotional songs both belong to this period. The poems reflect Mr Tilak's mental state during those days.

Mr Tilak used to say that he became a Christian intellectually first. It took him another ten or twelve years to become a Christian emotionally. This transformation was probably happening during our time in Rahuri. His poems bear witness to his inner turmoil. Gradually, his pride was breaking and its place was being taken by total surrender to God. His eyes would grow moist when he sang one song in particular. When we sing this song even today, it fills us with a strange emotion.

At long last I am at your feet, oh Lord
I have wasted my days so far
My pride said I was Your best disciple,
The cleverest scholar of Your Word.
It shames me to think of it now, oh Lord.
My ego deceived me, divided me from You.
Always and ever it was my will I adored.
I have no will, no strength, no knowledge now
All I have is You and You alone.
Hold me firm, let me not stray and fall
This I beg You, as I wait at Your door.

Gopaji

Once Mr Tilak's mind was occupied with an idea, he grew oblivious to all else. He was the intellectual. I was the clown. But his intellect did not stand in the way of my antics and my antics did not affect his intellect. My daughter Haushi had come home for her confinement. Sugandhrao Karmarkar and his wife Virginiabai, a north Indian, were also staying with us. She understood Marathi but spoke Hindustani. All in all, despite being out in the jungle, the house was always filled with eight or ten guests besides the four of us.

The eye specialist Dr Bhaskarrao Govande had come one day to visit us. He was massively built, light-skinned, light-eyed and abundantly whiskered. Sugandhrao's wife could have easily passed off as his sister. It was around nine in the morning. We had polished off abundant servings of snacks and tea and had now turned to our respective chores. Mr Tilak was writing, Haushi and Virginiabai were cooking, Dr Govande and Sugandhrao were lolling on the verandah chatting and I was leaning against the lattice keeping a watch on things. The lattice around our verandah was made of strips of iron. If you sat leaning against it, you saw everything that was going on inside and outside at one and the same time.

I do not think I have ever been troubled by formalities. I see my guests as part of my family. When I visit people, I promptly become part of their families. The poet Balkavi Thombre would always say, 'Lakshmibai, even if George the Fifth came to visit you, you would say, my dear man, can you close that gate behind you, please?'

Dr Govande and Mr Karmarkar were lounging near where I was sitting. Their eyes were closed but their ears were open. Just then I saw a man hurrying down the road. He was carrying something on his back. I recognized him by his walk. It was our Gopa. Mr Tilak had worked hard on him to make him presentable. His vision was weak, but he was now a schoolmaster in a nearby village and had been elevated from plain Gopa to Gopalrao. We considered him one of the family.

As he approached, the prankster in me woke up. Gopa caught sight of me and hurried over. Putting down the bundle he was carrying, he signalled towards the two men on the verandah and asked me in sign language who they were. Instead of answering with a silent signal, I deliberately raised my voice and answered loudly in Marathi, 'What can I do Gopa? I'm fed up. You can see how many guests we have. This fellow has just turned up. He doesn't understand our language and we don't understand his. He's a burden, always waiting to be fed. He's neither an idiot nor a savant.'

While I was sharing my secret with Gopa, Dr Govande looked at Mr Karmarkar with narrowed eyes. Mr Karmarkar looked back and winked. I had spoken so loudly that Virginiabai heard me in the kitchen. She rushed out. Angrily waving her hands about, she said in Hindustani, 'What is this that you are saying? Don't you know him? This gentleman is my brother. He lives beyond Tanjavur in Delhi. He has a big eye hospital there.' This said, she returned to the kitchen. Meanwhile, Dr Govande had risen and now sat cross-legged, watching us with a neutral expression. Soon Virginiabai came back with additional information about her brother. 'My brother does wonderful eye operations. His technique is amazing. He removes both eyeballs and puts them on a table. He dusts and washes them clean and puts them back in the sockets. I was a nurse in his hospital before I got married.'

'How was I to know this? Why don't you get him to examine our Gopa's eyes then?'

'Well, not now. But I'll tell him after lunch.'

That day the doctor acquired a new sister, dearer than his own younger sister. The responsibility of looking after him through the day was hers and hers alone. It was lunch time. Barring Gopa and I, everybody else sat in a single row. We sat facing them. Nobody said anything. Mr Tilak was deep in thought and Dr Govande appeared to have taken a pledge to stay mum. When he needed second helpings, he would call out to Dattu and jab his finger at the place on his plate where it was to be served. I would nudge Gopa to look at him.

'A haughty bird this one, isn't he? A proper tumbler pigeon,' Gopa said with a touch of his rustic dialect. 'Let me get him in my sights. I'll send such a sling-shot at him, he won't know what hit him.'

'What's this idiotic chatter, Gopa? Have you gone mad? Calm down and eat,' Mr Tilak said.

As far as the doctor was concerned, his face belied no knowledge of what Gopa had said. After lunch, Mr Tilak repaired to his room, leaving the rest of us free to riot.

I broached the subject of Gopa's eyes once again. 'You won't get any money. He's a poor man,' I began my defence.

Virginiabai and the doctor exchanged some words in a secret language and then the sister told us in Urdu, 'My brother is ready to do this operation for free.'

Preparations were made for the operation. Madam nurse brought things from the kitchen. Three seats were set end to end in place of a table; two large metal water pots, a basin, two handkerchiefs, a brand-new shining knife and a serving spoon were brought in.

'What's the spoon for?' I asked.

'That's to pour water in the sockets to wash them.'

'You mean you'll remove the eyeballs and swirl water around in the sockets?'

The doctor signalled to the patient to approach. He sat in veerasana with legs folded back under his buttocks, the knife in his right hand. The nurse stood behind the patient as support. The moment the point of the knife came near the corner of Gopa's eye, he knocked it out of the doctor's hand and ran. The doctor followed him like his nemesis. Gopa ran all over the house and outside with the doctor following him and the nurse running behind the doctor. We, the spectators, followed on her heels. The doctor could have caught Gopa, but he was deliberately keeping a short distance between himself and him. I was going on with, 'That's enough of your brother's surgery, woman. Get him to write a prescription for glasses.'

Virginiabai said, 'My brother is such a fine doctor that once he gets his hands on a patient, he will not let go till he's cured.'

When the fun crossed decent limits, Sugandhrao threw his arms around the doctor's waist and sat him down. Haushi's husband calmed Gopa. We returned to our places, laughing till we cried. I asked the doctor again through the nurse, 'Why don't you prescribe some medicine or give him glasses?'

Once again there was an exchange between the two in their secret language. The doctor nodded. He removed his own glasses and put them on Gopa's nose. Gopa saw everything clearly now. He was very pleased. The doctor wrote down a prescription for Gopa's glasses. He wrote the patient's name as 'Go Paji' which of course meant 'Go Rascal'. That was the last joke. We collapsed laughing. Gopa was livid. The doctor hugged him.

'Gopalrao, don't tell me you are seriously upset. We were only joking. Did you not understand that?' But now Gopa's volcano was about to erupt. He muttered angrily under his breath. The doctor gave him a rupee. Even that did not pacify him. 'I had brought tender jowar for you. I was going to roast it nice and hot for you,' Gopa said.

'But Gopa, the minute we set eyes on you, we also set your tender jowar on the fire to boil. It's been cooking away all this while. Admit it, your roasted jowar would not have been a patch on the fun we had.'

We burst out laughing again. Gopa joined in. Finally, Mr Tilak emerged from his room. When he found out what we had been up to, he gave us a good scolding.

Rebirth

When we were in Rahuri, Mr Tilak had gone to Jalna for a Christian convention. Our guests had dispersed. But Dattu was back from Pune for his holidays. The only people at home were Neelkanthrao Mama, his wife and two children, Chimbaba, Tara and me. Before Mr Tilak left, he had dismissed Shahaji Bhil from his job. As soon as he was gone, stones began to be pelted at the house and, on one occasion, the thieves came quite close to breaking in.

Neelkanth Mama gave them a chase. Our jowar had grown neck high. The chase went through it and heaven alone knows where it was taking them. We were following them with sticks and lanterns in the direction of the field where the jowar rustled in the wind. Suddenly, there the thief was, lying on the ground before us, having taken a good beating from Mama. Emboldened now, we raised our sticks to give him more of the same. The man pleaded, saying, 'I'm not the thief. He's escaped. I'm Mama. Honest.'

We hoisted him up and brought him home. Mama had been very fond of saying that no thief in the world would ever get away from him. But it was a different story that day. Shahaji Bhil was then reinstated as the watchman and we were not bothered by thieves again after that.

My health had improved greatly in Rahuri, which means I had grown so fat it was beyond describing. My bangles and necklaces had begun to bite into my flesh. In short I had become a hugely weighty wife. And why would I not be? I was the unquestioned mistress of the house and everything ran according to my wishes.

I had planted a beautiful garden in front of the house, which included a few castor oil plants. When they flowered, I stored the seeds in a clay pot. Now those seeds took possession of my mind. There were two things I was obsessed by. One was to put everything I had to use, and the other was to do whatever needed doing on my own. Fortunately, I found that Chimbaba shared these traits with me. Together we had woven ropes and mats with the leftover coir that I had stored. I had always been interested in making home remedies. So when I realized I had a pot full of castor seeds, I decided to put them to good use. 'Chimbaba, peel me a cup of castor seeds, will you?'

When he had peeled them, I ground them fine, added cinnamon and dry ginger powder and roasted the mix in ghee made from cow's milk. I made candy from this with sugar syrup. It turned out to be very tasty. When I make something, I like to share it. However, by the time the candy was made, everybody was asleep. Only Dattu was still awake. He had a bit of the crumbs. I finished off the rest of them. Then we fell asleep.

In the morning I woke Dattu up to study. 'You must study. Do you want to beg when you grow up? Chandekar is always complaining that you don't study.'

Dattu said, 'I'm telling you the truth, Aai. My head is spinning.'

'How is it that your head spins just when it's time to study?'

When he heard this, he forced himself out of bed and fell to the ground next minute. When I bent down to help him up, my head too began to spin. This was the beginning of our troubles. By the following day, we were like cholera patients. Chimbaba panicked. He suggested sending a telegram to Mr Tilak. But I sent him to Dr Ballantyne instead. Chimbaba told him what had happened. Dr Ballantyne was furious. He said, 'That woman is the limit. She's always making and eating these outlandish things. She gives them to her husband and her son. She sends them to me. Her husband's eyes are spoilt because she feeds him these nonsensical things.'

Dr Ballantyne was under the impression that I had made some festive sweets and eaten them. I had sent him some puranpolis and laddoos quite recently. This had given him the impression that I made sweets every day and fed them to my family and guests. But although this saheb was angry, he was also sympathetic. He gave us some medicines right away and kept us on a diet of sweet limes. Soon we began to feel better. Our misadventure happened on a Friday. When I went to church on Sunday, I was so changed that nobody recognized me. People kept asking, 'What did you do to lose weight? Please tell us.' I refused to divulge my cure, but I did not give the candy to anybody either. Chimbaba buried it deep down in the ground.

When Mr Tilak returned from Jalna, he was very surprised to see the change in me. But of course when he heard the story, he had to say, 'You are disgusting.'

When we moved to Rahuri, Sakharambhauji had also come along and had begun practising law. Mr Tilak went to see him before he went to Jalna. Rakhmabai asked him to get her a tawa, kadhai and other such things. Mr Tilak made sure he got them and went over to their place to give them. Rakhmabai asked him how much they had cost. Mr Tilak was very angry with her for asking. They quarrelled. Then Mr Tilak came home and forgot the quarrel.

After dinner, Mr Tilak went to bed. Just then a tonga came and stopped at our door. Sakharambhauji stepped out. He was sweating profusely. He looked like someone who had been seriously ill for six months. It scared me to see him.

'What's the matter, Bhauji? I hope all is well at home.'

'Yes. But how is Nana?'

'What do you mean? He's had his dinner and gone to bed. He's fine.'

'Look at this letter. I was handed this when I came home. He says this is his last letter to me. You will never see me again, he says.'

I immediately saw what had happened and explained the whole business to Bhauji. Bhauji went home, greatly relieved.

***

A poet once visited us when we were in Rahuri. He had recently bid farewell to his job with the police. He had not decided what to do next, but he had written a large number of poems and wished to write many more. One of his poems began, 'I shall not be a slave in the police.' He had many strange and funny things to recount about his years in that service. He would compose poems on the spot and recite them.

He took it into his head that he could write plays for a living and instantly began to write one. Dattu became his scribe. The poet would dictate his play rapidly and Dattu would take it down equally rapidly. The play was based on a story from an ancient chapter of north India's history. It contained a song that went, 'Some there were smeared with sandalwood paste.' The play ended abruptly at the end of the first act.

The poet had brought a wife with him. Being a Brahmin woman she naturally did not want to stay with us. She stayed in the Vithoba temple next door and did her cooking there too. She did not show herself much to us. I once said to the poet, 'Your wife is a Brahmin lady. Why doesn't she wear a mangalsutra then?'

He said, 'Bai, she grew up with Marathas. Perhaps that is why she doesn't wear one.' He was at great pains to show that he persecuted his wife. Once in a while he would go to the temple and beat her up. We would hear the sounds of his beating her and of her wailing. With it we would also hear suppressed laughter. I realized then that it was all play-acting, but I never let on that I had guessed. Anyway, in years to come, this poet became well known for his service to the Lord. He certainly deserved the fame that he got.

***

Mr Tilak was invited to Ahmednagar again. He was asked to take classes in Dr Hume's religious knowledge class. Mr Tilak had given up Mission work and we had settled down in Rahuri. But Dr Hume was very keen now that he should return to Ahmednagar and Mr Tilak consented to go. We returned to our old house in Ahmednagar, entrusting the house, the farm and the well in Rahuri to Shahaji Bhil's care.

Poets' Conference at Jalgaon

Bhaskarrao Kotak was a friend and admirer of Mr Tilak's. When Mr Tilak first entered the Christian community, many of its leaders were reluctant to accept him. They considered him an upstart. As for Mr Tilak, he was more than willing to take them on. He composed poems that took a sly dig at them. One of these men appeared to have made it the mission of his life to poison people's minds against Mr Tilak with concocted lies. Mr Tilak's poem, 'The Trumpet-blower' is about this individual. One line of the poem goes, 'Set fire to the rumour or, better still, to the mouth that spreads it'. The poem was written in such intense rage that later Mr Tilak regretted having written it.

Another poem entitled 'It Ran Away from Us' was also about one of these critics. The poem says:

The moon has risen.
All night it traverses the sky
As is its wont.
But dogs bark at it all night long
Till their lungs rupture.
When day breaks and the moon sets
As is its wont,
Dogs, happy with themselves, tell each other
It has run away from us in fear.

A third poem is entitled 'Daniel and the Lion'. It is based on the Biblical story in which Daniel, a great devotee of the Lord, is thrown into a lion's cave by his tormentors. But the lion does him no harm. In his poem Mr Tilak says, 'What use barking at a man who goes unafraid into a lion's den?'

Mr Kotak was a good reader of Marathi poetry and he particularly enjoyed poems like these which made him smack his lips in delight. He honestly believed that Mr Tilak alone had the capacity to bring those ego-driven leaders of the community down to earth. He believed in things like holy ash too, but he was a good friend to Mr Tilak.

Mr Tilak once received a telegram from Mr Kotak saying, 'I am dying. Come at once.' Mr Tilak borrowed money to go to Pune to see him. Mr Kotak welcomed him with a big grin. Mr Tilak was livid. Mr Kotak had felt a great urge to see Mr Tilak and also rag him a little. He said, 'You are such a great scholar. How is it you didn't understand what my telegram meant? It meant I am dying to see you. If I were really dying, would I have sent you the telegram? Surely someone else would have done it.'

They were far apart in age but very fond of each other.

Mr Tilak was extremely keen to edit a newspaper. So he started one called *Christian*. It used to carry the message of Christianity for non-Christians and of Hindu culture for Christians. This newspaper died after gobbling up a huge chunk of our money. But this did not mean that Mr Tilak's great urge to edit a newspaper died.

By the time we returned to Ahmednagar, the correspondence between Mr Kotak and Mr Tilak had grown greatly in frequency. Their meetings too became more frequent. Mr Tilak would up and go to Pune every now and again. On 15 December 1904, *Christian Citizen* was born. Bhaskarrao Kotak was the managing proprietor of the newspaper. The well-known grammarian Rev. Ganpatrao Navalkar was appointed editor of the English section and Mr Tilak of the Marathi section. All three possessed minds that were free and hearts that stood no nonsense. As a result, the newspaper created a big stir in the Christian community. It lived for three years. Then it died, leaving a huge debt on Mr Bhaskkarrao Kotak's head. However, when *Dnyanodaya* came into Mr Tilak's charge in 1912, he continued with the contents and policies he had chalked out for this newspaper. If you glance through the issues of *Christian Citizen* and of *Dnyanodaya* between 1912 and 1919, you will find many surprising things. For instance, you may gather from *Christian Citizen* dated 16

February 1907 that the original idea of the poets' conference that was held in Jalgaon was Mr Tilak's. A letter in this issue also reveals the purpose behind the conference. The letter says:

> By the grace of God, a conference of modern poets has been planned for 2 and 3 March in Jalgaon. The purpose in organizing such a conference is to ask and find solutions for vital questions about poetry such as what is the place of the poet and poetry in the history of Hindustan; have today's poets fallen from that place; if so, can they hope to occupy it again; why has no epic poem been written in the nineteenth and twentieth centuries; is there no possibility that such a poem will be written; why has *Kavyaratnavali*, the monthly magazine of modern poetry which has been in existence for sixteen or seventeen years, fallen into such dire straits; is there any chance that poetry will find patronage with the British government and our own principalities; could a committee of modern poets, if formed, be of any use. Intermittently during these debates, poets will present their work before the goddess of poetry, encourage each other in their common pursuit and forge bonds of friendship. We hope you and your readers will offer support to this work.
>
> On behalf of the managing committee
>
> Your humble servants
>
> Narayan Wamanrao Tilak, Madhavrao Laxman Khambete, Yeshwant Gangadhar Dixit, Narayan Narsimha Phadnis.
>
> Jalgaon
>
> 24-2-1907

Besides Mr Tilak's name appearing first, the style of the letter is also his. The comment the letter makes on *Kavyaratnavali* would never have been made by its founder-editor, Nanasaheb Phadnis. The conference kept our house so busy, it was almost as though we were celebrating Dattu's wedding. The conference marked the literary birth of Balkavi Thombre. It was also during this conference that an illiterate like me began singing her poems with greater confidence.

Mr Tilak was keen that I should go to Jalgaon, but I had a severe stomach ache. Besides this, we had kept a milch buffalo. Half my mind would have been with her and her calf had I gone away. But I did write a poem and send it to Jalgaon. Of course, Mr Tilak had refined it, but he had not touched the line for which people at the conference praised it. That line was, 'You are the poets, I only a beggar at your door'.

The poem was actually in praise of poets.

You are the blossoms on the tree of poetry.
Your laughter brings laughter to the world.
When you grow sad, there is gloom all around.
Your fragrance fills the air.
People clamour to partake of it.
Being with you is the only joy in life.
You, the flowers, have now gathered together.
It pleases the Creator to see this garland.
I would have come to bow before this gathering
had fate not stood in the way.
And so I greet you from afar.
Accept my salute with your innate grace.
You are my brothers, I, a sister in need of your protection.
You are the poets, I only a beggar at your door.

Two poets, Mr Tiwari and the late Mr Anantatanay, responded to my poem with poems. The latter's poem was published in the issue of *Christian Citizen* dated 15 March 1907. During the conference, somebody taunted Mr Tilak for being a Christian. Anantatanay was enraged and wrote a poem expressing his feelings. He demanded to know of the taunter why the flower which he said had flowered in a cemetery had less value than other flowers. Does this flower not have the virtue of other flowers which lure the honey bee with their tender touch?

Balkavi Thombre

Mr Tilak had a poet friend called Colonel Kirtikar. He presided over the Jalgaon conference. He was an army doctor who had seen many wars. In his letters to Mr Tilak, he would refer to me as 'that ever-dying wife of yours'. I was always ill with something or the other and had taken to my bed at the time of the conference. I should not say bed. It would be more correct to say floor. Because that is where I rolled and writhed about. The floor was bed enough and my arm, pillow enough. But that is enough of that.

Mr Tilak's exhaustive report of the conference for which twenty-six poets had assembled, appeared in the issue of *Christian Citizen* dated 15 March 1907. This is what he wrote about Balkavi (Child Poet) Thombre:

> The gathering was fortunate enough to hear poems composed on the spot by Tryambak Bapuji Thombre, barely thirteen years of age. Who can deny that his pure, fluent, charming language is not a divine gift? Hindustan must be giving birth to countless child poets, child saints, child warriors every day who go to waste later. Who is to scout for them and nurture their talents to maturity? Surely we, the sons of Hindustan, should do it? Meanwhile, let us pray that God will enable these young people to serve our country to the fullest extent. All we are busy doing at the moment is skirmishing with our tongues and warring with our pens.

At the end of the conference, an executive committee was formed to offer help to modern Marathi poetry and poets in a systematic way. It comprised the following:

President: Lieut. Col Kanhoba Rannchhoddas Kirtikar, I.M.S., pensioner.

Vice-President: Raosaheb Vishnu Moreshwar Mahajani, Director of Public Instruction, Varhad Region.

Minister: Narayan Waman Tilak

Assistant Minister: Narayan Narsimha Phadnis.

Members: Moro Ganesh Londhe, Chandrashekhar Gore, Kashinath Hari Modak (Madhavanuj), Narayan Siddheshwar Joshi.

The conference benefited Marathi literature in two important ways. One was by bringing Thombre to public notice and two was by mooting the idea of the poetry series, *Abhinavkavyamala.* Later Mr Tilak went to Pune and met Laxmanshastri Lele, Raosaheb Kanitkar, Vasudevrao Apte and N.C. Kelkar, with whose help the poetry series was started.

Even after the conference, Mr Tilak could not get Thombre out of his mind. He felt the boy should be sent to school, should have the chance to study, and that nothing should happen to cause his poetic genius to suffer. So he began to write to Col. Kirtikar in this regard. Col. Kirtikar was a rich man and also Mr Tilak's friend. He promised to give Thombre ten rupees a month, but on the condition that the boy move to Ahmednagar to be under Mr Tilak's supervision. The condition was fulfilled. Thombre came to live with us in Ahmednagar.

He came alone. The day before that, Mr Tilak had gone out of town as usual. As I have already said, I was ill. Before leaving, Mr Tilak had told me that Balkavi was coming and I was to look after him well. It was about ten o'clock on Christmas day. I was asleep. The children had gone to church. There was not a soul in the house or in the vicinity. Our servants and neighbours had all gone to church. It was at such a time that Thombre came.

I asked, 'Are you Thombre?' using the respectful plural address for the boy.

He said, 'Yes.'

'Please sit down. My children have gone out. When they come back, they'll take you to a Hindu eating place. Meanwhile, I can offer you milk and bananas if you don't mind accepting them from us.'

Thombre had milk and bananas without demur. After a while, Dattu returned along with his friends Muley and Parnaik. They took Thombre out for lunch. Throughout his long stay with us, Thombre continued to eat out. Mr Tilak returned a couple of days later. He went to the market and got cod liver oil for Thombre to give him a little more strength.

I addressed Thombre in the respectful plural only on the first day. The sense of formal distance between us soon melted away. By the next day, he had lost his gloomy look and I was addressing him in the familiar singular. He had been worried about the new home he had been thrown into. As he often told us later, he had been convinced that Christians were monsters and evil spirits. But within a day he realized we were human beings whom he could take a liking to. He became good friends with Dattu and his mates. His behaviour in the house was like any other family member's. I had 'taken to the floor' when he came. So I had told him, 'My child, open that cupboard and help yourself to milk.' When he left the empty cup where it was, I had said, 'My child, can you put the cup away, please?'

Years later, he would tease me saying, 'Lakshmibai, you will even tell King George the Fifth, "My child, please close that gate after you".'

My addressing him in the singular once gave rise to an awkward situation. Bhauji also started addressing him in that manner. After all, Thombre was Dattu's age, a child poet albeit a talented one. So surely there could be no problem addressing him in that manner? When Bhauji was visiting us one day and saw Thombre on the verandah, he said to him in the singular, 'Thombre, come here,' or some such thing. Ignoring him, Thombre came straight to the kitchen where I was cooking. He sat before me and said, 'Lakshmibai, I don't approve one bit of your brother-in-law's behaviour. Is he some great man? Everybody is respectful to me. Even Mr Tilak doesn't address me in the singular. Why should he? I'm going right out and telling him what's what.'

'Don't do that, son. I also address you in the singular, don't I?'

'You're different. You are like my mother. You cared for me day and night when I was ill. Did he come here and share that work? So who is he?'

'He's my brother-in-law. So for my sake, please don't say anything to him.'

Bhauji came to the kitchen. He wanted to find out why Thombre was quarrelling with me and why I was trying to pacify him. He asked Thombre what was going on. That caused him to flare up even more. Bhauji said, 'Thombre, I was addressing you in the singular because I thought it was the natural thing to do. I was wrong. I will never do it again. I didn't realize it would offend you so much.' From that day, I too began to address him in the respectful plural. But I could not keep it up for long and Thombre did not like it. He came and sat beside me one day and said, 'Lakshmibai, how much longer will you continue addressing me like this? Please call me once by the special name you've given me.'

So I said, 'Go away, idiot.' He laughed then and so did I. When I wanted to be particularly affectionate, I would call him idiot. He felt happy when I returned his honorific to him.

During the time Thombre lived with us, he suffered a long bout of intermittent fever. He tossed and turned for forty days. It was Mr Tilak's money, Rajabhau Dharmadhikari's and my care, Dr Sorabji's medicines and God's mercy that saved him. He lived to bring glory to Maharashtra. I did not sleep for entire nights during that time because I had to do everything for him. That is why he and his mother bore a special love for me. His mother would say, 'Lakshmibai, this child isn't mine. He's yours. He was reborn because of you.'

Thombre's behaviour around the house was like a family member's, no different from Dattu's. He followed me around the house, while with Mr Tilak, he put on an air of great solemnity. I was the first listener for any new poem he wrote. There I would be, giving instructions to a maid or talking to somebody and here he would be impatient for me to hear a poem. When I paid no attention, he would tear up the poem before my eyes. Dattu and Tara would then parody a popular stage song to tease him: 'Oh what a philistine is this lout / He tears up poems and then stomps out.' That would make him laugh and he would rewrite the poem. Thombre was given to tearing up poems. Several of the ones he had written before he came to Ahmednagar had gone that way. He would recite some of them to us. One was composed around the conceit of a fawn licking the moonlight off a boulder taking it to be milk.

There is a story that belongs to this time. When Thombre came to stay with us, he began going to school. He must have been in the third or fourth grade. Dattu was in high school then. When Thombre came back from school, he would get after me to tell him a story. It was a daily routine. Telling him stories tired me out. One day Haushi's mother-in-law came to stay. We got on well together because she knew a lot about herbal medicines. She also knew a lot of stories. The way she told them, they would last for hours on end. When Thombre got back from school the day she came, he said to me as usual, 'Lakshmibai, please tell me a story.'

I said, 'A relative of mine has come today. She knows lots of long, wonderful stories. She will tell you a story tonight.'

Thombre was thrilled. Between the end of dinner and bedtime, he made numerous trips from the front room to the kitchen and out again. Bhaskar, Dattu, Tara, I, our guest and Thombre slept as we always did—in a long row. My children knew all about our guest's stories. They pulled their covers over their heads and giggled under them at what Thombre was going to face. Thombre, overjoyed with the thought that he was going to hear a really long story that night, wangled himself a place next to our guest. He sat on his mattress, his legs crossed, ears pricked, all agog to hear the story. The story began: 'See bhau, there was a king in Ujjain. His first wife had a daughter and a son. His first wife died. He married again. His second wife didn't want to look after the first wife's children. She pretended she couldn't see too well. She said, "An astrologer told me both children should go into the forest, tear the heart out of a hyena and feed it to me. That will make my eyes well again."

'The king agreed and took his children to the forest and left them there. They went in search of a hyena. They crossed one forest, then a second, then a third...'

'Bai, they crossed one thousand forests. But what happened next?'

'Wait, bhau. Please don't rush me like this. They crossed five forests, six forests, seven forests. They met a swan. He gave them shade. He made them sit under a tree. He decided to build a house. They crossed one sea, then a second sea, then a third sea...'

'Bai, I can see they must have crossed seven seas, but please tell me what happened to those children.'

'Please wait bhau, don't rush me. The bird brought one twig, he brought a second twig, he brought a third twig...'

'Bai, he brought enough twigs to make a hill. Tell me what happened to the children.'

'Please wait, bhau. Why are you doing this? Then the bird began to collect pebbles. He brought one pebble, then a second, then a third...'

'I can see the pebbles making a mountain as high as Meru. But I want to know what happened to the children.'

'This is no way to behave, bhau. Let me tell the story.'

Thombre gave up. He was sleepy. When he lay down, our guest, still keen on telling her story, sat up and began shaking him. 'Get up, bhau. There's just a teeny tail left of the tale.'

We laughed till our stomachs were near to splitting.

Thombre said, 'I beg of you, bai, let me sleep now.' But she did not let him sleep till three in the morning. The moment his eyes closed, she would shake him awake and continue with her story. At last it ended. When the rest of us got up in the morning, these two were still fast asleep. I was in the kitchen when Thombre woke up. He came there and literally prostrated himself before me.

'Lakshmibai, I fold my hands before you, your relative and her story. She should have been an epic novelist. I wonder what fly got into that ointment.'

The unticketed drama that had been enacted that night entertained us for months afterwards.

House Gone, Buffalo Gone

I have written about the poets' conference and Thombre in the last two chapters. But through it all, funny incidents continued to happen in our family.

After leaving Rahuri, we returned to our old house at Fergusson Gate in Ahmednagar. We had brought our Chimbaba with us when we came. He was a good, straight and trustworthy man. Shahaji Bhil was looking after our house in Rahuri on a salary of six rupees a month. The first thing Mr Tilak did on arriving in Ahmednagar was to set up his office. He had brought as many of his books as he could from Rahuri. Only a few had to be left behind. Mr Tilak was standing on a ladder, arranging books in ceiling-high shelves while Dattu and Rambhau Dharmadhikari stood below passing them to him. Suddenly, Mr Tilak realized his Webster's Dictionary was missing. Together they turned the whole house upside down, but to no avail. Mr Tilak was sure he had seen it in Dattu's hand some time ago.

'Dattu, hadn't you borrowed the dictionary that day?'

'No, Papa, I hadn't.'

'You're lying.'

'No. I never lie.'

'I saw it in your hand.'

'No. It was left behind in Rahuri.'

'Rambhau, don't you remember seeing the dictionary here?'

This set Rambhau on the horns of a tricky dilemma. If he said yes, he would be in trouble, and if he said no, he would still be in trouble. He was speechless. But when Mr Tilak began shouting, he quickly decided to remember that he had seen it in Ahmednagar.

Mr Tilak roared, 'Dattu, you know whom you are facing, don't you? Out with the truth, now.'

'But, Papa, I did see it in Rahuri.'

'Tell me the truth. I won't hit you. Don't be afraid. Tell the truth.'

'It's in Rahuri.'

Now Mr Tilak lost his patience. He began throwing books at Dattu one after the other from the top of the ladder, while continuing to shout, 'I-saw-the-dictionary-in-your-hand. Are you trying to prove me wrong? Have all of you conspired to put me down?'

Even then, Dattu continued to say the same thing. At this point, our Manjulabai said to me, 'Go and save him.'

I said, 'I'm not the one to come between those two.' After some time though, the volcano simmered down by itself.

Two months later, when Mr Tilak returned from a visit to Rahuri, he called Dattu to him as soon as he stepped into the house.

'Please forgive me, Dattu.'

Dattu had forgotten the incident. He said, 'Why, Papa? What have you done?' Mr Tilak held him close and said, 'I beat you that day for no reason. The dictionary was in Rahuri as you were saying. I feel very bad about my temper. Have you forgiven me? How happy it would make me to have a pure, innocent nature like yours.'

After that day, not once did Mr Tilak raise his hand to Dattu.

In Ahmednagar, an ascetic came to stay at our house. He always spoke of other-worldly things. 'God is bliss. He alone is truth. All else is false. The world is an illusion. Man is voluntarily drowning in it. He does not know where he has come from or where he is going. It is all an illusion. But he is lured by the illusion and goes after it, abandoning God. Wives, children, money, all such attachments are pure illusion and must be abandoned.' Then he would say, 'Let us serve people together. If we sold your house in Rahuri, we could use the money to buy a shop and use the profits from it to serve the people. That would make the needy strong.'

I always listened very attentively to what the ascetic said. Mr Tilak had been feeling burdened by the house in Rahuri. He too began to say that if we sold the house we would be able to use the money for a lot of welfare work. One day, there was no water in the house. There was a severe shortage of water in Ahmednagar. I went to where Mr Tilak was resting. The ascetic was sitting by him. I placed an empty pot of water in front of the ascetic. 'Here you are, Buwa. You want to serve humanity, don't you? There's not a drop of water in the house today. Perhaps you, Dattu and Tara can go fetch some. Of course, it's all a dream. An illusion. So there's no reason to take it seriously.'

Buwa began to show a disinclination for the task. So I gave him another dose of medicine.

'See Buwa, when I am roasting bhakris and I burn my hand, the blisters I get don't appear to my eyes like an illusion. I can't bear the pain. But since everything is an illusion to you, fetching water should cause you no pain. What objection could you have to that?'

When Buwa saw that Mr Tilak agreed with my reasoning, he got up instantly. He fetched a couple of potsful of water, moaning and groaning all the way. Then I said to him, 'I realize that you have a deeply illusion-filled eye on our house in Rahuri. You'd best go your way tomorrow.'

Buwa left the next day but that did not save the Rahuri house from its evil stars. A certain Christian man was oppressed by debt. It was a rule in the American Mission that a man in debt should not be given a job. If this man lost his job as a result of his indebtedness, his condition would be worse. Mr Tilak's heart began to bleed. But what use was a bleeding heart? What did we have in the house that we could give the man? And so once again, the Rahuri house began dancing before Mr Tilak's eyes.

One day, Mr Tilak announced that he was going to Rahuri. He returned two or three days later. The day after he came back, he gave me six hundred rupees to keep. 'This is Dr Hume's money. Tomorrow such-and-such man will come to fetch it. Get him to sign a receipt for debt repaid and give him five hundred rupees.' I was determined to discover what was going on.

'If the money belongs to Dr Hume, why should we get an acknowledgement of debt? What does it mean?'

'It means that Hume Saheb wants to keep the debt he is giving a secret from Mrs Hume.'

The man who was supposed to come came the following day. I gave him the money and got him to sign the acknowledgement of debt received. I kept the remaining hundred rupees aside. Then I began to hear stories of the Rahuri house having been sold. It had gone in style, complete with a dowry comprising all the stuff in it: chairs, benches, shelves, tripods, lamps, cots, cradle, all the coir ropes that Chimbaba and I had woven. The baby went and so did the bathwater.

The well alone had cost five hundred rupees to dig and build. The well went and with it the farm and the house. But we now had one hundred rupees. Moreover, we were going to save the six rupees that we used to pay Shahji Bhil every month. That was no mean profit.

I said to Mr Tilak, 'Where is the money you got for the house?'

'It is safe. With Dr Hume. Now don't trouble me.'

'And all the stuff in the house?'

'Where were we going to keep it once the house was sold?'

'You mean we were in such dire straits that you had to sell off the lamps and the cradle as well? Sorry. That's unacceptable. I must have the lamps and cradle back. What inauspicious nonsense is this!'

'What idiotic ideas you have.'

'But what was the need to sell all those things?'

'Don't you understand? We were paying six rupees a month to Shahji, weren't we?'

Two days later, Mrs Hume came to see me. I said to her, 'Madam, I believe Mr Tilak has kept our six hundred rupees with you.'

'What six hundred rupees?'

'The price of our Rahuri house.'

'Not at all. Mr Tilak gave that money to that man to pay off his debts.'

My face was worth seeing then. I faced Mr Tilak with this when he came back. He said, 'Yes, I gave the money to him.'

'Why didn't you tell me this before?'

'I would have liked to. But would you have let me give the money to him then?'

And so we lost the house, and I a lot of water from my eyes. All that remained was the gleam of memories. The five hundred rupees too were lost. What remained with us till recently was the receipt of debt repaid. I deposited the remaining hundred rupees in the bank. I added twenty rupees to the sum and bought a buffalo. She was a fine, good-looking buffalo. But she produced only male calves and not much milk. That is why her owner had transferred the millstone to our necks. But later he regretted it. Because, when she came to us, she gave birth exclusively to female calves and produced abundant quantities of milk.

Mr Tilak used to take great care of the buffalo. One day he was washing her when a very rich scholar came to see him. The buffalo was on display in front of the house. Mr Tilak sent a message to the kitchen that a visitor had arrived, came indoors, washed his hands and went out to welcome him. This pampered buffalo was the cause for many quarrels between us. One day I said, 'I don't know what to do. When I put dung-pats out to dry, they get stolen.' Mr Tilak gave the problem some thought and came up with a sure-fire scheme for preventing the thefts. Dattu and Tara were sitting nearby when he said, 'We'll engage a servant to dry the dung-pats on a fire. We'll build a large clay stove, put a sheet of tin on top, roast the dung-pats and store them. That should do the job.'

All three of us burst out laughing at Mr Tilak's idea of a solution.

'You think I'm a fool? You think I know nothing?'

'You know a lot. There can be no two opinions about that. All I want to say is, the cost of having the dung-pats roasted will come to three times their price. Also when they are put on a hot tin sheet, they'll be reduced to ashes.'

'That's how you put me down every time. What do you say, Dattu?'

'I agree with what Aai is saying. If we are going to spend that much, we might as well buy firewood.'

Now Mr Tilak got really angry. He called Manjulabai and told her to light the stove and roast a dung-pat on a griddle and bring it to him. Manjulabai nodded and went off by another door. Mr Tilak went out for his work and the dung-pat affair fizzled out.

Once I said to Thombre, 'Can you give water to the calf, please?'

He did that and then, instead of leading the calf back to its place, he decided to have a bit of fun. He wound the loose end of the calf's tether around his own waist. The calf used to drink a lot of milk and had grown very strong. It began to pull Thombre and soon the two were going round and round the house, the calf in front and Thombre behind. I thought Thombre was leading the calf and only later realized it was the other way around. The calf was pulling him and he was laughing. But his laughter soon stopped when he stumbled and fell and the calf continued to pull. So Thombre went bumping along behind it like a log of wood and began to cry.

I ran out and untied the rope from the calf's neck to set Thombre free. He was crying and quarrelling with me. 'You're to blame.'

'What did I do? Did I tie the calf to your waist? And why didn't you call out to me when it began to haul you around?'

I put a plaster of turmeric over his bruises and fomented his legs. Finally, three days later, all signs of the calf's misdeeds faded from his body.

Our Days in Ahmednagar

One day Kalyani, our buffalo, broke loose and ran amok. Mr Tilak was taking a class in the lecture hall. Lady Kalyani set off from Fergusson Gate and went right past the lecture hall. Mr Tilak's eye fell on her. He stopped his lesson halfway, ran out of the class and went after her, dressed in trousers, coat and hat with a long cane in hand. The buffalo had no time for him. She would not be curbed. Finally, somehow, he managed to bring her home.

Mr Tilak said, 'It's not easy to turn a buffalo around. I know now what a tough job cowherds do. From tomorrow, we'll double our cowherd's salary. These people are poor. They don't speak up. That's why we make them work so hard for such small returns.' Accordingly, we began paying the cowherd more.

It was decided to hold a gathering in the mission school. A gathering is not complete without a play. The boys were told they could only do a play which had no female characters. Such a play could not be found. So Mr Tilak took it upon himself to write one and also to direct it. He had neither a plot in mind nor time to write. Most of his time was spent doing things for other people.

But the boys were not to be denied. The minute school got over, they would plant themselves in the house. The first day was devoted to christening the play. It was called *Sheelam Param Bhushanam* (Character is Man's Finest Ornament). Rehearsals were to take place in the evenings from five o'clock. But there was nothing to be rehearsed. When the boys came, some visitor would always drop in. Mr Tilak would then spend the evening talking to him. If nobody dropped in, he lost himself in reading or writing. Occasionally, he would engage the boys in a debate about some profound subject. The boys on their part worried only about when the play was going to be written and when they were going to start rehearsals.

Tea-making added to the general confusion. Mr Tilak

believed that nobody could make tea as he did, in a scientific manner. So tea-making was his monopoly. This is how it went. The stove was set in the middle of the room and around it were arrayed the kettle, cups and saucers, milk and sugar along with inkwell, sheets of paper, penholder, spoons, the parrot's cage, the cat and the dog in the doorway. The boys from the Mission school sat in the middle of all this. Six or seven days after the play had been named, Mr Tilak chose the boys who would play his characters. 'You will be Balasaheb, you Pillya, you Devdutt, you Charudutt.'

'But Papa, won't you give us lines to learn?'

'Can't you give me some time to have tea?'

'Of course we can. But if somebody drops in meanwhile, nothing will get done.'

One day, Mr Tilak gave each of the actors some lines to learn. When they clamoured for more, more were given. The play was written and directed in this fashion and completed just in time for the gathering. By then the boys had grown very impatient. They were not sure that the play was ever going to be completed.

Mr Tilak would say, 'Stop worrying. Of course it'll be completed.'

'Why don't you dictate it? We'll take down the lines.'

That is something Mr Tilak could not manage to do. Finally, the play turned out so well it became the talking point in Ahmednagar for days afterwards. Two or three boys who took part in it went on to shine in different fields. B.L. Patankar who is currently professor in a Nashik college played Devdutt. Rev. Ramkrishnapant Modak, the Member of the Legislative Council from Ahemdnagar, played an important role. The now famous actor Bapurao Pendharkar played Charudutt. He had a very sweet voice. Madhavrao Patankar, owner of the popular theatre company, Patankar Natak Mandali, said to Mr Tilak, 'If this boy makes theatre his profession, he will go very far.'

***

Around this time, Mr Tilak had taken to playing songtya. In this board game, the pieces are moved according to the numbers you get by casting cowries on the floor and seeing how many fall face down and how many face up. The game led to fierce quarrels. Mr Tilak would arrange the cowries in his hand surreptitiously before casting them in order to get the numbers he wanted. Soon people stopped playing with him. This angered him so much that he began playing by himself using the right hand as one player and the left as its opponent.

One day, all of us planned to play with him. He was very happy. But we made a condition. The cowries were to be placed in a bowl, rattled and thrown. On one side were Mr Tilak, Thombre and Tara. On the opposite side were Dattu, Bhaskar Krishna Ujgare and I. Mr Tilak was doing well in the first game. Only one of his pieces was left on the board waiting to go home. He needed to get two for that. If he got ten, the piece would have to go home, come out and then move back in with the risk of an enemy piece devouring it. If he could have thrown the cowries in his usual manner, they could have been properly arranged. But throwing them from a bowl made the risk real.

Mr Tilak threw the cowries. One fell on its back face up, the other fell on its side, facing us and backing him. Mr Tilak shouted, 'Two!' We shouted, 'Ten!' He said, 'How can it be ten?' We said, 'How can it be two?'

He tried forcing his opinion down our throats by banging his fists hard on the floor and shouting, 'Narayan Waman Tilak says it is two.'

I shouted back, 'How can it be two? Lakshmi Narayan Tilak says it is ten.'

He turned to Thombre and Tara. 'What numbers are the cowries showing?' Thombre said, 'Neither two nor ten, but one-and-a-half.'

Mr Tilak said, 'That makes it two.' We were angry but we were also laughing. Finally, we insisted that he play again. Mr Tilak was not happy to do that. What if he did not get two?

Finally he flung the board, the pieces and the cowries all out into the front yard, rushed to the ironsmith next door and told the people there to take all of the stuff away. This they did, happily. Why would they not?

***

Mr Tilak was constantly losing things. He would not keep them in their proper place, would not look in the places where he had kept them and would not allow anybody else to look for them either. The things he lost most often were his dentures, box of matches, cap, glasses and belt. His shoes, coat, cap, collar, belt and umbrella would also play hide-and-seek with him, particularly when it was time for him to leave for a class or a lecture or a journey. Meanwhile, the rest of us danced circles around him.

On many occasions, he was forced to leave without his cap or had to secure his trousers with the rope off the calf's neck in place of a belt. He would say, 'Nobody looks after my things. Everybody is busy with their own work. Nobody cares for me!' At which point we would all rush to care for him.

One day, he lost his dentures. What chaos followed! He said, 'This dog has filched my teeth. Or rats have hidden them under this tonne of wood shavings you've collected for the stove. Haul them out and throw them away everybody. She's only concerned about the house.' So all my fuel was dumped into the compound and we found his dentures on the table in their usual box.

Once he lost his cap. It was hanging on a peg over which he had hung his coat. Mr Tilak had to go out. In his hurry, he got into another coat and started looking for his cap. First he slammed the first coat down on the floor. The cap below it got thrown down with it. Then all our clothes came off their pegs and began to fall on the heap like the snakes who threw themselves into the sacred fire during Janmejaya's snake sacrifice in the *Mahabharata*. Along with the clothes, mattresses, rugs and blankets, all fell to the floor.

'Go call that Manjulabai. What's she doing? Tell her to look for my cap.'

Manjulabai came out and stood stunned by the sight of the mountain of clothes and linen.

'Manjulabai, what's the use of having you people? Are you vegetables for cooking? I want you to find me my cap this minute.'

'But, Papa, it has to be under that mountain.'

Nobody dared say another word. Manjulabai escaped to Mr Tilak's office to look for the cap and only came down when she saw him from the window striding out bare-headed. After that, we began to put the clothes away and found the cap entangled with the first coat. When Mr Tilak heard of this he said, 'Yes, of course. I'd hung it under the coat yesterday.'

***

Once in a while, Mr Tilak would send me to take his class. Something funny happened the first time I went. 'Go take my class,' he said.

I said, 'What should I teach them? How to make pickles and methkoot?*'

'No, silly. Just tell them about Hindu customs, that's all.'

There were thirty or forty students in the class. They were not little children but adults like us. They welcomed me when they saw me.

'Gurumauli, are you going to teach us today?'

'Yes, I've come in place of your guru.'

I blabbered away and managed to teach them something that day. When my lecture was over, one of them said, 'Gurumauli, may I ask you something?'

'Certainly. Go ahead.'

'Our guruji has told us that you beat him. Is that true?'

'How is that possible? He must have said something else

---

*Methkoot is a dry powder made from roasted and ground dals, wheat, rice and spices, generally eaten mixed with rice and ghee or rice and curd.

in some other context. Do wives ever beat their husbands? Words are enough to beat a wise man. In that sense, I do beat him once in a while.'

I said something along these lines to get out of the situation and came home. Mr Tilak was lost in making tea.

'So how was your lecture? What subject did you speak on?'

'It was a really exciting subject.'

'What was it?'

'Why do wives beat their husbands? Is it a good thing or a bad thing?'

'What is this nonsense you are talking about?'

'Not nonsense at all. This was really my subject.'

'So what did they say?'

'They said, no wonder Guruji was saying that Gurumauli beats him up.'

'What did you say to that?'

'Me? I told them the truth.'

'What?'

'I told them that I give him a good pasting when he doesn't heed me, does vanishing tricks with our money, gets angry without reason and doesn't come home on time.'

Mr Tilak believed my story completely. He said, 'I believed you were a wise woman. But today I'm convinced you are a fool. One day, I fear you will destroy my reputation completely.'

Kith and Kin?

We were in the habit of picking up and carrying on our hips people who could actually walk by themselves. I want to narrate a few such incidents. But let me first say that neither of us tired of doing these things. On the contrary, not doing them made us feel lost.

One evening, a lame man turned up at our house. He appeared to have had a paralytic stroke. We kept him with us. Rambhau and I took a lot of trouble caring for him. He had to be given heat treatment, served and sometimes even fed food and cleaned. Rambhau was a very good man. He came to us much before he converted to Christianity and continued to return to us for years afterwards whenever he needed shelter. But he was a past master at fibbing and running up debts. His conversion, marriage and the rearing of nine-month-old Chiki after his wife died, all happened in our house. When he had a job, he worked extremely well. But he did not last long in it because of the two flaws in his character. However, as far as serving people was concerned, he felt the same way as we did and always helped us in this kind of work.

With our combined efforts, our Tamburlaine's health improved. He used to require bidis worth two annas every day and tea three times a day. He got all of this on time. He stuck on at our house even after he began to feel better. Then he converted to Christianity. After that his mood changed. It was as though his hands had touched heaven. He sprouted wings. One day, the tea did not taste right. Another day, he had not been given his bidis on time. A third day, his food was cold. A fourth day, Tara was too noisy. Her mother had not brought her up well. Tara became a daily complaint. Mr Tilak tried his best to explain things to him, but he would not give up his point. He was pacified only when Mr Tilak scolded Tara.

One day, when Mr Tilak had gone out of town, our Gopa,

the teacher, came to see us. His knowledge of herbal medicines was great. He had a medicine even for paralysis. I said, 'Gopa, take this man with you to your village. A cure works best when the medicine, the doctor and the patient are together in one place.' I gave him five rupees for expenses and the two of them left. A letter came from Gopa by the same train as Mr Tilak. It said that the patient had flown the coop. Mr Tilak felt very sad for him.

***

After this character exited, another entered. Mr Tilak had just stepped out into the front yard after making himself a cup of tea and dragging the other tea-drinkers in the house out of bed to have theirs, when a very tall, broad individual came and stood before him. He had a lightish complexion, a flat, broad face, light eyes, matted hair coiled like a crown on top of his head, shaven cheeks and chin, a saffron robe reaching down to the ankles, a saffron turban and he carried a small bundle tied in saffron cloth. Standing before Mr Tilak he said, 'Are you Tilak?'

'Yes, I'm Tilak.' As soon as he heard this, he put his bundle down and extracted from it an enormous garland which he put around Mr Tilak's neck.

'I feel blessed today. My life has been worth living.'

Removing the garland from his neck, Mr Tilak said, 'Buwa, please don't touch my feet. God is great. I am but a puny creature.'

Buwa took up residence in our house. Like the chatak bird which thirsts for water, he would wait for every word that fell from Mr Tilak's lips. Mr Tilak became very fond of him. Nothing could separate the two. Mr Tilak would talk to him about Christianity. As he listened, Buwa would feel moved and tears would gather in his eyes.

Mr Tilak said, 'This is not an ordinary man. He will become as ardent a follower of Christ as Peter and Paul. When tears come to his eyes, they flow from the outer corners. That is a sure sign of true devotion and love.'

Tara said, 'What Papa says is true, Aai. His tears flow from the outer corners of his eyes. I have also read somewhere about what that means.' But I was not convinced. He reminded me of a story in which a goatherd cried because he said he had lost a goat.

This was not the end of it. Buwa began to work in the house like the rest of us. He never uttered a single rude word or grumbled about anything. He was a good, meek and affectionate man. He would help Mr Tilak wash the buffalo and take her out to graze. He behaved like a member of the family. As for serving Mr Tilak, he did it in the same spirit as a shishya serving his guru.

Many people believe that you get a lot of money when you convert to Christianity. I have not come across a single example of anybody getting money by converting. This belief springs from the fact that missionaries and Christians help the needy. But helping people is an important part of the religion. Our Buwa was also under this impression. One day, after evening prayer, he began to ask questions.

'How many children do you have?'

'You know how many.'

'How far will you educate them?'

'As far as they wish to go.'

'But you must have planned something.'

'They will graduate or else they will go to England or America.'

Buwa's mouth began to water. Then a little kitten came out of his bag.

'Maharaj, I know a poor woman who has two daughters. They are very eager to study. I have helped her a lot till now. I have admitted the girls to an institution. They are both clever. It costs me a minimum of fifty rupees every month to keep them. I have arranged for ten rupees. Please give the remaining forty. If you can afford to send a child to England or America, think of these two girls as your children and do this much for them.'

Mr Tilak said, 'Buwa, I'm hard put to educate my two children. How can I do this? You could send the girls to us here. We might be able to do something for them then. But I don't have enough money to send forty rupees in cash to them.'

'I'm not asking for it for myself. I'll give you the girls' address. You can send the money directly to them. If you can educate two, you should have no problem educating two more. Or you can deposit an amount in the bank in their name that will fetch forty rupees interest a month.'

After that, Buwa despaired and went away. He came to meet me after Mr Tilak had passed away. His headgear was now a pagdi. He had married one of the girls and was the father of some three or four children. He claimed that Lokmanya Tilak had arranged his marriage. True or false, who can tell?

***

Once Mr Tilak noticed a young Brahmin on the station at Mumbai. He was alone in the world, very clever but his appearance would have put even a seller of roast gram to shame. Mr Tilak brought Baba home and handed his charge to me. Baba's sacred thread was grimy, his teeth black with bidi smoke and his whole body covered in scabies. I heated water and got the servants to wash and scrub him till he shone. Then I gave him Mr Tilak's clothes to wear and restored him to human form.

Mr Tilak indulged him a lot. Baba used to call him Papa and me Mamma. But he being a Brahmin and we Christians, he used to imagine all kinds of things when we had our meals. He would look at a preparation of brinjals and cutlets, call it mutton and not eat. If I served him flax-seed chutney, he would push his plate away saying it was dried-fish chutney. Then Mr Tilak would give him four or five annas to go to the bazaar and eat what he pleased. Later Mr Tilak said, 'Serve him in my office, under my eye.' So I began to serve him in the office.

He used to want tea five or six times a day. I gave it to him. But he would take money from Mr Tilak and go out to have more tea. Mr Tilak would take money from Dr Hume, saved from his salary, for these expenses. Occasionally Dr Hume would refuse to give him money, because Mr Tilak would have taken an advance on his entire salary. Then he would secretly sell off old newspapers to finance this guest's needs.

This young man was full of fears. Our house was like a chawl with three blocks in a row. This young man was accommodated in the back room of one of the blocks. The other room in the block was used to store firewood. Servants were reluctant to fetch wood from there. For one thing, this youngster had started dirtying the place. He had also turned the front part of the block into a bathroom and the water from the tap would run under the wood. If we complained to Mr Tilak about it, he would say, 'You have too little tolerance for people.' The problem was serious. So one day I said to the young man, 'Bhau, if you're scared of the dark at night, please wake up Ranu. He sleeps close by and there's always a lit lantern for you to take along. This laziness won't do. And for every little thing that happens, you are ready to carry tales.'

Baba was enraged to hear me say this. He felt insulted. The next day, he put a lock on the door. He sat before the door quarrelling and not letting anyone in to fetch wood. 'You call me your son but you are so partial. Dattu has so many sets of clothes and shoes. I don't have anything.'

'That's because he goes to school. If you went to school, you would also get clothes like his.'

'I won't have that. When you buy him shoes, you must buy me a pair. Have you ever seen parents like you?'

'Absolutely not. There are no parents like us but there are also no sons like you. If I slap Dattu across the face, he will not utter a word. But you don't let me utter a word about your behaviour. You feel insulted by the smallest sound of disapproval I make. You claim to have passed the seventh grade. How then do you not have even an iota of sense? Come on. Hand over the key.'

'I won't. I don't know who you are.'

'Right. In that case, I don't know you either. Don't come for lunch.'

'I don't have to come for lunch. I will get my lunch here.'

'Let's see how you get it here.'

'Just watch.'

When Mr Tilak came home, he heard all the tales. Baba said, 'I took pity on her for your sake. I would not have tolerated her insult otherwise. I would have hit my own mother with my slippers. Why not her?'

Mr Tilak had to go to Mumbai that day. He asked him to get ready to go with him. He planned to make arrangements for him there. His highness gave away his clothes and bedding—all the stuff we had given him. They were to take a train that left at midnight. There was no money in the house. The bank was closed. We put together as much small change as we could. It added up to one person's train fare to Mumbai. But Mr Tilak was an optimist. He was certain he would get money at the station. As it happened, he met his great friend Raosaheb Sathe who was also going to Mumbai. He was an avid reader of poetry. Mr Tilak asked him for a loan. Raosaheb said, 'I have just enough for my fare.'

The train pulled into the platform. Mr Tilak and Raosaheb boarded it. Our son was still standing on the platform. The train began to move. Mr Tilak told him to go back home. In his confusion, Baba forgot to ask him for the tonga fare back. It was winter. The night was dark as pitch. He was alone. Tongas would come and pass him by. Down below, there was the occasional corpse burning on the pyre by the river. Our son was scared stiff. He found his way somehow to Fergusson Gate, his heart thumping all the way. As he stood there, the watchdog pounced on him. Ranu was sleeping on the verandah. He thought it was a thief and ran with his cane raised. But of course it was our son.

'Why have you come back?'

'Don't ask. And don't wake up Mamma.'

The following day, Ranu said, 'Our guest is back.'

I said, 'Fine. Don't any of you say a single word to him.' Everybody did as told and when their work was done, they had their breakfast. They did not call him. Finally he came uncalled.

'Mamma, I'm here.'

'Are you? Good. Now I'm the mistress of the house. Mr Tilak is away. You are not my kith or kin. I will not put up with your arrogance.'

My cannon fired round upon round while he listened in silence.

'Here's a water boiler. Those are the tea and sugar tins. Put all this stuff near your bed. Fire the boiler and bung all the stuff in. When you feel the urge for tea, just turn on the boiler tap so the tea falls straight into your mouth as you lie in bed. I am not going to dance attendance on you. You will have to do all the housework from now on since nothing I do pleases you. I will be the guest now. You see pieces of mutton in a brinjal and cutlet preparation. You smell dry Bombay Duck in garlic chutney. I don't believe you are a Brahmin at all because a Brahmin would not know such things existed. You must be one of those Brahmins who have tasted such things. You seem to be under the impression that we eat them. And under the impression that Mr Tilak concedes your every request. But that's because you don't know him. Once he gets angry, he'll pull apart every bone in your body.'

This dose had more than the expected effect on our adopted son. He promptly fell at my feet. 'Lakshmibai, please forgive me, I beg of you.'

From that day on, he really did begin to behave like a member of the household. Later he found a good job. Mr Tilak baptized him. We got him married. His wife had her first delivery at my place. He was lucky to have a really good woman for a wife. His children too turned out very well.

The Karanji and the Modak

The Diwali special issue of *Manoranjan* magazine published one of my poems titled 'The Karanji and the Modak'. Many readers liked the poem very much. It was an explanation of why Hindu women always make a small modak along with karanjis and a small karanji along with puranpolis. In my poem, I asked readers to look around and notice that nothing in the world stands by itself. The moon is not alone in the sky. Venus is right beside it. Rivers flow into the sea and creepers are supported by trees. A poet cannot compose without inspiration and man cannot live without woman. No wonder the karanji asks where is my modak and the puranpoli demands the company of a karanji. You might say women are mad to follow such customs. Yes, indeed we are mad. More than that, we are likely to drive others mad too.

Needless to say, Mr Tilak had refined the poem. One day, I received a letter from a woman in Pandharpur who asked, in a couplet, whether my poem had stood alone or had my husband supported it. The letter made me very angry with Mr Tilak. Why did he have to push me into the public eye and make me fall flat on my face like this? But Mr Tilak was nowhere near me to be scorched by my rage. He had taken it into his head to write an epic poem and had gone off to a place called Bhuinj near Wai to start work on his 'Christayana'.

I could not get that offensive couplet out of my head. I decided I would reply with a poem of my own. The result was my longest and most well-known poem 'Man and Wife'. Whole lines of the poem would come to me at night. I would scrawl them down on the floor with chalk. If I wrote on paper but did not have a penholder at hand, I would dip a matchstick in ink and write with that. In the morning, Thombre would transfer my night's labours onto paper. Bit by bit the poem grew to 275 lines. I sent it off, along with a strongly worded letter, to Mr Tilak. Dattu has preserved it to this day.

In my poem, I described the atmosphere in our house

where every person was a poet. I also referred to a man of sixty who had only recently begun to write poetry. This was a reference to Raosaheb Vinayakrao Sathe who had come to live in Ahmednagar after retiring and had started writing poetry. His son Waman was an excellent artist. Had he lived, he would have been famous. But he was snatched away when he was twenty-three or thereabouts. Mr Tilak wrote his second 'A Father's Tears' at this time. The first was written when our Vidyadhar died.

Raosaheb would come to our place every day and recite his poems to us. As with Thombre, so with him, I was the first listener. One day, he said he wanted to write to Mr Tilak. Dattu brought him an inkwell and a penholder. He and Thombre sat nearby. Raosaheb began to write. He would read out every line as he wrote it and end with the question 'Unh'? To this I had to respond with an affirmative 'Hun'. Thombre and Dattu laughed secretly at our duet. Raosaheb did not notice. The letter he was writing was very long. At one point, the boys could not hold back their laughter any longer. They ran out of the room. Finally the letter was done. Now Raosaheb wanted to know Mr Tilak's address. I called Dattu and Thombre in. 'Boys, just write out Mr Tilak's address for Raosaheb.' The boys got down to their task. One asked, 'Reverend. Unh?'

The other answered 'Hun.'

'Narayan, unh?'

'Hun.'

'Waman, unh?'

'Hun.'

'American Mission, unh?'

'Hun.'

'Bhuinj, unh?'

'Hun.'

'District Satara, unh?'

'Hun.'

The address was written. Raosaheb put the letter in his pocket and left. At night, I laughed to myself over the 'Unh-hun' chorus. But then I felt very bad. Raosaheb was older to us and had more knowledge. Was it right for us to make fun of him?

The next day, another such thing happened. Thombre and Dattu had climbed on to the roof of the house. Bhaskar and Tara were down below. When Raosaheb came, he began to scold them for climbing up there. Thombre made fun of him. The other children joined in. Raosaheb was very angry. He came into the house and told me about it. I went out and asked Thombre to come down. But that too was no use. So I settled down to listen to Raosaheb's new poems. Meanwhile Thombre went off to his restaurant for dinner. I gave Dattu and Tara a good scolding. 'I will not stand for anybody teasing Raosaheb. I will beat you if this happens again. I'm going to talk to Thombre when he returns. Nobody else will say a word to him.'

Everybody was already in bed when Thombre came back. Nobody spoke and nothing stirred. He went to each one's bed and tried to start a conversation. He even laughed out loud. But he got no response. He felt sad. He did not understand what this was all about. He came and sat before me and said, 'Lakshmibai, what has happened? I don't understand.'

'My boy, we have decided not to talk to you until you admit your mistake.'

'What wrong did I do?'

'You teased an elderly man. If you want to tease, find somebody your own age. We love you. You have no idea how bad we feel when someone criticizes you. If you tease Raosaheb, will he call you a good boy? Will I be pleased if he says you are bad? We like Raosaheb just as much as we like you. So, until you promise never to make fun of your elders, none of us will speak to you.'

Thombre was a child poet but often more child than poet. He felt very sorry. It showed on his face and in the water that gathered in his eyes.

'Lakshmibai, I swear at your feet that from now on I will never offend an elder.'

I hugged him and he smiled. He kept his promise too. Never again did he insult an elder.

Eight Years of Waiting

Dattu passed his exams. He had a tough time because he was studying for two exams at the same time. He was appearing for the school final exam and also for the drawing teachers' exam. After he passed his third grade of drawing, I had consulted Rajaramji Chandekar about what he should do. He said, 'Let him appear for the school finals and the drawing teachers' exam at the same time. Then if Mr Tilak suddenly decides to give up his job, Dattu will find one easily.' Rajaramji was my consultant in matters of education. So I did as he had advised.

A dozen students went from Ahmednagar to Mumbai for the teachers' exam. All of them cleared the first part, but came to grief in the second and returned home. Dattu had lost his chance of becoming a drawing teacher. Now my hopes were pinned on his passing his school finals and finding a government job.

Dattu had to go to Poona for his exams. The question was, whom was he to stay with there. In the end, it was decided that he would stay with Gharumai. Her husband Mr Barve was well-to-do, by which I mean, he was born well-to-do. He wrote to say I should also go along with Dattu. So I did. Once there, Mr Nanasaheb Barve claimed a monopoly over drawing Dattu's bath water for him. Every day when he did that he would say, 'Just past this exam and we'll be through.' Upon which Gharumai would whisper to me, 'You'd think he had spent on Dattu's education.'

Dattu cleared the exam. Mr Tilak was furious to hear this. 'Why do you do these things without asking me? Now he can't go to college. You always follow your own ideas. I want to send him to college. So now he'll have to stay another year in school to matriculate and get in. If he fails, it will mean one more year at school.' I felt very guilty. Once again I consulted Mr Chandekar. He said, 'There's a way out. Send Dattu to Nagpur. Allahabad

University does not insist on students passing board exams. School finals will do.'

Mr Tilak asked Dr Robert Saheb, who instantly agreed to admit Dattu. Fortunately, the fees were low enough for us to afford them. And in this fashion the path was unexpectedly cleared for Dattu's higher education. All of us went to the station to see him off. It was the first time he was going so far away. That saddened Mr Tilak. Both Tara and I also felt very low for days afterwards.

Dattu was about eighteen years. I began to dream sweet dreams. I saw him grow into the world's best scholar. He was now in college and he was such a fine young man that I—being his mother—could find no fault in him. It upset me that he was receiving no proposals for marriage despite his fine qualities. Actually, proposals do not come from the girl's family amongst Christians. The boy proposes. But not being used to this custom, I would keep forgetting it.

There was a matron in Ahmednagar called Rakhmabai Kukas. We often called on each other. I told her about my secret worry. She said, 'Bai, amongst us we ask for a girl's hand. And anyway, your son is not old enough yet.'

I could not accept this. I said, 'What is old enough? He will continue with his college. The girl will stay with me.'

That summer we decided to go to Nashik. Rakhmabai's brother Mr Krishnarao Sarode had also come there from Mumbai for a change of air. We were staying close to each other and had made arrangements for our meals to be delivered by the same woman. So for two months, neither family had to bother with shopping, cooking and cleaning. We met every day at mealtime when the woman came and served us in our home. Besides this, the Sarodes were very proud of the Marathi language and got along very well with Mr Tilak. The Sarodes were good, kind people and we became great friends during those two months. This was the time when Mr Tilak was putting together the second book in the series called *Abhinavkavyamala*.

He had collected a number of poems by different poets. This gave us the opportunity to read some unpublished poems of B.R. Tambe's. We would spend entire afternoons reading them.

I continued to be obsessed by my desire to get Dattu married or at least engaged. Had I been a Hindu, I would already have had a little daughter-in-law to help me. But that was not to be now. Since the custom was not for girls' families to propose, I decided to sound out prospective brides' families myself. And I did too, without Mr Tilak's knowledge. But I received the same response every time. 'Bai, the boy is still at college. Why are you talking about his marriage now?'

I could never accept this idea. While we were in Nashik, Dattu and the Sarodes' daughter Ruth became good friends. I began to think it would be lovely to have her as a daughter-in-law. She was a good girl and very intelligent. It was obvious that Dattu and she liked each other. Ruth was in the fifth grade of senior school and was only fourteen. This is not considered an age for marriage amongst Christians. Not even the age to think of marriage. Even amongst Hindus this age is no longer considered old enough for marriage.

Anyway, one day I took Ruth aside and asked her if she would agree to becoming my daughter-in-law. She said 'How can I say? You can ask my father if you wish.'

I nagged Mr Tilak. I agreed that the marriage could not take place just yet. But what harm was there in proposing it? At last Mr Tilak gave in and spoke to Krishnarao who said, 'I will consult my sister and let you know.'

Once more I became uneasy. How was I to hold my patience till the Sarodes returned to Mumbai and consulted Rakhmabai?

Summer was over. We returned to Ahmednagar. Dattu went back to college and there was no letter from Krishnarao. We waited for a couple of months and then Mr Tilak wrote to him, needless to say as a result of my nagging. He was in no hurry to get Dattu married. But I just could not wait for a daughter-in-law.

Finally Mr Sarode's letter arrived. He said they were willing to give the girl to Dattu but on one condition. Not a word was to be said about marriage till Ruth had given her matriculation exam. Mr Tilak wrote back to say he too was in no hurry till Dattu had got his Bachelor's degree. And so, although there was to be no wedding for the next four years, I was filled with joy.

They say that when young people are engaged, the thought of marriage distracts them from their studies. No such thing happened in the case of these two. Ruth passed her matriculation and won a scholarship for standing first in English in the entire university. Dattu too graduated but the idea of their getting married when he had completed college and she her matriculation was set aside. It happened only when she too had completed her higher education and got her graduate degree. I, who had not been prepared to wait even eight months for the marriage, ended up waiting patiently for eight years after the engagement.

New Pots and Pans

Dattu was in his final year. There were four days left for him to return to Nagpur after the vacation. We said our evening prayers and were sitting around chatting. It was around ten o'clock when we heard Rangubai, the ironsmith's wife, call out to us from across the street. 'Bai, someone has been watching your house. Be on your guard.'

The Mission had given us three residential blocks stuck to each other like a tenement. Dattu slept in the block at one end. Rambhau's daughter Chiki, the maidservant and I slept in the back room of the middle block. Mr Tilak slept in the front room and Rambhau on the verandah. Rambhau had been staying with us since his wife died when Chiki was only nine months old. He had now become part of the family. Our kitchen, storeroom and dining room were in the third block.

My household was not mine alone. I was looking after two other families. I would always say in my prayers, 'Dear God, I don't mind my belongings being lost, stolen or destroyed. But please keep the belongings of our other people safe.' Mr Tilak always scolded me. 'Who asked you to take on other people's problems?'

That night we stayed awake till midnight. When I got up at break of day, I went out through the front door and walked round to the back looking around closely. I noticed that the ground at the back was wet. I said to myself, 'See how our maids waste water. That's why we fall short.'

A little further, I saw our cradle turned upside down. To me this was an inauspicious sign. Who had planted this omen near my house? A closer look revealed that it was no cradle. It was the entire frame of the window dug out of the wall and thrown down. Beyond that gaping hole, the door was wide open and the room inside cleaned out. All my water storage pots were emptied of water and carried away. With them had gone every copper and brass vessel that we possessed, including spoons and ladles.

I hurried to the front and woke up Rambhau. 'Get up quick. We've been robbed. There isn't a single stick of anything left.' I had to shake Rambhau awake because he had slept so late at night. He said, 'Robbed? Who did it?'

'Thieves.'

'Where are they?'

'Once you're properly awake I'll show you.'

When he was properly awake, he marched over to Mr Tilak. 'Papa, get up. We've been robbed. Cleaned out.'

'Is that right? Good. Now for a few days at least we won't have to bother with locking doors.'

Mr Tilak's wishes had been granted, but so were mine. All the stuff that was stolen belonged to us. I had put the others' belongings in the middle block. So they were safe. In the morning there was nothing to eat or drink in the house. The milk pan had been stolen along with the milk. Our next-door neighbours made tea for us. Dr Hume heard about the theft and came to console us. But neither Dattu nor Mr Tilak nor I needed to be consoled. The only time I had felt afraid was when I thought I saw the cradle upturned.

Dr Hume said, 'Bai, don't worry. I'll send you a pan.' We thanked him for the offer but declined it. We had Kalyani. Since her coming, I had started selling milk. That brought me a good amount of money. I felt sure I could rebuild my kitchen on the strength of that. I had already packed a box of savouries and sweets in Dattu's bag. That had escaped the thieves' hands. The rest of the food was stolen. The following day I bought a whole lot of clay cooking vessels from the potter for one rupee. Nobody was going to steal those.

After Dattu went back to college, we received letters from the Pendses and Barves to say that Gharumai was very ill and I should go to see her. She was like a daughter to me. It was my duty to go. But my heart was in my home and my people.

Moreover, the police inquiry into the theft was underway. Mr Tilak kept saying to the police, 'Let what has gone be. I don't need those things.' But the police would not have it. Their investigation and questioning continued in full swing. Finally they recovered a spoon that we identified as ours. The investigation ended there. We did not see the rest of our belongings again. We were free of them and the police.

Mr Tilak prayed for the thieves. The prayer was published in the *Dnyanodaya* issue dated 6 July 1906. This is how it went:

> My dear Lord, my beloved mother, good and bad, happiness and sorrow are your twin breasts. You nurse us alternately on them. Today I am as grateful to You for my loss as I would have been for gain. I have lost belongings worth fifty rupees. But had the poor who live around me lost what little they had, that would have been truly sad. I thank you that this did not happen. This little theft has made me acutely aware of what it must have meant to the people of Belgium and Armenia to have lost all their possessions and suffered the death of thousands of innocents. My throat chokes over the thought again and again. We have been spared, and for this too I am grateful to You.
>
> The indestructible will of God says, 'Do not accumulate possessions on earth where they are likely to be stolen. Instead lay up a store of possessions in heaven where no thieves will touch them. For where your riches lie, there your heart will be engaged.' However well I understood Jesus Christ's message, I needed an experience like that day's for the heart to accept it and turn towards loving what is not destructible.
>
> You have fulfilled this need and for this I am grateful. Jesus Christ whom You have blessed with Your complete acceptance, has been my teacher, my support, my life, my friend. He is always by my side. How great is Your grace that he asks me to forgive these ignorant thieves and pray that they bow before You in repentance for their deeds.
>
> Does forgiving these ignorant thieves mean that I am

> encouraging them to harm the citizens of this town? No. You, the saviour of this world, do not say so. Kingdoms and justice, laws and the police, they are all part of Your design. To allow transgressions against them and thereby bring harm to my fellow citizens would be a great sin. Help me not to commit it.
>
> Let these thieves be caught. Let the law judge their guilt. But let me forgive them. Let experience show them that I am their well-wisher, their helper. By myself I do not have the strength to achieve this. Let me remain then in the embrace of my dear Lord Jesus Christ. When he is beside me, I will follow all Your wishes. You have ensured today that I am happy, calm, and close to You. For this I bow before You a hundred times.

This was the effect that the theft had had on Mr Tilak.

***

Meanwhile, Gharumai was writing letter after letter to me. Mr Tilak said, 'Why don't you go? I'll take you there. I will look after everything here.' But my heart was trapped in the running of my home with its web of human relationships. I was in a situation that is so well captured in the proverb 'If you hold it, it bites; if you leave it, it runs away'. Finally I made the decision to go. I packed away what was left of our belongings after the thieves had been at them. My collection of scraps of cloth, my tin containers of every size, I labelled them all and put them under lock and key.

I was worried about the family and the cattle, but they could hardly be locked up for safety. They were free souls and I had to leave them be. Mr Tilak came with me to Pune. Rambhau and Thombre stayed home along with the domestic staff. Dattu was at college and Tara had been enrolled in Hujur Paga, the girls' school in Pune.

The situation in Pune was terrifying. Both Gharumai and her husband were seriously ill. Gharumai had been diagnosed with cancer and Mr Barve had a growth on his backbone. Mr Tilak said, 'Don't leave them. Don't worry about home. I'll manage everything there.' Even Mr Tilak found it hard to leave. There's a saying, 'When the mother dies, the aunt at least must live'. I had to be there.

I stayed with my niece for two months. Both Gharumai and her husband began to feel better, so I decided to return to Ahmednagar. Gharumai was distraught when she realized I was going. For two months after that, letters flew from Pune to Ahmednagar inquiring about the state of things. The letters from Pune said all was well. But my suspicious mind would not believe it.

Although the locked-up stuff was safe back home, there was no sign of the cattle, or the fodder I had stored for them nor even the fodder-cutting machine. I was stunned. I was not sure if this was real or a dream. When I got over the shock, I was told that the buffaloes had been sold. It was purely by accident that we still had Kalyani's calf, Soni. She was saved because she had been taken out to graze. Even my hens had been sold. My milk-and-egg business had been a great support for the running of the household. But now it was shattered like Sheikh Ali's air castle.*

I was an expert at accounts. I asked Mr Tilak for every paisa earned and spent. He too delivered the accounts to the last paisa. He said he had paid off all our debts. That was a relief. Now we needed money only for the wedding. I consoled myself with the thought that being free of debt was not such a bad thing after all.

The buffaloes were gone. The hens were gone. The parrot had flown away. The only pets we had now were Blackie the dog and his lifelong mate, Champi. Blackie had been with us for thirteen years. When we were in Rahuri, a bitch had littered in our house. We had kept one of the pups. Champi had lived with him for the last four years of his life. With age, Blackie

---

*This is Sheikh Chilli, a character in children's literature. In all the stories about him, he builds castles in the air and comes to grief. In one story, he is dreaming as usual of becoming rich and marrying the princess when he absent-mindedly cuts through the tree branch he is sitting on.

developed many ailments. I got a stove to keep him warm and a cot on which he could lie. Champi was always there, near him. I used to massage Blackie, give him medicines and put drops in his eyes. People laughed at me. But he responded to my nursing like a human being. When the pain became unbearable, Blackie would moan and Champi would come running to me, tug at my sari and take me to him.

One day, she came to me around two o'clock in the afternoon and pulled me out. Blackie was moaning louder than ever. When he saw me, he climbed down from the cot, licked my feet and lay there to draw his last breath. His four pups began to jump all over him playfully. Champi howled. Mr Tilak and I could not bear to see her grief. We locked her in a back room and buried Blackie in the yard. As soon as we let Champi out, she found the exact spot where Blackie had been buried. She sat there crying for a month, refusing food and water. Finally, she died of a broken heart. A blessed soul.

A Story

I had started writing a novel on a social subject. Occasionally, I would stumble over a diphthong in which two half-letters formed a single consonant and my progress would be halted. Then I would take down book after book to look up the letter. When I found it, my train would return to its track. One day, while my novel writing was in full flow, suddenly the mule bucked and stopped. I could not write 'manushya', the word for man. The 'sh' and the 'ya' at the end made a compound letter and I was stumped. As usual, I looked up book after book but I could not find manushya anywhere. Here is the scene that followed. I am worried. I am surrounded by untidy piles of books. Household chores are calling out to me. Just then Thombre walks in. He looks askance at the scene.

'Lakshmibai, why are you sitting like this? Are you looking for something?'

'What's to be done? I'm looking for a manushya. He's nowhere in these books.'

Thombre stood before me, his hand on his chest. 'Why have you taken so much trouble? Here stands a manushya. If you want to see more, come out. The world is full of them. They are everywhere. There's no shortage of them.'

'I don't want men from the outside world. I want a manushya from a book.'

Both of us laughed. Then Thombre wrote ma-nu-shya for me.

When the novel was done, I asked Thombre to read it. He wrote down the following response:

> I have read this entrie novle. Such a novle has not been written anywhere in the langwage of Maharashtra.
>
> Signed: Trimbak Bapuji Tomre, Ahamand Nagra.
>
> Date: Fif tin Jun, Nintin hundered for tin.

> Buy now. A unik novle. Buy now. This opur tuniti will not come again.

I still have this review with me. I had not titled my novel. But Thombre had added a title page on which he had written in big bold letters 'Lakshumbai's Novel'. That page has been swallowed up by time. It is twenty-one years since this happened. In those days, my writing was the constant butt of jokes among the youngsters in the family. I write more correctly now.

One day we got a letter from Tara. She said she had not received a nice long letter from us for ages. She wanted a nice long letter. Thombre and I were the only ones at home. He wrote an answer to Tara's letter. He made strips of paper a few inches broad and stuck them together till the resultant strip was long enough to reach from Tara's head to her toes. Below is the letter he wrote on that strip.

> Ahmednagar, Tilak Wadi, middle block, near the water pot, next to the flour grinder, beside the narrow mattress on which sleeps Lakshmibai. 3-3-1914.
>
> Our many blessings are with you.
>
> In Neverland lived a man. He had a daughter. She wanted a long letter. How to write? When to write? What to write? It was the month of March. The date was the third. Should he make khichdi? Plain chapatis? Clarify butter? Cook lunch? Empty pans for the servant to wash? Lock the storeroom? Time for a nap. Lie on a rag. Cover with a scrap. It is nearly one. Why nap? To calm the body. Makes a long letter easy.
>
> Oh listen Tarabai, this tale is for you, Pune city, Hujur Paga school. In the hostel many like you. Some Mongolian, some Burmese, some Japanese, some Indians. Arabs have their mullah, Turks their Kazi, Greeks have their soldier, everyone has someone. The Russian from Russia came to the Konkan, went grey, sat in the yard, trembled with the cold. Cried aloud. Many saw. Washed him, bathed him. Get up Baba, grow up. Baba grew up.

Tara had written a poem, 'My Cat'. This cat had been gifted to her by Pradhan, a friend of Dattu's. So Thombre's letter went on:

> A cat littered in the engineering department. She had three kittens. The dog ate one. The cat took the second. Get up brother. Call Pradhan, Queen Tara wants a cat. What kind of cat? Sick and troubled, spindly legged, dancing all over the place? Pradhan gave the third kitten to the peon. The peon gave it to Queen Tara. Now Queen Tara had a cat. Where shall I keep it? Where shall I take it? Where will my cat stay? Shall I carry it on my shoulder? Shall I carry it on my head? Or take it with me to bed? Drinks two pails of milk. Eats two slabs of meat. Won't let me pour milk. Jumps into the milk pail and drowns. My cat, my cat. Breaks Banya Baba's hand, bares her teeth at Champi, hisses at Blackie.
>
> Tarabai, you spoke your mind, I heard what you said. Wrote a long letter with inkpot and pen. Always wanted to write a long letter. The wish has been granted. I feel better.

Scaredy Me

I was not really as fearful as some people are. But in comparison with Mr Tilak, I was a scaredy-cat. Mr Tilak's dictionary did not contain the word fear at all. Symposiums, serpents, sahebs, he took them all in his stride.

Once, in Ahmednagar, we had organized a huge dinner. There were two women schoolteachers among the invitees. They lived in the school hostel run by a white woman warden and worked under her orders. She was a good woman, poor soul, but a strict disciplinarian. She saw discipline as a starched and ironed garment. The tiniest wrinkle in it sent her into a murderous rage.

The teachers had permission to be out till eight o'clock in the night. But the dinners we give—do they ever end at eight? Moreover, I had requested the teachers to help with the serving. That meant they could go home only after two dinner sittings had been served, that is around ten or eleven at night. But madam descended on us just after eight-thirty and started quarrelling with Mr Tilak. 'Why did you not send the teachers back in time?'

To begin with, Mr Tilak answered calmly. 'Dinner isn't over yet. When it is, I'll escort them back.'

She flew into a rage at that. 'Who do you think you are? I won't tolerate our school discipline being broken like this. You will send my teachers back right now. They will not stay here a minute longer.'

Mr Tilak said, 'You may get out of my house right now. This is not the village square to fight. If you don't go, I will have to remove you physically. I will not send the teachers back before they've had dinner. Go do what you want to in your house.'

She left. The incident did not escalate further. But our guests were astonished at Mr Tilak's daring.

This woman had become fascinated by the Japanese

Jinrikisha on her way from America. She would go all over town sitting in the rickshaw while the poor school students pulled it. Mr Tilak found this intolerable. He said to her, 'This is not our way. In the old days, pious people would pull the chariots of gods in procession or the king's chariot as a mark of respect. But you are neither a god nor a king. It is not right for you to come to our country and oppress people. These boys may be from poor families and you may be helping them. But they are not your slaves. Stop using this rickshaw or else...'

She said, 'Or else what? My leg hurts. I can't walk. I won't stop using the rickshaw.'

'If you can't walk, aren't there tongas around?'

Back then automobiles had not arrived in a big way. The madam paid no heed to what Mr Tilak said. This annoyed him even more. He composed a poem called 'Jinrikisha' and taught it to the local boys. That was like putting a firebrand in the hands of a mad monkey. When the Madam went out in her rickshaw, a band of boys followed her reciting the poem at the tops of their voices. In the end, she complained to Dr Hume. Dr Hume summoned Mr Tilak. A huge argument followed in which the rickshaw came to grief. Never after that did anybody use this contraption in Ahmednagar.

Amongst the missionaries who lived in Ahmednagar, the Bissel family was very well known. Rev. H. Bissel and his two sisters Dr Julia Bissel and Dr Emily Bissel were very highly regarded. They spoke Marathi so well that had they stood behind a curtain and spoken, they would have been mistaken for upper-caste women from Pune. One day Rev. Bissel and Mr Tilak quarrelled. The cause of the quarrel was a letter Mr Tilak had written to Rev. Bissel, which he had ended too formally. The quarrel soon ended when Mr Tilak provided an explanation through a poem.

Dr Emily Bissel once found that she could not recite a poem of Mr Tilak's in the tune for which it was composed. So she changed a few words here and there and sang it that way.

Angered, Mr Tilak wrote the poem 'Poet's Plea'. In this poem he warned Dr Emily, 'However skilled and tender your hand / I cannot bear its touch upon my poem. / For me that is worse than death.' Although he had aimed that directly at her, Dr Emily Bissel never held it against him. Indeed, she often asked for his help. She came to him every day to have the hymns in her book corrected. She and Miss Hattie Bruce (Mrs Cooper) share the credit for publishing Mr Tilak's poems on and for children. Nobody was aware of these poems, which form a splendid hall in Mr Tilak's mansion of poetry.

Mr Tilak went into warrior mode at the very mention of snakes and rats. He killed many large snakes but rats, by and large, hoodwinked him and escaped. Once a snake swallowed a rat, coiled up and went to sleep. Mr Tilak approached it quietly with a large pan which he upturned over it. Then he arranged dried dung pats around it and set them on fire.

When we were in Vani, a large snake climbed up to the upper floor and entered the room where Mr Tilak was sitting from a window behind him. A student was sitting in front of him. He said, 'Guruji, a very big snake has just entered.' The snake slid behind two boxes. Mr Tilak lit two lamps on either side of the boxes, stood astride them and crushed the snake with repeated blows of a pestle. The snake was a man-and-a-half in length.

Mr Tilak did not have similar success with rats. At night, the smallest sound would wake him. Then there was no going back to sleep. The sound was generally made by a rat. That meant mayhem in the house. Lights blazed, sticks were collected, sleeping people were woken up, doors and windows were shut. The son would be at one door, the daughter at the other, Thombre by the window, the wife beyond him and Mr Tilak in the centre of the room, beating the ground with a stout stick. I would feel scared. 'Please, the stick might hit somebody on the head.'

'Yes, I suppose I've gone mad,' he would retort.

When the hunt had reached the height of excitement and the rat had run to the door, Dattu would open it a chink and let it out. That would anger Mr Tilak in the same way as a hunter is angered when his quarry slips away.

'Dattya, you let it go!'

'No, Papa. There it is, at the other door.'

There was much banging and thumping while the argument raged. Finally, exhausted by the exercise, all of us would fall asleep.

The town boundary wall ran right behind our house in Fergusson Gate. It spoke directly of Chandbibi.* Out of it emerged snakes which had lived through the historic times of the Nizam. One day, I felt a movement under my pillow. I said to Mr Tilak, 'Somebody is lifting my head. Can you pass me a box of matches?' Many boxes were stored right next to Mr Tilak. He said, 'Shut up and sleep. You imagine things. If someone is lifting your head at all, it is you.' The argument ended and we slept.

The following day, Mr Tilak took Dattu and his students to Dongargan. Only Tara and I were at home. Somebody had given Tara a horse belt and she was busy playing with it. There was nothing for me to do so I started cleaning the house. There was a box at the foot of the place where we slept on the floor and a large cupboard full of books at the head. When I began to clean this room, I discovered a huge snake behind the box. Its mouth was within inches of my big toe. I pushed the box back and went and sat next to Manjulabai in front of the stove. Not a word would escape my lips. I just sat there with my head between my hands. When I began to tell Manjulabai that I had spotted a large snake, she thought I was telling her a story and responded accordingly.

A little while later, Mr Tilak, Dattu and Bhaskar returned from Dongargan. I told them about the snake. They all pointed

*Chandbibi belongs to Ahmednagar's history. The sister of the sultan of Ahmednagar, she was a polymath, musician and painter. She is best known for defending Ahmednagar against Emperor Akbar's army in 1595.

to Tara's horse belt as the culprit and laughed. I persisted in claiming it was a snake with even more urgency. Mr Tilak got up then and said, 'Come, show me your snake.' Dattu followed him and both began looking around the room. Dattu saw the snake behind the cupboard. 'See, Papa, here it is. It is huge.'

Then everybody rushed around collecting sticks, umbrellas, lamps, whatever came to hand. Polishing his glasses, Bhaskar gave orders over everybody's shoulders. The snake turned out to be a man height long.

***

Ours was a fun-loving family. When Dattu and his friends came, the fun was doubled. Dattu and Tara came home during the vacations. Their friends would gather in the house. They played the whole day long. In the afternoon, they would do conjuring tricks. In the evenings, they would give lectures. There was no dearth of listeners. Mr Tilak, his guests, I and the women who came to see me, were their audience. The chief participants were Dattu, Thombre and Tara. Our adopted son, about whom I have written earlier, also played his part. He would sit in the opposition and raise doubts and objections. But once the games started, he would begin chain-smoking his bidis.

These children had made a bag with an invisible pocket. They would put objects in the pocket and open the bag for the audience to see. But there were no objects to be seen. This earned the children loud applause.

Another trick was with a ball. There were a couple of flexible canes that happened to be protruding from the sloping roof of the room where the boys played. They had tied a string to the back of a cane and passed it into the neighbouring room. When Thombre asked the ball to jump, the boy at the end of the string would give it a little tug. The springy cane would then dislodge the ball which would fall to the ground. But if someone from the audience ordered it to jump using the same words, the ball would not budge. The trick astonished the audience.

Bhaskarrao Ujgare said, 'They are fooling us. There's some trick here.' Thombre said, 'Bhaskarrao, stand in the centre of the room. I will break the lens of your glasses exactly in the middle, without touching it. I will just give the order and the lens will crack in two.' This was an empty threat of course. But Bhaskarrao said seriously, 'Magic tricks should not harm anybody. Do what you want to do with your bag and your ball.'

There was another trick they played. Dattu and Thombre would think of an object and ask Tara to guess what it was. They would make coded signs to her and she would guess right. One day the audience sent Dattu and Thombre out of the room and thought of an object. Tara guessed it right again. This time it was our adopted son who made the signs. The minute she touched the correct object, he would light a match. The audience became suspicious of the match. Somebody took away the box of matches. Even then Tara guessed right. Because the moment she touched the correct object, our adopted son would blow out a puff of bidi smoke. This was something nobody except Tara noticed.

Thombre would say, 'My magic isn't something to sneeze at. I can conjure up anything with it. I can get Dattu here from Nagpur if you so wish.' I would say, 'I know all about your magic. Don't fib.'

Once, eight days after Dattu had left for Nagpur, some people came to see Mr Tilak as usual. Suddenly, Thombre's younger brother Babu rushed in and muttered something incoherently. It sounded like, 'Lakshmibai, make something nice for dinner. Dattu is coming back.' Amongst the visitors was young Mulay. After Babu left, Mulay's younger sister also breezed in and breezed out. Some time later, Thombre got up and went out. When he returned, he was trembling with fear. 'S-s-s-nake. Hissing,' he said. 'Why don't you carry the lantern,' I said. 'You're such a scatter brain.'

Seeing Thombre so scared, Mr Tilak picked up his gun. The gun had been bought for the Rahuri house but was never used in Ahmednagar, although there were snakes aplenty around us. But that day it was going to be a big hunt and that called for the gun. We collected an assortment of weapons—sticks, umbrellas, brooms—and set off behind Thombre. Seeing all of us out and armed, our neighbours also came running. Some twenty or twenty-five of us were now walking cautiously towards the lavatories at the back. Mr Tilak asked Thombre, 'Where is the snake?' Thombre said, 'In the centre lavatory.'

There was a rattling sound from the lavatory built of tin walls. When people heard the snake rattling the lavatory walls, some of them clung to each other and others began to retreat. Mr Tilak raised his gun. Just then the lavatory door was flung open with a bang and Dattu walked out.

'Lakshmibai, have I not conjured up Dattu as I said I would?'

'What nonsense. There would have been a catastrophe if the gun had gone off.'

'Dear Lakshmibai, would we have let such a thing happen?' Everybody laughed out loud and dispersed to their homes. After Dattu had reached Nagpur, his college had been ordered shut because of the plague. He had let his friends know and they had planned this prank. When he came back he went directly to the Mulay's place with his luggage. The plan was to give him time to have some refreshments and then conjure him up. But Babu Thombre could not keep the secret. He muttered to me, 'Cook something nice today, Bhau is coming.' I said, 'Who told you?' 'Nobody. I just thought.'

After letting the cat out of the bag, he joined the other boys. Thombre realized what his brother had done. 'Babya, why did you go to the Tilaks' house?' Then Mulay's sister was summoned. She said it did not look as if the Tilaks suspected that Dattu was coming. Even then, because of Babu's extra smart act, the boys realized that the prank as previously planned might not work. That's why the conjuring act had to be dropped and replaced by this trick.

Memories of Balkavi Thombre

When Thombre was with us, he was a happy, playful, positive person. But whenever he returned after being away, he was a changed person. A few days later, he would be the old Thombre again. When he went away, it was generally to Khandesh or Pune. Much later, he began going to Mahabaleshwar for work. By then, he had become more even-tempered.

On one occasion, he started quarrelling with me the minute he returned from Khandesh.

'Tell me why all of you love me.'

'I don't understand what you're saying.'

'Naturally, you don't. Because you are hiding a secret.'

'I'm sorry, Thombre. I don't have secrets. Nobody loves on order or stops loving on command.'

'No. But there's a different motive at the root of this love.'

'What motive? I'm not aware of any.'

'Aren't you? Then tell me why you give me milk to drink.'

'Thombre, I am at a loss to understand your question.'

'You do understand. You are doing all this because you want me to become a Christian.'

'I would be very happy if you did become a Christian, Thombre. Because I am a Christian and I believe it helps the soul to evolve. But it is wrong to say that it is the reason why Mr Tilak and I love you. If there's a motive for loving, then it isn't love at all. It is play-acting. If you think the days and nights that we have spent and continue to spend nursing you is all pretence, then there is nothing further to say. So tell me, do you think we are play-acting? Who has put such an idea into your head?'

Thombre calmed down and returned to being his own self. This time, Thombre's younger brother Babu had come with him. He too started going to school. Both would eat in a Hindu restaurant and stay with us. When they came, Mr Tilak was away. My back was hurting badly so I had put a poultice on it. Now the poultice had dried and was pulling my skin.

The following morning, I called out to Manjulabai. 'This thing has troubled me dreadfully all night. Please heat some water.' She went away. Thombre and Babu were sleeping in the next room. Thombre got up and began banging on the door. I opened the door. He stood before me, hands on hips. 'Tell me how I have troubled you.'

'Who said you've troubled me?'

'You did.'

'I? And to whom did I say that?'

'To Manjulabai.'

'Did she say so?'

'She didn't have to. I heard it with these, my very own ears.'

'What did you hear?'

'This one has troubled me dreadfully all night.'

'Thombre, you should listen carefully before starting a quarrel. Look at this poultice on my back. I told Manjulabai, *this* thing had troubled me. Heat the water. Now I'll stand here. You go to the back room and ask Manjulabai.'

Thombre went to Manjulabai. She told him what I had told him. Then his temper, which had shot up so high, climbed down.

Two women, both called Manjulabai, had worked for us for many years. The hawk and dove factions were famous in politics in those days. Our children had named the two women Manjulabai-the-hawk and Manjulabai-the-dove. The Manjulabai of the foregoing story was the dove. I have a memory of her that will stay with me forever. During the time she was with us, somebody came and told her that her daughter had been murdered, hacked to pieces and thrown into a well. She let out a howl. I was nearby. I was so shocked that, although I was still young, my head began to shake involuntarily, and still shakes. But her weeping soon stopped. Her daughter was alive and well and even came to meet her.

Once when Thombre returned from Pune, he came and sat

on the rope swing we had put up in the back room. I was in the kitchen giving instructions to the cook. Thombre was twisting the rope of the swing. As the rope untwisted, the swing would spin fast. That momentum would make the rope twist the other way. His conversation twisted and turned in the same way.

'An axe handle threatens its own.'

'What does that mean?'

'It means the axe handle is made from a tree. But when the blade is fitted into it, it is capable of cutting its own roots.'

'Meaning?'

'Meaning you.'

Thombre's mind was like the swing, in a twist.

'I suppose I'm the handle.'

'That's right.'

'And you are the root? And what's the axe? Your traditions, I suppose. We have destroyed them and that has hurt you.'

Of course, in my usual way, I was laughing as I said all this. That made him furious.

'I am so enraged, but that means nothing to you. You are laughing.'

'See, Thombre. You are twisting the rope of the swing. Untwisting it is in your hands. I am laughing because there's no twist in my mind. If you decide to untwist yourself, you will also start laughing.'

Thombre was as dear to us as our children and he felt the same way about us. A few years on, he dropped out of school and began teaching Marathi to Europeans. He did this work in Ahmednagar. But occasionally he had to go to Mahabaleshwar in the summer. On the first occasion that he went, Dattu and Tara also went with him. They rented a house for themselves and cooked their own food. In those three months, they saw every street and corner of Mahabaleshwar. They climbed to Pratapgadh. They sat on slopes and dips along the way and recited poetry. Thombre wrote his famous poem 'Nishwas' during this stay. This was in 1913. According to Dattu and

Tara, when he recited the poem in the midst of the hills of Mahabaleshwar, it acquired a sublimity that was uncanny.

Thombre used to keep the money he earned with me. Once, when he was staying in Ahmednagar, I began putting aside small sums from it and collected fifty rupees. But later, when Mr Tilak had overspent, I put a little more money into this amount to plug the hole. Mr Tilak was quick to take loans and I to repay them. I said to Thombre, 'I have put aside fifty rupees from your earnings. May I use them? I need the money to repay a debt.'

'Please go ahead.'

'I don't know when I'll be able to return it, but I will do it for sure. If I pop off meanwhile, take the money from Dattu. But if you need it badly before that, give me a month's notice and I'll make arrangements to return it to you.'

'Just take it now. We'll see how it is to be returned later.'

After this, Thombre went to Pune. A few days later, Babu came from Pune and began asking for the money. 'I have to go to Khandesh and I need the money right now.'

I said, 'Mr Tilak isn't at home. Salaries haven't been paid. When he gets his salary, I'll send the money.'

But he would not have it. He said, 'Amrutrao, my eldest brother (our Thombre) has sent me and told me to bring the money back immediately.' I said, 'Babu, if I had the money, would I not give it to you?' Babu fumed and fretted and went away. He had come in the morning and left in the afternoon. Thombre came by the evening train. Dattu had gone out for a walk. He noticed Thombre walking from the station with his head down, weeping. So he turned back with him. The minute I saw him, I said, 'Thombre, I will send you the money as soon as Mr Tilak returns.'

Sniffing, Thombre said, 'Lakshmibai, I didn't send Babu to get the money. He did this wicked thing of his own accord. I've come to apologize. I couldn't stay back in Pune when I heard what Babu had done. I don't need the money at all.' Thombre was terribly upset by what had happened. When Mr Tilak returned, we wired the money to him immediately.

Thombre's mother was a very sweet-tempered woman. Thombre's temperament resembled hers. When you experienced her simple, straightforward, guileless nature, Thombre came to mind. And when you met Thombre, she came to mind. Thombre thought of us as his own people and so did his mother. She would say to me, 'Lakshmibai, had you not been there for him, our Nana would have slipped away from us. You are his real mother.'

When these people left for Pune, they kept all their ornaments and valuables with me. That was because they were first going to Mahabaleshwar from Pune before returning to Ahmednagar. But in all the hurry and scurry, I did not know where a necklace had been kept. Later we heard that Amrutrao's wife had taken it along. But nobody told me this. I was terribly worried. Thombre was very lazy about writing letters. I wrote four letters to him about the necklace but did not receive a single reply. Finally, Dattu sent a double postcard to him in Mahabaleshwar. On one card he wrote a single word in bold: 'Necklace?' On the other he wrote two words: 'Found' and 'Lost'. Below that appeared the instruction: 'Please erase whichever word does not apply and post this card.'

This pill worked and we got a long letter from Thombre. But Dattu had received his 'reply paid' postcard a day before, bringing the news that the necklace had been 'Found'.

Thombre would recite other people's poems with as much love as his own. Once he liked a poem, it became his. Not for a moment did he treat it as another's. This was the great thing about his love of poetry. There are poets who will turn their noses up at other people's poems.

Thombre used to love Mr Tilak's poetry. He would explain the poem 'Vanavasi Phool' with such fine understanding that only if you heard him would you see why it had the effect it did on listeners. Once he taught the poem to Mr Tilak's class. Mr Tilak himself sat with the students and was so overwhelmed to hear him speak about engagement with and disengagement from the life of the world that as soon as his lesson was over, he flung his arms around him and held him close to his chest.

When Mr Tilak was on tour once, Dattu at college and Tara at school in Pune, Thombre ran into an astrologer who told him he was going to die that very day in an accident. Thombre hurried home and came straight to the kitchen.

'Lakshmibai, an astrologer has just told me that I am going to die in an accident today.'

'Astrologers are cunning people. They talk a lot of rubbish. Anyway, don't go anywhere now.'

'But I must. How else can I disprove his prediction?'

When I saw he was determined to test what the astrologer had said, I put aside my work and sat with him. I called Dattu's friends over to sleep in our house. I bought mithai worth two rupees and we sat up all night eating it, talking, telling stories, singing and entertaining each other. We did not let Thombre out of our sight throughout that day and night. On that occasion, what the astrologer had foretold was proved wrong. But five years later, it was proved tragically right.

Many people came to our house, stayed and went away, but there was nobody like Thombre. Although he would quarrel with us occasionally, there was no guile in him, no hatred, no selfishness. He was an affectionate, friendly, happy person who loved to joke and play an occasional prank. When he was with us, his boyishness surfaced. There were lots of fun and games when he was around. There was horseplay, tree climbing, jumping on the house roof, fights, paper littered all over the place, poems written, poems read out, poems torn up in anger when listeners were not attentive enough, then laughter again and writing stories, reading them out, reciting other people's poetry with as much enthusiasm as his own, making fun of poems that did not measure up, organizing meetings at home, doing magic tricks, keeping an eye on Bhaskarrao's glasses, making fun of my writing, sleeping out at night counting the stars, apportioning the stars to each one of us, quarrelling over unfair shares, leaving things lying around in the house and tidying them up when I scolded, putting on a solemn face in front of Mr Tilak... So many things big and small that I keep recalling and grieving over.

Come drink these last two tears
Little bird, will you ever return?

The Lord's Court

There is a Congregational Church in Ahmednagar of which we are members. A congregationalist is one who holds Jesus Christ as the true and sole Lord of the Church and does not admit the authority of any individual or assembly of individuals in theological matters and the rules that govern the Church but invests that authority in the local church itself.

We needed to find an equivalent word in Marathi for Congregational Church. Two or three alternatives had been suggested. Mr Tilak had used the phrase 'Christacha Durbar' in a lecture. The word 'durbar' suggests a king meeting his subjects. It may therefore be understood as a place where Christ is the sovereign authority and his subjects work for the church, guided by his word. Mr Tilak also said that the word 'church' had become a symbol of a divisive rather than a uniting institution. It had come to stand for the dominance of the institution and its rules over the rights of the people and their work. The word 'durbar' had no such connotations. Why should we not use this word then, was his question.

It was clear that Mr Tilak's mind was in turmoil these days. He had begun work on a collection of keertans. He was making me commit the keertans to memory and giving me lessons on how to perform them. He had assembled a chorus to accompany me. The same year, he began to write his collection of abhangs for singing during bhajan meetings. He was convinced that the foreignness of Christianity would be completely wiped out if worship happened in the traditional forms of keertan, bhajan and readings from mythology. With regard to his collection of abhangs, this is what he has to say:

> We have repeatedly pointed out to our Christian brethren that keertans, bhajans and mythology are, in this country at least, important means for praying and spreading the word. We are overjoyed, eternally grateful to God that, within six or seven

> years of Rev. Harry Bissel first picking up a pair of castanets and making bhajans popular, hundreds of bhajan groups have sprung up all over Maharashtra, intensifying their devotion from day to day. However, the groups have no more than around 250 old and new compositions. To overcome this difficulty at least partially, we have been publishing keertans and abhangs from my collections in *Dnyanodaya*. Many will use them and for that we are grateful.

It was in this year too that he began a movement called Christacha Durbar, Christ's Court. Its origin must have lain in his mental turmoil and the lecture it had occasioned. It is possible to show through his writings and statements of the time that the turmoil had been going on in his mind for at least twenty years and had come to a head now. Mr Tilak made a resolve to complete his 'Christayana' and his collections of keertans and abhangs.

Thus poetry was helping the new movement. But Mr Tilak's hungry mind would not rest merely with that. He could not confine his ideas to paper alone. That is how the Christ's Court movement started. He found many followers for the movement in Ahmednagar. They composed songs especially for the Court. They belonged generally to the younger generation. People like Dr Hiralal Gaekwad, Chimanrao Gaekwad, Hiwale, Dharmadhikari enthusiastically propagated the use of bhajans in worship. Mr Tilak published his credo and spread the word amongst Christians in the whole of Maharashtra. The credo follows:

CHRIST'S COURT

> 1. Name: Lord Jesus Christ is establishing His kingdom in the souls and the world of men. The name of the assembly of individuals in whose souls the kingdom of God has been established is Christ's Court.
>
> 2. Motive: Without in any way standing against missionary churches and other Christian institutions, to unite through love and service followers of Christ, baptized or unbaptized,

in a bond of brotherhood, and arouse in them the feeling that, Jesus Christ being their teacher, all men and women are brothers and sisters and they must therefore serve humanity with love as He did, although He had to be crucified for it. This would make them true brothers and sisters of the Son of Man. They should become true friends of the world and true patriots. The brotherhood should become a universal family in the true sense of the word and the world should be able to see Jesus Christ once again in them. Jesus Christ, originally of the East, should be revealed as Jesus Christ of the East once again through them. The world should be able to witness Christian love, Christian independence, the power of Christianity that makes man master of his circumstances. Then Christianity will gradually lose its foreignness and become altogether Indian. The goal of this institution is to try and create such goodwill in our countrymen towards their Christian brethren that they will declare their intention to take care of them as their own.

3. Durbar Members: Any man or woman, baptized or not, who has been counted as adult by the government, who has accepted the credo of the durbar, has the recommendation of two members of the durbar and permission from the chief servant, may sign, or if illiterate put a thumb impression on the vision paper, and thus become a member of the durbar.

Exception (A): No person who has been excommunicated by his church for a sin that she or he has committed, or has been judged as a criminal by the government and punished for his crime, will be admitted to the durbar. If such a person accepts the vision of the durbar, then the durbar will accept him as a dependent in consultation with his church or the government. If government rules do not forbid the person from becoming a dependent of the durbar, it is to be taken as government's agreement.

Exception (B): No person who is not in agreement with all the clauses of the durbar vision, can become a member. However, he can become a dependent of the durbar if he so wishes and has the chief servant's permission. The dependent does not have the right to vote.

4. Patron: Persons who are neither members nor dependents of the durbar but are its well-wishers will be named its patrons.

5. Local Durbar: If there are five or more members of the durbar in any place, they are at liberty to set up their own groups for worship and service to the public. Whatever name they may give their groups, the groups will still be seen as local durbars. A salaried or volunteer worker should be appointed for each durbar and its work. The local durbar will decide what work is expected of him and whether or not he has a specific authority as part of or beyond this. Wherever a local durbar is set up, it will devote itself to working for all the local churches, for other legal institutions that serve the public and the local people. Most importantly, it must see itself as a representative of Jesus Christ and work towards establishing the Kingdom of God on earth. If, for whatever reason, despite having the numbers, a group of locals is unable to set up a durbar, they still remain, as individuals, members of Christ's Court. A local durbar is not a church. It is a concept that brings together all churches and is, as a group and as individuals belonging to the group, a member of Christ's Court. Since Christ's Court and the local durbar do not oppose any church or any legal institution devoted to public service, they are not likely to arouse hostility in anybody. In case of such hostility, the durbar members' motto should be, 'We will defeat evil through good.'

6. Propagators of the Lord's Kingdom: They will be the chief messengers who will carry the message of the Lord's Kingdom into the world. Our Lord will select the messengers. The messenger will be one who will not accept any salary from anywhere for his work. He will live partly by his own manual labour and partly on whatever his brethren in the durbar or others give him voluntarily. He will be more like an ascetic and will have made the following pledges to Jesus Christ:

i. Like You, I will live in poverty.
ii. Like You, I will serve humanity.
iii. Like You, I will not consider anybody my enemy.
iv. Like You, I will forever be prepared to be crucified.
v. Like You, I will give my all to fulfil the will of God.
vi. Like You, I will love all mankind.
vii. I will be near You through the power of faith. I will make Your world and mine one. I will strive to form myself in Your image and finally become one with You. I will thus, through personal experience, prove St Paul's assertion, 'For you have died and your life is hid with Christ in God.'

These are the men and women who will become the messengers of the Kingdom of God. It will be the duty of every member of the durbar to pray for them and help them.

7. The seat of origin of the durbar: This will be the permanent residence of the initiator or elder servant. The following work will be done here:

i. A register of all members and dependents will be maintained.
ii. Correspondence with local durbars and individual members will be conducted.
iii. Arrangements will be made for the training of servants of God's Kingdom and distribution of work to them.
iv. Literature about the Kingdom of God will be prepared and published.
v. Questions regarding Christ's Court will be attended to.
vi. The servants of local durbars will be the advisors to the elder servant.
vii. The Elder Servant—the one who first proposed the idea of Christ's Court is, of course, the Elder Servant and has been accepted as such by those who are already members of the durbar.

THE CREDO OF CHRIST'S COURT

As a father helps a child in every way to do his work, so must You too My Father and Lord, enable me, weak as I am, to fulfil the work I am setting out to do in Your name.

1. I have made Jesus Christ my guru. I shall therefore spend my time reflecting upon His life, His work, His purpose and His teachings.

2. In order to contemplate it the right way, I will study the Bible and other books on the subject regularly.

3. Jesus Christ said to his disciples, 'I am your life.' I shall therefore consider His life mine. I shall think and act in accordance with Him.

4. At the start, in the middle and at the end of my day, that is morning, afternoon and night before going to bed, I shall pray to my holy, my most loving Lord and Father, Almighty God.

5. I shall look upon every man and woman in Christ's Court as my brother and sister. I shall always look to their good, help them in their hour of need, console them in their sorrow, respect them and their families and consider their honour mine. My only aim would be to ensure that, seeing the brotherly ties of the members of Christ's Court, the world should be filled with astonishment and praise the Lord.

6. If there are one or more members in the place where I live, I shall, in my spare time and at a set hour once a week, be present with them and worship God with them.

7. My guru calls Himself the son of God but also the son of man and teaches me that service to God is not complete without service to humanity. I shall therefore serve mankind in every way I can, selflessly and without reward.

8. With the wisdom that God grants me through my prayers, I shall look upon my responsibilities towards the Court as personal needs and make regular monetary contributions to it.

9. I shall enrol at least one new member in the Court every year.

Narayan Waman Tilak
Elder Servant
Christ's Court
Christayanashram,
Satara

Christ's Court is established. It has gained many members but also extreme opposition. It is Man's nature to look with suspicion on anything that is new.

It was during this period that Mr Tilak resolved to move from Ahmednagar to Satara to find more time and more quiet to write 'Christayana'.

Satara

Ruth passed her Intermediate examination in 1916. Eight days after her result was declared, Dattu wired to say he had passed his B.A. examination. He was appointed to a teacher's post in the Mission High School in Ahmednagar directly after that. I was happy that our son had begun to earn. But he worked in Ahmednagar for barely four months. He was keen to do his Masters in Nagpur. He was looking for a way to earn enough for his tuition, books and accommodation there. Soon he found what he was looking for. He was offered a room free and fifteen rupees for some supervisory work and also found a student to tutor. This was enough to see him through. So he went to Nagpur and enrolled for a Master's and a Law degree.

Meanwhile, Mr Tilak was going through a rapid transformation. Only one thing had obsessed him from the time he was a child. He did not wish to be what he was. He struggled continuously till his last living moment to become a better person, and finally he managed to triumph over the biggest flaws in his nature. It is said that human nature is fully formed in youth and does not change after that. This was proved wrong in Mr Tilak's case. His growth continued till the very end.

Within a few days of Dattu's going to Nagpur, Mr Tilak had himself transferred to Satara. It was his greatest wish to find a place where he could complete 'Christayana', his epic poem on the life of Christ, which he had started many years ago. But given his nature, he had not been able to work uninterruptedly to finish it. So many people in Ahmednagar knew him and so many more knew that he lived there, that the number of visitors to our house to see him had been increasing by the day. If a discussion on any of his favourite subjects was begun, it meant saying goodbye to his work for the next few hours.

So he decided to go to a quiet place and finish 'Christayana'. Dr Hume was always there to do his best to accommodate

Mr Tilak's wishes. He wrote off at once to his daughter in Satara and she made arrangements for us to stay there. We were allotted a large bungalow which Mr Tilak named Christayanashram. He had a nameplate made which he nailed to the front of the bungalow.

Dr Hume's daughter, Mrs Lee welcomed us to Satara. We spent the first night at her place. Her husband Mr Lee had only recently passed away. There was just herself and her two lovely children in their house now. We moved to our bungalow the following day. Our lifestyle was still as austere as a dervish's, but here we were in a splendid bungalow. There were no possessions to fill the space. It was exactly like a mendicant's hut. The twelve doors of the bungalow were open to all comers. Anybody could come and anybody could go. Benji, a cousin of Dattu's betrothed Ruth, was with us and so also was Chiki, Rambhau Dharmadhikari's daughter who had been with us from the time her mother died.

I said, 'Why do we need a bungalow? We need company. This place is too far away from town for that. Benji isn't going to stay with us forever.'

'Why do you need company? We have Chiki and Tommy.'

Chiki was eight or nine and Tommy was a dog. But Mr Tilak had earned much merit and it helped. After we arrived in Satara, Dr Hume sent a clerk to assist him with his writing of 'Christayana'. Along with 'Christayana', he continued to work for *Dnyanodaya*. He had stopped taking payment for this from 1912. The clerk was to assist him on this work too. He had a lovely family. One of his two sons was a singer. Mr Tilak got him to teach me the scales. Occasionally he too would join me for lessons, because we had plans to go around the country at some future time performing keertans. Mr Tilak had sent for a blind youth called Limbaji from Miss Millard's school for the blind in Mumbai to accompany us in our keertans. He was blind and his wife one-eyed. But such was their love for each other that they managed beautifully with the one eye they had between them. We gave him a house and paid him ten rupees a month. I heard recently that he now earns forty rupees a month and there are nine eyes in place of one in his house. A poor Christian named Rambhau Sasane lived in Vambori. For years Mr Tilak had been sending him two rupees a month as help. But in the rush of moving to Satara, he had been unable to do that for the last two months. Indeed, it would not be wrong to say that there was no money to send now. A fortnight after we arrived in Satara, Sasane came hobbling to the bungalow, leaning on his cane.

'Salaam, saheb.'

'Sasane, what has brought you here?'

'A train.'

'Why?'

'For money.'

'For heaven's sake Sasane, would not a two-paise postcard have done the job?'

'People may remember, or may not remember. Thought I'd come myself.'

'That's fine. But what about the cost?'

'I knew you'd give me that. I borrowed the money.'

'Great, Sasane. That's really clever of you. After this, please don't come if the money is delayed. If you do, I'll stop giving it.'

Mr Tilak paid him ten rupees for his fare to Satara and back and four rupees for the two months he had not been paid and sent the old man on his way. The lesson had cost Mr Tilak ten rupees. He never again forgot to send Sasane his money.

After coming to Satara, Mr Tilak began making a garden in the compound of the bungalow. I did not show any interest in it and that made him angry. I said, 'I've made gardens so often before, but you never let a single one live. I'm not going to plant another garden now.' I was an enthusiastic gardener. But somehow my heart was no longer in it. So he watered and looked after the plants by himself.

'Christayana' was the reason why we had shifted to Satara.

But once again it got stalled. I said, 'What's the matter? You came here to write "Christayana" and you're doing nothing.'

'You are quite ignorant about these things. Writing poetry is a matter of inspiration. You can't write it on order.' And then he had vast amounts of other work to do. In addition to Christ's Court, he and Mr Kothari had recently started a society called the Deccan Rayat Samaj. He was a member of the regional executive committee and the work took him frequently to Pune. 'Christayana' was being pulled this way and that between Christ's Court for the Christian community and the Rayat Samaj for the socially backward non-Christian community.

Renunciation

Although we were now in Satara, Mr Tilak's tours continued and some very important things were happening in the course of his travels. He was invited to speak to the Christians in Dindigul in the Madras Presidency. He discovered something there that did not exist in the Christian community in Maharashtra. When converting to Christianity, those people had not shed their baggage of touchable and untouchable castes but continued to hold it close to their chests. So some people sat inside and some outside the church. Mr Tilak simply could not tolerate this.

One day, he sat with the people outside the church and began to address them without as much as glancing at the people inside. Feeling ashamed, they came out one by one. After that, Mr Tilak made it a rule not to speak before a congregation that practised caste discrimination. This had an excellent effect, and at least while he was there, he saw no signs of discrimination. During this time, the Christian businessmen of Rahuri had also organized a meeting where Mr Tilak was invited to speak.

Almost from the time he became a Christian, Mr Tilak had felt convinced that he should not be a salaried employee of the Mission. Even when he continued with some Mission work, he did not accept payment for it. But now that he wanted to take on work that was very different and onerous, he decided to give up Mission work altogether. Following is the letter he published from Rahuri on 1 September 1917:

PUBLIC STATEMENT

Saturday, 1 September 1917

For the sake of the country, Christ's Court and myself, I will hereafter not be part of any institution in any way other than through the bonds of love and service. Hereafter, the intended goal of my life shall pertain only to my bond with

Jesus Christ and with the welfare of the present. Therefore, respecting God's word, I shall not be a dependent or employee of the Mission or of any other human institution. I am now a Christian ascetic, that is one who pursues not detachment but attachment through love. From this day onwards, I wish to act solely under the instruction of God who is the soul. I appeal to all those who love Christ, Hindustan and me, to intercede on my behalf with God our Father.

Narayan Waman Tilak

Below this appears the following note, headed 'Clarification of Certain Doubts':

1. There are three reasons why I have published my resolve:

(a) If ever I am tempted to depend on human beings, this statement will rise before my eyes and curb me to some extent at least.

(b) It will afford encouragement to those amongst the Christians in Hindustan who wish to follow the same path.

(c) I need the prayers of many to fulfil my resolve.

2. What will happen to the work I have been doing?

(a) For me, the American Marathi Mission has literally taken my mother's place. If I have even a shred of gratitude in me, I will not bring my mother institution into difficulties. The only thing I do not want from it is a salary. What I do want is its love, sympathy and prayers. I shall continue to do the work I have been doing for it. I want the Mission's help even in my present transition, and I am certain I will get it.

(b) I am one who believes that service to humanity is service to God. This is enough to indicate which works will be included in my service for the welfare of the present.

N. W. Tilak

Mr Tilak stopped accepting a salary. He had become the kind of ascetic he had described. He took to wearing saffron robes.

He had only two, which he himself washed. We paid off all our household staff. He himself swept and swabbed the house right down to the kitchen. A Christian man wrote to him asking, 'Does your renunciation mean you have renounced your family?' He too wished to serve humanity like Mr Tilak; but he was encumbered by family responsibilities. Mr Tilak published his response to this gentleman and also wrote a note about the cloth bag he carried.

A LETTER TO REFLECT OVER

Praise be to Christ.

It is many days since I received your letter. I thank you for it. If while replying to it, a word, phrase or statement escapes my pen that is hurtful to you, I ask for your forgiveness.

Christian renunciation is not renunciation of the wife. It is to love one another selflessly and to help one another reach heaven while still living on earth as Lord Jesus Christ has willed and taught. It is a terrible calamity to let your family increase beyond your capacity to support it. I describe it as terrible because thereby the father and mother themselves destroy their children's bodies, minds and souls. Excessive procreation is not God's gift. Saint Paul counts the control of the body amongst the sacred rewards of a soul. This is to say that God, the holy soul, teaches husband and wife to control bodily desire. This means He teaches us not to procreate beyond our capacity. In Christian renunciation, a husband is not called upon to sacrifice his wife. On the contrary, the teaching is, 'What God has joined together, let no man put asunder.'

In short, if your family has already grown beyond your capacity and is likely to grow further, do not become an ascetic like me immediately, but pray to God at home and gradually decrease the desire you feel for your wife. This is the first step towards complete renunciation. To achieve this, there must be total cooperation between husband and wife. The more both of you immerse yourselves in prayer and meditation, the easier you will find it to renounce bodily desire.

Do not abandon your household even after this. Do not give up your work or income. Your family is large. If you forsake your children and let them starve, you will be committing a big sin. God looks after his devotees' welfare. They should not worry about it. This is the message and counsel given in many places in the Holy Scriptures, but the world has not properly understood it. All of this is contained in a single utterance of Christ: 'The labourer is worthy of his wages.'

Who is the one who will pay the labourer his just wages? Without doubt, the Lord Himself. But who will be his instrument to make the payment? The world for whom the labourer works. How much? Equal to the worth of the work. You will see from this that it is not he who meditates alone—for each one does that for his own spiritual growth—but the Christian ascetic who serves the world who may open his bag for what the world will give. This is not begging for alms.

I carry a cloth bag because I wish to serve Hindustan. I ask for just wages for the work I do. I ask for only enough for myself. If someone were to put one lakh rupees before me because they felt sorry for my family, I would not touch it. If the world rewards me with what is enough for me alone, I will give it to my family and starve. If it is more than enough for my family and me, I too will sit with my family and eat, returning to the world what remains.

You have asked me two more questions. I will not answer them because Christ has not instructed me to answer them, nor will you be satisfied if I do. However, with regard to your questions I can only say that I see in my restlessness, of which you and many others like you speak, a sign of God's grace. And for this, I have often thanked the Lord. My restlessness that you and many others like you speak of is something I see as a sign of God's grace for which I have often thanked the Lord.

I ask your forgiveness once again for the faults in my letter and take your leave.

Your humble servant,
Narayan Waman Tilak

PUBLIC STATEMENT

'...for the workman is worthy of his meat.' (Matthew 10.10). The one who provides the meat is God. He arranges for the man whose work the workman has done to give him his due. Accordingly, I, the undersigned, humbly inform my Christian and non-Christian brothers and sisters that:

I shall, if I need to, extend my cloth bag before those whom I may have served. I shall accept whatever God puts it into their minds to give, with gratitude to them and God. If the alms given to me exceed my needs, I shall instantly or later, use them for a charitable purpose.

For example, lately I was called upon to address five different groups of people. I had the right to hold out my bag on each of those occasions. However, while I was there, God had found other means to fulfil my needs. Therefore, I did not exercise my right to receive my due.

I do not call this begging. I do not wish to beg nor would I encourage begging. I am a Christian ascetic. I cannot abandon my family. I am tied to them by old bonds. I and my wife have experienced on earth what Jesus has said: 'What therefore God hath joined together, *let not man* put *asunder*'. And so, as long as we live, we shall live together. Our children will do likewise. Do not therefore, out of pity for me and my family, send me anything in charity. Please ask me to serve you. If I serve you, I shall ask you to put whatever you wish to in my bag. I shall not accept anything that people give without reason. For only 'the workman is worthy of his meat.'

Narayan Waman Tilak

An Acutely Felt Need

It was barely ten months since we had arrived in Satara when Mr Tilak gave up his job. He instantly wrote two letters, one to *Dnyanodaya* announcing his decision and one to Dattu informing him of it. Dattu was to appear soon for his M.A. Part One examination when this news reached him. He wrote to his father immediately saying, 'I am not asking you not to give up your job. I am merely saying do not announce it till I come home.' His father wired him, 'I am going to Pune to Mr Kothari's. Meet me there.' Dattu went to Pune and discovered that his father had already broadcast his decision. So, whatever he had wanted to say to his father remained unsaid.

What he had wanted to say was that his father should first get Tara married, make plans for his own and my future and then give up his job. But now it was clear that Dattu would have to give up the idea of a Masters, because he would have to support the family. His idea was to enrol for a law degree here while living and working in Mumbai. Mr Tilak would not have it. 'I am totally against my son becoming a lawyer. Choose any other profession.'

'What choice is there for me? I can't become a doctor now. The only other thing I can do is teach. I'll do that if that's what you want.'

At last he decided to work in Mumbai and also study for a law degree in the time that he could spare from his job. He went to Mumbai and found a job immediately at the Mission school in Byculla. During this upheaval, he had failed in his M.A. Part One. Later he thought of doing his Masters in Mumbai but did not get permission for it. As a result, he put aside all thoughts of ever doing his M.A.

Mr Tilak went to Ahmednagar from Pune. Of our livestock, only Kalyani's she-calf Soni remained. He sold her before returning to Satara. Whether he sold her or simply gave her away I do not know, because I certainly did not see the fifty rupees that he said he had got for her. What he did bring back, however, was a young 'bull' called Namya. Namya was gullible, hard-working and lisped. He came on the understanding that he would board and lodge with us and get clothes and a rupee per month. Mr Tilak began to spend time teaching Namya the Lord's prayer. He would say 'Our Father which art in heaven.' Namya would invariably say, 'Oul mothel's fathel in heaven.' But Mr Tilak persisted in teaching him.

Once, Barrister Athavale and his wife Meenabai came to stay. Namya said, 'Who is he?'

I said, 'That's my daughter and that's my son-in-law.'

'What family does the son-in-law have?'

'He has a brother,' I said.

'What does he do?'

'Why don't you ask him?'

Namya went to the Barrister, broom in hand.

'Mr son-in-law, what wolk do you do?'

'I am a barber.'

'And your blothel?'

'He's a butler.'

Namya was stunned to hear this. How could Mr Tilak have married his daughter to a barber? He came back to me and said in a tone of severe protest, 'What a son-in-law! A balbel and his blothel a butlel. And whele did you find the blide fol Bhau? In Mumbai. My Mama's daughtel would have been so much bettel for Bhau.'

This crazy chump was much loved in our house. But he and Chiki were always at loggerheads. Nothing that Chiki did pleased him. Once she was washing a clay pot in a basin of water. Namya wanted to find fault with that. He stood before her deep in thought. Then he said, 'Chiki, shall I tell Aai what you'll doing? You've dlowned the pot in that basin of wattle.'

Once I sent Namya to sleep at the place of a woman who was ill as company. The woman died early next morning. Namya came home immediately and went to sleep. Mr Tilak made tea and asked Tara to take Namya's cup to him. When she went to him, he was sitting up ramrod straight in bed, eyes fixed, and refusing to talk.

'What's wrong with you, Namya? Here's your tea.'

Namya remained mum. Finally when all of us gathered around him, he said, 'I couldn't talk. I had lockjaw like that woman.'

It was a year or more since Dattu had passed his B.A. Ruth was about to appear for her B.A. exam. He was earning enough to support himself and her. We began making plans for the wedding. But where was the money for the wedding to come from? How was the wedding to be celebrated without money? I used to teach Mrs Hegan Marathi. I had kept the fees she paid me with her for safe keeping. I expected it would add up to about a hundred rupees by the time Dattu got married. That would not have been enough. We needed more.

I knew no English so I would teach Mrs Hegan Marathi through Marathi. We were reading *Samrat Ashok* together. Somewhere in the course of reading it, we came across the word 'angvangkalingamagadhadi'. Mrs Hegan was so charmed by the lyrical sound of the word that she decided she would call her husband that. We had a good laugh when I told her the word was a string of place names.

Mr Tilak started preparations for the wedding with great gusto, which means he wrote down a new system of rites according to which the wedding would be conducted. Copies of the system were being made at home, and the house resounded with the activity. In Mr Tilak's view, having a wedding system in place was all that was required for the wedding to go smoothly. There was no need to worry about anything else.

There was a notice in the *Dnyanodaya* issue dated June-July 1917, announcing prizes of one hundred and fifty rupees for novels in Marathi which would serve as guides to the Christian community. In the issue following this announcement signed by *Dnyanodaya*'s literary committee, the following statement by Mr Tilak appeared:

CALLING YOUR ATTENTION

> In response to a query that a gentleman has sent to me, I would like all prospective writers of the Christian community to know that I am not competing for the prizes announced by the literary committee but hope that they will go to upcoming writers of the community.
>
> Narayan Waman Tilak

The gentleman who had sent him the query was no other than Dattu. He was very keen to try his hand at writing a novel. He had been writing short stories and poems but had not attempted anything bigger than that. When the son got a published reply from the father, he began to write his novel. He finished writing it in about ten days. Later, when he came to Satara in the Diwali vacation, he brought his manuscript along. He was very keen that his father should read or hear it read. That was not happening. Mr Tilak was always busy with something or the other.

One day, it turned out the time was right. Mr Tilak had lain down on his cot after lunch. It was a quiet time of the day with no outsiders around. Dattu sat in a chair beside the cot and said, 'Papa, you have time now. May I read my novel out to you?'

'All right, read,' said Mr Tilak and listened with closed eyes. A few pages into the reading and Mr Tilak had fallen asleep. Dattu was very upset. He said to me, 'Papa has gone to sleep. When he reads out his things to us, he gets so angry if we don't pay attention. He never encourages me.'

'He must be tired, dear. Read it to him some other time.' But Dattu was too angry to do that.

'I will never read it out to him again or even tell him what happens to this novel.'

Five or six months later, after he had collected the post,

Mr Tilak did not come out of his office for several hours. Hearing no sounds at all from the room, I went in to find out what had happened. I discovered that Mr Tilak was immersed in reading a book.

'Look at this,' he said. 'Dattu's done something extraordinary. Here's your book. He's written it and dedicated it to you and me.' I knew more or less what the book was about but Mr Tilak had forgotten completely that such a thing even existed.

'He's been awarded a prize of one hundred and fifty rupees for it. He has written it so well. I can't put it down.'

'But you fell asleep when he was reading it out to you.'

Mr Tilak did recall that but said nothing, only smiled and continued to read. That day he came down for dinner only after he had finished reading the book. His joy over the book was indescribable. He shot off a letter to Dattu there and then. He also wrote to the Bissels and many others about the book. He told whomsoever he met the story of the deaf and dumb woman who was scared that her child would also be deaf and dumb. So she banged down a great big stone near his ear and was overjoyed to hear him cry lustily. 'My joy is like hers when she found out that her child was not deaf and dumb after all.'

An Offering of Devotional Songs

The chief reason for Mr Tilak to come to Satara was to write 'Christayana'. But that plan made way for compositions of devotional songs. When he gave up his job, Mrs Lee said, 'How will you manage now?' He composed an abhang about this in which he said:

> The world inquires after me as it would after an orphan child.
> I fear that they might turn me away from my resolve.
> I become aware of my weakness when wicked spirits dance before me.
> Please God, please stay with me.
> I say to you the times are bad.
> I cease to understand what I have understood.
> I see darkness ahead.
> Let my ears be filled with your voice.
> Let me not hear ought else.
> If I do, please answer what is asked.
> Do not give me a chance to do so.
> Your servant says, do something now.
> May what you have given me still stay in my hands.

Mrs Lee was not content with offering mere words of sympathy. One day, after she had spoken to Mr Tilak, she quietly put fifty rupees before him. Mr Tilak returned the money with a thank you. Since he would not accept the money, Mrs Lee gave it to me and Mr Tilak composed an abhang in which he said:

> Why do you allow that which I do not want to pursue me?
> Tell me what you mean by this.
> Why do you allow all kinds of people to pull me
> this way and that and cause confusion?
> If you wished me to be stuffed into a hole in a tree,
> why did you allow my wings to grow?
> Am I to blind myself with my own hands?
> Or live with eyes closed?

> My spirit pushes me forward step by step; but my feet are chained.
> When will you free me dear Lord?
> I can no longer endure this life.
> Says your servant, this whining and complaining,
> why do you not end it once and for all?

Mrs Lee, Rev. Mr Hegan, Mrs Hegan were kind, sympathetic and obliging. But there was another missionary there who disapproved of everything Mr Tilak did. This was the same woman who used to ride in a jinrikisha in Ahmednagar. She and Mr Tilak came together again in Satara. I will not say the woman was evil. But she was a believer in strict discipline. Every task had to be done just then and just so. If she found that the task had been done differently, she would be deeply upset. This caused confrontations between her and Mr Tilak every day.

Mr Tilak sang bhajans morning and evening, with bells on his ankles, cymbals and castanets in hand and a tabla or pakhawaj behind him as accompaniment. When he started singing, his soul would go into a trance. Who cared then for the body? He would dance while singing, something that was not part of the western way of worship. But for this lady, the western way was the ideal way and she simply could not accept Mr Tilak's way. She forbade her workers from coming to our place and joining in this form of bhajan singing. They ignored her and came nevertheless. So there were quarrels between them and her. She dismissed a couple of them from service, but Mr Tilak quickly found them other jobs. He composed an abhang on this lady's harassment in which he said:

> Merciful God, I too have met my Mambaji, like the one who harassed saint Tukaram. Your grace be praised. Mambaji may live in your world but yours is a brave world. I have met my Mambaji and my spirit suffers. But the ego has no place in your world. It demands the immersion of the body. It is not by becoming a wise man's ass but an idiot's ass that leads you to understanding God. Here it is that one must climb the next

> step. This is where one meets God's grace. Says your servant I shall not call this persecution but a celebration of pure bliss.

Mr Tilak would not let us bolt the doors to the bungalow, leave alone lock them. I would say, 'Why do you do this?' To which he would say, 'We should have such devotion towards God that we should not be tempted to accumulate anything. What is ours must belong to everyone. There should be no distinction between mine and yours.' He composed an abhang to this effect:

> Come one, come all, take away everything I have. That will make me rich. Come one, come all, mock me. This is the honour I seek. Come, come. Nail me to the cross. That will make me immortal. Your servant says give me this much and no more. And it will make me whole.

Another one on the same theme was:

> Fathers, mothers, brothers, sisters live in every home
> But there is no place on earth untouched by my love.

Mr Tilak had put his short temper and rages behind him. Their place was now taken by compassion. If he heard of someone saying something against him or if somebody harassed him, he would say, 'Such things inspire me to do my work.' He composed an abhang on this theme in which he said:

> The more I am unloved, the more my goal becomes my own. The more I am criticized, the stronger I become. The more the world moves away from me, the closer I come to my God. Why fear when our guru is lord of the world? It is for him to do what he desires with us. There is nothing that is ours. His power rules over all. Says your servant, all is Christ. Nothing that once was me, remains.

He also composed several abhangs regarding certain types of Christians and missionaries. Meanwhile, Namya had developed a great urge to go to Mumbai. We used different arguments to make him change his mind. But one day he enrolled as an army recruit and ran away. Somebody told him that his job would be to pull a fan. Later, there was some confrontation between his officer and him and he was sacked. After Namya left there was no help in the house. Mr Tilak would share all the housework with me down to sweeping and swabbing. He would say, 'Christ had no servants. He had no multi-storeyed houses. He did not even have a place to lay his head. Why do we need to pamper ourselves with these things?' He composed the following two very well-known abhangs about this:

> You did not have servants, why should I burden myself with them? You were served frugal food. Why should I have rich sweets? You had no place to lay your head. Why should I have houses with flights of stairs? Why oppress this poor man with such possessions? Why grant me this dismal plan? What I have is a burden to me. All I want is the ocean of your love. I use angry words, but what can I do? You do not listen to me. Says your servant, dear Christ, make a place for me beside you.

> Evil men spat on your face. Who am I to deserve better? Canes made welts on your back. Why then should I not bear the same? You had to carry your own cross. Who then stops me from carrying mine? Your head was adorned by a crown of thorns. That should be my ornament too. You were nailed to the cross and killed. Why should I seek any other death? Says your servant, all will be a celebration of bliss, if you will allow me to stay with you.

Last Visit to Ahmednagar

Soon it was 1918. Ruth sat for her B.A. exam that year. Dattu had graduated two years earlier. He had enrolled for his Masters once again at Mumbai University. He had also enrolled for a degree in Law. But these were his secondary occupations. His chief work was teaching at the high school. He had a regular salary now and had saved some money. So there was nothing stopping him from getting married. I got after Mr Tilak to fix the month and date. I was not happy about either the month or the date that was eventually fixed. I did not want the wedding to be in the month of Chaitra. Ruth's father insisted on Chaitra because the summer holidays would begin after that and everybody would be free to enjoy them.

I was defeated even in the choice of the place for the wedding. I wanted it to be in Satara. Ruth's father said it would have to be in the girl's home town. As a matter of fact, Satara was not our home town nor was Mumbai theirs. It was all about customs and that was that. I wanted Satara because it would be difficult to find accommodation in Mumbai for the large number of wedding guests who would go with us. But Ruth's father said they would look after the accommodation. I gave in again.

Our in-laws helped Dattu find a house. In those days, there were not many houses to be had at affordable rents. But he found Dattu a chawl on rent situated between his and his sister's chawls in Byculla. All my pots and pans had been stolen. But I had some guest utensils. It struck me that I could set up Dattu's home with Benji's cookware which was kept with me. Dattu could replace it piece by piece till he owned the lot. Then I would return Benji's pots to Benji. It was still two or three years before Benji would set up house. Benji was Rakhmabai's son, that is our in-law's sister's son. Our in-law was in fact Benji's guardian. So I took Benji's permission and sent his stuff to Mumbai and Dattu set up his kitchen in his own, albeit rented, house. My joy knew no bounds.

It was going to be a summer wedding. Dattu visited Satara during the Diwali and Christmas vacations. It was a very happy time for all of us. One day, Mr Tilak challenged Dattu to walk with him from Satara to Wai and back. Mr Tilak looked frail but was very tough. Dattu, on the other hand, looked strong but lagged miles behind Mr Tilak in stamina. I cannot remember too many times when Mr Tilak had had to take to his bed. He simply was not in the habit of falling ill.

Father and son decided to leave for Wai at noon the following day. But somebody turned up to see Mr Tilak just then, and it also began to rain. Mr Tilak showed no signs of walking to Wai. Dattu laughed and said, 'Papa, it's raining. You've cancelled the plan of walking to Wai, right?'

Mr Tilak said, 'You think I'm afraid of the rain?'

'Of course, I don't. But you don't seem to be getting ready to go.'

What was getting ready for Mr Tilak? He was wearing his robe, his blanket was next to him, his cane was in the corner and his slippers were near the threshold. He collected all these things and said, 'Let's go.' Before the words were fully out of his mouth, he was standing outside in the rain waiting for Dattu. Dattu also got ready in five minutes and stepped out. I said, 'Who has asked you to go in this pouring rain?' Both laughed at me and left.

Mr Tilak and Dattu reached Wai when the rain was still coming down in buckets. As soon as they arrived, Mr Tilak escorted Dattu straight to the hospital and went on a tour of the town. Dattu had started a fever. 'Are you ready for the return trip?' Mr Tilak then asked Dattu. Dattu, lying in bed, folded his hands and said, 'I've lost the bet.' The next day, they came home by car.

I had worked very hard to learn how to perform keertans. Mr Tilak had given me many lessons and I had now begun to perform them. They even got talked about a bit. I was invited to perform in Ahmednagar. Mr Tilak was also scheduled to go there to take a class. We left together and stayed at Rev. Hume's bungalow. On the way there, we picked up Tara from Pune so she too was with us. It was Dr Hume who had made this plan so that we could all go back and meet our friends there. Mr Tilak too was eager to visit Ahmednagar but that was to meet members of Christ's Court. This was where the foundation of the Court had been laid so it was only natural that Mr Tilak yearned to go back.

When we arrived, my keertan was pushed into the background. Dr Hume started his own keertan. He said, 'Tara is a clever and good girl. I think she should start working. She is old enough now to help her father. I'll get her a job in Miss Bruce's school. She'll earn a hundred and twenty-five rupees a month.' Mr Tilak's salary had been the same. He had given up the salary but not the work. His work for *Dnyanodaya* had always been for free. Dr Hume had been worried about how we would manage without Mr Tilak's salary and that is why he had thought up this idea of giving Tara a job as well as Mr Tilak's salary.

Mr Tilak agreed. His difficulties were solved and he did not suspect Dr Hume's motives in suggesting the plan. He took what Dr Hume said at face value. But I had doubts. 'Saheb, will she get this salary regularly? If we interrupt her studies now, will she be able to go back to them later? My feeling is, once attention is deflected from studies, it is difficult to bring it back.' Dr Hume tried hard to convince me but I said, 'I do not think she is qualified today to earn more than fifteen or twenty rupees. This is quite clear to me.'

Dr Hume said, 'Lakshmibai, you don't recognize your daughter's worth. We do.'

'Saheb, you might give her a salary of one hundred and twenty-five or even two hundred now. But after Mr Tilak and even you have gone, will others value her in the same way? I don't think we should interrupt her education at this point.'

'Fair enough. But how far will you educate her and how will you do it?'

'I'll find ways to manage but I am determined to help her get a graduate degree.'

'All right. So what would you like me to do for her?'

'Pray.'

Mr Tilak was listening to this conversation quietly without interrupting us. But when we rose from the dinner table and went to our room, he said, 'You really don't know how qualified Tara is.'

'I do know. They will pay her your salary. Then why don't you take the salary for your work? This seems to be the reason why saheb has called us here from Satara.'

That might be so, but Mr Tilak's reason for coming was something else. Many durbaris had come to meet him after his arrival. Some people were opposing the Christ's Court. They had poisoned the missionaries' minds. They spread the impression that Mr Tilak was doing this to create problems in their work.

When we were having dinner the following day, the opposition party came and parked itself in the front room. Mr Tilak was not aware of this. After dinner, he went with Dr Hume to his office. There Dr Hume said, 'Bhau, now what is this that you have started? What's this that people are saying?'

'What people? What are they saying? Do I tell them to steal? To burgle? Do I encourage them to murder? Tell me what it is that I do.'

'Listen, bhau…'

'Who is saying what? Bring him before me.'

These remarks were made so loudly that we could hear them in the other room. The last roar was so loud that Mrs Hume closed the doors of the bungalow and took me to a room at the other end of the house. I told her to let me go, but she would not. She had never faced such a situation before. For me, it was an everyday thing. I tried to pacify her. 'Madam, let me go. I know his nature well.'

Dr Hume embraced Mr Tilak saying, 'Bhau, bhau.' Mr Tilak calmed down a little. The people sitting outside came in.

Mr Tilak prostrated himself before them, explained the work of Christ's Court to them in detail and they were satisfied.

When Thombre heard we were in Ahmednagar, he came running to meet us. He came with his entire family. He embraced us and said, 'It has been so long since I met my well-wishers. I missed you terribly after you left.' We went to have dinner with him on our last day there. His mother could not stop thanking Mr Tilak and me. She said, 'Tryambak is not mine. He is yours. You have done so much for him and seen him through a serious illness.'

I insisted Thombre should come for Dattu's wedding and he readily promised to come. Knowing that Mr Tilak had given up his salary, he said, 'Do you have money for the wedding? I can give you up to two hundred rupees.' He held out the money there and then. But I said, 'We don't need it now. I'll ask you for it if I do. Bring it with you when you come. If you give it to me now, I'll spend it on unnecessary things.'

'You'll need khanns to give away to the women of both families. I'll give you those. Take them at least with you.'

'No, not today. Bring them along with you as well.'

We stayed the night at their place. We chatted all night and did not realize how the hours flew by. The following day Thombre came to the station to see us off. As the train moved, his eyes grew moist and so did mine. Mr Tilak was also tearful. Mr Tilak was very miserly with tears. The monopoly of shedding them had been given to me. But that day his tears fell fast.

We knew Thombre's entire family. The only person we had never met was his elder sister. Thombre always said, 'She got me interested in poetry. She also writes poetry.' I had often said to him, 'Thombre, do arrange for me to meet your sister.' He would build castles in the air. 'We'll go. We'll do this. We'll do that.' But they all collapsed.

Balkavi Thombre left us suddenly for the eternally quiet place to write poetry, plunging into sorrow a loving mother, a devoted wife, a talented sister, an affectionate brother and a bosom friend. Mr Tilak bathed his memory in tears. Dattu and Tara had played and romped around with him. His memory still brings tears to our eyes.

> Come, drink up these last two tears
> Little bird, will you ever return?

Dattu's Wedding

By the grace of God I have many adopted children. One of them, Dr Earnest, lived in Satara. He was called doctor because his wife was a doctor. The date, time and place for Dattu's wedding had been fixed. And now we needed money for the wedding party—the groom's relatives and friends—to travel to Mumbai. Most were living with us anyway. I began collecting the money. I asked Dr Earnest to lend me two hundred rupees. The agreement was oral. The conditions were as follows: 'Dear boy, the only witness to the money you will give me is God. You will give me money in secret and I shall return it to you in secret. But we will set no time for repayment. If I happen to die, you will take the money from Dattu. Give me the money if you trust me. If you cannot give it, say so. I shall not feel bad. You will receive no interest from me on the loan.' My creditor accepted all these conditions and loaned me the money on the strength of my word alone.

Mr Tilak, on his part, was busy with another kind of wedding preparation. He had a clerk to assist him. With his help, he was churning out copies of a manual of wedding rites that he had evolved and later published in *Dnyanodaya*.

Dattu was in Mumbai. He did not come home even during the summer vacation. He was busy setting up his home with his parents-in-law's help, looking for accommodation for us and hiring cooking utensils for the wedding lunch. Mr Tilak's friend Dr Govande had promised to loan him the utensils, but did not do so because he fell out with Dattu's in-laws over some unknown matter. Nor did he come for the wedding. The invitations from both families were printed together in Mumbai.

This was the first auspicious event in my family. But it was obvious that none of my relatives would come. I would have loved to have a large party from the groom's side going with me. I would also have liked Dattu to be with us. But he was stuck in Mumbai. Our party comprised Dr Earnest, his wife and daughter from Satara; Manjulabai-the-Hawk and her daughter from Nagpur; Babu Patankar; my brother's son Vasudev; Benji; we three and Chiki. Of these, Babu Patankar was the only one whose train fare I did not have to pay. It was wartime. Fares had soared. I had to spend a huge amount on this trip.

I had collected a lot of grain and other foodstuff with the idea of taking it to Mumbai where we would need it. But we would have had to pay extra for the load. So I left it all behind. This meant that the money I had spent on it was, for the moment, dead money. I often boasted that I had more practical knowledge than Mr Tilak. But on such occasions I fell flat on my face.

And so we set off. Earnest was our boss. He was a clever man. He managed to reserve a whole compartment for us at Satara. We spread out comfortably. The train was bursting with passengers. But we reached Pune in great comfort. As soon as we drew into the station, Earnest began to fling our luggage quickly out of the compartment. I asked his wife why he was doing that. She said, 'It's something to do with reserving the compartment.' There was an equally big rush boarding the train from Pune. But once again Earnest managed to get a whole compartment for us. It felt like our ancestral property. We opened out our bedding rolls and lay down with our covering sheets pulled snugly up. Earnest alone sat by himself in a corner. A shrewd man entered our compartment at the station immediately after Pune. He sized up Earnest accurately. The shrewd man was followed by a horde of people. The compartment filled quickly to bursting. We were hard put to roll up our beddings and gather our luggage and ourselves together. We managed somehow till dawn. Then milkmen entered the compartment with their cans. I burst out laughing. Dr Earnest's face was worth seeing.

The groom is supposed to be part of the party going to the bride's place. We had written to Dattu asking him to join us before we got into Mumbai. So he came to Sion station with

Bhaskarrao Ujagare and waited for our train to come in. But neither of them had bothered to check the timetable. Our train was not scheduled to stop at Sion. It steamed past them, leaving them gaping after us. So now the groom's party was going to arrive before the groom himself. Dattu's father-in-law was at Byculla to receive us. But I was still upset about Dattu not being with us.

Arrangements for our accommodation had been made at the Methodist Mission Girls' School near Jacob's Circle. Dattu's in-laws lived on Belassis Road. Dattu's in-laws were civilized people. We came to an understanding with them that the cost for the wedding dinner would be shared. Each one's share came to one hundred and fifty rupees. I borrowed my share from them for the moment and returned the money soon after. The in-laws came to stay with us that night and returned home the following day. The wedding was scheduled for the evening. The bride reached the church on time. We too left in good time and waited for a tram. None came. Nor did we spot a horse carriage to take us to the church. So we footed it all the way. The bridegroom ran ahead to get there on time. We arrived later.

Mr Tilak conducted the wedding according to the new rites. He had composed the wedding songs which were sung by Patankar, Jai, my nephew, Bhaskarrao Ujagare and others. The day after the wedding, the bride and groom left for their honeymoon in Matheran. Our in-laws too went away for a change of air, taking their belongings with them. We, the bridegroom's party, shifted to a chawl. When it was time for tea the next morning, we longed for Satara. There was not a spot of anything in our new quarters to make tea with. Enough stuff had been laid up in Dattu's house to last a fortnight. But what use was that? His house was in Byculla and the key to the house was in Matheran.

It was only the day before that we had feasted on laddoos and sugared rice. And now there was not even a spoonful of milk for our tea. I was laid low after the hustle and bustle of the previous few days. But as I lay in bed I prayed. Dr Govande had gifted me fifteen rupees for a sari. I used the money to order rotis from the public cookhouse. There were some leftover laddoos and fritters too. That was our breakfast. We bid farewell to some of our guests, giving them half their fare back home. The rest of us stayed behind. It was no joke to provide tea and meals twice a day for ten or twelve people in a place like Mumbai.

A drawing teacher called Sadashivrao Dethe lived in a chawl quite close to our house. He had a wife and four children. He was the son-in-law of the man who had baptized Dattu and me. His house was small but his heart was large. He took over the responsibility of looking after us. His wife would cook and he would bring the food across to us. I shall be forever grateful to Sadashivrao and Krupabai for all they did for us.

During a wedding in a place called Cana, the wine ran out. So Jesus performed a miracle. He turned water into wine. I remembered that now. Dattu had instructed Benji to draw fifty rupees from the bank and give it to me on the day we were leaving for Satara. After some reluctance, he drew that money and gave it to me. We returned to Satara loaded with the grace of God.

Now I must narrate a story to show how I would get into a fix and put others into one as well. I sent a slice of the wedding cake to Mrs Hume in Mahabaleshwar requesting her to give it to all the missionaries and our acquaintances there. I had thought she would give a few token crumbs to everyone like the spoonfuls of copra-sugar mix that we give guests during religious ceremonies. But that is not the Christian custom. Mrs Hume was forced to throw a tea-party to distribute the slice of cake I had sent.

Meanwhile, even before we reached Satara, a guest had turned up there with his family. It was Mr Malelu, Ruth's aunt's husband. They were in Satara for a change of air. There were seven of them in all, including their maid and we were only three and Namya. The house was full to bursting. The shopping

I had done for the wedding and left behind now came in handy. Between us, Chiki, Tara, Namya and I made a strong team to look after the guests. Namya was perpetually scouring pots and I was perpetually at the stove. But they were happy days. By the time we struck the bottom of the grain storage bin, the vacations were over. The rainy season was round the corner. Our guests left. Ruth and Dattu came to Satara for a day before returning to Mumbai from their honeymoon. We were overjoyed to see them. Despite her college degree, Ruth did not find household chores irksome. She was as hard-working and efficient as her mother.

Namya had seen Mumbai for the first time during Dattu's wedding. He longed to go back. When Dattu and Ruth were leaving, he insisted on going with them. Dattu managed somehow to dissuade him, promising to give him whatever he asked for.

'Will you send me a lling? Shoes? A wlist-watch? A hat?'

'I'll do that the minute I get back.'

It was not difficult to send these things which would have cost a few annas, no more. But Namya became very anxious after Dattu left. 'What if the postal clerk steals the things Dattu Bhau sends before they reach me?' Once an idea was lodged in his head, there was nothing you could do to budge it. Namya now started picking quarrels, just to find a pretext to go to Mumbai. One day, Chiki was washing a clay pot in a basin of water. He looked at her, thought hard, bent down and said, 'What aal you doing? The pot will dlown in the wattle.'

She said, 'Let it drown. Papa is going to bring more pots with him when he comes back.'

'Leally? How many will he bling?'

'A cartful of pots.'

'But who will bling those pots home calefully? I'll go to the station.'

Nothing I said made any difference. He became so anxious about those pots that he went off to the station without dinner.

This was the time when they were recruiting men for the war. Namya enrolled and left for the war. Mr Tilak tried hard to convince the men in charge at the station that the boy was touched in the head and did not understand what he was doing. But to no avail.

On reaching Mumbai, Namya complained to the officers that he had not been told about fighting a war. All he had come prepared to do was pull a fan. So he was promptly chucked out. This is where Namya's story ended for us. I have no idea where in the general ocean of people this little drop disappeared.

Chiki

I have mentioned Rambhau Dharmadhikari quite often before this. After he got married he stopped visiting us. He did not even bring his daughter to show us. Although Rambhau had a lot of love and respect for us, his wife could not endure our relationship. She did not like the idea that we should have a claim on her husband's love. We were not blood relatives, so why visit us?

But God has His own plans. That poor woman died. Her daughter, whom she had done everything in her power to keep away from our sight, now had nobody but us to look after her. Rambhau brought Chiki to our house and both began living with us. Chiki was very young when she came. She grew extremely fond of us. Her nature was quite like her father's, affectionate and a little boastful. But there was not a shred of harm in her. She had many enthusiasms but nobody indulged them. On occasion, people in the house not only ignored her but even dismissed her rudely. That hurt her very deeply so she would spend all her time around Mr Tilak and me.

We had put her in school but she always stood last in her class. Her sole interest was in being at home and playing. She liked grooming herself, scrubbing her face, dressing up a little and showering love on everybody. When we moved to Satara, she went with us. Here too she went to school, but followed me around the rest of the time helping me with my work.

Chiki was always looking for occasions to boast about us. She called us Aajoba and Aaji. If she was asked, 'Chiki, have you had dinner? What did you eat?' she would reply with a ready list of delicacies fit for a rich man's table. In reality, we would have had the usual bhakri and vegetable.

One day I made some puran with jaggery and chickpeas. Chiki went to school and invited all her teachers over to have some. One day a teacher, knowing how much she loved me, said, 'Chiki dear, your Aaji's dead.' Chiki was so gullible that she left her slate and satchel behind and ran all the way home, crying her heart out.

I said, 'Why are you crying, Chiki? Why have you come home?'

She said, 'I'm crying because you're dead. My teacher told me you had died.'

One day, she was memorizing a poem which went, 'When sleep doesn't come a song is sung / The one who sings it is my loving mum.' She kept repeating the lines and tears flowed from my eyes. When she noticed this, she flung her arms around me. 'Why are you crying, Aaji?'

'I'm crying because you don't have a mother, my dear.'

'But aren't you my mother, Aaji? Where would I go if you weren't there for me?'

This sweet reply brought on more tears.

There was an ayah in Satara, who had been pensioned off by a missionary lady and was living a life of comfort. This old woman was of great service to me. She would spend a lot of time with us because she had no other work. I took advantage of this and got her to do my sewing, mending, and cleaning of grain. In return she had her tea and meals with us. Once in a while, she even made some money off us.

One Mother's Day, I had made some fried savouries. I had given her some, but had not given her the kadhai to clean. I was boiling water and tamarind in it to clean it of grease. I was in the kitchen roasting dals for thalipeeth flour while Chiki and Ayahbai sat outside cleaning grain.

Ayahbai asked Chiki, 'What is Aaji doing?'

Chiki said boastfully, 'My Dattu Kaka is coming so she's making all sorts of things like laddoos, anarase, karanjya, shankarpale.' This acted like the proverbial firewood in the hands of a mad monkey. The heat of the firewood burned into Ayahbai's brain through a loose screw in her head. She decided that I was making all this stuff on the sly, keeping it a secret from her.

Soon it was time for Mr Tilak's tea. He came in to collect all his paraphernalia. With him, making tea was an event. Fortunately, he made it himself. I was still roasting my dals when Ayahbai peeped in and said, 'What are you doing, Bai?'

'Nothing much. Dattu is coming so I'm making bhajani flour. He loves thalipeeth.'

'It is all right. Whatever you're making isn't costing me anything. It's your son, your money and your effort. What's in that kadhai?'

'Nothing. It's the one I made fritters in. I hadn't given it to you to clean.'

'That's not true. I cleaned it the same day.'

'No, really. I'm boiling water and tamarind in it to get it clean. Why would I keep such things from you? You're not going to take it away.'

'All I'm saying is, children don't lie. Not that it matters to me. But even the government takes what a child says as the truth.'

'I don't think I understand what you're saying.'

'Sure you don't. After all she's just a child. What does she know? Children don't know what they are supposed to say and what they are not.'

'Has Chiki said something to you?'

'It's all right. She's not to blame. A child will always tell the truth. You should have told her, poor thing, that she should not mention these things.'

'What things? What are you talking about?'

'Nothing much. She just told me about all the snacks you are making because your son is coming. She's not at fault.'

'For heaven's sake, nobody is at fault. What's got into your head?'

'Why would you know? It's not the girl's fault. She is bound to tell the truth.'

So far Mr Tilak had remained silent, although he could hear what we were saying. But now he called out to Chiki.

'What did you tell her?'

Chiki kept mum. I said, 'She just likes to show off. She always tells tall tales. Why take them seriously?'

'What does that mean? One day she might go around telling people that Aajoba has stolen a pile of money from somebody.'

Mr Tilak grabbed Chiki and started beating her. Ayahbai began singing, 'Let it be, saheb. She didn't lie. Children always tell the truth.'

'Bai, you have no sense. One day she'll cause a real problem for us.'

'There's nothing to it, saheb. Once you tell children not to say something, they don't.' The more Mr Tilak raged, the more the woman slid another piece of firewood into the flames. But meanwhile Chiki's back was turning into a blistering pancake. Finally I pulled her away.

'Do you want to kill her? Why should you beat our child because you're angry with somebody else?'

'It's you who've spoilt her.'

Ayahbai was still at it. 'Saheb, you shouldn't have beaten her. There's nothing wrong. Your son is coming so his mother has made eatables for him. Why should I object?'

Mr Tilak said, 'The woman's a raving idiot', and took Chiki to the bathroom to wash her face. Then he sat her down beside him, stroked her back and gave her tea. He also slipped a cup to Ayahbai.

Not Christianity but Christ

This was the last year of Mr Tilak's life, but it was worth more than ten. He said the country would not progress if it did not practise Christ's teachings. Hindustan had always paid more heed to the individual than to books and sects. He began to tell fellow Christians that it was not Christianity but Christ whom they should follow. His prayer to Christ was, 'Let my soul be a mirror in which the world sees you / Live in my thoughts, speak through my tongue, keep my actions pure and true.'

This new turn in his thinking brought him into conflict with those around him. He used to say that the Christian anywhere should be like Christ and the Hindustani Christian like the eastern Christ. He himself began to try and practise what he preached. He had been preparing for this turn in his life for the last ten years. It was ten or twelve years ago that he had said in a poem:

> I still fall short my Lord, much too short
> Not an ounce have I returned to my people
> Of the pounds I owed
> And to you I shall always remain indebted
> Oh saviour of sinners.

He was struggling very hard to fill the lacuna that he saw in himself. Over the years he had tried to overcome the failings that had accompanied him from birth. It would not be an exaggeration to say that they had disappeared almost entirely in this last year. To take just his short temper as an example, I do not recall his losing it even once over a slight or an insult. The only thing he still allowed himself was an occasional outburst of righteous indignation.

Mr Tilak was not doing paid work. He got a little money occasionally from his writing. That was all. We had always been poor, and we continued to be poor. The only difference between our earlier and present states of poverty was that we were free of debts now. By God's grace we were still surrounded by people. Our home was a meeting place for people of different castes, religions, ideologies, all bound together by goodwill. Amongst them were people who were still pondering over religion, others who had been coerced into or had willingly converted to Christianity. Together, we sang bhajans twice a day. We had acquired a gong. When it was struck, people from all over the wadi, and sometimes even from the town beyond, would congregate at our place. Even a casual passer-by might step in and join.

Having no money, Mr Tilak had taken to wearing saffron robes. It saved us dhobi expenses. He had had the robes made from old dhotis. People sat on the floor and sang. Mr Tilak alone stood. Everybody carried a small pair of cymbals and castanets. One person would keep the beat on a tabla or a horseshoe. Sometimes Mr Tilak would wear bells on his ankles and dance as he sang, losing himself completely in his devotion. This state culminated in a trance when the body was forgotten. The other singers were similarly affected and the singing would go on for hours.

In our home we did not discriminate between caste, age, religion or status. From the Brahmin to the sweeper, anybody could join in the bhajans. Christians would come and so would employees of the Mission. Whosoever came was like family to us. There was no question of them and us.

One of the Christians who came regularly had, like us, come to Satara from Ahmednagar. Later he went to Mesopotamia to fight in the war. We would remember him often but had no news of him. One day an official letter came inquiring about who this man's heir was. Mr Tilak's eyes filled with tears as he read the letter. When I heard the contents, I too felt very upset. Mr Tilak concluded that he had been killed. I maintained that he was hiding somewhere out of fear. But Mr Tilak was firm in his belief that he was not the kind of young man to hide. The man used to call me Aai and treat me as his mother. I cried the whole day as I did my household chores, thinking of his every gesture, speech and conduct.

The following day, I forced myself to cook. I made rice and a vegetable. I felt his presence all around me. He had eaten with us the day before he left. What did he go through after that? It must have been around half past one. We were both trying to console each other. We sat down to lunch. Once again our eyes filled with tears. Just then we heard a voice calling 'Aai'. I turned around and there he was. I said loudly, 'He's come to life.' After that the food that our tears had made impossible for us to swallow tasted like nectar because now we were shedding tears of joy. Today, this young man, Amrutrao Tribhuvan, has become an eminent lawyer in Ahmednagar.

I shall return here to the rickshaw lady who did not care for Mr Tilak's bhajan singing and had therefore sacked two of her employees who attended the assemblies. Mr Tilak had found them jobs. This became the cause for an all-out war. The lady thought her people had greater regard for Mr Tilak than for her. She felt she had lost her authority. Mr Tilak thought the lady had turned her Indian Christian employees into slaves. He wrote an abhang which said:

> Hindustan is not to be trifled with
> Its deeds stand true and tall
> On this soil were born great men of religion
> Before whom the universe quaked
> Faith was their life
> The universe was their home
> Why parade these ridiculous masks?
> Why play at absurd charades?

I was responsible for pouring oil on these flames. One of the members had been banned from the church for his inappropriate conduct. He had reformed and wished to be readmitted to the church. However, he was not prepared to apologize publicly and fulfil all the other requirements demanded by rules. So the disciplinarian lady missionary would not re-admit him. The people working under her also fell in line. Once when Mr Tilak was out of town, Dr Hume wrote asking him to mediate and have the man re-admitted to the church. If he were abandoned in this way, he was likely to go even further astray.

I agreed with Dr Hume and assumed the responsibility of seeing this task through myself, without waiting for Mr Tilak to return. When I spoke to a Mission employee, he said, 'Bai, we agree with you, but we are helpless before our lady boss. It might help if you took the lead.'

I went to the lady boss. She said, 'Why should we concern ourselves with these people's problems? It's better for us to stay out.' I returned home and prayed with all humility in order to find a solution to the problem. It was a Sunday. I sent a note to the priest during evening prayers. He read it out to the assembly. 'I wish to convey God's message to you. I request everybody to wait for five minutes after prayers. Yours, Aaji.'

I had marked the eighth chapter of St John and asked a young boy to read it. I stopped him at the eighth verse. 'He that is without sin, let him cast the first stone at her.'

I said to the congregation, 'Christ came down to earth to raise the sinner, to save him. He did not come to trample on him. What do you value more, a human life or a sense of your own greatness? If this man renders you a written apology and you exhibit it, will it make you feel greater? Why are you bent on branding a soul that has just cleansed itself through remorse?'

People muttered, this woman asked for five minutes and look how long she is taking. Despite this, what I said had a good effect. The man was re-admitted to the church. Mr Tilak and Dr Hume were very happy. Later I found the once-ostracized man a wife. They were happy. He had put four of his daughters in a hostel run by the disciplinarian. One day they came home saying they had been thrown out of the hostel. Mr Tilak arranged for them to stay in a hostel in Pune. The fifth daughter was teaching in the lady's school. She was sacked and told, 'Go to Aaji. She'll find you work.' She came weeping to me. I consoled her. 'God looks after the poor. Go back and don't worry.'

I was praying silently all the while. The next day, a guest from Ahmednagar came to stay with me. Her son earned one hundred rupees a month. He was single. The woman asked me if I knew of a suitable match for him. I was overjoyed that a proposal had come walking to my door. I brought the girl for her to see. She liked the girl. I looked after my guest with all the respect due to an in-law. Soon the young people were married.

From the start, we had been fortunate in acquiring two things of great importance—free accommodation and a doctor who was like family. We had Dr Sorabji in Ahmednagar, Dr Kelkar in Satara, Dr Gore in Nagpur, Dr Dandekar in Mumbai and now Dr Gupte in Nashik. I was to perform a keertan in town one day but had come down with a high fever the previous evening. Mr Tilak sent Dr Kelkar a note: 'She is not well. Come as soon as you can.' The doctor was not at home. He had gone on a visit to some village. He saw Mr Tilak's note when he returned. The note gave no information about what was wrong with me. It was ten o'clock at night. The doctor was without his assistant at that hour and he was ravenous. He could not decide what medicines to carry with him. Finally, he filled a huge sack with medicines and instruments for every illness he had treated me for as far as he could remember. His tonga was harnessed but the tonga driver had left. So he picked up the reins himself and drove to our house. By then my fever had gone down.

The doctor said, 'You hag, what did you have anyway? Did a snake bite you or was it cholera or what? I was scared out of my wits.'

I wanted to laugh but I was also feeling very sorry. I said, 'It's just that I have to perform a keertan tomorrow and I didn't want to have a fever.'

Instead of medicine, the doctor gave me two whacks on my back with his cane. Of course, since they were lovingly delivered,

I did not need any ointment to soothe me. Then he made some rice gruel for me to have. My keertan went off well the next day and some people who were present invited me to perform in other places. One of the invitations was from a European gentleman named Mr Frichley. He was not a missionary but a sculptor. He had heard about us from somebody and, being of a religious bent of mind himself, had invited us.

This was the first Christmas after Dattu's marriage. In my opinion, he and our daughter-in-law should have spent it in Satara. But Dattu wrote asking us to go to Mumbai instead. Mr Tilak never demurred over such things. He agreed instantly and we went to Mumbai. Before we arrived, Dattu had stayed up nights translating a book for which he was paid seventy-five rupees. Mr Tilak was very happy that Dattu had the sensitivity to do this in order to ensure that we would not fall short of anything during our visit.

Chiki was staying with Dattu, Tara was at college and stayed in St Colomba's Hostel. We reached Dattu's home in Byculla at break of day. He came downstairs to carry our luggage up. And there we discovered that Ruth was in bed. She could not keep down even a sip of water. But it was the kind of illness that makes grandparents happy.

I had come fully prepared for Christmas. All we needed to do was to fry the sweets and savouries and we would be done. Tara and Chiki took over that job. It was not as if Ruth could not have done it, or that she was shirking the work. She simply did not have the energy to do anything at all. Even then she did a few things with the girls' help. I was busy preparing for my keertan.

This was our last Christmas together. It was a very happy time for us all. Ruth gave her father-in-law a tea-set as a Christmas gift and gave me a nine-yard sari. Christmas went by very quickly. We had planned to go to Lonavala for New Year. Mr Frichley had invited us to sing bhajans and perform a keertan. We had exchanged letters and met a couple of times.

But that had been enough for us to get to know each other very well. Mr Frichley had begun to hold Mr Tilak in high regard.

We reached Lonavala on New Year's Eve. I performed my keertan. That night was Watch Night. We were Mr Frichley's guests on the first day of the New Year. When we left the following day, Mr Frichley put a cheque for five hundred rupees in Mr Tilak's hand. Our next stop was Pune where again I performed a keertan. After that we arrived in Satara with our stash of five hundred rupees. As soon as we got home, I secretly returned the two hundred rupees Dr Earnest had given me and felt greatly relieved.

Mr Tilak's habitual prayer was, 'Dear Lord, keep me poor. I don't want money.'

My prayer was, 'Dear Lord, I don't want debts.'

God had heard both our prayers. There is a poem of Mr Tilak's which goes, 'Let not my hands and heart be singed with money.' Our natures had been so formed as to make it possible for both of our prayers to be answered. I did not crave money so Mr Tilak's prayer was answered. Mr Tilak stopped borrowing money so my prayer was answered.

He had indeed given up borrowing money. We did not owe anybody a paisa and Dattu and I did not have to repay any debts later either. Despite this, I would complain. I would say, 'Bad times come without warning. We should have a little money put by at least to take care of our limbs.'

Mr Tilak said, 'Would He who has looked after us from before our birth not do the same now? What do you gain by worrying?'

Of the five hundred rupees Mr Frichley had given us, two hundred went towards repaying my debt, one hundred was spent on Christ's Court and I kept the remaining two hundred aside. It proved very useful when the time came.

Shadows Gather

We now entered a time when Nature assumed a grim aspect. Farmers ploughed their black soil and sat down to pray. People's eyes were fixed on the clouds like the chatak bird, yearning for rain. The clouds would thunder and flit across the sky. Like the black spot we put on a baby's face to ward off the evil eye, a tiny spot of black cloud would appear in the midst of those empty puffs of vapour, but no rain fell and people's mouths ran dry.

Mussalmans and Christians prayed to their respective gods. The Brahmins held rites to propitiate their gods. The idols in the temples were imprisoned in water to compel them to listen to people's prayers. The poor called upon God to save them. People lost heart. They panicked. The child became a burden to the mother.

Mr Tilak believed in prayer and fasting. He began having only one meal a day. At times, he would skip even that. When he sat down to eat, his throat would often get choked. He would say, 'How can I eat this food when I know my own people cannot afford it? I'd rather you gave it away to my starving brothers and sisters.' He began giving away whatever foodstuff there was in the house to the needy.

Another disaster struck on top of the drought. Fleas. Cages arrived in homes. The air was filled with the fumes of burning tar. Inoculations began. People left their homes. We got news of this one or that one going away. Mr Tilak heard about a preparation for fumigation which he got me to make. He began giving away fistfuls of it to whoever he saw. It was meant to drive away mice, rats, mosquitoes and fleas. By the grace of God and human efficiency, the plague had been held off. But disease inevitably follows drought and so it did. The disease we call manmodi, or dropneck, struck Satara first. It took away the last shred of courage left in the people. They were too shocked even to speak.

Manmodi was almost worse than the plague. In a family of ten, only one remained standing. The others were flat on their backs. The animals grazing in the forest could not be brought home and the animals at home could not be fed or given water. Families had no food to eat, no oil to light their lamps, no men to fetch their water. We heard the story of a penniless man who sold his cow in exchange for two pomegranates.

Conditions were so pitiable that Mr Tilak opened a small clinic and free kitchen. I used to brew three or four seers of a herbal infusion every morning. Mr Tilak would distribute this from eight to twelve in the morning along with milk, sago, sugar, kerosene and boxes of matches to all comers: Brahmins, Marathas, Mahars. His bhajan singing continued morning and evening. Meanwhile, every day, notices would come to us to vacate the free accommodation that had been allotted to us. But since there were no chains or cuffs on our wrists to compel us, we paid no heed to them. The people of Satara, brought to their knees by drought and disease, were liberated at last from both.

I have had a problem with my stomach since Dattu's birth. Sometimes the condition becomes acute. It was one of those occasions and I was in bed. As soon as Mr Tilak got up in the morning, he would first light the stove, put it under my cot and then make tea for himself. Nowadays he spent a lot of time speaking to me. Not that he had not done so earlier. But now he would find time when he really had none to sit by me and talk. But I did not like the things he said. Although I would go 'hunh hunh' most of the time, there were times when I said, 'Enough of your rambling. I hate it. You can never tell what's going to happen. But we should talk of auspicious things. God's messengers are out there, ready to pronounce, "So be it".'

He would say, 'But what I'm saying isn't inauspicious. When two people travel together, one might reach his destination before the other. That's all there is to it. There is nothing to fear. One needs a subject to talk about, so I thought of this. What's wrong with it? We don't know what's going to happen and when. We aren't sent a notice about it beforehand. Only a mother knows how long a child should play outdoors. When it grows tired, she picks it up and holds it close. She lulls it to sleep. That's what God does. He will pick you up, if not today then tomorrow. Instead of flailing against it, we should wait eagerly for the moment. People should strive to become a little bigger than their circumstances. If those who are left behind when their dear ones have gone, spend their time lamenting, they prove that they are the slaves of circumstance and show disrespect for God's will.

'When a woman's husband dies, she goes crazy with excessive grief. She forgets that she has children to take care of. She weeps at any time of the day and in any place. She is oblivious to the effect her show of grief has on others. And the women who come supposedly to console the woman, recall such virtues of the man as perhaps didn't even exist, so that, far from consoling her, they only pour oil on the flames of her grief. They give no thought to the needs of the dead man's family, the help they might require, the ways in which they could be made to forget their grief. Whosoever comes, makes the woman weep, takes the scabs off her wounds and turns the house into a place of permanent gloom. The woman goes blind with weeping and her children suffer in body and mind.'

Hearing him say these things was like having lumps of flesh gouged out of my heart.

'We know a Vaishnav by the mark he makes on his forehead. Similarly we know a family is in mourning by the black dresses they wear. I can't stand it. Black hearse, black horse, black coffin, black sari, black armbands, black borders around letters. What is all this? Is going to the home of God an inauspicious thing? Is it inauspicious to go to the One who is immortal and sacred? What is the sign of sacredness, black or white? If I go before you, I don't want you doing any of this. I want everything to be white.'

'I don't know why you're going on like this.'

'It would be better if I went before you.'

'I don't understand what's better and what's worse in this.'

'You'll understand in good time. I don't want you and the

children to give yourselves over to grief when I'm gone. We must go to God some day and that's nothing to lament about. It is He who will take me and He who will look after you when I'm gone.'

The Mambaji in Mr Tilak's life, like the original tormentor of Saint Tukaram, began to make things more and more difficult for him. She kept sending us notices to vacate the house. We did not obey her command. Bhajan singing happened in the house twice a day. Her employees, heedless of her orders and threats, would attend both times. After that Mr Tilak began giving sermons in the church. In those days, there was no separate building for the church. Prayers would be said in the school and the school was looked upon as the church for that duration. But Mambaji controlled the school, and she would make sure to keep it shut as often as possible.

Mr Tilak would say to the people, 'Build yourselves a church with your own hands even if it's a small place with a thatched roof. Stand together, endure suffering, but build your own church. How much longer will you drink from other people's hands? How much longer will you be abjectly dependent on others? It is a hundred years since you became Christians. Are you still babies crawling on all fours? Was this how your ancestors were? Should you not have pride in them? Why do you bend your heads before others?'

To the missionaries he would say, 'How much longer will you feed us with your hands? Let us stand on our own feet now. Don't interfere. Let us swim, go down, drown, let the current take us, let us die. But through it all, let us learn to float.'

To me he would say, 'Wait and see. These same Christians and missionaries will turn against me one day. But I will continue to say and do what I believe is in their interests. I will endure harassment but work for their welfare till my dying breath.'

However, except for one Mambaji, no Christian or missionary ever harassed Mr Tilak. On the contrary, they were always friends and family to him.

As the month of Magh came to an end, summer began to make itself felt. It was not the sun so much as the sand that gave out heat. At prayer time, Mambaji refused to hand over the keys. The school remained shut. Mambaji was determined not to part with the keys come rain or shine. People came to Mr Tilak complaining that the doors of heaven had been closed on them that day. He said, 'Let them be. God does not reside in the church. The Lord has said wherever two or three of you gather with one heart in my name, there will I be. Come, let us open a church under a tree on the common.'

Mr Tilak set off. The people followed. Mambaji saw this from afar. Instantly, a boy came running after them with the keys and turned them back. The church which had been closed was opened. The speech that Mr Tilak made that day brought tears to the listeners' eyes. The theme of his speech was, 'The servant says dear Lord, make some place for me beside you.' As his speech ended, Mr Tilak said, 'This will be my last sermon to you. I doubt if I will step into this church again. When I leave, I will not return to Satara.' People began to weep. What Mr Tilak said turned out to be true. This was indeed the last sermon he made in that church. But just see how inscrutable God's ways are. The very Christians who had had to gather in a school for their prayers in Satara were given a beautiful new church after Mr Tilak died and they called it the Tilak Memorial Church.

Death is like the cunning man who will find any pretext that will help him do his work. It is enough if you stub your toe or have a bout of hiccups. In recent times, sugarcane-juicing machines had mushroomed everywhere. We used to order sugarcane juice at the end of the bhajan session and occasionally Mr Tilak would also have some. Perhaps it did not suit him. He began to look like an ill man. However, this did not interfere with his work. He would still get up in the middle of the night to write.

I started nagging him again. 'We don't have a single paisa for illnesses and other emergencies. How can we remain so incapable of looking after ourselves? For you money is an enemy. But what will we do for medicines now?'

'He knows what we should or should not eat and drink. I am certain that He will not let us fall short of medicines. He will even provide for my funeral. He will even provide for you for a month after I've gone to allow you to mourn me. A month is enough time for mourning. After that you must fend for yourself.'

Now Dr Kelkar began making regular visits to the house. One day Mr Tilak got up at three in the morning and came to my room. He never woke me up when I was asleep because it set my body trembling more violently. But that day he woke me up and said, 'I have troubled you a lot all these years. Please forgive me.'

'Why are you saying that today? Are you not feeling well?'

I quickly lit the stove and went to call Mr Dhanaji from next door. When we got back Mr Tilak was sitting up, writing.

'How are you feeling, Guruji?'

'I'm feeling well.'

Mr Dhanaji left and I went back to sleep. That night Mr Tilak made his will. The reader might wonder what a man who does not have a paisa to his name says in his will. That is why I have reproduced some parts of it here. One copy of it was sent to Dattu, one to the Mission and one he kept for himself.

> If I had not been a believer in God, Christ and beauty of which I have my own definition, I would have been some other kind of man. Fame and public censure are both like bubbles. If people choose to criticize me after my death and doing so serves their purpose, so be it. It does not affect me in any way.
>
> How long someone lives does not define his life for me. It is the usefulness of the work he does that defines it. If a man does not do useful work, he might as well die. I see two things around me everywhere. Beauty and ugliness. I love beauty. The reason why I love Christ so intensely is because He is an ocean of beauty. Rather He is beauty. He is Himself

the epitome of beauty. The man who loves beauty in the hope of gaining heaven or escaping hell can never love it truly. Love has to be selfless. I love beauty for itself. I believe that heaven and hell are two states through which a man's soul passes to achieve a unified third state. If Christ's existence in the soul of the man who holds such an opinion is erased, the man will become a terrible being.

If my friends and well-wishers wish to erect a tombstone over the place where my ashes are kept, and wish to inscribe it, let the inscription be as follows: 'I still fall short, my Lord / I still fall very, very short.' There should be no honorific like Reverend or Mr before my name. I appeal to my friends from the bottom of my heart not even to use the word poet before my name. My name should not be inscribed in the English way as N.V. Tilak but in Marathi as Narayan Waman Tilak.

Nobody can tell when they will be called away by God. Nobody should waste time thinking about that. I will never refer to the call from God as death because it is God's will, His invitation. It is the birth of a new life. The thought of death never depresses me. I am not troubled by death and nor am I troubled by life. This is the basic principle of a Christian life and I am experiencing it to its fullest through Christ.

I love my country more than I have loved my parents, wife, children, friends, and why, even myself. I pray that Hindustani Christians will dedicate themselves to helping their churches grow, to make them truly independent and full of joy.

I would like to be cremated after death. Please forbid the use of black in the funeral procession. Please place my ashes in the Ahmednagar cemetery. My picture should hang next to Dr Hume's in the seminary with the word 'He' under Dr Hume's picture and the words 'Looked after him' under mine.

This too he had written in his will.

Mrs Lee, Dr Hume's daughter, was living in Satara at the time. Mr Tilak typed out the following letter to her:

Satara
4.12.18

My dear Mrs Lee,

I have suddenly become so very sick with a pain in my heart that I think I shall be called away at any moment tonight. I'm quite ready. I have the following wishes and messages.

1. THE MISSION, I hope will take care of my wife. She is an angel, but she has her weaknesses. Will you be her sister?

2. CHRISTAYANA is incomplete. Help Tara try to develop her poetical inspiration so that she may finish it one day.

3. DO NOT make much of me anywhere when I am gone. I have not accomplished even a thousandth part of what God had made me capable of accomplishing. I wish nothing from you all or from the world but pardon.

4. Burn my remains, and then if my friends wish it, take some remnant and bury it. If any monument is to be raised over it, say on it 'I still fall short my Lord / I still fall very, very short.' Write no name but only this: Here lies somebody who loved Jesus with all his heart and also his countrymen.

5. The following persons are very dear to me. My wife first, Tara and Dattu, Dr Hume, Hatty Bruce, yourself, Jaibai Gaikwad, Bhaskar Ujagare, Mr Edwards, Sir Narayan Chandavarkar, Bhadrabai Madgaonkar and Dr Macnicol. Tell them so.

My messages:

1. To India: Follow Jesus.

2. To my Christian brothers and sisters: Your life is in Christ; your life is Him and nothing else.

3. To Missionaries: Cease to be fathers and mothers, be real brothers and sisters. Know how to appreciate, trust people and take the place of India's revered Saints.

4. To All: I lived as a friend and died as a friend to all, and I am sure I am still both here and in the hereafter.

Yours sincerely,
N. W. Tilak

Why Fear When the Lord Is with You?

The day Mr Tilak posted copies of his will, he also wrote to Dr Daulatrao Gore in Pune. Dr Kelkar used to visit regularly. He had even offered to house Mr Tilak at his place. But he did not have a hospital. Dr Gore wrote back to say come any time. We will make all necessary arrangements for you. As Mr Tilak had predicted during his prayer meeting, he did not step on Ahmednagar soil again.

We left Satara. As promised, Dr Gore had made all arrangements for us in Pune. We had a special room, a ward boy, free medicines. Mrs Mathurabai Malhar took upon herself the responsibility of providing the few odds and ends we required—pots and pans, stoves, hot water for our baths. So far so good. The only thing missing now was a Damaji, like the saint of yore who gave away all that he had to the needy. And there he was, standing before us with folded hands. This was Govinda, Manjulabai-the-Hawk's son. He had heard of Mr Tilak's illness and had come to Pune specially to see us. He brought us some fruit and gave me fifty rupees. 'Use this for Papa. I have saved it from my salary.'

I was both happy and sad. Sad because he was so young and we should have been giving him things and looking after him instead of the other way around. I did not like to think that he was perhaps repaying us for the little we had done for him earlier. But I did not want to turn down his offer. So I took the money and kept it aside. From next day on, money started coming in from various sources. Our expenditure, including milk, soda, fruit and visitors came to about six or seven rupees a day. After spending that, I would still have a small balance left over at the end of each day. The amounts we got, except on Sundays, were anything between one and one hundred rupees. We had a maid to help us with the work and Rambhau Dharmadhikari. He, poor man, was on his feet most of the time.

This was a direct experience of a line from one of Mr Tilak's abhangs. 'The Lord is our father and mother. We shall not want.'

Here, too, Mr Tilak spent very little time in bed. He would visit the other patients and pray and sing bhajans. Chintamanrao Gaikwad, a courtier of Christ's Court, used to accompany him in the singing. Many abhangs were born here. Mr Tilak even made a few speeches. But there were times when he felt so uneasy that I would panic and run to fetch Dr Gore. He always came, even when halfway through a meal. The only time I could not catch him was when he was in the operating theatre.

We received a letter from Jai. This was Manjulabai-the-Hawk's daughter and Govinda's sister. She was a nurse in Nagpur. Mr Tilak loved her like a daughter. She left Nagpur for Satara before we left for Pune. But she fell ill on the way and had to return to Nagpur. Her letter said, 'Papa, here I lie, seriously ill. And there you lie in the same state. The doctors have given up all hope for me. I don't think we'll ever meet again.' She wrote to Govinda too, asking him to visit her if he could. He came to us with the letter. We pressed him to take the fifty rupees he had given us and go to Nagpur.

Pandita Ramabai sent Manoramabai to meet us. She brought some eats with her and a hundred rupees. In all, there was plenty as Mr Tilak had predicted. Tara took a few days off and came. Dattu too took a few days leave to come and see us. Ruth was not well but despite that she made some sweets and sent them with Dattu. Mr Tilak felt great joy during his illness at the thought of becoming a grandfather. In all that hustle and bustle, I had started sewing things for the baby. Mr Tilak had made a patchwork quilt. Often I would ask Mrs Gore to do some of the sewing and that poor soul would happily oblige.

The incurable illness that had afflicted Mr Tilak was nothing more than piles. But it used to make him extremely uneasy sometimes. He kept after Dr Gore to operate on him. But he also had a touch of bronchitis. Dr Gore said, 'I won't be able to give you chloroform in this condition. Medication will cure you gradually.' He consulted a couple of other doctors about Mr Tilak's case and they too agreed with him.

The more Mr Tilak's illness troubled him, the sweeter were the abhangs he wrote. He wrote around thirty abhangs during his stay in the Pune hospital. We heard of Jai's passing away there and he wrote an abhang about that. The poem he wrote on poet Govindagraj's death also belongs to this time.

After some time, he began to feel better. The children returned to Mumbai. Yet, although he was better, his mind thought otherwise. He was eating, drinking, writing, reading, walking around and giving speeches; but he still wanted to be operated upon to remove the piles. Around that time, Dattu's father-in-law wrote to us about a very good surgeon who had joined J.J. Hospital. This letter was followed by one from Mr Frinchley. He said the excellent surgeon who had recently joined J.J. Hospital happened to be a good friend of his. He offered to make every arrangement for us to go there.

Everybody in the Pune hospital was against Mr Tilak's going to Mumbai. Dr Gore told him a hundred times, 'Don't go. I will look after you here. An operation may precipitate a crisis. I don't think you should go in for surgery.'

Mr Tilak's response was, 'I have a lot of work to do. I want to get completely well. There is "Christayana". There is Christ's Court. Please don't stand in the way of God's will.' This silenced Dr Gore.

Ruth had now begun to feel better, but Dattu had fallen ill. We had heard that he was only mildly unwell and was being treated by Dr Dandekar. But he was actually down with typhoid and Ruth was six months pregnant.

Finally, Mr Tilak's plan of going to Mumbai materialized. Mr Frinchley booked a second-class compartment for him. The people in the Pune hospital felt very sad when Mr Tilak left. There were tears in Dr Gore's eyes. He was convinced that he was seeing his Gurumaharaj off on his last journey. He and his wife Harrietbai used to call him Gurumaharaj.

We boarded the train at Pune station at night and were in Byculla the following morning. A stretcher had been sent to the station from J.J. Hospital to carry Mr Tilak there. He began to laugh when he saw it. He sent the stretcher back and went out himself to hire a horse buggy. We got off in front of Dattu's house. Mr Tilak was about to climb up when Malelu the priest said, 'Don't stop here now. Please go straight to the hospital.'

Mr Tilak said, 'Let me meet Dattu. Let me finish my morning ablutions.' But that was not to be. The Great Reaper was calling him. He did not climb a single stair. He walked to J.J. Hospital wearing the same robe in which he had travelled. On the ninth day after Mr Tilak walked to the hospital, he came out on the shoulders of four men. Tara and I went upstairs to Dattu's. Mr Tilak's illness shattered me and all the strength drained out of my limbs. When I reached upstairs, I found Dattu had been down with typhoid for six months. I looked at him and my mouth went dry with fear. I was not ill, but I could not get out of bed. Ruth had to do a lot for Dattu. Nobody in the house was even thinking of Mr Tilak. We had lost him and he had lost us the moment we stepped into Mumbai.

Somehow, I had sensed what was going to happen. I sent word with Malelu to the doctor to say Dr Gore had been against surgery. The surgeon's return message was, 'Do I practise the barber's profession then?' Who can teach know-alls? Whatever profession he practised, he left for England three days after he took up Mr Tilak's case. So how could an illiterate woman like me be expected to see the difference, if any existed, between a barber's kit and this man's surgical instruments?

J.J. Hospital used to be full of students. As many prospective doctors as a patient had organs would gather around to examine him. Mr Tilak was appearing for his own examination in J.J. Hospital while our home had become the breeding ground for illness. My daughter-in-law had grown weak, my son was in bed, I had also taken to my bed soon after we reached Mumbai. The climate of the city did not suit Chiki and she was barely holding on. By the grace of God, Tara was well. Nobody else around was in good health.

Tara used to visit the hospital and come back with news. Prof. Patankar was in Mumbai during that time. He would come to help us whenever he found time from his own work. Many of our friends had gone away for their summer vacation. The rest were busy with their lives. Dattu's in-laws had gone to Matheran. Ruth was their only daughter, and she was not well. Naturally, they would have liked to take her along. But she did not wish to go. So she stayed back.

What Tara, Babu Patankar and Manoharrao Ujagare did for us in those days was invaluable. Five days after we arrived, Tara persuaded me to go with her to the hospital. There too Mr Tilak was writing as he lay in bed. He wrote articles and abhangs for *Dnyanodaya* while he was fighting death. Our final meeting and the conversation we had while he was still in a conscious state, happened because of Tara. 'I feel better now,' he said. 'I'll soon recover completely. Don't worry. I still have two big tasks to complete. "Christayana" and Christ's Court. Guess which is my favourite song?' And he recited a song that went: 'The enemy might lay siege to you, but who cares? / When your Father is with you, no mountain is tall enough to stand in your way. / 1919 is going to be a memorable year.'

I realized that the song was his message to me. My heart grew heavy with sorrow. I did not wish to let him see the tears in my eyes so I left the room and cried my heart out. Ruth went to see him the same day. He held her close and blessed her, 'You are going to give birth to a son.'

The following day a friend of Dattu's from the medical college came over to tell us that Mr Tilak had fever, but we should not worry. Then his temperature went up to 105 degrees. On the third day Babu Patankar sat by his bedside the whole night. On Friday, 9 May 1919, Tara went to the hospital. Dattu and I were in bed. Dattu's heart was prodding him to go and see Mr Tilak. He had not got up from his bed for a long time. But he rose, came to me and said, 'Come, let's both go.'

I did not have the courage to go. But we set off on foot, he supporting me and I him. Somehow we managed to reach the hospital. Tara was standing at the gate leaning against a tree. We went directly to Mr Tilak's ward. He had been given an injection of morphia. Manoharrao Ujagare and another friend P.V. Kashinath Raghunath were standing by him along with one or two others. Finally Mr Tilak met his son. He could not speak but he gestured towards his mouth. Dattu fed him a spoonful of water and his soul left his body.

Tara was outside. I hugged her. 'Tara, think that your mother has gone and your father lives. I will not let you lack for anything. I will see to it that you complete your education.'

We came home. A little later, Manoharrao Ujagare and others brought Dattu home. Chiki was waiting for us at the door. She said, 'How is Aajoba?'

'He's better now.'

'Then why don't you take me to meet him?'

'You'll meet him tomorrow.'

There was no sign in our home that death had entered. Our neighbours had no inkling of what had happened. So far we had managed to follow Mr Tilak's wishes. God alone knows whether Manoharrao felt rested in body and mind, because he voluntarily took upon his shoulders the responsibility of seeing the funeral through. He sent telegrams, called up people, went to the printers, decided on the time—he did all this with Malelu's consent.

The Missionaries from Mahabaleshwar wired saying everything should be done according to Mr Tilak's wishes. That's when we remembered his will. Manoharrao asked, 'So what shall we do?'

'Do what Mr Tilak wished to be done.'

On 10 May, Mr Tilak had been brought back to the home where not more than five months earlier he had celebrated Christmas. Now Chiki understood everything. Although many people were out of town, newspapers, telegrams and telephone calls told them the news and they came from Ahmednagar, Alibaug, Pune, Lonavala and other places. Black was banned in accordance with Mr Tilak's wishes. There was no question of the hearse being black or white because people decided they would take turns at carrying the coffin on their shoulders all the way.

The Byculla Church was filled to bursting with mourners. There were Hindus as well as Christians in the gathering. I was not weeping but I was not in my senses either. After prayers, the mourners carried the coffin to the crematorium at Worli and brought back with them some ashes in a wooden casket. The mourners had selected one of Mr Tilak's bhajans to sing during the funeral procession. Sixteen years on, the words and the tune of that bhajan still echo in my ears. The bhajan went like this:

Why fear when the Lord is with you?
When all words except the Lord's name are forgotten?
Such a man lives in the world but does not belong to it
Impoverished here, he has riches to reap
The body is his, but the soul is Christ's
Such a man is above sickness and death.
Why fear when the Lord is with you?

PART FOUR

A New Age

The moment Mr Tilak's ashes went into the casket, I became acutely aware of my new identity. I began receiving letters of condolence from the very next day and felt deeply saddened to see the honorific that now preceded my name. I was no longer 'saubhagyavati', the woman who was fortunate to have a husband. I was that unfamiliar thing called 'shrimati', which meant, simply, lady. Although shrimati was also a respectful title, I found it extremely inauspicious. Poetry, which had consoled me after Mr Tilak converted to Christianity and had been my companion till she saw me happy again, now returned to hold my hand. I wrote a long poem that expressed my anguish at what had come to pass. The refrain went, 'The happiness of the woman whose husband lives is over.'

It was about two o'clock in the afternoon. The five of us sat facing each other lifelessly. Ruth, Tara, Chiki, Dattu and I, sucked into our individual vortexes of sorrow, surfaced occasionally only to look blankly at the ceiling. Our bodies had been immobilized because Dattu was still ill, Ruth was nearing her full term, Tara was missing out on her college and Chiki was playing hide-and-seek with ill health, but our minds were working full-time. Mumbai, crowded and bursting with activity, was like a vacuum to us. We were surrounded by wide empty spaces in which there was not a single person we could call our own.

That afternoon Dattu was lying in bed; Ruth was sitting with him talking; Tara, Chiki and I were sitting on the floor leaning against the wall, when an individual rushed in and collapsed before us. He was panting, his throat was dry, he was streaming with sweat and his eyes were closed tight. We wondered what new catastrophe we had been presented with.

Sakharambhauji had left Pune intending to visit Mr Tilak. He had not heard about his illness but had felt a sudden urge to see him. When he arrived at Karjat, he decided to make a detour to Vengaon to see his sister who lived there. However, even while he was there, his entire attention was fixed on seeing his Nana. He was worried about him. His mind would not rest till he saw him. His own health had not been very good in recent times. His sister said to him, 'Stay with us for a few days. You're very weak.' But he would not heed her or anybody else. Finally, three days after Mr Tilak had passed away, he had his tea and left for Karjat station. Waiting for the train, he read about Mr Tilak's death in a newspaper. The news shattered him. He had loved his brother very deeply.

He had no idea where we were staying. He arrived in Mumbai and inquired his way to the house. He found it at around three o'clock, came upstairs and collapsed. He had left Vengaon with just a cup of tea in him. Already weak in body, he had travelled from there to Karjat and from Karjat to Mumbai with nothing but that inside him. Then he had walked around in the heat of Mumbai to look for our house. We were upset to see the state he was in. What could we do for him? The moment of shock when he had read the news left a mark on him for the rest of his life.

True, we had no relatives in Mumbai. But we had friends who came to console us. Dr Bhaskarrao Govande and his wife Ramabai took us to their house to spend a few days with them. Nanasaheb wrote, inviting us to go to Nashik. Although Dattu had not recovered fully, we agreed to go. Dattu, Tara and I went. Ruth stayed back alone. We left Chiki with the Govandes.

When we left, Bhaskarrao gave me a piece of advice which I will never forget: 'Please understand. You are out in the marketplace now. You will have to take many knocks. You will need to be very careful when choosing what to buy. If you allow your mind to focus on the crowd in the market, you might as well forget shopping. Just remember my words.' I have been experiencing the significance of his words ever since.

I have many relatives in Nashik. I met them all. We rented

a house in Sharanpur for ten rupees. My sister's son Vishnu and daughter-in-law Kashi set it up for us. They ensured that I did not want for anything. My two brothers and their children were in Jalalpur. They would come to see me once in a while. But Nanasaheb and Vishnu would visit every day without fail.

Dattu's health improved after we came to Sharanpur. Here we received two letters. One was from Pandita Ramabai in Kedgaon and the other from Dr Emilybai Bissel in Mumbai. Panditabai invited us to spend a month with her. Emilybai wrote to say they had found a job for me in Mumbai and I should go back by the first of the month.

I had never done a regular job before. We had no clue about the nature of the work I was to do. What could it be except performing keertans? I was after all an illiterate woman. So we did not give it a thought. The tide of our grief had not ebbed. I had run through my reserves of money. But our hearts were numb, like fingers which are bound tight and then freed and still feel nothing. Grief had frozen us.

Dattu had a job in the Mission High School in Mumbai which fetched him a salary of seventy-five rupees. How could all of us manage on that in the city? As far as the missionaries went, with the exception of one Mambaji, nobody was against Mr Tilak. They had taken it upon themselves to arrange something for us, and we did not think it right to ask what kind of work it was. Dattu was feeling well now. So he returned to Mumbai and reported to work. Tara and I went to Kedgaon where Ramabai looked after us and helped us immensely. Everywhere in Kedgaon, girls were singing Mr Tilak's songs. That added to our depression.

We met many women. Their belief in God, the presence of Christ in their lives in all His grace was evident. We stayed for just four days but it was like being in another world. We saw there how God looked after everybody, the old, the young, the orphans and the disabled, the small and the big, He held out His hand to anyone who was in trouble. It woke us to the fact that we were not the only orphans around.

Ramabai wanted us to stay there permanently. But Tara had to return to her college and Dattu was in Mumbai. So I was not very happy with the idea. Dattu had now resolved to study for his Law degree. I too had been called back to Mumbai for work. Why then should we shilly-shally? I turned down Ramabai's invitation. After four days in Kedgaon, we received a letter from a woman in Satara asking us to stay with her for a few days. I saw straightaway what that meant. I knew exactly who was behind the invitation. I said to Ramabai, 'I must leave. I will have to go to Satara. This is an indirect notice. Please pray for me.'

When we left, Ramabai gave us four saris and several pieces of flannel for jackets. In addition, she also gave me thirty rupees. With my great urge for charity, I contributed five rupees for Ramabai's work. In short, I took water from the Ganga and made a sacrifice from the same water to the river.

Although I was still in Kedgaon, I could only see Satara. I knew what was awaiting me there. I said to Ramabai, 'Give me some provisions. The Satara market is far away and there's nobody to help me.' Ramabai gave me all that I required and saw me off.

My constitution had become like a child's now. If I slept I slept forever or not at all. I ate and drank like a child too. A child needs its mother. Now Tara had become my mother. She had to look after me in every way. Meanwhile, the clouds were gathering to attack. We were enveloped in darkness. Nature had turned dark. My mind had turned dark. There were countless stars in the sky but not a single one was allowed to shine through the powerful army of clouds that stood guard over them. The train rumbled, the clouds thundered, my heart pounded. Nobody had the power to stop any of that. It was in this state of mind that we alighted from the train at Satara at around one thirty in the morning.

Until now we had always made the journey from the station to our home by car. But now we had to cut our coat according to the cloth. So we hired an open carriage. We climbed into it with our baggage of disaster and grief. The night was dark as pitch. Clouds reigned over the sky. To make the scene more fearful, lightning flashed and glow worms flickered. Then the rain came down. We opened our umbrellas for what little protection they could give.

The carriage stopped before the gate of our bungalow. An old memory surfaced. Mr Tilak had sworn never to return to drink even a sip of water in Satara once he left the place. And here were his wife and daughter, returning to the same place to collect belongings of little value.

When we left Satara, we had handed over our keys to a neighbour. To wake them up in the middle of the night would not have been right. So we went around to the back verandah and using our hands in place of eyes, groped around to find a dry spot. Our saris which had become wet were now dry and they warmed our frozen bodies. Once again our umbrella gave us much support.

But sleep was difficult. The darkness was so dense that even if you had dug your fingers into your eyes you would not have seen a thing. But we pictured every corner of the house that lay behind the wall. In that darkness we even began to see a bit of past history clearly. Writing, reading, singing bhajans, visitors, tea, these and many other happenings unrolled before our eyes. We tried giving each other courage. But I had no strength to give anybody courage. We were to each other like straws to drowning men.

As soon as day dawned, the neighbours realized we were back. The people from our wadi came to meet us. A teacher brought us breakfast. News of our arrival reached our landlady's ears. She hurried over immediately to see us. She said three sentences which were supposed to console me.

Sentence number one: I am sorry to hear about Mr Tilak.

Sentence number two: When will you vacate the bungalow?

Sentence number three: I'll leave now. I have lots of work to do.

Obviously, she did not expect replies to sentence one and three. I replied to sentence two promptly: 'It is already vacated.'

At ten o'clock a question came our way: 'Have you packed your belongings?'

'No. If you have a carton, please send it across.'

A carton came. It was so small it could not have contained more than half-a-dozen cups and saucers. I was in bed. Tara was managing everything. The provisions Ramabai had given us came in handy. They served to fill the emptiness in our stomachs. At three o'clock, Madam returned. 'You still haven't packed! I need the bungalow desperately. When will you clear out all this stuff?'

'If you need the place so desperately get a coolie to put our stuff out on the road. What stays will be mine. What goes I don't care about. Possessions can be bought. Mr Tilak can't be brought back.'

Madam left. I suppose her employees were forbidden from coming to help us. I could not move from my bed. Tara had to deal with everything. I sent a message. 'Can we hire a room for a few days to store our luggage?'

Back came the reply, 'We are ourselves short of space. I'm sorry about that.'

Raobahadur Joshi was a neighbour of ours. When he heard about our problem, he sent his wife to help us. He sent men to help us empty the house. My Christian brothers, poor souls, were full of regret. But they were helpless. They had to think of their livelihoods. They could not show the same rebelliousness now that had been possible when Mr Tilak was alive. In those days they were sure that if they lost their jobs here, Mr Tilak would find them other jobs elsewhere.

The woman who had written to me inviting me to stay with her for a few days heard I had come but did not bother to visit. She was not obliged to. Perhaps she had decided that my grief would be too hard for her to bear.

Tara wrote to Dattu to say we were in Satara to vacate the

bungalow. Two days later Benji came. Just before that, some Hindu and Christian friends had decided to help us. Our belongings were packed. The question of renting a vehicle to transport them remained. I called a contractor and said, 'I do not have money. If you trust me, please send this stuff to Mumbai at your expense. Send the bill to Dattu. He will pay you.'

We kept some heavy things at Raobahadur's place. Not heavy in price but in weight, like the grinding stone. Mr Tilak was no more. But we felt his presence around us all the time. Perhaps the soul stays with loved ones for a while before it goes to heaven. Dr Kelkar, Raobahadur Joshi and most of our Christian brothers and sisters were sad to see us go.

Mumbai

I had spent my entire life from age eleven onwards, with and around Mr Tilak. We had been separated for five years, but even during that time, not for a moment had he shifted from before my eyes. Nor had I shifted from before his. I am what I am because of him. He would set his goals and I would follow them with closed eyes. He composed poems, I sang them. He begged, I walked alongside with his begging bowl. Sparks flew between us only when I could not keep up with him. My state was like that of an old cart tied to the back of the Deccan Queen, keeling and pitching as the train gathered speed. But when I could tackle his speed and had time to mull over and understand his ideas, our carriage proceeded smoothly. His body contained the self-generated power of the engine and mine drew its power from that energy. But once my carriage had managed to get on to the track, there was no stopping it.

The one who had held the strings of my life in his hands was now no more. A new world rose around me. A new life began. I had not been invited to Mumbai to perform keertans. The work allotted to me was the kind widows generally did. I was offered the job of a matron of a girls' hostel at forty-five rupees a month, with spacious accommodation attached. There was space for Dattu also to move in. My joy knew no bounds. I was happy that although Mr Tilak had gone, my son, daughter-in-law and daughter would be with me.

Missionaries were always criticized. Even their good work was twisted to look bad. But my experience with them was very different. They come here out of love for Christ and are anxious to do as much as they can for the welfare of the people. Looking for some way to ensure my livelihood, they had found me this job of a matron. Dattu told me the whole plan when I returned from Satara. It was a satisfying prospect. I would have a good salary, a place to stay, a home job and lots of people to work under me. That was the carrot, but there was a stick that went with it. I had to step down to the kindergarten class for it. I began at the beginning of all things. The alphabet. There was a time when I had taught children. Now I had to teach myself. The hostel accounts which I had to check were written in English. Dattu would go off to work. Tara would be at college. Ruth was at her parents'. But Dattu and Tara taught me a few things, numerals and a trick to recognize items in the accounts by their initial letters. So 'C' was coconut, 'S' was sugar, 'P' was potatoes, 'T' was tea. That is how I checked accounts.

Another part of my job was to open the letters that the girls received, read them and then hand them over to the girls. That was easily done when the letters were in Marathi. But I had to apply to Dattu and Tara for help when they were in English. The world has always been kind to me. I have never lacked assistance. Here, too, there were enough people to help me. About two hundred and fifty girls, big and small, lived in this hostel. The older girls looked after some of my jobs. They took over work like sweeping, dealing with the clothes that the washerman took and brought back and keeping an eye on the man who made our bhakris.

The Madam who supervised the hostel would make two rounds every day. This was the first time I was doing this kind of a job; so I had no idea why she came. The girls told me that the practice was for the matron to carry tales to Madam at least twice a day. The tales were about this girl receiving a surreptitious letter, that girl's eyes straying and another answering back. The girls were then punished according to the level of their crime. How could all the girls be equally good? There were two hundred and fifty girls from as many parts of the country. Even children born to the same parents and living in the same house are different from each other. But that is the fun of it. What use would it be if all the girls were little Pune dolls? Without the bad, we would never recognize the good.

There were many mischievous girls in the hostel and others learned naughty tricks from them. Some were experts at imitating men's voices. I knew nothing about this. Once during study time, I thought I heard a man's voice upstairs. When I went up I saw only girls. I came down but once again heard men talking upstairs. I went back up. I was going crazy. Finally, a girl told me the secret and spoke to me in a man's voice.

Everybody called me Aaji. I was not a grandmother yet, but Chiki had christened me Aaji long ago. By and large, the girls behaved very well with me. But that did not mean they did not rebel once in a while. One day a girl said to me, 'Aaji, let me see the letters.' I could not show them to her. There was a reason for this. Often people would write obscene anonymous letters. I would offer them up to Lord Narayan in a fire sacrifice. I did not show them to hostel officials to prevent the girls from being punished. And I did not show them to the girls to prevent them from being adversely affected. But this girl took my refusal as an invitation to harass me. Her nastiness escalated to the point where she burned my saris under a pile of dried leaves. There was a smell of burning in the air. I could not make out where it was coming from. But there it was. Lord Narayan, not satisfied with a burnt offering of letters, had devoured my saris too.

Every day at dinner and prayers I would plead, 'Dear girls, let me remain in one piece as I came. Don't run away or anything like that.'

The girls would say, 'We promise not to make trouble for you, Aaji.' And sure enough, in the three years that I was there, there were only two such incidents. Nobody ran away from the hostel, but one girl ran away from school and the other from church. Those who did, married the men with whom they had eloped and lived very happy conjugal lives. If the officials in charge had had the wisdom to marry them to the men they loved, they would not have needed to elope. They went from right under the officials' noses. I was not held responsible for what happened.

Mr Tilak's wish was granted. He used to say, 'Don't cry for me when I'm gone. I will leave money enough to last you a month. Beyond that each one must earn and eat.' We came to Bawkar Hall a month after he was gone. I had one rupee left.

After that, nobody had the time to mourn. The days were filled with work and the nights with fear.

Bawkar Hall had a basement. If you peered into it through the cracks in the floor planks, you would think it was a tomb. There was an army of cockroaches there. They would crawl up through the planks at night and jump around, their feet making clicking sounds on the wood. In your half-sleep, you would imagine somebody was walking around. The girls' empty heads were filled with stories about ghosts. As a result, they themselves would behave like crazy spirits. There was no dearth of amusing incidents happening in the midst of my heavy workload.

I once conducted an experiment which worked. I could not bear to raise my hands against the girls. If a little girl did something naughty, I would stand her in front of me and cane myself. It upset them to see their Aaji suffering. That would stop them from playing pranks. I would make the older girls stand in a corner. One girl refused to come to terms with this punishment. So she decided to punish me.

I had kept some hens in a corner of the Bawkar Hall compound to help me take care of my household expenses. What other business could an illiterate woman like me do? So I ordered hens for twenty-two rupees from Rahuri. The girl who was waiting to punish me, got up in the middle of the night and sneaked up to the hens. She picked them up one by one, swung them round her head and dashed them to the ground. She killed seven or eight hens in this way, venting her anger against me on them. But she was very contrite the following morning. Her anger had subsided. She caught a parrot and gave it to me. 'Aaji, see how big and beautiful he is. Here, take him.'

I put the parrot in a cage. He ate half a chapati at one go, drank water and then began looking around. Who knows for how many days he had starved. When Dattu returned in the evening, I said, 'Look at this parrot. I had so wanted a pet bird. I bought this one. Mr Tilak always said he would get me a cockatoo from Zanzibar. But now we have this fellow.'

'Aai, money is tight right now. How much did you pay for him?'

'Sixty rupees.'

Even as we spoke the parrot had begun to talk exactly like a human being. He whistled. Then sang. But the language in which he talked and sang was beyond us. We were astonished. He stayed with us till 1932. He used to imitate the voice of every person in the family and speak exactly like him or her. At long last, my desire to own a bird had been fulfilled.

There were a lot of thieves running around outside, but they did not get to lay hands on a single thing in the house. But the thieves in the house had a field day. One day, a friend of Dattu's from Nagpur came to see him. He had large eyes, sharp features and a commanding personality. Dattu said to him, 'Bapu, I want you to turn into an impersonator. Nobody knows you here. My sister and I will assist you.'

News got around that there would be a show of hypnotism in the hostel. The only outsiders who came to the show were Madam, a couple of officials and Dattu's father-in-law. The remaining people, including teachers, were from the hostel. The girls were very scared. Dattu's friend strode in. Some girls broke into a sweat at the sight of him. He said, 'So who will be my first guinea pig?' Nobody answered. Tara said, 'I'll be the first.' He began to work on her. She shut her eyes tight. Her lips began to move. 'Tell me. What's on your mind?' Bapu asked. Tara said, 'I've stolen food often. I've stolen money from Aai to buy stuff to eat. I stole a book once.' As her confessions progressed, the girls became more and more scared. Dattu's father-in-law said, 'Please stop this experiment now. Bring the girl back to her senses. She looks very scared. Now call some other girl.'

Tara 'came to'. The atmosphere became very grim. Not a single person spoke. So then one of the officials said, 'It's very late now. Please come another time and do a show.'

The audience dispersed. The show had its effect. The next morning all the things that had been stolen reappeared magically in their respective places. Nothing in the house was stolen after that.

Joy Wrapped in a Pall of Gloom

It was almost three months since Mr Tilak died, and this was my first happy day. I was expecting to be called to the hospital. I got busy completing my chores as fast as I could with the girls' help. I went to the hospital around twelve o'clock. It was a Sunday so I could leave some chores to the girls. When I arrived, Ruth and her mother were already there. My heart was caught in a conflict of grief and joy. It was difficult to hold back my tears. It was around four o'clock when I set eyes on my grandson. I celebrated the event instinctively with a long poem which began, 'As I was drowning in sorrow / A wave of love lifted me / And brought me gently to the shore'. It ended with the lines, 'Standing atop this peak of joy / Hope showed me the old fort / Whose pinnacle was now forged in gold and diamonds / In the form of the infant before me.'

This was the second poem I had composed after Mr Tilak's going. The children said, 'Aai, it's good you've written the poem. At least now people can't say what they used to—that Papa wrote all your poems.'

I said, 'Who knows? Perhaps he imagined these events and wrote poems about them in advance for me!'

Ruth stayed in the hospital for ten days. From there, she went to her parents' home where she stayed for another thirty days. On the fortieth day, the baby was baptized and Ruth came home. The baby was named after his grandfather as Mister Buel and others had pressed us to do. We did not celebrate his christening in a big way. We gave the girls jaggery mixed with ghee and distributed ten rupees worth of pedhas.

There is a strange story about Nana. Mr Tilak had been brought home from the hospital before his funeral. Ruth had cut a few hairs from his beard to keep as a memento. When Nana was born, he came with a few hairs below his chin exactly in the place from which she had taken Mr Tilak's hair. He still has them as a grown-up boy.

We had tried, as far as possible, to do everything according to Mr Tilak's last wishes. We had cremated him and preserved his ashes in a small box which was in Rev. Malelu's keeping. He had wanted his ashes to be buried in the cemetery in Ahmednagar. Now we were a little more relaxed than we had been. Moreover, the annual conference was also coming up in Ahmednagar. We planned everything with Rev. Dr H. Fairbank. Dattu, Tara and I left for Ahmednagar with Mr Tilak's ashes. We were going to be away for just four days. Ruth was going to substitute for me during my absence. Benji and Balubai were there to help her.

The night before we were to leave, the girls had created a ruckus. We had switched off the lights at ten-thirty according to rules. However, soon after the power was switched off, a teacher started shouting. Then the girls who were half asleep joined her. It was only when we switched the power on again that everybody calmed down. The girls wanted the lights to be kept on all night. That night they were.

We reached Ahmednagar on the last day of the conference. Diwali was on and this day was dedicated to worshipping Saraswati, the goddess of learning. Mr Tilak's ashes were taken to the church where prayers were said and other rituals conducted. Many people made speeches. Sakharambhauji also spoke. The ashes were then taken to the cemetery in procession with people singing bhajans all the way. Mr Hivale and Dr Hiralal Gaikwad, both courtiers of Christ's Court, led their bhajan group in singing Mr Tilak's composition, 'Where did you have servants?' Rangoli patterns had been made and lights lit on both sides of the road in honour of Saraswati. Some people said, Mr Tilak, who had devoted his life to learning was being incidentally honoured. Dr Hiralal sang the abhang with ardour and the last line seemed particularly appropriate to the occasion: 'Your servant says Dear Lord, make me a little place beside you.'

The uproar that the girls had created the night before we left was repeated several times thereafter. Every time it happened,

I would want to laugh but also felt very scared. Fortunately, although my circumstances had changed, my original nature remained unchanged. I never abandoned my early upbringing and Mr Tilak's teachings. When he was alive, our house was there to welcome all comers, but its doors were always open for those who wanted to leave. Mr Tilak never insisted on anybody visiting him. But if people came he was there for them.

I have never become accustomed to the western manners that have entered some people's lives with Christianity. I have never greeted people according to the time of day, or thanked them, or knocked on doors and entered only when I was asked to come in, or asked for official permission if I wished to entertain a visitor. I continued to be independent.

One day, a destitute old woman came to our house. I kept her with me. But she would talk a lot and very loudly in her sleep. I used to be tired with the day's work and needed some sleep. Dattu was studying and so was Tara. Both needed rest. And with her in the house, sleep was difficult. So I said to her, 'Tarabai, please sleep near the girls now.' The girls were asleep. The old woman went over in the dark and began to feel around. The girls' heads were already full of stories about ghosts and the fear of thieves. The old woman tugged at a girl's covering sheet. The girl let out an instant yell. She touched her neighbour and that girl decided the hand belonged to a ghost. So it went on, one touching another in the dark and the other screaming. The hall was full of sleeping women, each one afraid for her life. One would pull another's hair, another would tear the jacket off somebody's back, some tugged hard at someone's sari, some girls crawled around in fear, some wailed, others shouted, 'Help, I'm dying' or called upon God to save them. That night of shouting still rings in my ears and I want to laugh. I switched on the power and went into the hall. A woman was crawling towards me, her whole body trembling. Her hair was flying around, some clinging to her face. Her blouse was torn to shreds, and her sari into ribbons. Her eyes were weeping but her mouth was laughing. She was drenched in sweat. She was very angry with me but also amused. She waved her hands at me saying, 'Aaji, you better make that old woman sleep beside you from tomorrow.' I asked Tarabai what she had done. She said, 'What did I do? Nothing. I was only fiddling with my bedding.'

***

Mr Tilak always told his Christian and non-Christian friends that changing your religion did not mean turning your back on your country. He never fought with anybody over religious differences. People of all religions and castes came to meet him and he too visited them in their homes. He even wrote an abhang that spoke of this goodwill amongst the people of his country, ending with the lines, 'Says your servant, my Mother is large of heart / And like her is her family.'

However, our Christian brothers and sisters seemed to believe that too much fraternizing with Hindus was a sign of the Christian adopting Hindu ways. We used to have many Hindu visitors. Sometimes they stayed with us. We were in a girls' hostel where ideas about Christian-Hindu differences were rampant. We were caught on the horns of a dilemma. We were like the proverbial mendicant who says please do not give me alms if you do not wish to, but for heaven's sake hold back your dogs. One day, a young man came to see us at around two o'clock in the afternoon. Dattu was not at home. The man was dressed like an aristocrat in a knee-length coat, slim-cut pajamas, expensive shoes, ring and watch and carried a cane.

'Does Mr Tilak live here?'

'Yes. Where have you come from?'

'Indore.'

I thought perhaps my Rambhau uncle had heard of Mr Tilak's death and sent this man. This uncle had sent me money for Dattu's thread ceremony. So I said, 'Who has sent you?'

He said, 'Nobody. I've come of my own accord.'

'Whom do you want to meet?'

'Lakshmibai and her son.'

'Please take a seat. My son has gone to work. My daughter to college. My daughter-in-law and grandson are at home. And here I am. Lakshmibai. But to tell you the truth, I don't recognize you.'

'You wouldn't.'

'What is your name then?'

'Vitthal Dattatreya Ghate.'

I was overjoyed to hear the name. He was a writer and the son of a poet who had been a dear friend of Mr Tilak's although I had never met him or his family. During times when we were away, the family always looked after Mr Tilak's needs, helping him with any problems he might have. This young man was just a child then. Overcome with happiness, I embraced him while tears of joy streamed down my face. I asked after the rest of the family. 'Only two of us brothers remain. Everyone else is gone.'

'Tell me, do you write poetry?'

'I do.'

'Will you please recite one?'

The poem he recited was beautiful beyond description. I asked him for another. He said he would return in the evening with his notebook and read out all his poems to us. Then he left.

When Dattu and Tara returned, they too were very happy to hear of this visit. He returned at eight in the evening as promised. We had finished our chores and were waiting for him. He sang his poems till one o'clock in the morning. The poems captured our hearts. They overflowed with love, reflecting his cheerful nature. Dattu published the one Ghate had recited in the morning in *Dnyanodaya* and it soon became part of our repertoire of hymns. Thus the bonds that had tied our two families together were renewed.

Although Ruth had been born and brought up in Mumbai, Bawkar Hall did not seem to suit her health. Even Nana did not keep particularly well. So she went to Ahmednagar and stayed with my sister Shahabai Misal. She and her husband looked after her very well, but Nana began to feel even more poorly there.

So Ruth shifted to Rahuri where again Dr and Mrs Ballantyne did everything they could for her and the child. She stayed there for six months, returning to Mumbai only for Benji's wedding.

Nana was an early talker. He loved to draw. It was like a game for him. Give him a chalk and he would instantly start drawing his favourite things—Fearyman and Choochootrain. When the girls asked him, 'What has your mother studied?' he would say 'Beyay.'

'And your father?'

'Beyay.'

'And your aunt?'

'Beyay.'

'And what has your Aaji studied?'

'Big round pumpkin.'

When Fate Takes a Hand, Good Sense Takes Leave

Nana was a toddler. A great big market used to be set up outside Ruth's parents' place on Nag Panchami, the day snakes are worshipped. Ruth had taken Nana to see the fun. The girls from the hostel too could have gone. But our community and the hostel officials did not approve of Christians going to see Hindu festivals and fairs. So the poor girls were deprived of the fun.

In recent times, our Madam and her husband had taken enthusiastically to swimming. Convinced that what was good for them was good for everybody regardless of what and when, they had begun to take the girls swimming too. That day, it was a school holiday and they were eager to go swimming, so they decided to take the girls along.

The Sahib had already selected a quiet and deserted spot. It had been decided on the previous night that all of us, the girls, teachers and I, would meet and go together. We got up at dawn and completed our morning ablutions and chores. At such times even adults tend to behave giddily, so the girls' excitement was not surprising. They had a few quick mouthfuls of breakfast, cleared up, got dressed and were ready and waiting by six o'clock. They had already removed all their jewellery the previous night and handed it over to me to look after. They did not have much jewellery, but all their odds and ends together made quite a pile. We walked most of the way because it was not possible to hire enough cars for all the girls. But we took a train for the intermediate part of the journey. The Sahib drove up to Mahim by car while Madam went with us by train up to Mahim. Then she got off and went with her husband by car. We walked from Mahim.

At Mahim station, the father of one of the girls met us and talked with us for a long time. Although he had several sons, this girl was his only daughter and the tail-ender. She was very brainy which made people want to be with her. I had never been in command of anything, so I was not used to being authoritative. I was like an elderly aunt or granny to the girls and that is how we behaved with each other. We walked along merrily, the girls pulling my leg all the time. 'I wonder how Aaji runs,' said one.

'What? She can't even walk fast.'

'What if she falls?' said another.

'I'll pick her up if she does.'

'You think you can do it single-handed?'

'We'll find four hefty men to help.'

'And what if she's badly hurt?'

'We'll bandage her.'

'And what if she drowns?'

'We'll fish her out.'

'And what if she dies?'

'We'll cry.'

'Hey, stop talking that way about Aaji.'

I said, 'Say what you like about me but for heaven's sake take care of yourselves. One should always speak of good things. What is destined to happen, happens anyway.'

We reached Juhu beach at around ten-thirty. We sorted out our things. Some girls spread out their dhurries and lolled, some read, some cavorted around. Kids and calves are alike. Show fodder to a calf and there it goes prancing. Give a child a wide, open space and there it goes dancing. Madam said, 'We've never been to a place like this and will never go again. It is truly memorable.' Looking back, that sounded like a prediction.

I was born and brought up on the banks of the river Godavari. I was not acquainted with the sea. I had merely seen it. When we left, many people had tried to stop us saying it was Nag Panchami and it would not be wise to be on a beach at high tide. But somebody had told Madam and Saheb that the tide would only come in at two in the afternoon, and that is what they were relying on. When we arrived at the beach, there was no water to be seen. I was used to seeing a full Godavari. This expanse of sandy desert filled me with wonder. I said to myself, 'There's not enough water here to soak your ankles. Where are they going to swim?'

The girls said, 'We're hungry. Give us something to eat.' It is the custom in our country that if someone is hungry, you do not let them go without food. The custom in the west is not to bathe after food. Madam and I had a difference of opinion on the matter, but she ordered the girls to swim first and eat later. So the girls set off, one behind the other. Some of the older girls walked a great distance from us collecting shells. Some girls who were of an age to learn swimming accompanied Madam. The very small girls, some thirty or forty of them, came wading with me. I was feeling sorry that Dattu and Tara had not come. A young day scholar had also come along with us. He was his parents' only child. There were also students from the blind school.

It was eleven o'clock. The water had started coming in, but it was very placid. Then it rose just high enough to move from the ankles up to the knees. It was muddy and warm. In my fertile brain, I calculated that it must be noon and the mills must have closed, letting their effluents out into the sea. Now the sand began shifting from under the girls' feet and I heard a loud shout, 'The tide's coming in. Get out.'

There was not a single grown-up with me. I had neither cane nor stone for support. It was just an empty expanse. Nobody else heard the shout. Madam was busy swimming. The older girls collecting shells were far away. Madam had said this was the best place for the girls to swim because it was deserted with not a bird or man in sight. I experienced the truth of this description at first hand. Mumbai was a few miles away, crowded with people, but there was not a soul in this place. Meanwhile, the water was quietly rising from ankle to knee and knee to waist. For the girls who were with me, that was neck high. The water was calm so I did not recognize the terrifying danger of the situation, I dragged all the girls who were with me out, catching them by their hair, or blouses, or armpits or wrists. Some fishermen arrived with their boats. They saved a blind boy who was drowning. The blind school was close to ours and only that morning one of the students had fallen off a coconut tree.

We were all women. All the small girls were with me. But there was a girl called Veeraswamy who was weak and ill, so she was sitting with our stuff. I drove the little girls who were with me to where she was sitting. I had barely reached her when another problem cropped up. The guard said, remove all your stuff from here. There was no grown-up man or woman to help me. We had brought our lunch in huge pots. Plus there were the girls' belongings, umbrellas, slippers, saris, suitcases, cloth bags, money. My mind was spinning. The guard was shouting. I remembered what Christ had said: 'The son of man has no place to lay his head.' Somehow I mustered enough strength to shift all the stuff, driven by sheer will power.

Meanwhile, the girls with me were running helter skelter. We could see the girls who had gone shell-collecting very faintly in the distance. They had raised their hands and were saying something, but we could not hear them. Some had climbed up on rocks and were waving their hands. The sea had assumed a menacing look now. The fishermen were asking for five hundred rupees to rescue the girls. I said, 'I will give you the money but first get those girls out.' But they said, 'Give us the money first.' I should not have expected them to trust my word. I was, as always, in threadbare clothes. If a person is worth one, his clothes have to be worth ten for anybody to heed him. My clothes were threadbare but I happened to have two-and-a-half thousand rupees insurance money on me. I was certain that Mr Tilak would not have objected even if I had given away the entire lot, nor would Dattu have said a word about it. But the fishermen wanted an assurance from Madam. She had pulled out the girls near the shore and run off to call up her husband who had gone away for a while and was going to come back later.

This entire drama had begun at eleven-thirty. The tide which was supposed to come in at two had arrived at ten-thirty. The girls came ashore at twelve. I had been thinking they would be pulled out on the other bank and we would punish them good and proper afterwards. But the sea does not have another bank. Nor could it keep down the girls it had swallowed. So it washed them ashore of its own accord. It was twelve-thirty. Nobody had eaten since the morning. The girls were famished. Saheb came. He unwrapped their private lunch and they began to eat. Gradually, people from the nearby buildings came out a few at a time and stood in a circle around us. They began to ask us, 'How many girls were there in all? How many have drowned? Did they have families or were they all orphans? You should not have come today in the first place. It is Nag Panchami. How will the god tolerate this? And how can you sit and eat?'

When Madam heard the last sentence, she and Saheb put down the food that was halfway to their mouths. I tucked my pallu in, stood in the middle of the circle, hands on hips and delivered a thundering lecture. 'Have you lifted even a finger to help us? You've gathered here just to see a tamasha. Get out of here. We will have to bear our burden ourselves.' The circle broke up and the crowd dispersed. The first girl who was washed ashore was in the sixth class. Her mother had died when she was still a child. Her father and sister had looked after her. Yesterday was her birthday. The flowers that I had put in her hair were still intact. I had put the bangles on her wrists just three days ago. One after the other, eleven girls and one boy were washed ashore.

Was this real or was it a nightmare? I pinched myself. It was no nightmare. We put the bodies in a cart and sent them off to J.J. Hospital. My knowledge fell short. I thought the hospital would put them on a potter's wheel, spin it till they threw out all the water they had swallowed and they would be fine. I asked Saheb, 'Will they get well?'

He said, 'They will.'

A few girls remained after most had been packed into a cart. Saheb accommodated some of them in his car. He said to me, 'Aaji, you must be tired. Come in the car.'

I said, 'No I can't. The girls with me are grieving. I can't leave them to walk while I ride in a car myself.'

Further along, the police stopped the car. The laws are the same whether you are a Saheb or a common man. Saheb was let off and allowed to go. We walked all the way home. But the joy and enthusiasm with which we had left had vanished now. A terrifying darkness filled us instead. Our feet were leaden, our hearts pounded, our minds tense with worry. We walked mechanically and did not feel like opening our mouths to talk. We saw those girls before our eyes. We remembered something one of them had said and something another had done. One would not wish such a fate on one's worst enemy.

We reached the station. That girl's father was there again. 'Where's my daughter?' he asked. Phone calls had already spread the tragic news everywhere even before we reached the station. The man asked first this girl then that where his daughter was. The girls pointed to me. Naturally, as a senior I was responsible. A stone weighed down my gut. 'Why don't you speak, Bai? What happened? I can't see my daughter anywhere. Don't keep things from me.'

What could I say? I would not have had the heart to tell even an enemy about such a terrible event. Dear readers, you can imagine the state I was in. Should I tell the truth or lie? It would be a sin to tell the truth but also a sin not to tell it. The story would come out soon enough anyway. I said, 'I'm not too sure where she is. She may have gone ahead or she may be coming after us.' Then, somehow, we managed to get into the train. We reached home at seven. Saheb had also reached his house around that time. He sent us a message from his bungalow. 'Lock the gates. Don't let anyone in. And don't allow any girl to go out without permission.' Dr Gurubai Karmakar and Mr Buel came to meet us. Dattu's parents-in-law came. They said,

'Thank heavens this happened in the presence of the officials. Imagine the burden of responsibility that would have fallen on you otherwise.' There was a man who had studied in Dr Hume's school. It was because of his efforts that a good school had started in Wadala. He treated me like a mother. When he heard the news, he came running to offer help. This young man's name was Narayanrao Deshmukh.

We were slaves to orders from the higher-ups. We locked the gate. Jahagirdar the sentry sat in his cabin with a thick cane in hand. He was a Muslim and had watched over the hostel honestly and dedicatedly for forty years. A huge crowd gathered outside the gate. We could hear sounds of the cane being used. There was a continuous shower of stones on the walls. The crowd was shouting, 'Open the gate or we'll break it down, come what may. We don't care even if we die. What's the government doing? Show us our daughters or blood will flow.'

Inside, the girls and others were crying. Outside all hell had broken loose. There were only three men to give us support, Dattu, Deshmukh and Jahagirdar. I wished the earth would split and swallow me up. Two of the women workers were sunk in their own grief. One had lost a sister and the other an adopted daughter. There was plenty of food in the house but no hand rose to take it and no mouth opened to receive it. The older girls, curled up into balls, dotted the floor. The little girls huddled near the teachers. If adults were petrified by the mayhem, how could the girls not be? Finally, in the midst of all the shouting, I went to the gate and said to the crowd, 'I will open the gate. You may do what you like with me. I am not afraid. But please don't riot. I cannot recognize all the girls. I will switch on the lights. Please come in and see them for yourself.'

I unlocked the door. The crowd entered like an unstoppable torrent. The girls' relatives poured in. Shevantibai Kotak also came to inquire after me. The relatives cursed the officials and me. Many took their daughters away. I said, 'The officials have ordered us not to let the girls go. Please take their permission.'

They said, 'We don't care a rotten fig for your officials and you. Pour kerosene over yourselves and strike a match. How did you people live when so many girls died?'

The enemy was out in full force that night. Dattu, Narayanrao, Tara and I were on our feet all night. And so was Jahagirdar outside. People from the city itself and outlying areas were streaming in to inquire about their girls. The little girls were terrified. Some had already been ill; others became ill.

Many other things added to the chaos. Some people wanted tea, some coffee, some soda. The evil eye had to be warded off so stoves and mustard seeds were called for. Hot water, bread, butter, you never knew what would be asked for next. In addition to climbing up and coming down dozens of times, our guests had to be pleaded with, consoled, given courage, pacified and sent away. I spent twenty-five rupees just like that in one night. The ball in the stomach remained. The little girls would suddenly let out a yell, 'Aaji, sea, sea.'

Shridhar Gaikwad was our manager. During weddings, a young family member might ask an elder, 'The bride's side wants this or that, should we give it?' Similarly Gaikwad asked me as an elder, 'How many coffins will we need? Roughly what dimensions should they be?' How would I have answers to those questions? I simply said yes to everything he said.

Saheb came in the morning. 'Aaji, will you be able to recognize the girls?'

'Yes.'

'Will you name them?'

'Yes. But where are they?'

Saheb went away, leaving my question unanswered. My heart began to pound. Worry ran crazy circles in my head. What if I did not name the girls correctly? I went to J.J. Hospital at around eleven o'clock. Saheb was with me. He told me the girls' names. This was my first visit there after Mr Tilak had died. The road outside was packed with cars, buggies and bicycles. There was no counting the number of people who had come on foot.

A virtual sea of people surged there. I could not recognize a single girl. But as it happened, I was not asked to.

Call me lazy or slovenly, but I was still wearing the same sari I had worn when I went into the sea. Its loose end was still tucked in at my waist. Drenched in water, it had dried on my body. The terror of the occasion was making my whole body shake. My neck used to tremble in any case, but now every part of my body joined in. I was like some swaying pinnacle on top of a mausoleum.

I have experienced many things in life but I had never before crossed the threshold of a law court. I did that now. When I got out of the tonga, Chiki's father had to lift me down and carry me into the court. I saw one dear face in that crowd, Gurubai Karmarkar's. I sat beside her. When my name was called, this trembling bird entered the cage. I clutched the railing of the witness box while my body heaved and spun like a churner in a pot of buttermilk. My hair hung loose down my back and my head banged helplessly on the railing. I was like one of those women possessed by a goddess. All that was missing was incense and camphor to get this apparition talking. People waited for my deposition to begin, but not a word would escape my lips. Then Dr Gurubai stood up and said, 'I would like to ask the court for permission to stand behind this lady. I shall not prompt her. I will merely hold her head. That will allow her to speak.' She was granted permission and she stood behind me like a chaperone.

When I was able to look up, I saw Raobahadur Athavale before me. Our questions and answers proceeded as follows:

'How high was the water when you reached?'

'It was nowhere in sight.'

'Who was with the girls?'

'Two of us.'

'How did you not drown?'

'What can I say to that?'

'Where did the water come from and where did it go?'

'I know no geography. But it came from the left and went out on the right.'

My testimony ended. I did not return to J.J. to see what was happening to the girls. It is beyond my powers to describe the scene there. Mothers and sisters had flung themselves down on the stony ground. I cannot endure even the memory of it.

Thus ended our picnic at Juhu. But its echoes continued for months afterwards with the girls suddenly breaking into screams and shouts.

Through the Shadow of Death

In the grim drama of death that had been played out in our house and in our close circle of friends, the first to go was Thombre. Then Mr Tilak. Fast on the heels of Mr Tilak's death and even before we had had time to settle properly into our new life in the hostel, came the sad news of my eldest brother Keshavrao Mama's death. Our Chiki followed. After her Bhauji, then Ruth's aunt, then the eleven girls who had been like daughters and granddaughters to me, then Mr Mitra, Mr Rendalkar, Kakasaheb Mirikar, Pandita Ramabai and finally Ruth's father. Altogether, Time snatched away some twenty or twenty-two of our dearest people within a short span. We were passing through the dark realm of death. There was no knowing who would be picked up next.

One day a letter came from Bhauji. I am coming. Pick me up from the station. Dattu fetched him from the station. I have already written about the effect Mr Tilak's death had had on his mind. He was no longer the same man. He would say the most awful things to people. He had taken it into his head that his sister-in-law was responsible for his brother's death. He also began to believe that he was now going to be an excellent poet. He would sit up all night writing poetry.

Dattu, Tara and Ruth made every effort to keep him in a good mood, doing whatever he asked for and always agreeing with whatever he said. The man who had never in his life pronounced a single rude word to or about me, now began to quarrel with me. If the children were around him, he would begin to scold them. He did not need a reason to get angry. One day, he got some food from the market and slapped it down in front of me. 'Take this. Eat. You devoured my brother.' And he went off to the station in a huff. I sent Jahagirdar after him. He managed somehow to persuade him to come back.

Jahagirdar whispered to me, 'Uncle had set up shop with currency notes.' I said to Bhauji, 'How much money do you have on you? Let me keep it safe.' This upset him and he went off again in a sulk. This was our first and last quarrel. We did not meet after that. Soon we heard that he had passed away.

Dattu's father-in-law went to Wai for a change of air. He fell seriously ill there. The doctor wrote to us, 'Krishnarao's health is critical. His daughter should be with him now.' Ruth, Dattu and Nana went to Wai. Dattu left Ruth and Nana there and returned. Then we received the news of Mr Sarode's death. It was as if, having taken Mr Tilak, Death had gone berserk.

Ruth returned from Wai. Four months later, she went into hospital again. It was a Sunday. My second grandson was born at around six in the evening. I met Benji on my way home from the hospital. In my excitement I said, 'Benji, you have a second uncle now.' He burst out laughing. But I was so absorbed in my own joy that not for a moment did I wonder why he was laughing.

Before Nana was born, we used to eat a lot of spicy food made with lots of condiments. But we had changed our diet later. We had begun eating bland food with little or no spices. We also introduced salads into our meals. In addition, Ruth would eat a lot of sprouted beans. She did so throughout her pregnancy. And so, unlike Nana who was thin and weak, the second boy was born strong and healthy.

By God's grace, my home now echoed with the sound of children's voices. Nana and Sona were like Bheem and Arjun. Of course, Sona was not his real name. A woman called Harnabai who used to work with me used to call him Sonya. That's how everybody started calling him Sona. But when he grew up, he went on a satyagraha, demanding to be called by his given name, Ashok. Even before he was three months, he was turning over and tugging at whatever he saw before him.

Ruth went to Rahuri. There Rev. Ballantyne prayed over Sona and christened him Ashok. Back from Rahuri, Ruth was cutting raw mangoes for pickles. I was sitting nearby preparing the pickling spices. Just then Ashok threw up. I said to Ruth, 'See, the mangoes have given him a cold.' She said, 'I haven't even touched him with these hands. How can I have given him a cold?' Nana was sitting beside him. He was about a year-and-a-half. He kept saying, 'Baby is putting Aaji's powder on.'

We were too busy to pay attention to him. Ashok was sneezing, throwing up and Nana was babbling. Finally Nana shouted, 'Baby has eaten Aaji's black powder.' So far we had been thinking of face powder which I had never used in all my life. But when Nana said 'Aaji's black powder' we looked around. Ashok was playing with a packet of spices that was lying around and eating it.

This baby was born mischievous. He too began to talk and walk in his ninth month. Nana would sit in one place; this one would run all over. Crying at night was an unknown thing to him. All you had to do was leave the light on. This little mouse would wake up and go to work, peeling a couple of bananas and polishing them off. Then he would go and sleep beside one of us. Once I was having an afternoon nap. I felt something fall on my face. I woke up and saw it was a handkerchief. There was nobody in sight so I went back to sleep. Again a handkerchief fell on my face. My bed was placed against the wall between two doors. What the prankster was doing was running in through one door and going out the other. Finally I got up.

Chiki had been unwell even before Mr Tilak died. During that disturbing time, she was badly neglected. I cannot stop feeling terrible about this now. Work chased me and worries ran ahead. During the Diwali vacation, the girls left for their homes one by one. Chiki also wanted to go somewhere. She loved doing things, strolling around, going on picnics, sitting out under the stars, going out of town. But it was impossible to let her do these things. Where was the time or the money to give her what she wanted? Her father was constantly taking up jobs and losing them. He had married again. Chiki was after me to send her to Pune to stay with her stepmother. This mother had never as much as set eyes on this daughter. But on her insistence, I sent her with a girl who happened to be going to Pune. This change of air turned out not to suit her. When she returned, she was even more ill. Now I had some time to look after her. I put her on Dr Dandekar's medicines. But it was like shutting the stable door after the horse had bolted. Dattu, Tara and Ruth took very good care of her. She did not spend all her time lying in bed. The doctor visited every day. One day she said, 'Aaji, Roman Catholics have such lovely deaths with candles, incense sticks and lots of flowers. I would love to die like that.'

Tara said, 'Chiki, you had better not die, I'm telling you. If you do, Aajoba will give you a good beating.'

'Will he, Aaji? How will he do that in heaven? If he does, I'll hide under the table.'

Before she died, she insisted that I give her a bath. I was busy so I said, 'Don't be like that, Chiki. Let Aunty or Bai bathe you.'

Chiki said, 'I know you have a lot of work, Aaji. But I like you to bathe me. I like the touch of your hands.' I did bathe her but rather impatiently.

She took the maid aside and said, 'Look here, you must keep my Aaji's bed ready every night. Wash her drinking tumbler clean. She gets so tired by night that she eats any old thing and goes to bed.'

Chiki used to take great care of me. Not just me. She helped everybody in the house, even the girls. She was full of love for everybody.

Before she breathed her last, she said in her sweet voice, 'Aaji, I'll leave now. But I'll come back soon, all right?' I still hear those words and feel very sad. The medicines had cost forty rupees. I went to Dr Dandekar's to pay him, but he would not take a single rupee. He said, 'Aai, you did so much for her for so many years. I only gave her some medicines. That's nothing.'

My darling Chiki whom I had brought up since she was a nine-month-old baby gave me a lot of happiness till she died at the age of twelve. The 15 July 1920-issue of *Dnyanodaya* carried a tiny obituary about her. 'A small, loving girl, was called away by God on 11 July. Whoever had met this young child, from the youngest to the oldest, will miss her terribly. The name of this little one who travelled briefly on this earth was Subhadra Rambhau Dharmadhikari.'

Visitors

The girls were scared only at night. They never shouted and screamed during the day. But a day dawned when they did this too. A monkey couple had turned up unexpectedly in the compound. The moment the monkeys arrived, they began to wreck and demolish things. Dattu, who had loved birds, animals and children from the time he was a child, was trying hard to win them over with love. But the Saheb next door was a stranger to love. He picked up his gun and shot the female. With the wife gone so suddenly, the husband disappeared. He returned after three days of mourning. Dattu gave him a chapati and a banana. Soon he would sit at the window and inch forward. Once within reach, he would stretch out his hand and take the chapati from Dattu. But the girls would get scared and scream. Thus began a new era of daytime shrieking and squealing.

One day when Dattu was at school, I paid a monkeywala eight annaṣ to catch and tie up our visitor. Even then nobody dared go near him. When Dattu returned, the monkey looked at him and put his hand to his forehead in a series of salutes. When Dattu went near him, he put his head down and clung to his leg. Dattu picked him up, patted and stroked him, took him to the compound wall and tied him to a nearby tree.

From this vantage point, the monkey would scan the surroundings, and pick whatever pleased him off the heads of passers-by. A stretch of the hand and a cucumber, a corn cob, a bunch of leafy vegetables or the odd fruit would be claimed by way of toll. And if a street vendor stopped near the wall for a chat with somebody, the basket on his head would be totally emptied before half his conversation was done. With great presence of mind, the monkey would toss his loot into the compound. When the man who had lost his goods, sank to the ground in shock and looked up to God for help, there he saw his lordship, looking down at him and mocking him with a chee-chee-chee. Jahagirdar had a new job now—to collect the goods that our prankster had thrown into the compound and return them to the owners outside.

One day, there was a fire outside. People thronged to watch. Many unfortunates stood by the wall. There was no counting the number of caps and turbans that fell into our compound as a result. Those who lost them would grope their heads in confusion. All that their hands encountered were tufts and bald pates, because what had been there was now in the monkey's hands. The poor souls had no idea how this had happened. While the leaping flames of the fire were being treated to buckets of water, no cooling agent had been available for their heads till our little soldier had exposed them to the breeze in an act of social service. Jahagirdar stood outside, calling out in a loud voice, 'Cap, cap, cap. Whose cap is this? Turban, turban, turban. Who does it belong to?'

The girls used to be at home over the weekend. That is when our prankster invariably broke loose and created mayhem. The girls would shout, 'Tie him up, Aaji, tie him up.' I would rush out. The minute he saw me, the scamp would leap up and sit on my shoulder. The girls would cry out, 'Aaji, this monkey of yours is a nuisance. Please tie him up.' With the monkey on my shoulder, I would slowly creep towards the wall where his chain hung. As I neared it, he would leap down and off he would go to worry the girls. So back I would go and back he would leap onto my shoulder, back I would creep towards the wall and back the devil would jump down and run off. This could happen seven or eight times over till my shoulder ached and I decided life was not worth living. It was only when Dattu returned that the monkey allowed himself to be tied up.

One day Dattu got after me to take Nana out for a bit. I had lived in many other places but Mumbai scared me. Even now, I do not go anywhere alone in Mumbai. If I go visiting, I always take an escort who will pick me up and drop me from one house to the other. Dattu said, 'I will put you on a tram in which you just have to stay put. It will take you to the terminus. It turns around there and comes right back with you still sitting where you were.' The tram stop was just outside our door. But I went into a round of yes and no before I let Dattu put me and Nana on a tram. I had some ten or twelve rupees with me but no idea what to do with them. Dattu had thought the tram would go up to the end of its journey and come back. Instead it stopped halfway, told all the passengers to get off, went into a large house and settled down to rest.

I said, 'I'm not going to get off. My son told me to stay put and return with the tram. I want to go to the Khada Parsi.'

The tram driver said, 'Your son was mistaken, Bai. This tram isn't going back.' My head spun. Where was I to go now? Where was I to stay? What was I to eat? How was I to look after this child? He was so small. He was not even walking or talking yet. In that respect we were in the same boat, except that he wanted everything he saw to play with or to eat. He even wanted milk from the milkman who passed by. So there I was, a child on my hip, tears flowing freely from my eyes and not an idea in my head about what I could buy and what I could give him.

I looked around and caught hold of a man. 'Bhau, will you take me to the Khada Parsi? I'll give you four annas.' He agreed and disappeared into the crowd. I met another man, a good Samaritan. He said, 'Aajibai, where do you want to go?'

'To the Khada Parsi.'

'Come, I'll take you.'

'I'll give you four annas.'

He took me a long distance. When he spotted a Parsi who was standing by the roadside waiting for somebody, he said, 'There's your khada Parsi. I'll be off now.' He too disappeared into the crowd. I was so angry I wanted to give him two tight slaps. But he was not there to receive them. My feet were walking, my eyes were crying, my mind was worrying. 'If we have to spend the night out, we'll have to sleep on the pavement. I could do that, but what about Nana? His parents will be worried to death.'

A thousand such thoughts ran through my mind. Meanwhile my feet kept walking, with God as my guide. The road looked familiar. But in Mumbai all roads looked alike to me. I passed Bawkar Hall on leaden feet. I heard a familiar chee-chee behind me. But I kept on till the chee-chee became insistent. It was our scamp calling us back, wondering why we were not coming home. I had been looking at the place. Now I turned around and my heart which had shrivelled up into a ball, grew large again.

It was around this time that a poor woman, who had been cheated, turned up at my door. She was young and had only one eye. Somebody had taken advantage of her and abandoned her. She delivered a boy seven months later. She stayed with us till then. The baby needed a lot of looking after. She was herself a child and had no idea what to do. She was so weak that she could not even nurse the baby. So I looked after her baby and she looked after my cooking. I named the baby Chhotya.

I have found that people are ready to share somebody's grief, but have problems being happy for them. I do both. Young Champa went to the hospital from my home. She delivered a son. People are so happy when a son is born. But what could that poor child do to celebrate? I too could not afford pedhas. But I distributed sugar liberally for which many women teased me.

Once I got a letter from Alibaug, from Bhaskarrao Ujagare. 'Sarah-amma, I am very worried about Sonu. This is her first pregnancy. We would like her to come to you for her delivery. There are many good hospitals there.' Bhaskar used to call me Sarah-amma, Mr Tilak Abraham-papa and Dattu Isaac-baba. He had composed a song which he would sing out of Mr Tilak's hearing but within Dattu's and mine. 'Abraham-papa, will you cut up Isaac-baba?' The song referred to the story in the Old Testament in which Abraham is about to sacrifice his son Isaac's life for the love of God, when God saves him. Since Isaac was Abraham's only son, the family names fitted us perfectly.

Anyway, Sarah-amma wrote to this nephew, Lot, telling him to bring his daughter to her in her seventh month. Accordingly, the family came when Sonu was in her seventh month. After dinner we sat around chatting. I told them of all the amusing incidents that had happened to us here. 'Bhaskar, if you are fortunate, you'll experience some real fun here. But you need to be lucky.'

Resting both his palms on the floor as he was in the habit of doing, Bhaskar said, 'Really? What kind of fun is this?'

'You have to see it first-hand. But, as I said, you have to be lucky.'

'We are leaving tomorrow. I hope it'll happen today.'

'Yes, but it's not something that can be ordered.'

Bhaskar turned out to be lucky. Everybody went to bed. Bhaskar was sleeping in the room which had the power switch. Suddenly, he heard girls screaming. A thief had entered and was sitting by a girl's head, eyeing her necklace. Then she saw him move to another girl's bed. She saw his hand approach her neck. That's when she found her voice and began screaming. Bhaskar got up and made for the door. But he could not find it. The power switch was at his feet but he did not know. We were outside saying, 'Open the door.' He was inside saying, 'How? I can't see it.' We banged on the door to guide him. But there was so much noise everywhere that he could not hear the banging. At last Dattu held a lantern up to a crack in the door and Bhaskar opened the door by its light. We switched on the power. There was sudden light everywhere. We looked around for the thief. That poor fellow had escaped long before.

There are grades amongst thieves too. A thief's grade depends on how often he has been to prison and how long he has stayed there. These are material inquiries without which a girl's father does not give her to him in marriage. I do not know which grade the thief who visited us belonged to. But he soon found out that the girls possessed nothing worth stealing. So he decided to turn his attention to the matron. Dattu's table is at the foot of his bed. It has cupboards on both sides. The thief assumed this was our treasure chest and began fiddling with it.

What can thieves find in Christian homes? Some clothes and some odds and ends.

That night, the pitch and timbre of the shouting had changed. There was a lot of thudding around and a single syllable repeated over and over 'Thi, thi, thi.' I was listening from my bed. Was somebody playing a pipe? Was somebody playing catch-catch? The floor boards resounded to running feet. I switched on the power and at that very moment the thief slipped out of Dattu's hands. Dattu and the thief had been playing catch-me-if-you-can while Ruth had been trying to shout 'Thief.' I think Mumbai thieves plaster themselves with grease before setting out on business.

Illness Comes from Four Sides

Once again, Ruth and the children were unwell, so once again we sent them to Rahuri. We used to send them fifty rupees a month. I had invited Manjulabai-the-Hawk's daughter-in-law Radha to stay with us. I had not seen her since her wedding. Dattu had enrolled for a Bachelor's degree in law around this time. It became a cause of friction between him and his boss at school. The friction surfaced even in church.

The Prince of Wales was to arrive the following day. Plans were being made about who and how many of us would go to the harbour to see him. It was decided that the older girls and teachers would go. They would leave at six in the morning and return by eleven. They did accordingly after gulping down a few mouthfuls of food. Radha too went with them, and so did Jahagirdar. The smaller girls stayed back.

I wanted Dattu and Tara also to go, but both were busy studying at home. I got Champi to make a large amount of rice and bean curry, because I was sure the girls would return home ravenously hungry. Some time after the girls had gone, an older girl who had stayed back came running in to say, 'Aaji, look what's happening. People are shutting the windows of the building in front.' I went out and sure enough that is what I saw. Soon stones started being pelted at the windows from the street. I told the gardener to go out and see what was going on. He was guarding the place that day since Jahagirdar had gone with the girls. He closed the gate and came in. Immediately after that we heard shouts hailing Mahatma Gandhi. There were some thirty or forty children with us. They too joined in the chorus hailing Mahatma Gandhi.

Before the girls left, a hot argument had raged between two groups. I had warned them, 'Girls, there will be plenty of time later to argue. When you're on the road today, please don't utter a single word.' I managed to make the older girls understand, but the young children with me were impossible to convince.

Just then some people outside began to bang on the gate violently. It was our Christian brothers and sisters who were shouting, 'Let us in quick.' We let them in. They gave us more information about what was happening outside. I put our forty Gandhi devotees in the flour-milling room. When I came out, I heard a lot of shouting on the road. Our guests said, 'They've cut the tram cables, knocked down lamp-posts, broken cars and scattered their parts. All doors and windows of houses are shut. Two rival gangs are walking the streets. We returned halfway. We didn't dare go on.' They were still panting and drenched in sweat as they spoke.

Now Dattu and Tara were suddenly keen to go.

'Coming Tara? I want to see this.'

'Please, don't both of you go.'

'You're such a scaredy, Aai.'

Both went off. I was already anxious about the girls and the teachers and Radha, who was my guest and wearing gold worth two or three hundred rupees. And now it was Dattu and Tara. These two walked around Bhendi Bazaar, Pydhonie, Chowpatty, Null Bazaar, Byculla and New Nagpada. The roads were totally deserted. They were surprised. If a riot was supposed to be going on, why was Mumbai not even its normal self but abnormally quiet? Dattu was bare-headed. Tara was wearing a six-yard khadi sari. When they arrived at the Khada Parsi statue, they were stopped by both gangs. But they got away because the pro-government gang would not touch Tara, she being a woman; and the pro-Gandhi gang let her go because she was wearing khadi. Dattu and Tara reached home safely in the evening.

Somebody was stabbed on the road right outside our American Mission church. The Saheb there locked all doors and sat in the church. Our own Saheb and Madam were trying their best to keep the girls safe in all this chaos. The weapons that the gangs were using were no more than sticks, canes and stones, but they were enough to terrorize Mumbai. Our Jahagirdar kept the entire herd of girls and teachers together and escorted them to Canon Joshi's compound. Canon Joshi was a man of great piety. Around four o'clock in the afternoon, he fed all the girls and teachers with a bun and a cup of tea each.

Our gardener was busy putting his eyes and ears alternately to a crack in the gate and coming back every five minutes with news. Every piece of his news was fresh and spicy. Now the girls had been caught by a Pathan. Now they had been locked up by street ruffians. Now a tram had been overturned and all the girls had been crushed under it. All his news related only to our girls. Around nine at night, our Saheb managed to reach the hostel, nipping into shadows to hide along the way. He said, 'Aaji, no need to worry. All the girls are safe with Canon Joshi. They might come soon or tomorrow morning.' It was only when they came back at around ten-thirty and stood before me in flesh-and-blood that I breathed a sigh of relief.

I received two reply-paid joint postcards the next day. Both were inquiries about us, requesting a response by return of post. One was from my sister Shahabai Misal and the other from Mathurabai Malhar in Pune. She had heard a terrible rumour about Dattu.

The illness for which Ruth, Nana and Ashok had to be sent away to Rahuri now attacked Tara. It was not a very serious illness but Tara's constitution could not endure it. She had not fallen ill very often in her life, but when she did, the illness had squeezed everything out of her. First it was plague, then a fever that came and went and now it was ague. She would shiver and the temperature would rise; while it lasted, she would continue to shiver.

She had to appear for her Bachelor's degree examination during this illness. She went to write her first paper, but came back halfway through. Her temperature was still high the following day when again she insisted on writing her paper. 'Please let me go. I don't want to miss the exam.'

I managed somehow to keep her home. I gave her some home remedies, but when they did nothing to bring down her fever, I started her on Dr Dandekar's treatment. He did all he could. I have no account of how much ice I must have put on her head. Soon she was so weak she could not even sign her name.

The Diwali vacation started. The girls and the teachers left for their homes. Dattu went to Rahuri. The whole place was deserted. Even thieves did not visit. I continued to be worried about Tara whose fever would still not settle. The doctor said, 'Give her fish broth and take her away for a change of air.' Now where was I to get her fish broth from? And where was I to take her for a change of air? A good woman named Yashodabai used to live next-door to us. She was kind enough to bring Tara fish broth for fifteen days, and it was she who suggested I take her to Matheran for a change of air. Matheran is very close to Mumbai. I began making preparations to go. I bought all the food we would require so I would not have to go shopping there. Incidentally, Champa, who had delivered a boy and whom I had adopted as a daughter, decided around then to run away. She took the boy with her. Afterwards, she sent me a message: 'Aai, I'm fine. Don't worry.' But she has not come to see me since.

I took an orphan girl with me when we left for Matheran. She was about seven or eight. My brother's daughter Sonu lived in Neral, at the foot of the Matheran hill. I wrote to her asking if we could come for a few days. She wrote back promptly, saying, 'Please come. I'll look after Tara and you.' Benji put us on the train. In Tara's case, put is the right word because he literally carried her in. Sonu and her son came to Neral station to receive us. After two days there, when Tara's fever and my anxiety were still at the same level, Sonu said, 'Aunty, you stay here. We'll send Tara to Matheran every day. It's the high season now and you won't be able to afford the rates of accommodation.'

I remembered that Dattu and Ruth had come to Matheran for their honeymoon. I sent Sonu's son to Matheran to look for the place where they had stayed. The man who owned the place sent word back, 'Tell Dattopant's mother to come any time. The house is hers.' We left for Matheran in the morning. There were no tongas on the hill-station, only hand-pulled rickshaws. We put Tara in a rickshaw and we footed it. In keeping with our barber friend's message, his house was indeed mine except that there was no place to put my foot in. It was a small house with many families living in it. But I was of Brahmin stock. I threw myself body and belongings into the crowd and allowed them to find their own place. So body and belongings landed in the back verandah. There was just enough place there to set up three stones to cook on and a five-foot-by-five-foot space to sleep skin to skin in. I would get up at six in the morning, rush through my morning routine, cook lunch, pack it and leave for the town with Tara and Lakshmi the orphan girl, returning only in the evening. Our evening meal was cooked by our hostess. Nobody has ever turned down anything I have asked for. The world is my oyster!

There was plenty of free air in Matheran but little water and practically no milk. But that did not affect us. Although I was named Lakshmi after the goddess of wealth, I had never lived up to my name. In short, we did not need tea. Tara's milk was stopped. As for water, I would buy a large pot of it for three annas. Clothes were washed and baths had according to how much water was available. We would spend the whole day under a tree, shifting as the shade of the tree shifted.

Our place on the verandah was where others in the house went out and in. At night when we slept, the poor things would go in and out by a roundabout way. All the barbers who lived in the house were good people. It was the height of the holiday season, so they did not have a chance to put their razors down for even a single minute during the day. By night, the men would be exhausted. So they would drop in at the distiller's on the way home as a reward for their labours. If their hands were busy through the day, now it was their mouths loosened by alcohol. But their womenfolk did not encourage their blather for too long.

Next door to us was a nurse who had come from Mumbai

for a holiday. I found in her a kindred soul and we got on like a house on fire. When we left the house, we would tell her which way we were headed. She would finish all her work by four in the afternoon and come looking for us. My English was limited to yes, no, cat, dog, come, go. But she was very keen to learn the language and I promised to arrange for her to learn it. There were three graduates in our house so she was very pleased. When she joined us, we would sing together. She used to admire my voice. I was rather proud of it myself. My songs were the ones Mr Tilak had composed. She sang folk songs.

One day when we were lost in our music, some three or four Muslim ladies came there, following the sound of our voices. They looked very well-to-do. They sat down near us but we continued singing. There were two serving women with them who were making paans for them. The women ate them but their entire attention was on our singing. My nurse friend began talking to them in their language, Hindi.

'Have you ever heard Gauharjan sing?'

'Sure we have. But have you heard our Gauharjan Senior sing?'

Another woman said, 'Your Gauharjan's singing only makes men lose their senses. But when our Gauharjan Senior sings even the serpents in the jungles sway.'

The nurse said, 'Let's hear your Gauharjan Senior sing. I've heard Gauharjan. People pay ten rupees per head to hear her. Nobody is a match for her, I can assure you.'

'Listen then.' And so their Gauharjan Senior began to sing. Her singing was divine. People gathered around us. She sang four songs. Then she said, 'I am the same Gauharjan you are talking about.' This woman, who was so rich and such a great artist, talked to us as if we were old friends. I have read somewhere that rich people need to be with good people. But we kept moving away from them as though they were an infectious disease. Hard as she tried to persuade us, we refused to go to her bungalow. Finally she gave us her address in Mumbai. She must have been sixty or sixty-five at the time. Soon we parted company. She made her way to her bungalow. The crowd that had gathered around us dispersed. We walked back to our home.

We spent three weeks in Matheran. When we left, I put twenty rupees in the owner's hand. Tara had gained enough strength now to speak. But her fever continued unabated. We reached Mumbai on the 1st of June. Soon the girls and teachers began to arrive one by one from wherever they had gone. Dattu also came back with his family from Rahuri. It was not a good idea to continue to stay in Rahuri. The rainy season would soon begin and there were no hospitals there. Ruth would soon need one.

We were together again. Just when I thought I did not need to worry about anybody now, Ruth and the children went down with fever again. With the three of them and Tara, we were bound in a four-sided box of illness. My work routine would soon begin. Dattu too would be back at school. Having four ill people in the house was beyond my capacity to manage. Since Ruth could not be sent back to Rahuri, I wrote to Mrs Hume in Ahmednagar, asking her to give Tara a place in her compound and find a woman to look after her. I said I would send ten or fifteen rupees to her every month. Mrs Hume wrote back immediately. 'Let Tara come to me. She will stay in the bungalow with me. You are not to worry at all. I am only saddened by your offering to send money. I don't want a single paisa to look after her.'

That good woman took care of Tara. She nursed her personally. At the end of three months, Tara's fever disappeared.

Wanted, a Daughter

Around this time one evening when it had started to drizzle, a Victoria stopped outside our door and a voice called from within, 'Mrs Tilak lives here, doesn't she?' As soon as the lady heard an affirmative answer, she hopped out of the carriage and came straight in. Behind her came her baggage. The Victoria driver was paid. He saluted the woman and went away. The woman pushed her baggage to the side of my bed. Nobody had a clue who she was and why she was here. Was she someone I should have known or someone Ruth should have known? Whatever be the case, the woman turned out to be a kindred soul of the arch *Mahabharat* plotter, Sakuni Mama. As soon as she arrived, tales about the mother-in-law were whispered in the daughter-in-law's ears and vice versa. Fifteen days later, we still did not know whose guest she was. Fortunately for her, the confusion did not lead to her being fed by neither. But the tales she carried were enough to fill both Ruth's ears and mine.

To add to our problems, she was in purdah. That meant she did not show herself to the menfolk of the house. Even when she ate, it was from behind her purdah. One day my brother's son, Babu came. He said, 'Attya, who is this woman in purdah that you've brought home?'

I said, 'I have no idea. Ask your sister-in-law.'

He asked Ruth, 'Who is this woman?'

She said, 'How would I know? She must be one of your attya's guests.'

He said to me, 'Attya, what is this mystery?'

'It's a mystery to me too. But this much I can tell you. The woman has been a terrible nuisance. Dattu is too polite to say anything. And he's busy with his books. Tara is away in Ahmednagar. I worry about her. There are patients in the house too.'

'I see.'

Then Babu went out. He hired a Victoria, loaded the woman's luggage in it and said to her, 'Okay, get going. The carriage is waiting.'

She got into the Victoria quietly and left. I said, 'Babu, what have you done? She's a young woman and this is Mumbai.'

'Wasn't it Mumbai when she came?'

I paid no attention to what he said. Another son of my brother's, Vasudev, happened to be there at the time. I sent him after her to the station. He came with the report that she was buying her ticket.

My daughter-in-law never gets ruffled. That's her nature. It is balanced and steady. She is a faithful person. She is loyal to one town, one house, one person and so on. Once she is pleased with an idea or situation, she is anxious not to let anything change it. It is the same with medicines. When Nana was small, our Tatya introduced us to the Rajshri Kunhe medicine. This happened when Nana was down with severe dysentery. Not a single medicine would work on him. That is when Tatya suggested we try the Kunhe treatment. Later, when Ruth went to Rahuri, she came across a book by Mahatma Gandhi which recommended a similar treatment. Doctors had already given up on Nana's health. So Ruth immediately put a mud pack on his stomach and his dysentery was cured.

Tatya was an old friend of Mr Tilak's. He was generally lazy about writing letters. But when we wrote to him about the children's illnesses, his replies would come by return of post. At times he would even write every day, and we would follow the treatment he recommended. My daughter-in-law who had gone on a diet of sprouts during her second pregnancy was hardly going to balk at the things Tatya told us to do. Now, with Ruth and both children ill, we thought of him and instantly wrote him a letter. No reply. We wrote a second letter. There was still no reply. Then we sat together and discussed what to do. We came to the conclusion that I should go to Tatya's place with the two children. It was impossible for Ruth to go. Dattu had his job. Tara was in Ahmednagar. That left only me. I said to Dattu, 'But how will I manage?'

'There's nothing to it. I'll put you on the train. Don't get off anywhere midway. Get off at the right station. Get a coolie to carry your luggage and tell him you want to go to the post office. Done.'

Nana was two-and-a-half. Ashok was one-and-a-half. And I was an illiterate bumpkin. But the three of us set off. The compartment was not crowded. Illness had made Nana very cranky. He was curled up on my lap. Ashok was also ill but active. So while my lap took care of Nana, my eyes followed Ashok. He was like a spinning top. He would not sit still in one place and I could not control him. There was a Marwari couple in our compartment. I had taught the boys several games. Peekaboo was one of them. Ashok thought the Marwari woman in purdah was playing peekaboo with him. So he would keep running to her, putting his hand inside her purdah and shouting, 'Boo.'

She was furious beyond words. The more she shook off his hand, the more excited he became by the game. What excited him further were the things he saw behind the purdah which he had never seen before. Glittering gold ornaments—a nose-ring, a choker, a long necklace, a large ornament on her forehead and a set of red paan-stained and gold-filled teeth. This battle continued for a long time, throughout which she kept saying, 'Take charge of your child' and I kept wanting to laugh. I was also angry with the woman. Look at the age of the child. Was he of an age to get angry with? In her place I would have picked him up. The child was running around happily like the wind, his hair flying around his face, his little mouth babbling. Who would not be tempted to pick him up and pet him? I must say though that in looks he is like me.

Certain customs run deep in Christian people's blood. I have begun to get used to them. I have learnt lessons in proper behaviour and manners from my daughter-in-law. But my lessons don't always translate into action, as in this instance for example. I presented myself at Tatyasaheb's door with two children in tow without having informed him. I had brought a woman along as house-help. She was not quite the kind that would fit into a high-caste Hindu household. Tatyasaheb was a high-ranking government officer. He used to move around amongst equally high-caste Hindus. Even his subordinates were high-caste Hindus. Our woman would obviously be out of place in such an environment. When we turned up unannounced in Tatyasaheb's front yard, he was very surprised and when he set eyes on the woman he even looked a little angry. Tatyasaheb's wife addresses me as Bai. She said, 'What brings you here, Bai? You should have written to us.'

'Dattu wrote several letters to you. There was no response from Tatya. Everybody at home is ill. So I picked up the children and came.'

'But your daughter-in-law is due to deliver soon. You shouldn't have come.'

Tatyasaheb then explained to me the treatment we should give the children. He gave me a lecture on how the treatment worked. Then we all slept. Ashok woke up in the middle of the night as he was in the habit of doing and went on his patrol. He went directly to Tatya's room and attempted to wake him up. Tatya was tired from a day's hard work. He was not particularly pleased with Ashok's patrol. He was very upset. When we got up in the morning, he said, 'Bai, please go away with the children.'

'How can I do that? What have I come here for? Dattu has asked me to rent a place and stay.'

'You will not get a place to stay here. Just give the children the treatment I've prescribed and they'll be fine.' The crucial point in his treatment was to ensure that the children's bowels were clean. It is true. If we control our tongues, that is eat and quarrel in moderation, we might avoid many of our mental and physical problems. Of course, I only preach.

Tatya sent Dattu a telegram, put us on a train and saw us off.

Dattu came to the station but he could not spot me and I could not see him. I hired a coolie to carry the boys, but neither of them would go to him. At last I handed our bundle of belongings to the coolie and, grasping each child by the armpit, struggled to alight. Just then Dattu spotted me and relieved me of the burden.

We started the boys off on Tatyasaheb's treatment. The next day we dunked Nana in a tub of water and put him to sleep wet. Then we gave Ashok the heat-and-mud pack treatment. We did this for five or six days running. Meanwhile Ruth had stopped shivering, although she still had temperature that would reach as high as 105 degrees. Nana and Ashok recovered but Ruth continued as before. We put cold towels on her head all day. She was nearing her due date and we heard many women in her condition were running a similar fever. Ruth's mother would stay with us overnight.

One day I had boiled a lot of peas in their pods. Ruth did not look good that day. I said, 'You're not looking well. Did you eat too many peas?' Sure enough, when I woke up early next morning, there was a tonga standing in front of the house with mother and daughter already in it. I too got in. We reached the hospital at six o'clock and little Meera arrived fifteen minutes later. Many babies born around that time were running high temperatures. Not our Meera who came through fighting fit. We had hoped this baby would be a girl. That is why Ruth had not cut Ashok's hair. Mother and child came home after ten days.

Around that time, my sister Shahabai Misal's daughter Tarabai wrote to me. 'I have to come to Mumbai to give an exam. Another student will also come with me. I will have to stay with you. Please let me know by return of post if we may.' Tarabai was a doctor. She had opened a big nursing home in Karachi. Dattu and Ruth replied to her letter. 'Come whenever you want to. Treat this house as yours.'

Our Tara had recovered with Mrs Hume's dedicated nursing. She came home. Chiki's father Rambhau also came from Parole. Meera was three weeks old. Dattu was busy with his teachers' training examination. The Diwali vacation was around the corner. Ruth said to Rambhau, 'What is the climate like in Parole?'

Rambhau said, 'Excellent.'

'How big is your house?'

'It's very large. The water supply is plentiful. There's a good stock of foodstuffs, groceries, tea and sugar in the house, and firewood.'

'Then can we come to stay? Dattu's exam will be over in a couple of days. We can go immediately after that.' Rambhau agreed wholeheartedly. Like Chiki, he too never let people in on shortfalls. Like father like child. Both bragged but also backed up their bragging with action.

Dr Tarabai came with the student she had spoken of. He used to eat with us but sleep elsewhere. The day Dattu's exam got over he, his wife and children left for Parole. Now there was only the recently recovered Tara, our two guests, I and my worries at home. I worried about Ruth who was only three weeks gone after delivery, with two toddlers, a newborn baby, and an exhausted Dattu. But what chance does wisdom have before a mind that is made up? Once children grow up they acquire the power to decide for themselves. With so many people away and no children running about, the house suddenly felt very empty.

Independence

Tarabai used to wear a vermilion kumkum mark on her forehead. Our community was opposed to wearing kumkum. She was married to a man from a different community. That made her even more suspicious. To top it all, she was accompanied by a Hindu student. Now we began to be seriously watched. People would peep in casually, wait to catch us doing wrong so they could spice up stories about what they saw and serve them to the officials. The officials were only too happy to eat what they were served because there was already friction between them and Dattu over one thing and another. But no official had the courage to come out openly and say what was bothering them. The officials and some other Europeans came by to see Tarabai and the student with her.

Now suddenly everybody began to show a lot of anxiety about my health. I was not ill, but these people's anxiety was sure to make me so. Actually, they were the ones who had been affected by us and were looking for a way to recover without taking medicine. Whoever came to meet me would say, 'Aaji, you must go away for a change of air.'

I would say, 'But why should I? There's nothing wrong with me.' And yet, I was beginning to be affected by this show of anxiety. There was no reason why people could not speak out frankly. But they were stopped by rules of politeness. Best not to crack the glass and break the stick is how their thinking went. The problem was that nothing in our house was done on the sly. Whenever spies came, they saw us living life in full view with nothing to hide. The doors and windows to where we sat talking were always wide open. I detested curtains. It was only when no amount of peeping and spying and eavesdropping revealed any wrongdoing that this campaign to urge me to go away for a change of air was launched. After all, the missionaries were foreigners. Their knowledge of our language was as good as non-existent. Their connection with us was through our own people. These people were responsible for poisoning their minds and misleading them.

One day a woman dropped in, all politeness, persuading me to go away. 'Aaji, you don't look too well.'

I said, 'Look here, all of you are under the impression that I don't understand what's going on. But I do, all of it. I know exactly why everybody has suddenly become so anxious about my health. This is what I have to say about it. I would like to continue doing this work without salary till Dattu finishes his college term. I need a place to stay till then.'

The polite woman said, 'But, Bai, I want to start a clinic here.'

I said, 'So start it. I have capable hands. I will set up a mithai shop and put up a signboard with my name on it.'

The woman went away. The next day the parish priest came. He too advised me to go away. Now I lost courage. Dattu was far away. To top that, he had fallen ill. And I had to listen to this constant nagging. I thought I would really become ill and have to go away.

Tara said, 'Don't worry, Aai. Meera has brought us good luck. We are now going to be independent.'

'How, with two small children in a place like Mumbai? Where can we get a place to stay?'

Tara said, 'I have studied enough now. We'll manage. Don't worry about a job.'

Dr Tarabai said, 'Maushi, would you like to come to Karachi? I can find jobs there for Tara and Ruth. Then Dattu will be free to concentrate on his law books.'

'Why only to Karachi? I'd be ready to go even to England. A thief at home has no problem being a beggar in foreign lands.'

I had no news of Dattu who was ill in Parole. The children kept these things hidden from me. Telegrams flew between Tarabai, Patankar, Tara and Parole. Fruit parcels were also sent without my knowledge. But Dattu got all the news from Mumbai.

After her exam, Tarabai returned to Karachi. She began to look for jobs for the girls as soon as she arrived there. Dattu recovered and came back with his family. All of us were together again. Nobody was ill. The only worry that remained now was of livelihood. But since this illness was caused by the human germ, the doctor could do nothing to help.

Soon a letter came from Tarabai. We had been waiting for it as one does for examination results. Our luck was being tested. And joy oh joy, we had topped the class. The letter said jobs had been found for Tara and Ruth. Tara would get one hundred and thirty rupees and Ruth one hundred and fifty rupees a month. A house too had been found for thirty rupees a month rent. Tarabai wanted to know if these offers were acceptable to us. Our joy on reading the letter knew no bounds. That same day Rev. Edwards had brought us seventy-five rupees as remuneration for some article of Mr Tilak's that he had managed to get published. And we were not complete paupers even otherwise. The insurance money was grinning happily at me.

A telegram was sent to Karachi and we got down to packing. We also shopped for provisions. Still, there were two worries left. One was about Dattu and the second was to do with our belongings. Dattu would not be able to come with us, and over the years, we had collected an excessive amount of stuff. Dattu found accommodation in his parents-in-laws' home. Actually, a room could have been found for our stuff in Bawkar Hall itself. But with our experience in Satara still fresh in our memories, we did not even think of this option. If you've scalded your mouth on milk, you are wary of drinking buttermilk.

We asked Bhaskarrao Ujagare. He was actually a nay-sayer. But once he decided something was the right thing to do, there was no budging him. When we told him of our Karachi plans, he treated it at first as a joke. But we were four against one. We were not going to laugh it off. I said, 'Dear man, let's forget jokes for the moment. Just tell me what we can do with all our stuff.'

'My house is large. Put it there.'

Bhaskarrao was the parish priest at the Ambroli Church in Girgaum those days. So he had a larger house than people normally did in Mumbai. It even had a junk room. We did not give him a chance to have second thoughts. We shifted our stuff immediately to his place. Tara dealt with this work. Dattu had his job, I had my work and Ruth had her children. So Tara was the only free spirit.

From the time I started working, I had never invited my bosses for a meal, nor had I sent them special dishes in covered plates. Doing this was considered part of a matron's job. I believed that, more than food, you kept your bosses happy with the quality of your work. But now that our plan to leave had been finalized and all preparations made, I invited our Madam and Saheb for the first and last time for a meal. Although it was against my nature, I let Dattu persuade me to invite them exactly a month before we were due to leave. None of us spoke about work during the meal. We spent the time happily together. When Madam and Saheb were leaving, I put my resignation letter with one month's notice in their hands. They were stunned to see it.

'But where will you go?'

'Wherever God takes us.'

'What will you do with all this baggage?'

'We've made arrangements to store it.'

Madam said, 'We'll send you a certificate.'

'I won't need it. This was my first job and it'll be my last. I had never served anybody till now and don't intend to again.'

The Christmas vacation was about to start. The first of December was to be my last day at work. The girls had to report for work in Karachi on the second of January. We sailed three days before Christmas. Dattu was going to escort us. Bhaskarrao Ujagare, Manoharrao Ujagare and Lakshmanrao Padale had come to see us off. They had not come with garlands and bouquets. We were not going away to achieve great things. They had come to help us with the children and the luggage.

The ship blew its horn. It was taking us to the source of our food. We were looking excitedly at Mumbai and our friends ranged on its shoreline as they receded. The sea was calm. Its colour changed from time to time. So did the thoughts in our minds. For the world, we were going to Karachi. But for us, it was like going to England. Three women and three children were going to spend three years in that far away foreign land. Dattu would return and we would be left with no male support other than the two who were with us. One was two-and-a-half, the other one-and-a-half. But we were independent. I remembered a poem of Mr Tilak's:

> Where shall I look for you, oh freedom—
> As one in a crowd or solitary in a desert?
> Spin me round the world
> Reduce me to starvation
> But dear freedom, be mine.
> Without you the world to me
> Is bare, broken, incomplete.

Karachi

We had a lot of luggage, including the children's things. Popu our parrot too was travelling with us. We spread our beddings and arranged our luggage neatly and had soon made a cosy home for ourselves on the ship. I had heard about ships making you sea-sick. We had made advance preparations for it. But this ship had no effect on us. We were in great spirits, chattering and laughing, with the children and Popu taking part in our conversation.

The first place we stopped at after leaving Mumbai was Dwarka. It is a beautiful place. We went up on deck turn by turn to take in the sight. As we gazed upon it, Dwarka seemed to float on the water. Then our ship moved and Dwarka gradually disappeared from view. We were now approaching Mandvi in Kutch. We saw a motor launch there. Dattu and Ruth had gone up on the deck with the two boys. Tara, Meera and Popu were with me down below. Meera was not walking yet. She was lolling on the floor. Her milk bottle was lying near her feet.

When Mandvi harbour hove into view, our ship dropped anchor. Just as a litter of kittens clings to the mother cat's side when she returns to them after a long absence, so it was with our mother ship. As soon as she anchored, dozens of little boats and launches rushed towards her and clung to her sides. Some passengers alighted from these boats but were far outnumbered by porters. They were like a flash flood crashing into the ship. We had heard about pirates attacking ships. Those attacks were probably like this. The porters pounced on the luggage of passengers getting off and also of those not getting off. One of them stepped on Meera's milk bottle crushing it to powder. His other foot was about to land on her stomach when Tara pulled her away. Meera was saved in the nick of time, else Kutch would have spelt the end of everything.

We were on the ship for two days and two nights. We

arrived in Karachi on the third day, which was Christmas day. It was winter. The days in Karachi had grown short. The clock showed eight in the morning but it still felt like five-thirty or six. Tarabai and her father Gyanoba Misal had come to receive us at the docks. They helped us alight with our luggage. Tarabai sent us off with her father to her place, while she went to our rented house with the luggage. My sister, Tarabai's mother, was waiting at home, all set to receive us.

It was Christmas day but our heads were still swimming from the sea journey. We had felt no discomfort on the ship, but on shore we began to feel quite strange. Added to this was Karachi's severe cold. We were shivering from head to foot. After lunch, we read from the Bible and prayed at home and then set off to inspect our new home. It felt like morning, but it was afternoon.

The building was four storeys high. Our flat was on the ground floor. The rent was thirty rupees and the location seemed convenient. A dry canal ran in front of the house, properly plastered with cement and clean. A strip of road ran between the canal and the entrance to our house. Two steps led up to the house. Inside was a small yard. Beyond was the living room, spacious enough to accommodate a large double bed and still leave a pathway for going in and out. Beyond that was another yard with a verandah running round it. This backyard was planned as a convenience for our upstairs neighbours and an inconvenience for us.

There was no social discrimination or untouchability in Karachi. Everybody sat together in a row for meals. The rooms in the flats were also built in a row. Only the landlords' flats were designed differently. In the rest of the flats, the kitchens, lavatories and bathrooms stood next to each other. In our house too these rooms stood together on one side of the yard.

It took us two days to arrange our stuff and stock up on provisions. We entered our house on the third day. Dattu saw us settled and returned to Mumbai. Ruth and Tara started their teaching jobs. Now one old woman and three children reigned over the house during the day. Before we left Mumbai, Patankar had written to a friend in Karachi about us. When we shifted into our new house, the friend's father Mr Malik came to see us. He said, 'Ask me for any help you need. Please don't feel awkward about it.' I did not need another invitation. I said, 'Could you send two men to put up our bed? The other thing is, we don't know the local language so buying vegetables every day might become a problem.' Mr Malik instantly sent the men and himself escorted to our place a bullock-cart piled with vegetables which the vendor sold from door to door every day. So our bed was up and our vegetable supply fixed.

In Karachi, Hindu women, like Muslim women, did not go out unescorted. But they had a way of buying vegetables while remaining indoors. They would lower a basket for the vegetables that they wanted and then pull it up. The basket then went down with the money. Being on the ground floor, we bought vegetables directly from the man. There was just enough place for the cart to come through on the narrow strip of road outside our door. When I stepped out to buy vegetables, the boys would tail me and get up to tricks. One day, Nana lay down flat on the road beside the cart wheel. Neither the cartman nor I noticed. We were too busy buying and selling. Even the bullock was standing motionless. Ashok kept tugging at my sari, saying, 'Aaji, look where Nana is sleeping.' But I was counting my annas and paisas. Just then Nana's hand touched my foot and I panicked. I picked him up and told the vegetable man not to come again. There was nobody else in the house but me. If I stepped out, the children were bound to follow me. Why take the risk?

In time, we discovered that living on the ground floor meant we lived in hell. Heaven was the floors above us which we came to detest. The denizens of heaven sent their garbage down in cascades to land before our eyes. Wherever you are, in Mumbai or Karachi, there is one birth-right that people everywhere claim, the right to ignore the rights of those below you. We did not want to be anywhere near this high-placed heaven.

The children would start stirring early in the morning and calling out to Aai, Baba, Aaji. One day, a man staying on the topmost floor came down. His face was glowing with pleasure. 'I've been hearing familiar words from my country so I had to find out who had come to stay here.' We shared his joy in finding somebody from our parts who knew our language. Every time we met a Marathi speaker, our hearts would leap.

We decided to shift from this house. There was no male in the house and women, whether they were Hindu or Muslim, did not go out. On a bitterly cold day, Tara and Ruth set out on a campaign to find us a new home. They returned with the good news that flat number five in Karimji Manzil was going to be vacated soon. The rent was thirty rupees. The following day, the girls went out again. They climbed five flights of stairs and knocked on the door of flat number five. A young Sindhi man who was shaving, opened the door. The girls barged in and took a good look around the flat. The man was still shaving. When the girls finished their tour and returned to the front door, the man said to them quietly, without interrupting his shaving, 'This house is not going to be vacated. Number twelve is going to be.'

The girls knocked on the door of flat number twelve. An aged man opened the door. His mouth fell open as he gaped at them. The girls took a thorough look at this house too. Then they went down and climbed five flights of stairs of the building next door. But they discovered that the rent of the flats in that building was forty rupees, which was beyond our means.

The following day, I went with the girls to look at number five and twelve. Unfortunately, number five was not available. It was much better than number twelve. But the old man there was prepared to rent it out to us. So that is where we decided to shift. The old man asked for thirty-five rupees as advance on rent. We were not confident about the transaction. We asked my brother Gyanoba Misal to conduct the business. We had already begun packing. Gyanoba came around ten-thirty to say that number twelve was not available. We were sorely disappointed.

He then gave us the good news which he had withheld. Number five was now available. We were overjoyed.

A Bohri man came in the morning and took Ruth's and Tara's signatures on a printed piece of paper and asked them to accompany him. There was a group of other Bohris there. They offered the flat on an eleven-month lease. The girls did not know what lease meant. They thought they were being asked to pay eleven months' rent in advance. The men said, 'Have you done your matriculation?' The girls said, 'We have done our B.A.' The men did not know what that meant. It turned out that they were not asking for any of the things like mithai and pugdee that Mumbai landlords asked for. We got the flat without these things. So within a month of arriving in Karachi, we moved out of our first house into the second.

We had succeeded in the first skirmish in the battle for a home. All the dealings were with men. We did not see a single woman. We found that the men here behaved extremely respectfully with women. Even when the girls went to the market they had the same experience. All the shopkeepers understood English. The fact that these two were teachers in the Indian Girls' School impressed them. The school had a very good reputation in Karachi.

Our new flat was on the fourth floor. This house too was built to suit women in purdah. Once you closed the front door, the house became an invincible fort.

The design of the house was similar to the first, except that it was more spacious. Also, there was no heaven above the terrace that adjoined our flat. All we saw above was a clear blue sky. We had the sun for company in the day and the moon and stars at night. We saw aeroplanes flying overhead, but not a single other building.

Our Days in Karachi

A fortnight or so after we arrived in Karachi, we sent for Manjulabai-the-Hawk. There was no house-help available here. Not that we thought of Manjulabai as a maid. She was more like the children's third granny. The new house was lovely, but you had to climb sixty stairs to get to its heavenly heights. The terrace at the back was a good place for the children to play in. This was also where we could enjoy that thing called sunshine which had become such a rarity. In the first house, our upstairs neighbours would throw water down into our yard. We endured that without a word. In the new place, we ourselves once inadvertently did the same. Within a trice there was a loud knock on the door. Ruth opened it. A woman in a full flowing skirt entered. Behind her came another, then another and then yet another. Each had a child either attached to her hip or to her leg or hanging at the back. They half-filled our living room.

Some of us knew only Marathi. The girls also knew English. But the women began talking at the tops of their voices in a language none of us understood. However, their gestures and expressions were enough to tell us that this was about the water we had thrown down. We remembered our earlier experience and never again repeated what we had done.

Being high up meant we did not see people. If you wanted to see them you had to go down to the street. Peeping out of the window or from the terrace did not help. When the children looked down from this height, all they saw and found amusing was the turbans of men walking down below. Up here the children saw nobody at all except us four women. The only bit of excitement that came our way was aeroplanes. When Manjulabai heard their distant rumble, she would shout, 'A plane, a plane!' Then everybody, but particularly the children, would run out to look. At least four or five planes would fly overhead every day and the children threw their heads far back to look at them till they disappeared.

Babu Patankar's friend Gurdayal Malik belonged to Karachi. But he lived in Santiniketan where he was a teacher. Babu had written to Gurdayal who had told his father about us. That is why his father had come to see us soon after we arrived. He helped us a lot, and being what I was, I took all the help he offered. Meera began to teeth and fell ill. Grandpa Malik took her to the doctor who started to treat her. He used to take Nana and Ashok for a stroll. He and his second son ran a business. Physical culture was very important to him. As a result, he was fitter than either of his sons. He never needed medicines. When we shifted from the first house to the new one, he sent three men to move our luggage, for which I paid them no more than two-and-a-half rupees.

The children loved Grandpa Malik. Our first house was close to his so he made frequent visits. But once we moved, his visits became less frequent. One day we heard a loud knock on the door and a voice calling, 'Nana.' The boys were so excited, they forgot to open the door. Instead, they folded their hands in greeting and danced singing, 'It's Grandpa, it's Grandpa.' Finally when they let him in and he sat down, Nana brought out all his toys and set them down before him. Next, he brought his shoes. Then he got him an unwashed cooking pot and picked a raisin out of the dust and presented that to him. Grandpa held the raisin up to his eyes, took a handkerchief out of his pocket, wiped it clean and popped it in his mouth. Then Nana gave him his lozies and bikkis (lozenges and biscuits). Grandpa ate them and belched in appreciation.

Since both boys were close in age, when one did something, the other would copy him. Then Meera would make sounds in her language or cry. Nana bombarded us with questions. He got angry if our answers did not satisfy him. He often trapped us in our own words. I have taken the following conversations between him and his mother from letters I wrote home. Once Nana was asking his mother about prayers.

'Aai, do we have to pray to our Father before sleeping?'

'Yes, otherwise God will get angry.'

'Aai, does God pray every day? Who does he pray to?'

'Well…'

'Aai, who is God to you?'

'My Father.'

'Who is he to me?'

'Father.'

'Who is the man in Mumbai to me?'

'Your father.'

'I have two fathers?'

'Go to sleep please. I have work to do.'

'How many fathers does God have?'

'Please sleep.'

'Aai, who is my Mumbai father to you?'

'You tell me.'

'Who is your father to me?'

'Grandfather.'

'Is my father your grandfather?'

'No.'

'Why not?'

At this point Ruth lost her temper and he went to sleep.

Ruth had not had Ashok's hair cut because she had wanted a daughter after him. Ashok was plump, toddled around and lisped. Please read the next bit of conversation with that picture in mind. Ruth was doing some school work. Ashok was meddling with things around her. Nana and Meera were asleep.

'Aai, I want to write.'

'Go and sleep.'

'I go? I sleep?'

'H'm.'

'Sleep on the bed or sleep on the floor?'

'Sleep anywhere. See how good Nana and Meera are.'

'Aai, are good children good?'

'Yes, pet.'

'Aai, are naughty children naughty?'

'Yes. Ashok is very good.'

'Not very good. Little good.'

'Alright. Little good. Go sleep.'

'No, I won't.'

'Then go dance.'

'I dance? Where? I dance here?'

Ruth and I burst out laughing. Ashok danced. Then he said, 'Shall I stop?'

'Yes, that's enough. Now sleep.'

'I'll sleep on your hand.'

At this point, Ruth gave up on her work and went to sleep with Ashok.

Meera was doing very well in Karachi. She was teething fast. When Ruth spotted a tooth coming out, she would start giving Meera a sitz bath. This prevented her from getting the ailments babies normally get when they teeth. She would just get a low fever. She was very fond of Manjulabai. She would leap into her arms from ours. Ashok used to call her 'Meeya'. When Meera began to speak, her first word was 'Alla' for Ashok.

Ashok would stand before Manjulabai, hands on hips and lisp, 'Drink tea. Eat paan. Eat lime. Pick teeth. Pick ears.' Throwing a dishcloth over his shoulder, he would say, 'I'm going to the market.'

Ashok kept us laughing with the things he said and did. But once in a while, we would get angry with him and tell him to keep quiet.

'Why do you say keep quiet?'

'Then what should I say?'

'Say be quiet.'

'All right. So be quiet.'

'Why do you say be quiet?'

'Then what should I say?'

'Say keep quiet.'

We had taken a phonograph with us for our entertainment. When we played records, Ashok danced to the beat of the songs. One of the songs went, 'Don't leave me and go.' One day Manjulabai got angry with him and raised her hand as if to hit him. He sang, 'Don't leave me and go, my left eye is filled with tears.' Manjulabai collapsed laughing.

Once the Marathi film *Sinhagadh* was being screened. We used to tell the boys lots of stories about Maharashtra. So we took them to see this film. The film had such an impact on them that it entered all their talk.

'Ashok, you know we are from Maharashtra. We aren't Sindhis. Our place is so beautiful. There are big big rivers and big big forts on the hills. There's only one small dirty river here, and one mud fort. Our Maharashtra is very beautiful. We'll go there one day alright?'

'We are Marathi people. Marathi people don't cry. Sindhi people cry. Punjabi people cry. Even Bengali people cry. I am Tanaji. Aai, did Tanaji cry? Never.'

'Meera, don't cry. We are Marathi people.'

'Oon oon oon.'

But these brave Marathas would run scared of hens. They had not seen much of the outside world. Occasionally, I would take them downstairs. If they saw a hen, they would cling to my legs crying, 'Cococo.'

One day we were sitting in the living room. Nana, Ashok and Meera were on the terrace playing in the sun. There was a door between the living room and the terrace and the other rooms behind it. We were busy talking and the children were busy playing. While playing, Nana shut the door. Then, standing on tiptoe he bolted it. There was no way I could talk to the children or make signs. They too did not know what had happened. We heard Meera crying. I was at wits' end. After nearly two hours, I somehow managed to make Nana understand what he had done and guided him to unbolt the door.

I was very angry with Nana. I ran to him with a rolling pin, pretending I was going to beat him. He did not know what crime he had committed. So he too got angry with me and scolded me, 'Hey girl!' I leaned on the rolling pin and laughed.

We had not seen Babu's friend Gurdayal because he was staying in Santiniketan. Grandpa Malik always talked about him. Then we heard that he was coming. One day a small-made man turned up at our house with Grandpa Malik. He was dressed in a Bengali-style khadi dhoti-jhabba. He wore wooden clogs on his feet, gold-rimmed spectacles on his nose and nothing on his head. A look of goodness and purity glowed on his face. The children hit it off with him within a few seconds. He promised to come and see us every day but on condition that we would not insist on feeding him and would ask him for any help we required. We agreed to his conditions but he did not come again. We realized later why. He was very shy.

Grandpa Malik and his older son Ishwardas were in a business together. Grandpa Malik's hard work had helped the business grow. Gurdayal was the exact opposite. He was a scholar, a connoisseur of the arts, dedicated to service and pious. He was a great favourite of Dr Tagore's. Gurudev was his guide. All his plans and all his beliefs came from Gurudev. He had no interest in worldly things. He did everything that he was duty-bound to do. But his real happiness lay in serving people. While doing so he even neglected his own health.

Grandpa was a fit man. His hair and moustache were grey but his face bore the glow of youth. As against this, his two sons, particularly Gurdayal, kept indifferent health.

Once some races had been organized. The old man was one of the organizers. People persuaded him to run one race, just for fun. Gurdayal was also taking part in it. The old man won the race. Gurdayal came last.

> Fathers, mothers, brothers, sisters are found in every home
> Yet on earth no place exists, untouched by my love.

How the Story Ended*

From the Postscript by Ashok Tilak

Lakshmibai Tilak's *Smritichitre* ends abruptly at an indecisive point of her sojourn in Karachi. It is important for readers who have found her journey so far engaging to know how it continued and ended.

Lakshmibai, Ruth and Tara spent two years in Karachi. Soon after their arrival there, Lakshmibai took ill. Gurdayal Singh and his family gave her invaluable help during this critical time. From the very moment she stepped onto the ship that took her and her family to Karachi, she had yearned to return to her beloved home, Maharashtra. Dr Hume knew this only too well. When he returned from America, he moved heaven and earth to find a teaching job for Ruth in Ahmednagar and to facilitate Tara's departure for England where she wished to go. Devdutt went to Karachi to fetch the family back and they sailed home together in October 1924. The family went to Ahmednagar and Devdutt returned to Mumbai to continue his law studies.

Ruth was transferred to Nashik within six months of her appointment in the government school in Ahmednagar. The move fell in neatly with Devdutt's plan of settling in Nashik once he had passed his law examination. It was in that year, 1924, that Lakshmibai, urged by family and friends, began to write her memories of her husband Narayan Waman Tilak and her life with him. At first the memoir was titled, simply, 'Memories'.

---

*This is where Lakshmibai Tilak's *Smritichitre* ends. In the brief epilogue that follows I have completed her story, choosing relevant facts from the much longer epilogue that her son Devdutt (Dattu) Narayan Tilak appended to the edition of *Smritichitre* which he had modified slightly. This epilogue was incorporated by his son Ashok Tilak in the exhaustive, faithful edition of *Smritichitre* edited by him in 1973, published by Popular Prakashan, Mumbai.

She wrote the memoir continuously for the next seven years. However, there was absolutely no plan then to have it published.

When the family arrived in Nashik, they experienced the usual discrimination that had dogged every move they had made since Mr Tilak converted to Christianity. Although the town was full of friends and relatives, the family had to face much humiliation in finding suitable accommodation where their religion would not come in the way of their using facilities like kitchens and toilets to which every human being has a right. It must have been a new and joyous experience for Lakshmibai when Devdutt built a house, Shanti Sadan, in Nashik, finally ending the series of obligations under which the family had had to live wherever they went.

In 1931, an event took place in the family that disturbed and deeply saddened everybody. Tara who was back in Mumbai, married a man who was already married. Since bigamy was considered an unpardonable sin in Christianity, the man got around the problem by converting to what the family refers to as 'another religion'. Shocked, Lakshmibai took to her bed. For two months she did not come downstairs to the family rooms. Devdutt took everything she required up to her in her first-floor room.

The press naturally carried reports of the marriage, since Tara was the daughter of the well-known poet and radical thinker Rev. Narayan Waman Tilak. The news brought a spate of letters of sympathy to Lakshmibai. Amongst them was one that was to change the course of the remaining five years of her life. It came from Rev. Thorat who wrote, 'Rev. Tilak used to say, "My daughter Tara will complete 'Christayana' after me." And look how she has completed it.' For days and weeks after this, a disoriented Lakshmibai continued to grieve. Then she pulled herself together and resolved to complete 'Christayana', come what may. She went down on her knees and took a vow: 'From now on I shall not write a single word by way of letters or poems. I will not spend time reading or visiting people, worrying over trifles or writing my memoir. Dear Lord, I pick up this penholder before You. If it be Your will, make me the instrument of working for Your glory. If not, let me die doing this work.'

Dr Hume had died in 1929. His wife Katybai Hume, between whom and Lakshmibai there had always been a strong bond of friendship, was living in Wai with her son. Devdutt wrote to her about his mother's vow. Katybai instantly offered to look after Lakshmibai in every way possible if she wished to stay with her in Wai. Lakshmibai went to Wai and wrote a large part of 'Christayana' there. By the beginning of 1936, the entire sixty-three chapters of the epic, written in verse set to the traditional ovi metre, had been completed.

The years between 1933 and 1936 were the most important in Lakshmibai's public life. In 1933, a poets' conference was held in Nashik under the chairmanship of the poet Madhavrao Patwardhan, who wrote under the pen name Madhav Julian. Lakshmibai was invited to make the welcome speech. She spoke extempore in a strong voice without faltering or stumbling anywhere. The audience was stunned at her chaste language and substantial content. The speech was so highly appreciated that it was published later as a booklet and distributed free. She made another powerful speech as president of the Christian Literary Meet in Nagpur in 1934. In 1935, encouraged by eminent playwright Shripad Krishna Kolhatkar, the first part of Lakshmibai's memoir, now entitled *Smritichitre*, was published. Part Two and Three were published in 1935. Acharya P.K. Atre, speaking on the occasion of their release, bestowed on Lakshmibai the title 'Sahityalakshmi', the goddess of literature. The fourth part of the memoir was published posthumously in 1936.

In February 1935, Lakshmibai was busy going over 'Christayana' to make last-minute corrections and changes. Her handwriting was terrible, so Devdutt had arranged for an amanuensis to prepare the manuscript. Since their house was always full of visitors who came to see Devdutt, Lakshmibai took a room in the Vaishampayan's house across the road to do her work in peace. On one side of her room lived poet Bahinabai Chaudhuri's son Sopandev Chaudhuri. On the other side was an elderly lady named Maisaheb Bedarkar. Maisaheb and Lakshmibai soon became sisters and would spend some time every evening sitting together and chatting. The rest of the time, Lakshmibai worked without pause on 'Christayana'.

In February 1936, Lakshmibai decided to go to Jalgaon. Narayan Narsimha Phadnis, an old friend of Mr Tilak's and the publisher of *Kavyaratnavali*, had recently lost his son. Lakshmibai had been very upset at the news of a man in his prime going so suddenly. When she received an invitation to attend the thread ceremony of his second son in Jalgaon, she felt she had to go. In Jalgaon, she visited every single person she knew or was related to. Next, she wanted to go to Khamgaon and then to Akola, also to meet friends and family. Perhaps she sensed her end was near and wished to see her loved ones for the last time. However, this desire remained unfulfilled. She took ill with influenza in Jalgaon. The doctor advised her to return to Nashik immediately. Devdutt sent his older son to fetch her back. But while she was in Jalgaon, she said to a friend with whom she was spending a few days, 'So many people come to visit me just because I have a little fever. But the one I'm waiting for doesn't come. Death. There is no reason for me to live any longer. I have finished writing *Smritichitre* and "Christayana". I had vowed not to put my pen down till I had finished "Christayana". Now it's done. Nothing else remains to be done.'

When she returned to Nashik, she appeared to have recovered from her illness. She set off instantly to see all her loved ones in Nashik. When Sopandev went to Mumbai for work, she stayed with his wife Leelatai who was alone. During that time, literally a few days away from death, she went with Leelatai to see a nine o'clock show of V. Shantaram's film

Dharmatma, in which the celebrated female impersonator of the Marathi music stage, Balgandharva, had played his first male role. Devdutt scolded her for going and made her promise she would return home as soon as Sopandev came back from Mumbai. As it happened, there was no time for that. That same day, around three o'clock in the morning, word came to Devdutt that Lakshmibai had taken very ill and was shivering so violently that no amount of warm covering seemed to be helping.

The doctor's diagnosis said malaria. But he also felt a lump in her stomach which suggested an intestinal obstruction that would have to be surgically removed. Lakshmibai was completely prepared for this. Even as she lay on the operating table, the family could hear her talking and joking with the doctors. At first, the operation had been conducted with a spinal injection. But then she was administered chloroform. The surgery lasted for two-and-a-half hours. It was successful. She appeared to have pulled through. But within two days, her chest became congested, and on the morning of 24 February, she passed away peacefully. She was sixty-eight years old when she died.